AMERICAN CLIPPER SHIPS
1833-1858

"Surprise," 1261 tons, built at East Boston, in 1850
From a painting by Charles R. Patterson, reproduced by courtesy of
Doll & Richards, Boston

AMERICAN CLIPPER SHIPS
1833-1858

By

OCTAVIUS T. HOWE
and
FREDERICK C. MATTHEWS

VOLUME I

ADELAIDE—LOTUS

DOVER PUBLICATIONS, INC.
NEW YORK

Published in Canada by General Publishing Company, Ltd., 30 Lesmill Road, Don Mills, Toronto, Ontario.
Published in the United Kingdom by Constable and Company, Ltd.

This Dover edition, first published in 1986, is an unabridged republication of the work originally published as Publication Number Thirteen of the Marine Research Society, Salem, Massachusetts, in 1926–27. A few obvious typographical errors have been tacitly corrected. In the original edition the frontispiece of each volume appeared in color.

Manufactured in the United States of America
Dover Publications, Inc., 31 East 2nd Street, Mineola, N.Y. 11501

Library of Congress Cataloging-in-Publication Data

Howe, Octavius T. (Octavius Thorndike). b. 1851.
    American clipper ships, 1833–1858.

    "Originally published as Publication Number Thirteen of the Marine Research Society, Salem, Massachussetts, in 1926–27"—T.p. verso.
    Includes index.
    Contents: v. 1. Adelaide—Lotus—v. 2. Malay—[etc.]
    1. Clipper-ships—United States.   I. Matthews, Frederick C.   II. Title.
III. Series: Publication no. 13 of the Marine Research Society.
VM23.H62   1986   623.8'224'0973   86–1986
ISBN 0-486-25115-2 (v. 1)
ISBN 0-486-25116-0 (v. 2)

INTRODUCTION

THE clipper ship and the American clipper ship captain introduced into marine transportation the modern idea of service to the shipper in order to make dividends for the shipowner. These clipper ships set the pace for a short time as an American merchant marine and this pace was then picked up by Great Britain to capture the marine carrying trade of the world. The period of American maritime ascendancy was identical with that of the clipper ship, whose performances are the principal contribution of America to merchant marine history.

The clipper ship was a sailing vessel of peculiar construction, designed for great speed rather than for capacity. It had a long sharp bow, generally flaring outward as it rose above the water, and a long, clean run aft. The entrance lines were hollow, the masts were set with a great rake, and the yards were very square. A great sheer enhanced the appearance of a beautiful model and in every way the clipper ship ranked among the most handsome vessels ever put afloat.

It is generally conceded as a fact that the clipper model was developed in America from the fine, fast vessels of war built in France, which, prior to 1800, had the reputation of being superior in speed to any other sailing vessels afloat. In 1812 America became famous for fast vessels of small tonnage, some of the best of which were built in Baltimore, many being used as privateers. After the end of the war these vessels, ranging from the schooner of 100 tons to the ship of 350 tons, were put in overseas trade and they proved remarkably successful.

The first ship, called large, to be built on these lines, was the *Ann McKim*, 494 tons, launched at Baltimore in 1833. In her prime she was considered the fastest merchant ship afloat. The *Rainbow*, 757 tons, built at New York in 1845, was the second. The success of these two led to others being constructed of sharp model, principally for use in the China trade.

The full development of the clipper model did not, however, actually commence until 1850 when the demands of the new California trade put designers and builders on their mettle to turn out the fastest ships possible. The discovery of gold in Australia served as a further incentive to build clippers. After a few years the feverish activity in these trades lessened, freight rates dropped and the rage for vessels of high speed, built irrespective of cost, passed the flood, and the keels of no extreme clippers were laid in American yards after the end of 1854. The type of medium clippers was then elaborated and these models continued in vogue until the late 60's. Many of this latter class have records nearly equal to those of their 18 knot predecessors.

The American clipper ship was built of oak and other hard woods and was entitled to class A-1 for fourteen years. None were of the Colonial type of "soft wood" ships. Although the demand for clippers was so great and they were constructed with all possible speed, by builders from Maryland to Maine, it was not at the expense of either material or workmanship. The keel of the *John Bertram* was laid on Oct. 8, 1850, and ninety-one days thereafter she was at Boston, fully laden and ready to sail for San Francisco. She saw hard service for thirty-two years before meeting her fate. The character of the construction work is attested by the longevity of the *Young America, David Crockett,* and others too numerous to mention here.

To classify the clipper, medium, or, in some instances, the full models, has been a difficult task. Naturally shipowners were anxious to have their vessels rate as clippers, and often they were advertised as such, irrespective of merit. Frequently an ordinary merchant ship which had had the good fortune to make a fast passage was thereafter referred to as a clipper, disregarding the actual meaning of the word. Referring to the original *Akbar,* such an excellent clipper ship authority as Capt. R. B. Forbes wrote, "She was a good carrier and a fair sailer. Under command of Captain Dumaresq she might have deserved the name of clipper."

A criterion of the sharpness of any vessel, listed in this work, is the proportionate decrease from her original registered tonnage to her new measurement, per rules effective Jan. 1, 1865. Another test is the percentage of actual carrying capacity over the original register. Some clippers could carry barely their registered tonnage in dead weight and but little over it in mixed weight and measurement cargo. The *Panama*, 1130 tons, carried 1483 tons of mixed cargo, while the *Guiding Star*, of 899 tons, loaded as high as 2063 tons. The *Ganges*, advertised as a clipper, loaded 2413 tons against her register of 1258 tons.

It is confidently believed that all American-built ships which might fairly be classed as of sharp or clipper models, are mentioned in this book, while, *per contra*, there may appear some called mediums which were ordinary cargo carriers. Except in a few instances no vessels are described that were built after 1856, and not any built later than 1858.

With the advent of the clippers came the display of a great amount of ingenuity in the invention of their names. "Formerly," as an old account on the subject reads, "merchants were satisfied with a plain, prosy, modest nomenclature, calling their vessels after their wives, their friends, or some ancient worthy or modern hero, or by some homespun adjective expressive of strength or safety." This however was now all changed. There appeared for names *Typhoon*, *Hurricane*, *Simoon*, *Tornado*, *White Squall* and others descriptive of the action of the elements. Then there were names possibly egotistical but expressive of owners' pride; *Paragon*, *Peerless*, *Climax*, *Invincible*, *Queen of Clippers*, *Pride of America* and the like. Words pertaining to fleetness were naturally favorites as *Winged Arrow*, *Shooting Star*, *Sweepstakes*, *Flying Arrow*, *Staghound*, *Winged Racer*. In the realm of old ocean there were *Neptune's Car*, *Neptune's Favorite*, *Dashing Wave*, *Sparkling Sea*, *Flying Scud*. The most notable however were the many fantastic terms such as *Herald of the Morning*, *Witch of the Wave*, *Romance of the Seas*, *Wings of the Morning*. Referring to this last named ship, George Francis Train, writing home from Australia in 1854, said that he was "tired with these always-a-little-faster names" and suggested that "*Snail, Tortoise* or *Drone* be substituted just for a change." That the phraseology was, however, taking and catchy is evidenced by the fact that our cousins across the border in Canada were so favorably impressed that many of the ships they subsequently built bore the names of our most prominent clippers and this fact necessitates extreme care in tracing records.

The information contained in the following pages has been obtained from original sources contemporaneous with the vessels described. As early as 1877 research work was begun in San Francisco and it has been continued ever since. One result of this work was the compilation of a list of all deep-water arrivals and departures at the port of San Francisco, from the year 1849. It is the only list extant as fire and earthquake have destroyed most of the original records. Boston, New York and San Francisco newspapers have been carefully examined; private papers and correspondence of Eastern shipping firms have yielded a store of information and many letters have been written to foreign owners of American-built clippers. Much valuable information has been obtained from the "Percy Chase Papers" in the Harvard College Library and also from Lieutenant Maury's "Wind and Current Charts and Sailing Directions."

Mr. Charles R. Patterson has kindly permitted the reproduction in color of his painting of the *Surprise*. This has been possible through the coöperation of Messrs. Doll & Richards of Boston. Mr. Patterson's painting of *The Gold Seekers, 1849,* has been utilized on the jacket of this book through the coöperation of the Columbian Rope Company of Auburn, N. Y. The Peabody Museum, Salem, Mr. Robert C. Vose of Boston, Mr. A. G. H. Macpherson of Alverstoke, England, and Mr. M. B. Brainard of Hartford, Conn., have generously placed their collections of ship pictures at the disposal of the Society. A number of the ship portraits here published for the first time have been specially reproduced from paintings upwards of seventy years old. Such pictures are now very difficult to locate and, even when found, not always easy of access. The number of living actors in the drama of clipper ship life is practically nil.

ILLUSTRATIONS

AMERICAN CLIPPER SHIPS
1833-1858

AMERICAN CLIPPER SHIPS

ADELAIDE

MEDIUM clipper ship, built by A. C. Bell, son of Jacob Bell, at New York; launched Nov. 22, 1854. 218 x 41: 5 x 28: 2; 1831 tons American, 1694 tons British measurement. She was built to be operated as a Liverpool packet, had three decks and could carry some 3500 tons of cargo. She was very strongly built, had handsome cabins and cost $128,000. Her figurehead was a female in flowing white garments.

On account of the demand for tonnage to California, she was first put into that trade and on her initial voyage, Capt. James Hamilton being in command, she reached San Francisco, May 21, 1855, 114 days from New York. When 104 days out she was 500 miles from the Golden Gate. She then returned to New York, in 106 days, with wheat and barley which is said to have netted its shippers nearly 50 per cent profit. On her second voyage she arrived at San Francisco, Apr. 29, 1856, 124 days from New York, being within 500 miles of destination on the 110th day. Capt. Edgar Wakeman, who had assumed command at New York, reported that the voyage started auspiciously, the line being crossed 18 days out, while on the 28th day the ship was hove to, off Rio, in a heavy gale. On the return passage she took guano from Callao to New York in 91 days. On her third voyage she reached San Francisco, Sept. 29, 1857, having had much light weather and being close to the California coast for a week. On this run all of her crew of 26 A.B.'s were negroes and as the ship was docking at San Francisco, mate Lewis knocked one of the men from the topgallant forecastle overboard and the man was drowned. Lewis was arrested but was cleared. However, he was murdered by one of the crew while the ship was at Elide Island the following March. The negro murderer was tried by a court convened from officers of various ships then in port, was convicted and hanged aboard the *Adelaide*. Completing her voyage the ship left the Island, Mar. 28, 1858 and was 87 days to New York.

The *Adelaide* left New York, Aug. 30, 1858, and was 133 days to San Francisco. Loaded guano at the Chincha Islands and sailed from Callao, Sept. 10th; arrived at Hampton Roads, Nov. 14th, an excellent run of 65 days. Captain Wakeman reported that his run from Cape Horn to destination was 38 days only. He then sold his interest in the ship and retired from sail, the ship going to Mobile and thence to Liverpool where she arrived Apr. 12, 1860, after a run of 27 days from the Southern port. She then entered the trade for which she was built, that of a packet between New York and Liverpool, and soon established a good reputation for seaworthiness and speed, which was consistently maintained. Under command of Captain Cutting she arrived at New York, Apr. 6, 1861, 22 days from Liverpool, and the four following westward passages were made in 27, 25, 30 and 25 days respectively.

In 1863 the *Adelaide* was reported sold to go under the British flag but as her purchaser, Mr. Guion, was a member of the firm of Williams & Guion, her former owners, it was thought that there really occurred no actual transfer. On June 9, 1864, she left New York and on the 27th reached Liverpool, a run of some hours under 18 days. In 1874 she appears as hailing from Liverpool, with A. G. Linn as owner. In 1875 she was reported lost.

That the *Adelaide* was a fast ship is unquestioned, but some of the published statements respecting her runs cannot be substantiated, particularly a passage of 12 days, 8 hours, New York to Liverpool, in 1864, on which occasion she is stated to have been passed in New York harbor, outward bound, by the steamship *Sidon*, also leaving port for Liverpool, the *Adelaide* arriving out first. As a matter of fact the *Adelaide* in 1859 left New York in company with the clipper ship *Great Republic*, both bound for San Francisco. They continued together for eight days when they parted by going on different tacks. Off Pernambuco the two ships again met and were in company two days. The *Great Republic*, however, reached San Francisco

13 days before her rival. During his four years of command of the *Adelaide,* Captain Wakeman was always accompanied by his wife and the ship has, perhaps, the unique experience of having two children born aboard to the master of the vessel. The first born was very appropriately named,—ADELAIDE SEABORN Wakeman.

ALARM

MEDIUM clipper ship, launched from the yard of E. & H. O. Briggs, at South Boston, Mar. 18, 1856, for Baker & Morrill of Boston. 172 keel; 182, deck; 190 over all x 37: 6 x 23; 1184 tons; rounding of sides, 12 inches; sheer, 4 feet; dead rise, 12 inches. She had a long buoyant floor, concave lines below water line, good clean ends for sailing and an oval stern. A female blowing a trumpet was her figurehead. Her lower masts, counting from her foremast were 75, 80 and 70 feet; topmasts, 42, 44 and 33; topgallant masts, 22, 24 and 19; royal masts, 15, 16 and 13; skysail poles, 11, 12 and 8 feet. She is said to have closely resembled the *Starlight,* a former product of the same builders for the same owners.

She first left Boston, Apr. 7, 1856, Captain Matthews in command, and was 24 days to the line; was off the Cape, 65 days out and crossed the equator on the 91st day; then had a long spell of light northerly winds, with no trades, and was 39 days completing her passage, arriving Aug. 16th, 130 days from Boston. From San Francisco she went to the Chinchas, took on a load of guano and made the passage to Hampton Roads in about 93 days, reaching New York, May 13, 1857, 99 days from Callao. After completing a round voyage to the West Coast of South America, she loaded at Boston for San Francisco and took her departure early in April, 1860, Captain Howes in command. She was 36 days to the line; in latitude 30° South, Atlantic, lost her maintopsail-yard in a hurricane; in 40° South, was hove to for three days under a close-reefed maintopsail; was 89 days to the Horn; on July 7th, while hove to off the Cape, shipped a sea which carried away the figurehead and washed the long boat off the house; made the Horn five times before she was clear and northbound in the Pacific; was 35 days from the equator crossing to destination and on arriving off the Golden Gate had but two days allowance of water on hand. Anchored in San Francisco harbor, Oct. 5, 1860, 182 days from Boston. She then loaded 1799 short tons of wheat for Liverpool, and for the following two years was engaged in trade between England and India.

On Nov. 3, 1863, the *Alarm* left Akyab for Singapore and three days later encountered a hurricane; the wheel house and everything movable on deck was washed overboard. The hurricane continuing, on the 7th and 8th, she sprung a leak. On the 15th she struck on the south end of Preparis Reef, her bow sliding high out of water and soon there was 11 feet of water in the hold. Two boats were launched and all hands landed on a small coral island about five miles distant. Three days later they were taken off by the ship *Sultana*, from Aden for Amherst. It being discovered that the *Alarm* had slid off the reef and was floating, Captain Howes boarded her and found three feet of water in the between decks. He decided that it was impossible to take her into port and she was abandoned. The captain and his crew were landed at Maulmain, Dec. 1st. She was insured for $55,000.

ALBONI

CLIPPER ship, designed and built by Mason C. Hill, at Mystic, Conn. Launched in October 1852; named after the celebrated Italian singer, then at the height of her fame. She was described as an exquisite specimen of shipbuilding and admirably proportioned. Length between perpendiculars, 156 feet; over all, 182 feet; extreme breadth, outside, 37: 6 feet; depth of hold, 21 feet; tons, old measurement, 917; new measurement, 837. Her figurehead was the image of a dove with an orange branch in its beak. She was purchased shortly after being launched by James Bishop & Co. of New York, the consideration reported being $55,000.

The *Alboni* was credited with being able to show good speed but unfavorable conditions on her various voyages prevented her from making a good showing, or, according to available records, from making any passage shorter than average. On her maiden voyage she left New York, Nov. 21, 1852, and was 131 days to San Francisco. Captain Littlefield, in command, reported being 65 days to the Horn and 99 days to the equator in the Pacific. When 113 days out she was within 300 miles of the Golden Gate, being close to the coast in a dense fog for the final seven days. From San Francisco she was 51 days to Callao, thence 85 days to New York with a guano cargo. On her second voyage she arrived at San Francisco, Sept. 1, 1854, 150 days from New York; had a hard time off the Horn, being driven back 700 miles and obliged to go around the Falklands twice; was hove to on one occasion for nine days. Had very light winds all the way up the Pacific, carrying skysails for 60 days after getting clear of the Cape. From San Francisco she was 52 days to Shanghai; left there in December, the monsoon favorable, and was 98 days to New York.

Captain Barnaby now assumed command and on his arrival at San Francisco, Oct. 21, 1855, reported his best day's run as 251 miles, off Tierra del Fuego, which day was the only one on the passage that there was any kind of a fair chance. When 24 days out from New York was in five degrees North latitude but was then becalmed for 17 days so that she was not up with the line until the 41st day; passed Cape Horn, 90 days out; had 18 days from 50° to 50°; in heavy gales in the South Pacific sprung the foremast and for 53 days thereafter had nothing on the foremast above the topmast. Several men were lost overboard and for the greater part of the rest of the run, the captain, two officers and two seamen were the only ones fit for duty. The equator in the Pacific was crossed 127 days out and for 38 days thereafter nothing but light and unfavorable winds were experienced, the ship being within 500 miles of the Golden Gate for 19 days; total time from New York, 165 days. She then crossed to Shanghai in 59 days, thence reaching New York, May 19, 1856, 112 days out, 93 days from Anjer. On her fourth and last passage from New York to San Francisco, she arrived out Nov. 7, 1858, in 150 days; passed Cape Horn on the 70th day out and then had 15 days of heavy westerly gales; crossed the equator 114 days out and then had 36 days of light winds and calms to port. Went to Shanghai in 53 days; thence to Singapore, and finally to New York, via London, arriving Jan. 12, 1861, being 61 days on the last section.

She then engaged in trade between New York and Bremen and Antwerp and Captain Blanke had command for one voyage after which Captain Hoyer took her. On her westward passage in June 1861, Captain Blanke reported having fallen in with several icebergs and soon after a terrific thunderstorm was encountered during which the ship was struck by lightning, and, although not damaged, yet the smell of sulphur was so strong between decks that the passengers were in a panic. On her westward passage in February 1862, she had a heavy gale lasting five days, terminating in a hurricane; was under bare poles for 12 hours, and nearly on beam ends. Feb. 22nd the mainmast was struck by lightning but no particular damage was done; had thunder, lightning and hail squalls until midnight when it moderated to a heavy gale but with a tremendous sea which shifted the cargo in the between decks. Between Feb. 17th and 24th, the ship drifted to south and east from 48°: 20-31°: 20 to 46°: 20-27°: 20.

About January 1863, the *Alboni* was sold to Theodore Ruger and went under the flag of Hanover, as *Elsie Ruger*. She was continued principally in trans-Atlantic trade although it is noticed that she left New York, in April 1864, for Hong Kong. In 1868 she was listed as still owned by Ruger, but hailing from Geestemünde. In 1874 registers her name does not appear.

ALERT

BUILT by Metcalf & Norris, at Damariscotta, Me., in 1850; 764 tons. Crocker & Warren of New York, owners. Sold at Calcutta in 1857. Lost near Formosa, October 1858.

ALEXANDER

BUILT by Hayden & Cudworth, at Medford, in 1852, 143 x 29 x 20; 596 tons. J. A. Baxter & Co., Boston, owners. Went under British flag, 1861. Struck Frederick Rock in the Straits of Rhio, Feb. 5, 1864, was beached and became a total wreck on East Island.

AMPHITRITE

BUILT by Samuel Hall at East Boston in 1853, 206 x 39 x 24; 1687 tons. Owned in Boston. Sold to go under the British flag, 1855; renamed *Result*.

ANDREW JACKSON

MEDIUM clipper ship, launched from the yard of Irons & Grinnell, at Mystic, Conn., in March 1855, under the name of *Belle Hoxie*. She arrived at New York, Apr. 4th and was soon sold to John H. Brower & Co. who renamed her *Andrew Jackson*. 220 x 41: 2 x 22: 3; 1679 tons, old measurement. She was a very strong and particularly well-built ship and always delivered her cargoes in first class condition. Her figurehead was an image of the soldier-statesman for whom she was named. She was well sparred but free from flying kites, crossing only one skysail-yard, the main.

The *Jackson's* record for fast passages compares very favorably with those of clippers of extreme model. She made seven runs from New York to San Francisco, as follows: in 1855, 128 days; '56/57, 105 days; '58, 101 days; '58/59, 103 days; 59/60, 90½ days; '61,

103 days; '62, 114 days. These give an average of 106⅓ days, against 105⅚ days for the seven passages made by the *Flying Fish* and 103⅓ days for six made by the *Flying Cloud*. Her best time from New York to the line was 18½ days; to the Straits of Le Maire, 43 days; to 50° South, Pacific, 52 days, all made on her run of 103 days in 1861. In 1865 she was 36 days from 50° South, Pacific, to within 700 miles of the Golden Gate, and on her next trip was 16 days from the equator crossing to San Francisco. She made four passages from San Francisco to New York, in 88, 101, 87 and 101 days respectively. Homeward bound, on her first voyage, she was 92 days from Altata, Mexico, to New York; in 1860 she was 43 days from San Francisco to Callao, thence 63 days to New York, in ballast. Completing her last voyage as an American ship she went from San Francisco to Puget Sound and loaded a cargo of spars for Spain; sailed from Port Townsend, Oct. 6th and arrived at Ferrol, Jan. 12, 1863, reporting her run as 95 days from Cape Flattery. From Spain she crossed to New York, arriving Apr. 11, 1863, after a boisterous passage of 25 days, during which she encountered much ice and thick weather and was obliged to stand to southeast for 24 hours to get clear. Between her 5th and 6th Cape Horn voyages she is said to have made a round between New York and Liverpool, her homeward passage being made in 15 days from the Rock Light, but dates verifying this passage are not now available.

The *Jackson* broke no records, either on a whole passage or over any of its sections. It has frequently been published that her run from New York to San Francisco, in 1859/60, was 89 days, 7 hours (also given in some instances, 89 days, 4 hours), which would be eclipsing the *Flying Cloud's* two fastest runs, but these statements are proven to be mythical. On the passage in question, the *Jackson* hove up her anchor at New York at 6 A.M., Dec. 25th, and passed Fort Lafayette at 8:45; discharging her pilot at noon. She received her San Francisco pilot at 8 A.M., Mar. 24, 1860, and anchored in San Francisco bay at 6 P.M. Thus her passage is 90 days, 12 hours, anchor to anchor; 89 days, 20 hours, pilot to pilot; which is the third fastest of record to this date. Distance sailed, 13,700 miles, as against the 15,091 miles covered by the *Flying Cloud* on the record run of 89 days, 8 hours, anchor to anchor. In 1858, the time of the *Jackson* from New York to San Francisco was represented as being 99 days, but as she had sailed Jan. 16th, and arrived out Apr. 27th, her actual time was 101 days, or 100 days, 16½ hours from dropping Sandy Hook pilot to passing Fort Point, Golden Gate. At the same time the *Twilight* was 100 days, 20 hours, between the same points but she had led the *Jackson* seven days to the Pacific equator crossing, or 74 days against 81. It appears that the fast passages of the *Jackson* were due to hard driving and also to a succession of winds favorable to her running near to a direct course, rather than to her ability to move through the water rapidly and there is no record of any great day's run to her credit.

After her arrival at New York from Spain, in 1863, the *Jackson* was sold to go under the British flag without change of name. Captain McCallum was given command and he continued in the ship until she was lost. On Sept. 30, 1863, she left New York for St. John, N. B. On Mar. 2, 1865, she arrived off Dover, from Soerabaya, Java (Dec. 3, 1864), bound for Amsterdam. On Sept. 13, 1868, she was at Shanghai and when homeward bound she went ashore on a reef in Gaspar Straits, Dec. 4, 1868, and became a total loss. At that time she hailed from Glasgow, her managing owner being given as H. L. Seligman.

Capt. John E. Williams was in command of the *Jackson* from 1855 until 1860; after which Captain Johnson was in charge until she was sold in 1863.

ANGLO SAXON

MEDIUM clipper ship, built by F. W. Rhodes at Rockland, Maine, in 1853. 868 tons, old measurement. She was sold to E. M. Robertson of New York, for $50,000. Was called a handsome ship, of fine model, and quite sharp lines, although force of circumstances prevented her from ever making any fast passages.

On her maiden voyage the *Anglo Saxon* left New York, May 14, 1853, Captain Leeds in command, and arrived at San Francisco, Oct. 12th, in a 150 days passage. Had very heavy weather off the Platte, received some damage and lost her deck load. Off the Horn had bad weather for 26 days, losing jibboom; was not in the Pacific, clear of the Cape, until 98 days out and then had light winds to destination. From San Francisco went to Callao and was 102 days thence to Baltimore. Her second outward passage was to the west coast of South America, the return being 84 days from Callao to Hampton Roads. Her third voyage was 120 days from New York to San Francisco, arriving Mar. 16, 1856, Captain Mayo in command. Was 15 days rounding the Horn and 52 days running up the Pacific. Went to Calcutta and was 109 days thence to New York, arriving Dec. 12, 1856.

On Sept. 21, 1858, she reached San Francisco under command of Capt. Henry Manter of Edgartown, 164 days from New York. Had generally light winds on the passage except for 41 days between the 50's, in very heavy weather. This voyage was completed by her taking a cargo of whale oil from the Sandwich Islands to New Bedford. On this run she was in competition with four other ships, she beating the time of the *West Wind*, but all had quite slow passages. She again went out to San Francisco from New York, her time being 139 days and arrival, Nov. 12, 1859. Captain Manter reported being 70 days to the Straits of Le Maire and 26 days rounding the Cape. From San Francisco she went to Mazatlan and thence to Europe with dye woods. Crossed to New York, and under command of Capt. John M. Cavarly, formerly mate of the clipper ships *Shooting Star* and *Golden Eagle,* she went out to San Francisco in 127 days, arriving Mar. 15, 1861. On this occasion she was 18 days rounding the Horn and 50 days running up the Pacific. Completed this voyage by again going to Mazatlan and Europe.

She reached San Francisco for the last time on Aug. 30, 1862, 171 days from New York, Captain Cavarly reporting a bad weather trip. Was 39 days rounding the Horn in terrific gales from south to southwest, making it almost impossible to get sufficient southing to clear the land. Was not clear of the Cape until 109 days out; thence had 29 days to the equator and was within 700 miles of the Golden Gate for 18 days, in a constant succession of light airs and calms. She then went to Howland's Island to load guano for Europe; struck the reef there and had to run back to Honolulu for repairs, which cost $15,000. An attempt was made by unknown parties to burn her but the fire was discovered in time and extinguished before much damage was done. Sailed from Honolulu, Dec. 25, 1862, and from Howland's Island, guano laden, on Feb. 17, 1863; arrived at Queenstown, June 23d, and at Liverpool, June 25th.

The *Anglo Saxon* sailed from Liverpool, Aug. 17, 1863, with a cargo of coal for New York. Four days later, when off Kinsale Head, she was captured by the Confederate privateer *Florida*, Lieutenant-Commander Maffitt, and was burned. On Aug. 24th, the *Florida* landed Captain Cavarly and his crew at Brest. A claim was filed with the Geneva Convention for the destruction of the *Anglo Saxon*, totaling $63,695, of which $42,710.79 was for value of vessel. The amount recommended as settlement, in the British tables, was $42,-711.

After the destruction of his ship, Captain Cavarly gave up sail and entered the employ of the Pacific Mail Steamship Company, becoming one of the best known and most highly honored commanders operating in the Pacific. Coincidentally, it is noted that J. N. Maffitt, former commander of the *Florida*, also became prominent as a captain in the service of the Pacific Mail.

ANN McKIM

CLIPPER ship, built in 1833, at Baltimore, by Kennard & Williamson, for Isaac McKim, a wealthy merchant of that city. Length on the water line, 143 feet; beam, 27: 6 feet; depth of hold, amidships, 14 feet; 494 tons. Her draft forward was 11 feet only but she had what was called a long leg, drawing a full 17 feet aft.

She had considerable rake to both stem and stern-post; large dead rise and fine entrance and clearance lines, slightly convex. Her freeboard was small and she had very little sheer. According to her registration papers, filed at the Baltimore Custom House, Aug. 21, 1833, she had "a square stern, round truck, no Jannenes and with a woman's bust as a figure-head." She was the first large vessel built on practically the lines of the brigs and schooners then known throughout the shipping world as "Baltimore Clippers." She was named after the wife of her owner and in her construction no expense was spared to have everything of the best. Fancy hard woods, with plenty of brass trimmings, were in evidence and she was equipped with a number of brass cannon. In her early days she was the best known American ship afloat.

It has been impossible to obtain details of any of her voyages, during her prime, but she was conceded to be the fastest merchant ship afloat. Dana, in "Two Years Before the Mast," classes her as the equal of the celebrated Baltimore brig *John Gilpin*, although at the time he was writing, the *McKim* was hogged. After the death of Mr. McKim, in 1837, she became the property of Howland & Aspinwall of New York, who operated her in trade with the West Coast of South America and between there and China. In 1847 she was sold to parties in Chile and was at Valparaiso when news was received of the discovery of gold in California. On Jan. 20, 1849, she arrived at San Francisco in 51 days from Valparaiso, via Guayaquil, where she had made a short stay, this being a very good run. Thereafter she made several round voyages between Chile and San Francisco, in 1850 making the run to Valparaiso in 47 days. In September 1851, under Captain Van Pelt, she left North American waters for good and is reported to have been dismantled at Valparaiso the following year.

ANTELOPE, OF BOSTON

MEDIUM clipper ship, built in 1851 by J. O. Curtis at Medford, Mass., for William Lincoln & Co., of Boston, who subsequently sold her and at the time of her loss she was owned by J. Morewood & Co., and hailed from New York. She was a small ship of but 587 tons, old measurement, equivalent to about 425 tons present-day style. Her dimensions were 140 x 29 x 19 feet and her draft when loaded, 17 feet.

Her maiden voyage was from Boston to San Francisco under Capt. Tully Crosby and it was prophesied that she would make the run out in 130 days or less, but her friends were disappointed for her passage footed up 149 days. She then crossed the Pacific in average time and completed her first voyage by running from Shanghai to New York in 118 days. The following year, 1853, Captain Snow was in command and had a passage of 128 days from New York to San Francisco; thence 54 days to Callao and from there 104 days to New York. Then followed a round voyage to the West Coast of South America after which she went into trade direct with China.

Under Captain Clarke, she left the outer anchorage of Bangkok in July 1858, with a full cargo and some passengers for China and at 6:30 A.M. Aug. 6th, at high tide, with no breakers nor rocks visible, struck on Discovery Shoal, Paracels Reef. It soon being evident that the vessel was doomed, Captain Clarke, with four passengers and 13 seamen left the ship in one boat, while the mate, one seaman and ten Chinese passengers took the other. During the first night the boats parted company. Four days later Captain Clarke fell in with a Chinese fishing boat and offered its inmates $20 to tow him to a place where he could refill his water casks. They agreed but it was soon evident that they were not keeping faith, so Captain Clarke cut the tow rope and endeavored to escape but the Chinese pursued and attacked the boat with stones, compelling surrender, as the shipwrecked crew were without means of resistance. The boat was robbed of everything of value, two of the Chinese armed with spears standing guard; but the attention of the pirates being distracted, while dividing the plunder, two of the American seamen sprang aboard the Chinese craft and succeeded in dispatching all her crew. Captain Clarke, who attempted to follow his men, fell between the boats but was rescued. The junk was well provided with rice and water and a course was steered for Hong Kong and that port was reached on Aug. 14th.

ANTELOPE, OF NEW YORK

EXTREME clipper ship, built by Perine, Patterson & Stack, at Williamsburg, Long Island, in 1852; launched Mar. 27th. 187 x 37 x 21: 4; 1186 tons, old, 1055 tons, new measurement. Owned by Henry Harbeck & Co., of New York.

The first two voyages of the *Antelope* were rounds between New York and San Francisco under Captain Shinn, and were respectively, 149 days outward, 112 return, and 115 days outward, 129 return. The third voyage, 1854/55, was under Captain Mooers, and was 135 days outward, the return being by way of Shanghai and to Manila. On all of these passages, the ship contended with adverse conditions of wind and weather and had no opportunity of showing her sailing ability. Her fourth voyage, however, brings her name in the list of vessels which have made the Cape Horn run from Eastern ports to San Francisco in two figures, these passages to this date, numbering 21, made by 20 different ships, the *Flying Cloud* having two to her credit. On this run, the *Antelope,* under Captain Cole, left New York, Dec. 8, 1858; was 19 days to the line; was up with the Straits of Le Maire when 47 days out and 12 hours getting through; was forced down to 59°: 28′ South, but was in 50° South, in the Pacific, when 54 days out, which was within a few hours of the time made by the *Flying Cloud* on her famous record run to San Francisco of 89 days, 8 hours. From here on, the chance of the *Antelope* to make a 90-day run was spoiled by a continuance of light winds and from 30° South to 4° North, she was under skysails and royal stunsails, not a sail being altered. The equator was crossed 81 days out, and 13 days thereafter she was up to the latitude of San Francisco, but could not make port until the 16th day. The passage figured some hours over 97 days and she arrived 12 days before the *Tornado* which had left New York two days before her and which she had spoken when in the North Atlantic. Even though the larger and more powerful *Tornado* was handicapped by light winds and calms in the North Pacific, she appears to have been distanced on each leg of the passage by her smaller competitor.

The fast passage quoted was the last Cape Horn run made by the *Antelope,* at least while she was under the American flag, her operations thereafter being in the China and East India trade. In 1862/63, under Captain Lavender, she went from Liverpool to Calcutta, and was 100 days on the return run to New York. Her arrival was May 4, 1863, and she appears then to have changed her nationality as she sailed on July 1st, following, for Shanghai, under Captain Smith, as the British ship *Antelope.* In 1864 she received new masts and rigging and is registered as owned by Harbeck, Halsey & Co., the hailing port being Cape Town, with Captain Lavender in command. On Jan. 29, 1866, she arrived at New York with another very fine passage to her credit. Captain Smith reported leaving Calcutta, Oct. 26, 1865, taking his departure from Sand Heads five days later. Stopping at St. Helena, Dec. 22nd, 52 days out, and sailing the following day, he crossed the line Jan. 6th and furled topgallant sails off Cape Hatteras, 81 days out, for the first time after leaving Sand Heads. Passage claimed to be 88 days, including one day at St. Helena, although dates show 90 days gross, 89 days net. On Dec. 6th, when 36 days out, in the South Indian Ocean, she spoke the *Young Mechanic* which had sailed in company with her from Calcutta and which arrived at Boston the same day the *Antelope* reached New York. Six days later, the American built, British owned ship *Longwood* reached New York, also having made a short run from Calcutta, 86 days, so that season appears to have been favorable for fast passages on this route.

In 1870 she appears on the register as the British ship *Antelope,* of Cape Town, owned by W. H. Leland.

ARAMINGO

MEDIUM clipper ship, built in 1851, by Aaron Westervelt, at New York. 152: 4 x 34: 6 x 22: 6; draft, loaded, 18 feet. 716 tons, old, 729 tons, new measurement. Owned by Chamberlain & Phelps of New York.

Sailing from New York, Jan. 12, 1852, under Captain Sylvester, she arrived at San Francisco, May 29th, in 138 days. Thence crossed to Shanghai in 47 days, where the command was taken over by Captain Chadwick, formerly of the *Hoogly*, which was lost about this time, while bound up the river to Shanghai. The *Aramingo* left Shanghai, Oct. 6th, passed Anjer, Nov. 1st and reached New York, Feb. 1, 1853, 118 days from port of departure and 92 days from the Straits of Sunda,—a slow passage. Captain Drinkwater now assumed command and on arrival at San Francisco, July 23, 1853, reported an eventful passage of 133 days from New York. Was off the Horn for 20 days in heavy gales and within 700 miles of the Golden Gate for 13 days in light winds. June 1st, in the South Pacific, the ship had been in collision with the British bark *Regonwald*, from Callao, and while in contact, her captain, two mates and six seamen, jumped aboard the *Aramingo*, leaving seven men on their ship. The following day a vessel was seen, supposed to be the bark, but in a short time she disappeared. The ship had her mainyard damaged, foresail split, lost running rigging and one anchor.

This was the last appearance of the *Aramingo* at San Francisco. She thence went to Callao in 45 days, loaded guano at the Chinchas, and was 76 days from Callao to New York, arriving Mar. 16, 1854. She was thereafter principally used in trade between the Indies, England and the States and appears to have had a fair share of misfortunes. Under Captain Cassin, she arrived at Liverpool, Apr. 25, 1861, from Philadelphia, in a leaky condition; had been obliged to jettison cargo and had mainmast sprung. Then went out to Madras, having a long passage; proceeded to Calcutta and loaded a cargo, principally saltpetre, for New York. While outward bound, in tow of tug *Powerful*, she was stranded near Futlah Point and on floating

"Adelaide," 1831 tons, built at New York, in 1854

From a lithograph by Currier & Ives, 1856, showing the ship off Sandy Hook, "Hove to for a pilot"

"ANDREW JACKSON," 1679 TONS, BUILT AT MYSTIC, CONN., IN 1855
From a painting at Sailor's Snug Harbor, Staten Island, N. Y.

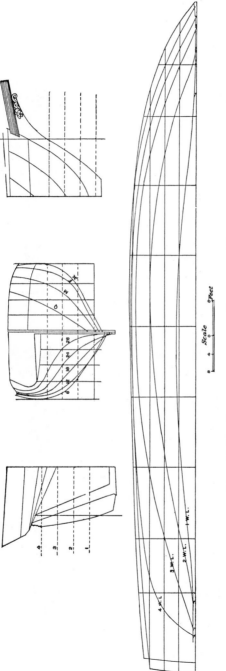

"ANN McKIM," 494 TONS, BUILT AT BALTIMORE, MD., IN 1833
Lines from Hall's *Ship-Building Industry of the United States*, 1884

"ARCHER," 1095 TONS, BUILT AT NEW YORK, IN 1852

From a Chinese painting showing the ship off Hong Kong

off she came in contact with her tug, both being considerably damaged. She finally got away from the Sand Heads, Apr. 21, 1862, and when near Ceylon, took officers, crew and passengers, 64 persons in all, from the British bark *Defiance*, of and for Madras, from Maulmain, with lumber, which had sprung a leak and was on beam ends. Landed the rescued party at Trincomalee. Off the Cape of Good Hope, July 5th, spoke clipper ship *Starlight*, which had left Sand Heads, May 8th, 17 days later than *Aramingo's* departure and which arrived at Boston, Aug. 25th, five days before the *Aramingo* reached New York.

In September 1862 she was sold at New York, the reported consideration being $25,000. She then crossed to England and in February 1863 was sold for £4650 sterling, having been repaired and newly coppered. Her new owners were Julius Ruhland & Co., of Bremen and she was renamed *Matador*. As the Bremen ship *Matador* she cleared from New York, June 23, 1863, for London. In December 1871, the *Matador*, Captain Kimme, on a voyage for London, put into St. Helena, leaky, and landed 300 tons of her cargo. This brought the leak above water and she sailed Dec. 23rd and reached her destination in safety. The German schooner *Margarotha* arrived at St. Helena, Feb. 4, 1872, and was chartered to take the cargo left by the *Matador*, to London. In 1875, the *Matador* is listed as owned by Gildermeister & Ries of Bremen.

ARCHER

CLIPPER ship, launched Dec. 29, 1852, by James M. Hood, for Crocker & Warren, New York. 176 x 37 x 21: 6; 1095 tons, old; 905 tons, new measurement. In May 1862 she was sold at New York to William Perkins of Boston, and was taken to that port for extensive repairs and a thorough overhauling, the total cost of which is said to have been about $25,000, leaving her practically rebuilt. Later on she was reported as being owned by Samuel G. Reed of Boston, who sold her in 1876, to Captain Crossman, for $12,000.

Among her different masters were Captains Bursley, Thomas, Osgood, Crowell, Josiah P. Cressey, Edward R. Power, Richard Evans, who died a few days after leaving Manila in October 1872, for Boston, and Moses Pike.

The *Archer* always had the name of being a fast sailer. Between 1853 and 1872 she made 11 passages from New York or Boston to San Francisco, which averaged 118 days; two of these were 146 and 144 days, due to light winds and also to long spells of heavy weather off Cape Horn. The average of the other nine runs is 113 days, two being of 106 days each, one of 108 days and one of 112 days, on which occasion she made the land near Monterey, California, when 108 days out. Her fastest run from port to the line, in Atlantic, was 19½ days; to the Horn, 51 days; to the equator, in Pacific, 83 days, on two occasions; from the equator to San Francisco she was singularly fortunate, having an average of 23 days for the 11 runs; six were particularly fast, as follows; 15, 16, 17, 17 18/24, 18 and 19 days; the slowest was 38 days, on her maiden trip.

From San Francisco she twice went to New York direct in 99 and 108 days respectively. To Hong Kong or Shanghai she made six runs; fastest, 45 days; slowest, 65 days and average, 54 days. From Hong Kong to San Francisco she had one run of 42 days. On two occasions she went to Callao in 42 and 49 days from the Golden Gate and thence to Hampton Roads in 75 and 85 days respectively. Among her passages from the Far East, homeward, may be noted; 127 days from Shanghai to London in 1855, taking her departure during the unfavorable season; Rangoon to Falmouth in 109 days, 1858; Foo Chow to New York, 106 days, 1865. In 1855/56 she was 106 days from Portsmouth, England, to Calcutta, returning to London in 107 days.

On her second run from New York to San Francisco, 106 days, in 1854, the *Archer* was beaten by the *Flying Cloud*, 17 days. The *Archer* left New York, eight days before the *Flying Cloud*, but the latter had more favorable winds and overhauled the *Archer* off the Horn. Both crossed the line, in the Pacific, the same day but the

Archer was two degrees further west and ran into light winds and calms while the *Flying Cloud*, favored by fine trades and good winds, was but 14⅓ days to port against *Archer's* 23 days. The *Flying Cloud's* time on this passage, was 89 days, 8 hours, the fastest on record from any Eastern port to San Francisco, to the present time. Eight years later, Captain Cressey, then in the *Flying Cloud*, commanded the *Archer*.

The *Archer* had many mishaps. In 1865 she was put on a sand bar in the river Min, by her Chinese pilot, and had to be docked. In March 1866, from Foo Chow for New York, she was struck by a hurricane off Cape Hatteras and thrown on her beam ends; lost her foretopsail yard and its double-reefed sail, was strained and otherwise damaged. In 1856 she was off the Horn for 30 days, having her bows started and everything forward loosened so that no head sail could be carried for 15 days; one pump was thereafter continually going until her arrival at San Francisco, 144 days from New York. In January 1865 she lost jibboom and had foremast sprung off the Horn, besides which she was struck by lightning, though not materially damaged thereby. Shortly after leaving New York, Oct. 14, 1866, she had a heavy gale for two days which opened up her seams and caused a leak and she put into Boston, on the 27th, for repairs. The damage to ship and cargo was $12,000. She resumed her voyage Dec. 10th.

In the South Atlantic, in 1867, bound to New York from San Francisco, her fresh water supply was found to be only 75 gallons, due to a leaky tank. A condenser was improvised from odd material including lead pipe from the head pump and about 10 gallons were obtained daily. The *Herald of the Morning* was later fallen in with and furnished three casks of water and soon after heavy rains gave a bountiful supply.

On Feb. 12, 1880, the *Archer*, then bark-rigged, foundered at sea while on a passage from New York to Havre. Captain Harris and his crew, exhausted from pumping, had just been taken off by the steamer *Naworth Castle*, which landed them at Sunderland.

ARCHITECT

THE *Architect*, although of but 520 tons register, was the largest of three ships built in Baltimore in 1847/48, of sharp model and designated as clippers but, of course, they were not in the same class as the extreme clippers later developed to take care of the California and China trade which was soon to rank first in importance among ocean trade routes. All these three, the *Architect*, *Gray Eagle* and *Greyhound*, established from the start good records for speed and became prominent in trade, principally with Rio Janeiro. They were also among the earliest vessels to take gold-seekers to California in 1849, being, indeed, the first clippers to be so employed.

The *Architect* was at New Orleans in January 1849, under command of Captain Gray, and soon filled up with passengers and freight for San Francisco. Like many other vessels in the early months of 1849, only one of her foremast hands received pay and that one was William Downie, who later founded the town of Downieville, California, and became prominent in the development of the northern part of the state. The voyage of the *Architect* to the Golden Coast proved to be eventful and tedious. Cholera broke out, causing several deaths among the 56 passengers aboard. Dissensions arose and the ship was obliged to put in to Rio. Sailing again Mar. 18th, she made slow time in the South Atlantic, had bad weather off the Horn and was reported to have put into a Chilian port for supplies. She arrived at San Francisco, June 28, 1849, reporting 160 days from New Orleans and 101 days from Rio.

There are no records showing when she left San Francisco or where she went, but she returned there in April 1850, reporting 45 days from Valparaiso. She then crossed to Hong Kong, under Captain Tibbetts, in 42 days, an excellent run, and was reported to have been sold by Mr. Gray, her original owner, for $24,000. Captain Dearborn assumed command and took his charge to New York in 108 days, a very fast run for a vessel leaving the China coast in the month of August. On arrival at New York, in December, she was reported as having been purchased for the California trade, for

$30,000. Captain Caspar was placed in command and the prediction that she would go out to San Francisco in 120 days or less was fulfilled as, allowing for 13 days spent in port at Talcahuana, she made the run in 116 actual sailing days. Captain Caspar reported that on May 28th, in 46° South, 82° West, they experienced a hurricane from the east lasting 12 hours, during which the ship scudded under bare poles 200 miles, by observation. This would make her time from New York to the location stated, as 66 days, an excellent run. From San Francisco she went down to Sydney, Australia, in the fast time of 46 days.

The *Architect* returned to San Francisco in May 1852, from Hobart Town, passage 77 days. Captain Coggins then took her back to Sydney in 54 days, and thence to China. In May 1853, she was reported lying idle at Hong Kong, Captain Hedges being in command. However, she was soon after taken up for London, with tea, and under Capt. George A. Potter sailed June 25, 1853, passed Anjer, July 21st, and arrived in the Downs, 107 days from Whampoa, and 80 days from Anjer. This passage, in itself, was not extraordinary but owing to the fact that she arrived out ahead of the British tea ships she was able to command the highest freight the following season.

The *Architect* crossed to New York and thence went out to Hong Kong in 102 days; sailing date, Mar. 1, 1854; arrival, June 11th; had been 24 days to the line and crossed the meridian of Greenwich, 47 days out, both good runs for the season. She was later reported sold at Hong Kong for $23,000, to sail under the British flag and for a few years, at least, continued in trade between London and China, but her name does not appear in the register of 1857/58.

AREY

BUILT by Williams & Arey, at Frankfort, Me., in 1856. 177 x 37 x 23; 1129 tons. Williams & Arey, Frankfort, owners. Sold to Wakeman, Dimon & Co., of New York, and renamed *Caroline*. In 1873 was ship *Nautilus*, of London, England.

ARGONAUT

BUILT by Samuel Lapham, at Medford, Mass., for John Ellerton Lodge, one of Boston's best known shipping merchants engaged in commerce, chiefly with China. Ready in October 1849, for her maiden voyage, the demand for vessels to go to California was so great that she was diverted in that direction and it is stated that before she left port her freight and passage money had more than equaled her cost. Designed before the necessity for, or the development of, the clipper model, she was an excellent specimen of the merchant ship of that period and the record of her performances is alike creditable to her builder and her commanders. She was quite small, of but 575 40/95 tons, old measurement; length of keel, 123 feet; deck, 148; beam, 32; depth of hold, 20; draft, 17 feet; dead rise, 15 inches. She was well sparred but carried no flying kites.

On her first voyage she arrived at San Francisco, Mar. 13, 1850, Capt. William Nott reporting his passage as 133 days, including a few days spent in port at Valparaiso. Crossing the Pacific to Hong Kong she loaded teas and left Whampoa, Aug. 27th; was 32 days to Anjer, thence 76 days to London with a total of 107 days. She beat the Aberdeen clippers *Countess of Seafield* and *Reindeer* and all other vessels leaving China for England about the same time, with the exception of the American clipper *Oriental*, whose time to London was 97 days. In their beat down the China Sea, against the southwest monsoon, the *Oriental* had the best of the *Argonaut* by 11 days, but from Anjer to London, the latter cut down this lead by one day. On their return voyage to China, the *Reindeer* left London late in December 1850 and was 130 days to Hong Kong. The *Oriental* sailed Jan. 14, 1851, and was 117 days going out. The *Argonaut* got away Feb. 27th and went out in 107 days, thus handsomely beating both her rivals. After loading for New York she took her departure from Whampoa, Sept. 4, 1851, and made the homeward run in 105 days, beating everything sailing from two weeks before her to two weeks after her, by from 7 to 25 days. The list included the *Houqua*, *Sea Nymph*, *Ariel* and *Isabelita Hyne*, all classed as fast sailers.

The third outward voyage of the *Argonaut* was from Boston to San Francisco and was the last one she made over the course; arrival out, July 4, 1852, 134 days passage. She passed through the Golden Gate a few hours after the *Staghound* and the *Sea Nymph*, whose runs from New York were 124 and 120 days respectively, all three vessels reporting light winds and calms the greater part of the way. Completing this voyage, the *Argonaut* crossed to China and loaded at Shanghai, and arrived at New York, Mar. 30, 1853, after a passage of 117 days; 100 days from Anjer. Captain Nott then turned the command of the *Argonaut* over to Capt. Nathaniel Hale, in order to take charge of Mr. Lodge's ship *Don Quixote*, then in process of construction at Medford. Leaving Boston, Apr. 27, 1853, Captain Hale took his charge to Canton in 119 days, the return being 116 days to London, arriving Apr. 3, 1854.

The *Argonaut* continued in trade with the Far East, her passages averaging well. In 1856/57 she was 99 days from Boston to Shanghai in spite of her slow run of 38 days from port of departure to the line and the season being that of the unfavorable monsoon. Her run of 106 days from Boston to Hong Kong, in 1860, was also made in the poor season. She left Boston, Feb. 2, 1861, for Shanghai and on May 19th was towed into Singapore damaged by collision with the steamer *Madras*. Captain Norton was in command, Captain Hale having been transferred to the *Sancho Panza*. After making necessary repairs the *Argonaut* proceeded up the China coast and loaded at Foo Chow for New York. She sailed Jan. 9, 1862; passed Anjer, Feb. 4th and arrived at her destination on May 17th.

On Apr. 29, 1864, the *Argonaut*, Captain Norton in command, while bound from Manila for New York, put into Mauritius, leaking badly in her upper works; discharged cargo and repaired. On arrival at New York, the following October, she was sold to go under the Norwegian flag without change of name, her new owners being Ruger Brothers of Geestemünde. In 1866 she is listed as owned in Christiana by P. Stranger. A few years later her name was dropped from the registers.

ASA ELDRIDGE

MEDIUM clipper ship, built in 1856 by E. & H. O. Briggs, at South Boston, Mass. 199 x 38: 10 x 25; 1324 tons, gross; 1296 tons, net. Her keel was 183 feet; dead rise, 15 inches; swell of sides, 12 inches. Her entrance lines were slightly concave below, becoming convex above but were comparatively short. For a figurehead she had a bust of the well-known packet commander after whom she had been named and who lost his life in the Collins' steamship *Pacific*. On her first voyage this figurehead was started from its fastenings by the heavy seas off the Horn and nearly lost. On rounding the Cape in 1861, it was entirely carried away but later recovered. On this occasion the bowsprit was broken off at the knightheads.

The original owner of the *Eldridge* was Henry Hallet of Boston, who sold her, in 1865, to W. F. Weld & Co., of the same place. That firm operated her in trade with San Francisco and the East Indies, until 1873, when she was purchased by Blim, Main and Montgomery. In February of the same year she was sold to English parties for £7000 and renamed *Norfolk*, hailing from Liverpool. Her first captain was Moses R. Coleman, after whom came, successively, Levi Howes, Captain Kelley and Captain Baker, the latter being in command for the five or six years prior to her sale abroad.

While credited with having fair capacity for speed, a résumé of the passages made by the *Eldridge* reveals the fact that generally they were longer than those made by ships also claimed as medium clippers. Outward bound to San Francisco she made nine runs from New York and one from Boston, the average of the ten being 140½ days. Her first arrival out was May 8, 1857, in 123 days, this being her fastest run over the course. The last time she passed through the Golden Gate, inward bound, was Sept. 20, 1872, 157 days out, this being her slowest run. Of return passages, two only were made direct from San Francisco to Atlantic ports, viz.; 120 days to Boston, in 1865, and 115 days to Liverpool, in 1872. She made four runs homeward from Manila and an equal number from Callao or a Pacific guano island, none of which could be considered better than average. In 1859 she was 17 days from Élide Island, Lower California, to the equator; 34 days thence to Cape Horn; 30 days to the line and 30 days thence to New York, a total of 111 days,—slow running time over every section of the course. Of passages between ports of the Pacific, her run of 28 days from Honolulu to Hong Kong, in 1866, may be considered as good, contrasting with her 44 days, Shanghai to Honolulu, in 1863, and her 69 days, San Francisco to Melbourne, in 1861. In registers as late as 1880, the *Norfolk* still appears as hailing from Liverpool.

ASPASIA

BUILT by Maxon, Fish & Co., at Mystic, Conn., in 1856. 145 x 31 x 20; 632 tons. N. G. Fish & Co., of Mystic, owners. Sold to Bucklin & Crane of New York. Resold in 1863 to go under British flag.

ASTERION

MEDIUM clipper ship, built by Stetson, at Chelsea, to the order of David Snow and others, of Boston, and launched June 28, 1854. 188 x 36 x 34; 1135 tons, old measurement. She was adapted for carrying capacity rather than speed, although her passages averaged fairly fast. About 1860 she was bought by Bucklin & Crane of New York and put in the California trade. Her original cost was $67,000 but at the time of her sale she was valued at the price of $46,000.

Soon after her launch she was chartered for $17,000 to go to Liverpool and return. On Mar. 11, 1857, she sailed from the Chincha Islands with a cargo of 1400 tons of guano, drawing 21 feet aft. She was insured for the voyage at seven per cent and one per cent additional for her guano charter. Capt. Moses Gay was in command. She sailed from Manila, Aug. 31, 1859, passed Anjer, Oct. 8th, was up with the Cape of Good Hope, Nov. 11th, but was driven back by a heavy gale and did not get clear, northbound, until 11 days later; arrived at Boston, Jan. 26, 1860, Captain Snow in command. She then crossed to England and loaded at Cardiff for San Francisco. Arrived out Apr. 22, 1861, Captain Gardner, who was in command, reporting a passage of 139 days. She later loaded guano at Baker's Island for Hampton Roads.

From Pernambuco, Captain Gardner wrote to his owners, under date of Sept. 16, 1861;—"I arrived off this port the 15th, 75 days from Baker's Island, and came to the outer roads this morning. I think you had better insure, even at the extra expense, as the *Asterion* is not a clipper and will be a bon prize for the Southerners. I shall sail this evening and take a new route for Hampton Roads." Captain Gardner's letter left Pernambuco, Sept. 19th, on the brigantine *Joseph Parke* of Boston, which was captured Sept. 25th, by the *Sumter*, whose captain, Semmes, was rather amused at the tenor of the letter. The *Asterion* arrived at her destination in safety, Oct. 16th, and later proceeded to New York where she loaded for San Francisco.

Captain Hurd assumed command and made the passage out in 131 days, arriving May 14, 1862, and returned direct to New York in 116 days.

On her last voyage, which was destined never to be completed, the *Asterion* reached San Francisco, June 2, 1863, 151 days from New York, Captain Hurd reporting unfavorable weather conditions throughout; 35 days to the line; 67 days to the Straits of Le Maire; 23 days rounding the Horn in very severe weather; and 33 days from the equator to destination. After loading a cargo of guano at Howland's Island, she was lost Sept. 24, 1863, soon after sailing, on the reef at Baker's Island. Capt. W. H. McLain, in after years one of the most respected and competent commanders in the Pacific and long employed by the Pacific Mail Steamship Company, was a member of the crew of the *Asterion* at the time of her loss and the following account is taken from his "Reminiscences" published in a San Francisco paper.

In 1863, at the age of seventeen, he sailed from San Francisco in the *Asterion*, bound for Howland's Island to load guano. After taking on her cargo and starting on her passage, the ship was lost on Baker's Island, some fifty miles distant from Howland's. The crew had great difficulty in fighting their way through the surf to the beach. A few stores and some wreckage drifted ashore and out of the latter rude huts were constructed. For over two months they dragged out a miserable existence, their principal food being snakes, which they dug from holes in the ground, and sea birds which they caught. A constant lookout was kept for passing vessels and finally a sail was sighted which they were able to signal and which took them off. It was the *Herald of the Morning*, from San Francisco for Howland's Island, and they were taken thence. From there they got to Honolulu, arriving Dec. 25th.

A Sydney, Australia, newspaper of Feb. 8, 1864, contains the following: "Chief officer Aldrick and three of the crew of the *Asterion* arrived here yesterday in the *Clarence Packet* from the South Sea Islands; their ship was wrecked on the night of Sept. 24th, on Baker's Island. Mr. Aldrick with six men left in a boat for Howland's Island, to engage a vessel to take the crew and what was saved from the wreck, to the Sandwich Islands. They missed Howland's and were obliged to bear up for the Kingsmill Group, where they arrived after ten days. Here they found the *Clarence Packet*. Captain Hurd and 17 of the ship's crew had been left on Baker's Island. The ship was insured in New York and had 1600 tons of guano aboard."

ATALANTA

CLIPPER ship, built at Baltimore, in 1852, by Gardner & Palmer, for Montell & Co., of that city. 200 x 37: 6 x 21: 6; 1289 tons, old measurement. She is described as of a beautiful model and was the largest vessel built at Baltimore up to that time. During her short career as an American ship, she proved a fast sailer but had many mishaps. On her first passage, Baltimore to New York, Capt. William Williams in command, she had all three topmasts carried away in a squall and reached destination in a disabled condition.

She sailed from New York, Apr. 14, 1852, under Captain Wallace, and was 142 days to San Francisco and thence 40 days to Hong Kong. She left that port, Dec. 16th, had a fine run down the China Sea and was clear of Java Head on the 25th, nine days out; had only moderate winds in the Indian Ocean, passing the Cape, Jan. 28th, 43 days out and 34 days after clearing Sunda Straits; was thence 23 days to the line, 66 days out,—good time but nothing near a record,— had a fine run from the line, 18 days to pilot, about 40 miles from Sandy Hook, March 10, 1853, a total of 84 days from Whampoa,— excellent time, but 75 days from Java Head,—a fair passage only. The same day, at 10 P.M., 13 hours after receiving her pilot, she grounded on Romer's Shoals, running her bows well up out of water. Tow boats were immediately sent to assist but it was only after nine days lightering cargo that it was possible to release her from her very dangerous condition. Being very strongly built she was not seriously damaged and after repairing she sailed from New York, June 20, 1853. On arrival at San Francisco, Captain Wallace reported his passage as 124 days. Went thence to Valparaiso in 44 days and from there to Talcahuano, thence returning to San Francisco in 44 days; was 500 miles from destination when 34 days out and was within 100 miles for the last three days. Then went back to Valparaiso in 46 days and was 80 days thence to Boston, arriving Oct. 30, 1854.

Capt. F. M. Montell now took command and until she got into the Pacific had a fine run; on the 13th day out from New York made 338 miles by observation; was 19½ days to the line, 46 days to 50°

South and 10 days later was in 50° South, Pacific; thereafter had only light and baffling winds, with no trades and did not reach San Francisco until June 30, 1855, a 127 days' passage. Went again to Valparaiso; thence to Callao and from there to Valencia, Spain, and proceeded to Marseilles. Her crew of Italians mutinied, stabbed the mate, locked the officers in the cabin and proceeded with the ship towards the Levant. Becoming short of provisions they put into Marseilles where they were captured by the *Constellation*. The *Atalanta* finally reached New York, July 29, 1856. From New York she went to Palma, Spain, arriving out, under Captain Ellis, Nov. 26, 1856, and was sold there, going under the Spanish flag as the *Marguerita* of that port, H. A. Coit, owner.

The *Atalanta* must not be confused with two other ships of the same name, one built in Amesbury in 1850, which foundered off Cape Flattery in 1890; the other, built at Richmond, Me., in 1857, and sold, foreign, in 1872.

ATMOSPHERE

MEDIUM clipper ship, built in 1856, by George Greenman, at Mystic, Conn. 190 x 41:1 x 22:8; 1485 tons, American measurement, old style; 1378 tons, British measurement. Owned by John A. McGaw of New York, until 1863, when she was sold at auction at New York and shortly after was resold, going under the British flag without change of name; W. Tapscott & Co., of Liverpool, owners.

After a round voyage to England, the *Atmosphere* was put on the berth at New York for San Francisco and arrived out Dec. 1, 1857, in 150 days. Capt. William H. Lunt, subsequently in the *Prima Donna*, belonging to the same owners, was in command. She sailed from San Francisco, Jan. 20, 1858, and the following morning a whirlwind carried away the jibboom, the foremast, close to the deck, and the maintopgallant-mast; she returned to port, refitted, resumed the voyage and was about 60 days to Hong Kong. Returned to San Francisco in 60 days, thence back to Hong Kong in 55 days. She then went to Calcutta; left Sand Heads, Oct. 9, 1859, and arrived at New York, Jan. 9, 1860. She then crossed to Liverpool and loaded a cargo of railroad iron for Calcutta. On arrival out, about Nov. 16, 1860, she went ashore on Melancholy Point and her cargo had to be lightered. She continued in trade between England and India and letters from Bombay, dated June 27, 1861, reported that in getting under way for London she ran into an iron ship lying at anchor, losing her figurehead and sustaining other damage. Completing this voyage she arrived at New York, Dec. 10, 1861, from Liverpool.

In 1864, the *Atmosphere*, Captain Freeman, sailed from Liverpool for New York, via Cardiff, where she took on board 1800 tons of railroad iron, and soon after leaving the latter port, encountered a hurricane which compelled her to put back to Liverpool, discharge cargo and go into dry dock for repairs. In 1869 she arrived at Liverpool, July 2nd, from Bombay, via Queenstown, where she had been forced to put in, short of provisions and with most of her crew sick. In 1882, while on a voyage from Liverpool for Valparaiso, she sank off Pernambuco after collision with the British ship *Thyrstira*.

While under British colors she was commanded by Captains Smith, Oram, Koven and Costello.

AURORA

E XTREME clipper ship, built by John Taylor, at Chelsea, Mass., in 1853; launched Nov. 5th. Owned by Pickman, Silsbee & Allen, of Salem. 204: 2 x 38: 6 x 24; 1396 40/95 tons, old measurement; cost of ship and outfit, $83,400. She was of fine model, had a long sharp entrance and at times showed great speed, although on no occasion did she have such continued favorable weather conditions as to enable her to make a complete passage of any particular note. Calms, light and contrary winds, are frequent entries in the records of her various voyages. On one occasion she was 47 days out from Sandy Hook to the equator, while in nearly all of her passages to San Francisco, she was fated to experience light winds in the Pacific, particularly off the California coast. As will also appear, there fell to her lot from her initial voyage, an undue number of mishaps and misfortunes.

Her four direct Cape Horn passages to San Francisco averaged 126 days; fastest, 112 days (in 1856), on which occasion she was 500 miles from the Golden Gate when 105 days out; the slowest on this run was 139 days, in 1861. On her two other voyages over this course she was forced into Rio, the first time being on her initial trip (1854), due to mutiny in the crew; again, in 1857, she had to put back, from near the Falkland Islands, to repair a broken rudderhead. These two runs from Rio to San Francisco were made in 72 and 105 days respectively. Of her passages between California and Hong Kong, three were westward, in 43, 48 and 47 days and two returning, in 49 and 48 days respectively, all being better than average time. Her five homeward passages from the East Indies were all made from Manila; the two fastest being 101 days, 78 from Anjer, to Boston (in 1863), and 103 days, 88 from Anjer, to New York (in 1854). It is noted, however, that her departures were generally made during the unfavorable seasons. In 1861, with a cargo of 1483 short tons of wheat in bags, which put her down to her maximum draft of 21 feet, she made the run to Queenstown in 122 days. While beating down the harbor, outward bound, she had touched on Blossom Rock, but came off quickly, and a survey showed she was not damaged.

On her passage from San Francisco to Hong Kong, late in 1862, she arrived at her destination in company with the bark *Lillie Knowles*, from New York for Shanghai, with whom she had been in collision. The bark was badly damaged but the *Aurora* only slightly. As a result of the importation of coolie laborers into California, about this time, suit was entered by the State against all ships engaged in the trade, for transgression of the passenger laws, and in company with the others, the *Aurora's* charterers were forced to pay $3 a head for those she landed.

Shortly after her arrival at Boston, in May 1863, the *Aurora* was reported as being sold, terms private. She went to New York in ballast and as the British ship *Aurora*, sailed Aug. 21st for Melbourne, thence going on to India. Was thereafter engaged principally between Calcutta, Bombay and England. In August 1865, while on a passage from Calcutta to Boston, was forced to put back for repairs and was docked, stripped, caulked and remetaled.

While under the American flag she was commanded by Captain Brown for the first three years; later by Captain Clough, and in 1862, Lloyd's Register gives her as under command of Captain Hopkins. Under the British flag she was owned for several years by Fisher & Ricardo, the hailing port being Bombay, with Captain Geit in command. In 1868, Bixkell & Company of Liverpool, owned her and the register of 1870 gives her owners as G. & R. S. Walker of London, with Captain Harriot in command.

Some time in or after 1870, the *Aurora* was burned not far from Bombay. She was found to have been loaded with bogus cotton and the captain and officers were accused of setting her on fire and afterwards tried and convicted.

AUSTRALIA

BUILT by William H. Webb, at New York, in 1852. 192 x 40 x 27; 1447 tons. Williams & Guion of New York, owners. Wrecked near Ayab, May 1864.

B. F. HOXIE

BUILT by Maxon, Fish & Co., at Mystic, Conn., in 1855. 187 x 40 x 23; 1387 tons. N. G. Fish & Co., Mystic, owners. Captured and burned by the *Florida*, June 1862.

"ARCHITECT," 520 TONS, BUILT AT BALTIMORE, MD., IN 1848

From a painting by J. E. Petersen, in the possession of Robert C. Vose

"ARGONAUT," 575 TONS, BUILT AT MEDFORD, MASS., IN 1849

From a painting by a Chinese artist

"Asterion," 1135 tons, built at Medford, Mass., in 1854

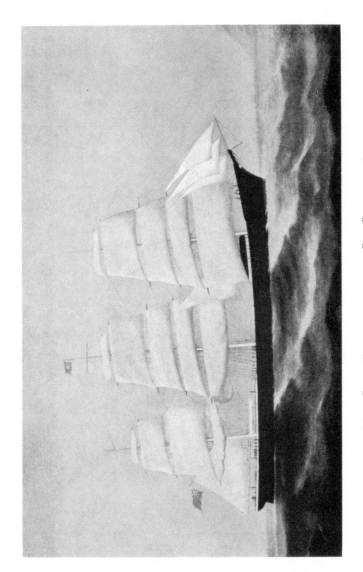

"BLUE JACKET," 1790 TONS, BUILT AT EAST BOSTON, IN 1854
From an oil painting in the Macpherson Collection

BALD EAGLE

EXTREME clipper ship, launched from the East Boston yard of Donald McKay, in November 1852. Keel, 195; over all, 225; x 41: 6 x 22: 6; tonnage, 1705, old measurements, but she could stow 2200 tons of general merchandise. She had very sharp lines; the bow had neither head nor trail boards and was of magnificent appearance, sweeping upwards as gracefully as a Venetian gondola. A gilded eagle on the wing was her figurehead. The stern was slightly elliptical in form, neatly ornamented and had a handsome, light appearance. Her lower masts, in order, were 85, 90 and 80 feet in length, all being made of sticks of selected hard pine, the pieces being dowelled together, bolted and hooped. The standing rigging was of 11 inch four-strand patent rope of Russian hemp. She spread 10,500 yards of canvas and was built to the order of George B. Upton, a prominent merchant of Boston, whose fleet of clippers, especially constructed for the California trade, also included the *Staghound* and the *Romance of the Seas,* with others of lesser fame. The command of the *Bald Eagle* was given to Capt. Philip Dumaresq, one of the best known masters in the China trade. His principal employers had been the Perkinses and the merchant-captain Robert B. Forbes, and the latter, in his book "Ships of the Past," refers to Dumaresq as the "Prince of Captains."

On her maiden voyage, the *Bald Eagle* left New York, Dec. 26, 1852, and made the passage to San Francisco in 107 days. The New York clipper *Jacob Bell* had arrived the day before in 122 days. The *Bald Eagle* crossed the line 28 days from Sandy Hook, averaging 144 miles per day. From Cape St. Roque she had but 19 days to 50° South and was only 10 days rounding the Horn. The Cape itself was passed Feb. 16th, 52 days out. In the Pacific she had 28 days from 50° South to the equator, and 19 days thence to San Francisco. She was in port until May 8th, when she sailed for New York, arriving out, Aug. 13th, in 96 days. Her competitor, the *Jacob Bell,* had sailed the day before her and reached Philadelphia on Aug. 3rd, thus somewhat retrieving on the homeward run, the beating she got on the passage out.

At New York, Captain Dumaresq took command of the new, Mc-Kay-built clipper *Romance of the Seas*, and Captain Caldwell took the *Bald Eagle* and had a run out to San Francisco of 115 days, arriving Jan. 25, 1854. The clipper *Pampero* reached port the same day in 109 days, while the *Jacob Bell* was 122 days from Philadelphia. The year 1854 was remarkable for fast runs from eastern ports to San Francisco;—the *Flying Cloud* was 89 days, 8 hours, the record to this day; while the *Romance of the Seas*, the *Witchcraft*, the *Hurricane* and the *David Brown* all made the run in under 100 days. The *Bald Eagle*, however, had not the favorable weather conditions her competitors experienced. She was 33 days to the line and passed Cape St. Roque on the 35th day; was 18 days thence to 50° South and 19 days rounding the Horn; crossed the equator 93 days out and was within two days' sail of San Francisco for six days. After discharging her inward cargo, she was partially reladen with merchandise similar to what she and other clippers had taken out, the Pacific Coast markets being glutted through excessive importations. Passing through the Golden Gate, Mar. 1, 1854, she anchored in New York harbor on May 19, a passage of 78 days, 22 hours, the fastest eastward run on record for a cargo laden vessel and within three days of the fastest time made by a ship in ballast.

The third voyage of the *Bald Eagle* was 117 days to San Francisco, arriving Feb. 23, 1855. She passed Cape Horn on the 57th day and was on the equator in the Pacific when 87 days out. Her time was beaten three days by the medium clipper *Southern Cross* and equalled by the *Sweepstakes*. She beat the *Pampero* eight days and the *Phantom* four days. At San Francisco, Captain Treadwell took command of the *Bald Eagle* and was 47 days to Hong Kong. She then took some 700 Chinese coolies from Swatow to Callao, reaching port Nov. 26th; and then went to Philadelphia, arriving May 4, 1856. She left New York, July 18, 1856, and was 120 days to San Francisco. Had light or baffling winds nearly all the passage, except off the Cape. Sailed from San Francisco, Dec. 7, 1856, and arrived at Calcutta, Feb. 5, 1857,—a passage of 59 days, which is very fast and possibly the record. From Calcutta to Boston she was 98 days, arriving Aug. 2, 1857.

The *Bald Eagle* made no further Cape Horn passages but was engaged in the China trade. In common with other fast clippers operating on that route during these years, she encountered generally unfavorable weather and her runs were rather long for a ship of her capability. Leaving Boston, Sept. 21, 1857, she was 109 days to Hong Kong and remained on the coast of China until August, 1859, when she sailed from Woosung and had a passage of 120 days to Liverpool. Under command of Captain Nickels, formerly of the clipper ship *Flying Fish*, she sailed from Liverpool, Feb. 21, 1860, with coal and stores for the British naval forces at Foo Chow. Arrived at Anjer, May 24th, 93 days out. Was at Shanghai, June 25th. On Apr. 25, 1861, she arrived at San Francisco in 41 days from Hong Kong,—an excellent passage. Sailed from San Francisco, June 16th; hove to off Honolulu on the 29th, and arrived at Hong Kong, Aug. 25th, having had nothing but light winds and calms the whole voyage. Captain Nickels was succeeded by Captain Morris and the *Bald Eagle* sailed from Hong Kong, Oct. 15, 1861, for San Francisco, with a full cargo of rice, sugar and tea and $100,000 in treasure. She was never thereafter heard of and as no trace of wreckage was found, it is supposed that she foundered, with all hands, in one of several severe typhoons which were experienced in the China Sea about that period. She was still owned by George B. Upton and was in good condition, being classed A 1½. The insurance paid on vessel and cargo was $300,000.

BELLE OF THE SEA

MEDIUM clipper ship, built by Ewall & Dutton at Marblehead, Mass., in 1857. 189: 4 x 37: 7 x 23: 6; 1255 tons, old measurement; 1165 tons, British measurement. Owned by T. B. Waters & Co., of Boston; and later by Edward Kimball. In 1862 she changed hands at New York; consideration $45,000. Early in 1864 she was sold at Liverpool for $43,000, and renamed *Strathpeffer* with hailing port Liverpool. In 1869, William Grant is listed as owner. In 1871, after leaving Callao for the Channel, she put into Valparaiso in distress and was condemned and sold. However, she appears in Lloyd's Register, in 1874, as the *Strathpeffer*, of South Shields, H. S. Edwards owner.

On her maiden voyage, the *Belle of the Sea* left Boston, Apr. 26, 1857, under command of Capt. Christopher R. Lewis, whose new, Marblehead-built ship *Southern Belle*, had been burned at sea. On arrival at San Francisco, Aug. 31st, Captain Lewis reported his passage as 126 days; was 58 days to the Horn and came around in nine days; crossed the equator 88 days out, but then had light winds and calms for 38 days to port. Returned east via Calcutta. She was then engaged in trade with Australia and India and is reported to have made one very fast passage from London to Melbourne, some 64 days. However, no dates or other confirmatory evidence is now obtainable.

On Apr. 19, 1861, the *Belle* arrived at San Francisco, 139 days from New York, Capt. W. P. Sigsbee in command. Was 33 days to the line; 65 days to 50° South; 106 days to the equator; the winds and trades were very light throughout the whole passage. Sailed from San Francisco, June 24th, and arrived at New York, Oct. 9th, in a passage of 106 days. Had made the coast in 103 days but then had heavy northwest gales, losing the maintopgallant-mast and some sails. Sailed from New York, Jan. 3, 1862, and in the North Atlantic carried away the mizzenmast with everything attached; had sails split, boat stove, etc. Was 62 days to 50° South and 15 days rounding the Horn; crossed the equator 101 days out and arrived at San Francisco, May 14th, 131 days from New York. Was within 175 miles of the Golden Gate for five days and had the main skysail set for 50 successive days. Sailed from San Francisco, July 16th and went to New York in 117 days.

Capt. William Low Foster, who had been for a time in command of the clipper ship *Morning Star*, of Boston, now took the *Belle* and sailed from New York, Jan. 18, 1863, for San Francisco. Shortly after leaving port had a heavy gale, during which the foremast was badly sprung and the ship started to leak. Put back to New York, arriving Jan. 25th. Discharged cargo which was found to be but slightly damaged; repaired and recoppered at a cost of $15,000 and resumed the voyage Mar. 18th. Had a good run of 22 days to the line and passed through the Straits of Le Maire, 57 days out; then had 30 days of very heavy weather, it blowing a perfect hurricane at times. Lost sails and part of deck load; crossed the equator 119 days out and was thence 31 days to destination, being 800 miles from the Golden Gate for 15 days. Reached port Aug. 16th, 150 days from New York. Sailed from San Francisco, Oct. 4, 1863, and arrived at Liverpool, Feb. 20, 1864, in 139 days passage. She was then sold as previously stated.

BELLE OF THE WEST

EXTREME clipper ship, designed by Samuel H. Pooke, of Boston, and built in 1852, by the Shiverick Brothers, at East Dennis, Mass., for account of Capt. Christopher Hall; launched Mar. 25, 1853. 178 feet long, over all, x 35 x 20: 6; 936 tons, old measurement; dead rise, 18 inches. The small fore-rake of her stem, with a lively sheer of 27 inches, and but slight flare of bows, gave her a most saucy and coquettish appearance, which was further enhanced by her graceful elliptical stern and handsome figurehead, a female image in flowing white garments, fringed with gold. She was very sharp; when about half loaded her water-line was practically straight from stem to abaft the mainmast; her run was long and clean. Two authorities who are now living, both conversant with all the extreme clippers, and one of whom was in the *Belle* as mate for four and one half years, assert that she was the sharpest ship they ever saw, and also the most beautiful. On her first appearance at Boston, and also at San Francisco, the newspapers called her the handsomest ship that had ever appeared in those harbors, saying, "Whatever bright-eyed little flirt she is named after, need not be ashamed of her appearance."

Capt. William Frederick Howes, of East Dennis, was appointed master of the *Belle*, early in the course of her construction and had his leg broken by the parting of the hawser when the tugboat started to tow the ship to Boston to be rigged. He, however, was able to assume his duties before the ship was ready for sea. That the *Belle* was heavily sparred is evidenced by comparison of her masts and yards with those of *Flying Cloud*, whose length between perpendiculars was 63 feet greater and who registered tonnage 846 tons larger. The following figures are for the mainmast, the *Cloud's* being given first. Lower masts, 88 feet and 85 feet—topmasts, 51 and 50—topgallants, 28 and 20—royals, 19 and 14—skysail masts, 14½ and 9. Main yards, 82 and 72—topsail yards, 64 and 63—topgallants, 50 and 53—royals, 37 and 40—skysail yards, 24 and 31. As the *Belle* had Forbes' rig, double topsails with topmasts fidded abaft the lower mastheads, these latter were much longer than those of the *Cloud*, they being, on the mainmast, 23 feet against the *Cloud's* 14 feet. Relatively, the same proportionate difference existed in masts and yards of fore and mizzen, showing that, while the *Belle* was not quite as lofty a ship and had not the lower spread of canvas carried by the *Cloud*, yet this was nearly made up by her much squarer yards from topgallants upward.

Capt. William F. Howes was in command of the *Belle* until 1859, when he was succeeded by his brother, Allison Howes. He was a skillful navigator but not a "driver" and the *Belle* has no particularly fast, complete passage to her credit; yet authorities say that she was never outsailed at sea. She made two runs out to San Francisco, the first being her maiden voyage in 1853, when her time was 132 days from Boston. Contrary or light winds prolonged her time to the line to 36 days and she was 19 days rounding the Horn; from 50° South, Pacific, she did well to the equator, 19 days; thence 24 days to destination. In 1859, her time was 133 days from Boston, a fair run of 26 days to the line being offset by heavy weather from off the Platte to 50° South, Pacific, which position she reached June 10th, 68 days out; from there, however, she had the excellent run of 17 days to the equator, crossing June 27th. Off Cape Horn she was in company with the *Young America* and again spoke that ship off the California coast but the latter had the advantage in subsequent light winds and reached San Francisco nearly two days in the lead.

In the fall of 1854, the *Belle* was 85 days from London to Melbourne. The ship *Swallow* went over the same course at the same period in 76 days and her captain, Tucker, was much elated at having beaten a ship conceded to be much faster than his.

The *Belle* made a number of voyages to Calcutta and other Indian ports. In 1864 she was sold by Glidden & Williams, of Boston, who had all along been her managing owners, to Mowjee Huny Doss, at Calcutta, and renamed *Fiery Cross*. She traded locally between Indian ports until 1868. In May/June of that year, then owned by Gopaul Canjee, of Calcutta, and bound thence to Muscat with a cargo of rice, etc., she foundered in the Bay of Bengal.

BEVERLY

MEDIUM clipper ship, built by Paul Curtis, at Medford, Mass.; launched Apr. 19, 1852. 151 x 31 x 21; 676 tons, old measurement. Originally owned by Israel Whitney and William Perkins of Boston. She was a good carrier, yet has some very fast passages to her credit.

Her maiden voyage was from Boston to San Francisco, 144 days, Capt. Perry Jenkins in command. Her best day's run was only 260 miles; had 12 days of calms and was 20 days off Cape Horn. From

San Francisco she went to Shanghai in 46 days; thence 100 days to New York. In 1855, she was 83 days from Boston to Melbourne, thence going to Calcutta. Left the Sand Heads, Oct. 13th and arrived at Boston, Jan. 4, 1856, in 83 days, the second fastest passage on record. On Aug. 29, 1857, she sailed from Boston and arrived off the Sand Heads, Nov. 23rd, a passage of 86 days, which is believed to be the record over that course. From Calcutta she went to San Francisco, arriving Sept. 4, 1858, in 80 days. A curious feature of this run is that her time of 14 days from Calcutta to Singapore and 66 days thence to destination, are neither fast runs, although the combination of 80 days is within one day of the record. She then loaded lumber at Puget Sound for Valparaiso and made the run down in 52 days. Captain Chase was in command at this time.

For some years the *Beverly* continued in trade with Australia and India. In 1862, under Captain Melville, she went to Calcutta from Liverpool and on the return passage reached Boston, June 15, 1863, 108 days from the Sand Heads. In 1864, she had the unique experience of being chased by the Confederate privateer *Florida*, but was fortunate enough to escape capture. About this time she was sold, becoming the ship *Alexander*, of Batavia, although Coolidge & Slater, of Boston, were reputed to be owners. In 1867 she is listed as belonging to A. A. Reed. Later, her name was changed to *Argonaut*, of Port Louis, Mauritius. In February 1868 she was purchased by W. F. Weld & Co., of Boston, who operated her until September 1872, when she was sold to L. E. Baker, of Yarmouth, Nova Scotia. Her name does not appear in Lloyd's Register for 1874.

BLACK HAWK (1)

BUILT at Black Rock, Conn., in 1853; 1100 tons. Owned in New York. Dismasted and foundered in 1854. Was launched under the name *Chief of Clippers*.

BLACK HAWK (2)

MEDIUM clipper ship, with rather full lines, built in 1857 by William H. Webb, at New York. 178 x 38: 5 x 23: 9; 1109 tons, old measurement; 1059 tons, new measurement; carrying capacity, 1600 tons, dead weight. She had a half poop deck running to the forward house and a square stern; was a neat appearing ship, although not the beau-ideal clipper. Her record as a fast sailer is, however, fully established and for years she was a successful and popular ship. Aside from one run from New York to Melbourne, thence to San Francisco via Hong Kong, in 1878/79, her career while under the American flag was spent entirely in trade between California and New York and England, including a few homeward passages via guano ports.

Between 1857 and 1880 she made 20 passages around Cape Horn to San Francisco, of which two were from Liverpool and 18 from New York; average for the 20, 124½ days. Those from Liverpool were 118 and 134 days; fastest from New York, 107 days in 1861 and 110 days in 1875; in 1867, her 113 days' run was the fastest for that year with the exception of the *David Crockett's* 110 days. Of her passages from New York, eight were made in under 120 days, their average being 115 days. From San Francisco, direct, eastward, her record is also very good; one run to Boston of 97 days and four to New York in 95, 100, 101 and 102 days respectively; to Liverpool, 101 and 104 days and to Queenstown, 113 days. From Jarvis Island to New York, she was 93 days, and from Baker's Island, 84 days, both including detention at Hampton Roads, where she called for orders. On Jan. 19, 1859, she left San Francisco Heads at 4 P.M. and hove to off Diamond Head, Honolulu, at 11 P.M. the 28th, a nine days, nine hours' passage. In 1869, on her passage to New York in 101 days, Captain Hallet reported crossing the line in the Atlantic, 69 days from San Francisco and being within 900 miles of Sandy Hook, 84 days out. In 1858 she had 18 days from the Pacific equator crossing to the Golden Gate.

The original owners of the *Black Hawk* were Bucklin & Crane of New York, who sold her to George Howes & Co., of New York and San Francisco, during the middle 60's. The latter firm retiring about 1880, the ship was sold and was operated in trade in the Atlantic, principally between New York and ports in Germany; her owners were D. H. Waetjen & Company, her hailing port being Bremen. May 2, 1888, the *Black Hawk*, under command of Captain Wachsmuth, left Bremen in tow and collided with a barge, going ashore. She was got off, however, and sailed for Baltimore. Her name does not appear in shipping registers thereafter.

While under the American flag the *Black Hawk* was commanded by Captain Bowers for the first five years; by Capt. Seth Doane, about the same length of time; had Capt. Milton B. Crowell from 1866 until 1874, except for one homeward run under Captain Hallett; Captain Baker then had her for about three years and was succeeded by Captain Howland.

BLACK PRINCE

MEDIUM clipper ship, launched Apr. 6, 1856, by George W. Jackman, at Newburyport, Mass., for Bush & Wildes of Boston. She was about 180 x 36 x 22 feet; 1061 tons, but could carry 1400 tons, dead weight cargo. She was moderately sharp and is said to have somewhat resembled the *War Hawk, Daring* and other products of the Jackman yard. During her short career she had to her credit only one passage worthy of note, that of 38 days from San Francisco to Hong Kong, in 1856, which time was the same as that made by the *Meteor* and *Western Continent*. Unfavorable conditions seem to have prevailed on practically all of her other voyages.

Of her three passages from Boston or New York to San Francisco, the fastest was 146 days, in 1860; losing jibboom, cutwater and figurehead on the passage. In 1858 she was forced to put into Rio, when 39 days out from Boston, due to mutiny of the crew, and her whole time to San Francisco was 167 days, 125 from Rio. From

Hong Kong to San Francisco she made three passages in 55, 50 and 48 days respectively. Crossing the Pacific in the opposite direction, her time was 38, 48 and 63 days. In 1856 she was 96 days from Java Head to Boston, and in 1858/59 was 83 days going over the same course. In 1862 she had a very long passage from New York to Shanghai, reported as 167 days. On arrival she got ashore at Woosung and had to discharge her cargo in lighters,—got off hogged.

On Oct. 13, 1864, she left San Francisco with 700 tons of copper ore and 600 tons of other cargo, for Boston. On Feb. 15, 1865, in latitude 38° North, 67°: 54″ West, she was supplied with provisions by the British schooner *Eliza*, then reporting that she had three feet of water in the hold and had jettisoned 80 tons of cargo. The following day the *Eliza* encountered a severe gale and as the *Prince* was never thereafter heard of, it is thought that she went down with her complement of 25 people. Her cargo was valued at $320,000 and the loss to insurance companies is said to have been $230,000. She was commanded by Capt. Edwin Chase, who had succeeded Captain Howes, who in turn had taken the ship from Capt. Charles H. Brown, her first master.

BLACK SEA

BUILT by Lupton, at Greenpoint, N. Y., in 1855. 150 x 34 x 20; 791 tons. French & Meincke of New York, owners. Sold to go under British flag in 1863. Renamed *Jupiter;* hailing port, London.

BLACK WARRIOR

MEDIUM clipper ship, launched late in 1853, from the yard of Austin & Company, Damariscotta, Me., and immediately purchased by William Wilson & Son of Baltimore, for $90,000. 234 x 42: 6 x 30: 8; draft, 23 feet; 1828 tons. Had three complete decks; was of a beautiful model and in every way an attractive looking ship, heavily sparred. Captain Murphy was placed in command and continued in the ship until she was sold.

Her first voyage was from New York to London where she loaded 2600 tons of general cargo and then ran out to Melbourne in 76 days; best day, 365 miles, while running her easting down. From Australia she went to the west coast of South America and sailed from Callao, Mar. 29, 1855, arriving at New York, June 23rd, in 86 days; had touched at Hampton Roads, 79 days out, for orders. It was on this voyage that the admirers of the Quebec-built ship *Ocean Monarch*, made public the fact that their ship had sailed seven days after the American ships *Black Warrior* and *John Stuart*, but had caught up with and led them 12 hours round the Horn and several days to the equator. The sequel, however, was that both the Americans made better time on the whole passage than did the *Monarch* on her shorter run to Cork.

The *Warrior* loaded at New York for San Francisco and took her departure Sept. 6, 1855, making the passage in 124 days, of which 35 days were spent in rounding the Horn in heavy gales; split sails, lost foretopsail yard and was otherwise damaged. Was within 280 miles of the Golden Gate for 10 days. From San Francisco she made a round voyage to Hong Kong; was 42 days going out and 36 on the return, which latter is within three days of record time. She then went to Valparaiso and Callao and thence to New York. Again loaded for San Francisco and ran out in 114 days although becalmed 27 days on the passage. Was thereafter, August 1858 to May 1860, trading between San Francisco and Hong Kong. Finally left the California port in June 1860, proceeded to Altata, in the Gulf of California, to load dyewoods for Europe. She arrived at Queenstown, Jan. 10, 1861, and in entering the harbor collided with a British bark and was damaged considerably in her upper works, necessitating eight or ten days' repairs.

In 1862 she was sold to James Baines & Co., and went under the British flag as the *City of Melbourne*. In 1870 she is registered as owned by W. T. Heron of Liverpool. She caught fire on Feb. 1,

1868, while at Williamstown Pier, Port Philip, Australia, and was scuttled. Three days later she was refloated and repaired. In 1877 she was used as a hulk at Melbourne.

BLUE JACKET

CLIPPER ship, of sharp model, though not of the extreme type of those put out a year or two earlier. Built by Robert E. Jackson, at East Boston, and launched Aug. 27, 1854. Keel, 205; over all, 235; beam, 41: 2; depth of hold, 24; draft, 22 feet; 1790 tons, old measurement; 1403 tons, new measurement. A very beautiful ship in every way, with magnificent cabin finishings; her half poop deck was 80 feet long. Had double topsails on fore and main, and unlike most clippers of her time, did not cross skysail yards. Her first owner was the prominent firm of Seccomb & Taylor, of Boston, who, however, soon after her first arrival in England, sold her to John James Frost to run in his "Fox" line of Australian packets out of London. Some years thereafter she came into possession of Pilkington, Wilson & Chambers, who operated the "White Star Line" between Liverpool and Australia.

On her initial passage, the *Blue Jacket*, Captain Eldridge, left Boston Oct. 2, 1854, and reached Liverpool on the 20th; her run from land to land was 12 days, 10 hours. Captain Underwood then took the command and had the fast run of 68 days to Melbourne, having beaten the initial passages of *Red Jacket, Lightning, Champion of the Seas, Sovereign of the Seas* and *Donald McKay*. Her time up to that date had been equaled only by the *Marco Polo* and beaten only by the *James Baines*. From Australia she went to London, by way of Madras, returning to Madras from London in 92 days. Thence went to Mauritius, where her arrival was noted as follows;—"The splendid *Blue Jacket*, now owned in London, arrived yesterday, landing 600 coolies from Madras at three pounds a head. Is now loading for London with sugar at three pounds, ten shillings per ton. The Immigrant Agents prefer American clippers because they make the shortest voyages and deliver the coolies in better condition than vessels of other nations. The model, finish and build of this vessel, with her cabin arrangements, have completely astonished the people of this island."

Details of subsequent voyages of the *Blue Jacket* are not at hand with the exception of two instances; one being a run from Melbourne to London, in 69 days; the other from Lyttleton, N. Z., into the East India Docks at London, in 63 days, in 1865. Capt. Joshua N. Taylor, of Orleans, Mass., was sailing master, under Capt. James White, in the latter instance, and the following details are from his narrative;—"Early one morning we hove up anchor; a heavy southwest gale followed us for several days, and running our easting down, we averaged 20 knots at times, with all sail set; at times the patent log even showed 23 knots. These gales carried us until we had passed Cape Horn and hauled up to 'norrard, and up to this time we had averaged 384 nautical miles per day, beating all records ever made by a sailing ship up to that time. We crossed the equator on our 42nd day from New Zealand and were in the East India Docks on the 63rd day. Captain White was a great man to carry sail and boasted that he had never taken a topsail off her at sea, while he had had command. The ship was equipped with a powerful steering gear with double wheels, and under ordinary conditions, one man and a boy could handle her. On one occasion on this passage, in a stiff gale at night, under topgallants, with four men (two at each wheel), in a heavy sea, with wind quartering, the ship often got away and broached to; it required all the men's strength to get the wheels over, so she would pay off on her course. Captain Taylor ordered topgallant halliards let go, fore and aft, but Captain White, coming on deck, had them again hoisted, when she took a sea on the quarter, flooded decks, burst companion doors and filled the main saloon two feet deep, causing a panic among the passengers. The topgallants then came down for good."

On her last passage, Captain White still in command, the *Blue Jacket* left Lyttleton, Feb. 13, 1869, with a cargo of flax and other colonial produce; her passenger list was 32 and her crew 39 men. On Mar. 5th, 20 days out, she passed Cape Horn and when off the Falkland Islands smoke was noticed coming from the hold. Every effort was made to subdue the flames without avail and finally all took to the boats. On Mar. 16th, all being in a very exhausted state from hunger, thirst and exposure and reduced to a mouthful of water and a tablespoonful of preserved meat in 24 hours, a sail hove in sight and they were rescued by the Baltimore-built but Bremen-owned bark *Pyrmont*. In "Colonial Clippers" the following interesting item appears;—"On December 8, 1871, the *Blue Jacket's* figure-head was found washed up on the shore of Rottnest Island, off Fremantle, Western Australia. Part of it was charred by fire, but there was no mistaking its identity, which was described as a man from waist up, in old sailor's costume, a blue jacket with yellow buttons, the jacket open in front; no waistcoat; loose shirt and a large knotted handkerchief round the neck; a broad belt and large square buckle and cutlass hilt at the side. On either side of the figure-head was a scroll, saying;—'Keep a Sharp Lookout.' "

BONITA

MEDIUM clipper ship, launched May 12, 1853, from the yard of E. & H. O. Briggs, at South Boston, Mass. Capt. James Huckins, of Boston, was both designer and owner. Keel, 167½ feet; deck, 182; over all, 192 x 36 x 22: 6; 1127 32/95 tons. Dead rise, 27 inches; swell of sides, 4 inches and sheer 3½ feet. Her lines were convex; no head or trail boards and her sharp bow terminated in a gilded billet. Stern oval and ornamented with scroll work.

She sailed from Boston, June 21, 1853, under command of Capt. Charles F. Winsor, and arrived at San Francisco, Nov. 9th, a passage of 141 days. The return to Boston was made in 131 days. On her second passage to San Francisco, Capt. L. G. Hollis replaced Captain Winsor and the *Bonita* left Boston, May 25, 1854, arriving out, Sept. 26th; passage 124 days. Captain Hollis reported a fine run of 48 days to Cape Horn and off it 20 days in heavy gales; crossing the equator in the Pacific, Aug. 25th and then light winds to port. From San Francisco she went to Singapore in 53 days; thence to Calcutta and arrived back at Boston, May 24, 1855, having been one year on the round voyage. In 1856 she went to Shanghai and thence to London.

The *Bonita*, Captain Hatch in command, sailed from London, Apr. 17, 1857, with a cargo of railroad iron, for Calcutta, and put into Algoa Bay, June 18th, leaky. She was condemned and the cargo forwarded by other vessels.

BOSTON LIGHT

MEDIUM clipper ship, built in 1854 by E. & H. O. Briggs, at South Boston, Mass. She was 1154 tons, old measurement, being some 40 tons larger than the *Northern Light*, although practically of the same model. Both vessels were owned by James Huckins & Sons, of Boston, and the *Northern Light*, also a Briggs production, is famous for having made the passage from San Francisco to Boston in 76 days, 8 hours, a record to this day.

The *Boston Light* sailed from Boston, Dec. 30, 1854, and on arrival at San Francisco, Apr. 11, 1855, Captain Callaghan reported his passage as exactly 30 minutes over 102 days; was 24 days, 20 hours to the line, sailing 3614 miles; passed St. Roque, 27½ days out, and was 22 days thence to 50° South; 11 days later was in the Pacific, northbound and 21 days thereafter crossed the equator, 83 days out; was thence 19 days to destination. From San Francisco she went to Sydney, N. S. W., in 63 days and from Australia to China. Sailed from Shanghai, Dec. 15th, cleared the Straits of Sunda, Jan. 2, 1856; was off the Cape of Good Hope, 54 days out, and arrived at New York, Mar. 25th, 102 days from Shanghai, 26 days from the equator crossing.

Under command of Capt. Elkanah Crowell, of Hyannis, she left New York, June 8, 1856; crossed the line, 27 days out, and passed

Cape Otway, Aug. 24th, 77 days from New York; arrived at Melbourne the following day. In June 1858, she reached San Francisco after a fine run of 41 days from Hong Kong; thence back to Hong Kong in 51 days, returning to San Francisco in 44 days. Sailed again Mar. 5, 1859, and arrived at Hong Kong, Apr. 13th, in the fast time of 38 days. She then proceeded to Calcutta and loaded for New York where she arrived Mar. 12, 1861, 98 days from the Sand Heads. Captain Holway, who was in command this voyage, reported having very light winds all the way to the Bermudas, after which had a heavy gale. While scudding across the Gulf Stream had several sails split, the bulwarks stove and several men injured. Capt. Sturgis Crowell, brother of Elkanah Crowell, assumed command and took his charge out to San Francisco, arriving Nov. 1, 1861, 163 days from New York. Made Staten Island, Aug. 2nd and passed Cape Horn six days later; then had violent westerly gales and was hove to for eight days under close reefed maintopsail, being forced back to the eastward; had sails blown away, bulwarks and boats stove, decks swept of everything movable and rudderhead sprung; passed Cape Horn again, Aug. 16th, 86 days out; from Aug. 20th to Sept. 3rd had very heavy westerly gales; washed away the figurehead; while hove to, had the rudderhead carried away; for eight days the ship was headed to the south'ard with no control whatever over her; was driven down to 59°: 30′ South; had to jettison 100 tons of cargo to lighten the ship to get at the steering gear. During the voyage the mate was stabbed by one of the crew and died of his wounds.

The *Boston Light* sailed from San Francisco, Dec. 1, 1861, for McKean's Island where she loaded a cargo of guano for Mauritius, arriving out May 24, 1862. She thence went to Calcutta, proceeding in September to Hong Kong and from there to Bombay. On arrival at the latter port, in January 1863, she was sold for 70,000 rupees and renamed *Tulga*. For some years previously had been owned by Henry Hastings of Boston. Captain Crowell was succeeded by Captain Sheppard, who was one of her purchasers and she was kept in the local Indian trade.

BREWSTER

BUILT by Currier & Townsend, Newburyport, in 1855. 171 x 35 x 23; 984 tons. W. Clark and others, Boston, owners. In 1886, was the Norwegian ship *Fama* of Langesund. Sold to N. Y. in 1861. Last report in 1890.

CANVASBACK

MEDIUM clipper ship, built in 1854, at Baltimore, by Abraham & Ashcroft. 153 x 32 x 19: 6; 731 tons, American measurement, 673 tons, English measurement. The original owners of the *Canvasback* were Oelrich & Lurman of Baltimore and she was operated under their name until 1863, when she was sold to George Stanton, of London, to sail under the British flag; purchase price, $28,000. In 1871 she is registered as owned by Oswald & Company, hailing port, Sunderland, England. In 1875 her hailing port is given as St. Thomas. She is described as a handsome vessel and a credit to her builders.

The *Canvasback* left New York, Dec. 19, 1854, and arrived at Rio, Jan. 31, 1855, a passage of 43 days. Sailed from Rio, Aug. 27th and was 36 days to New York. She made several more voyages between New York or Boston and Rio and was then employed in the China trade. In 1857, on a voyage from Liverpool for Boston, on Mar. 22nd she put into Fayal, leaky, and had to discharge part of her cargo. She had experienced a severe gale during which she had to jettison some of the cargo and had been damaged in hull and rigging. Captain Clark, her original commander, and who remained in charge until her sale abroad, was very sick on the run. She then went out to China and sailed from Shanghai, Feb. 12, 1858, and arrived at New York, May 21st, a passage of 98 days. Cleared from New York, May 27, 1859, and was 104 days to Hong Kong. Left Canton for New York, July 20, 1861; passed Anjer, Aug. 26th and arrived at port of destination, Dec. 1, 1861. In 1863, as has been stated, she was sold abroad.

CARRIER DOVE

MEDIUM clipper ship, built by James Abraham, at Baltimore, in 1855. 220 x 42 x 24; 1694 tons. She was owned by Montell & Company, of Baltimore, and is said to have been of beautiful model. On her maiden voyage she left New York, Oct. 5, 1855, under Captain Conner, and on the 8th day out, in a terrific hurricane, was thrown on her beam ends and lost her mainmast near the eyes of her rigging, also the fore and mizzen topmasts and all attached. Notwithstanding, she managed to get into Rio, Nov. 9th in only 55 days from New York, a perfect wreck above deck. She remained at Rio about two months, repairing, and, continuing her voyage made a good run to the Horn, off which she was 22 days in strong gales, and arrived at San Francisco, Apr. 25, 1856, 98 days from Rio.

In an advertisement in the "New York Herald," it is claimed that in 1858, the *Dove* went from Liverpool to Melbourne in 73 days and round the world in ten months. In 1859 she was 159 days from New York to San Francisco, thence to Callao and was 92 days thence to New York. In 1860 she was 126 and in 1861, 158 days, from New York to San Francisco. On the latter passage she had light and unfavorable winds and from time of leaving port, until she entered the Golden Gate, did not make 1000 miles in any one week. In 1862, Capt. F. M. Montell, formerly of the ship *Atalanta*, had her and she sailed from San Francisco, Jan. 15, 1862, with a cargo of wheat and arrived at Queenstown, May 19th, in 124 days. She then made a number of trans-Atlantic voyages under Captain Nash and later Captain Jackson. In 1863 she went ashore on the Irish coast, near Valentia, but got off with ten feet of water in the hold and after repairs was put up at auction and bid in by her former owners, Trask & Dearborn. The same year she was sold at auction in New York for $67,000. In 1865 she left Shields, May 24th, for New York, with coal and general cargo, the largest that had ever left the Tyne; arriving off her port of destination she went ashore on Gov-

ernor's Island and her cargo had to be lightered. In 1868 she appears
as owned by The Union Navigation Company, and was captained by
I. Maxey. In 1870, J. D. Fish & Co., of New York, are given as her
owners, her captain being E. Fish. In 1873, under command of Captain Merriman, she was 125 days from New York to San Francisco,
returning to New York in 119 days. In 1875, John W. Elwell & Co.,
of New York, appear as owners and she went out to San Francisco in
129 days from New York, thence to Liverpool.

On Mar. 3, 1876, the *Carrier Dove*, while on a voyage from Liverpool for Tybee, Philadelphia and San Francisco, went ashore on
Stone Horse Shoals, near Tybee, and became a total loss.

CARRIER PIGEON

MEDIUM clipper ship, built in 1852, by Hall, Snow & Co., at
Bath, Me.; launched Oct. 18th. 175 x 34 x 21; 843 92/95
tons. Owned by Reed, Wade & Co., of Boston. For a figurehead she
had a finely carved, gilded pigeon. Is said to have had a fine model,
and while considerably narrower, for length and depth, than most of
her contemporaries, she proved to be a good sailer on the one only
passage she made, she having, at the time, over 1300 tons of California cargo aboard.

She sailed from Boston, Jan. 28, 1853, under Capt. Azariah
Doane, for San Francisco. All went well until arrival off the California coast, when for several days dense fogs were encountered. During
the night of June 6th, when 129 days out from Boston, and supposedly off the Farrallons, she went ashore about 50 miles to the
south'ard, near Point Ano Nuevo, or New Year, and became a total
loss. All hands were saved but the money loss was severe, there being
insurance of about $195,000 on vessel, cargo and freight money. The
ship was valued at $54,000, and was sold with the cargo, as she lay,
for $1500. The point of land where she went ashore has ever since
been known as Pigeon Point, and on it was erected a fine lighthouse
and fog signal station.

CELESTIAL

EXTREME clipper ship, built in 1850, by W. H. Webb, at New York, for Bucklin & Crane of that city. 158 x 34: 6 x 19; 860 tons. She was the sharpest ship built up to that time and was the first clipper to be launched especially for the California trade. Capt. E. C. Gardner was appointed commander but left her after the first round voyage to take the larger and finer clipper ship *Comet*, a product of the same yards and belonging to the same owners.

The *Celestial* was launched June 10th and left New York, July 17, 1850. For a time, after going to her loading berth, Pier 4, North River, freights were rather slow and two-thirds of her cargo was secured at quite moderate rates. When the ship was nearly loaded news arrived of a large fire at San Francisco and the ship soon filled up at better prices. When hatches were caulked, an anxious shipper wanted space for several cases of cigars each containing 5000 "Noriega's." The shipper was persistent so Captain Gardner utilized four unused staterooms in the cabin by taking out the berths and opening up the cases which were too large to go through the doors. For this privilege, the cigar merchant remunerated the ship to the extent of $3.50 per cubic foot and the contents of the four staterooms added about $1000 to the ship's freight list. She arrived at San Francisco, Nov. 1st, passage 105 days, having come up to the Golden Gate in 38 days from 50° South, Pacific. From San Francisco she went to China and was reported as reaching Hong Kong in 33 days, a run only once or twice equaled and never surpassed. Went on up the coast, loaded at Shanghai and was 117 days thence to New York.

The second voyage of the *Celestial* was made under Captain Palmer, 108 days from New York to San Francisco, with light winds throughout; 55 days from San Francisco to Shanghai and about 115 days thence to New York, she having, as also on her previous homeward run, left the China coast at about the most unfavorable season. The third voyage was from New York to San Francisco, 120 days; thence 42 days to Shanghai; thence 96 days from Foo Chow to Liverpool. The fourth voyage was her last in the California trade; 130 days outward; 50 days, San Francisco to Shanghai. Left Shanghai, Apr. 5, 1855, the bad season; had a long and tedious passage down the China Sea, being 51 days to Anjer; arrived at New York, Aug. 25, 1855. Loaded for Melbourne; sailed Oct. 12th; arrived out, Jan. 5, 1856, 85 days' passage; arrived at Hong Kong, Apr. 1st, from Melbourne. Went up the coast to Shanghai and loaded for New York. Sailed Apr. 26th, the unfavorable season again; was 44 days to Anjer and thence 83 days to destination, arriving Aug. 27, 1856. She then went back to China, having a long passage of nearly 150 days; loaded at Foo Chow and made the run thence to London in 98 days, arriving Jan. 11, 1858. Shortly thereafter she was sold to sail under the Spanish flag. In 1861 she was owned in New York by B. Blanco.

CELESTIAL EMPIRE

BUILT by Jotham Stetson, at South Boston, Mass., in 1852. 193 x 38 x 29; 1630 tons. C. H. Parsons & Co., New York, owners. Abandoned Feb. 20, 1878, on voyage from Bremen to New York.

CHALLENGE

IN 1850, the "London Times," in an article on American clippers, stated that a noted shipbuilder of New York had recently received an order from certain merchants of that city to build a mammoth clipper ship, regardless of cost, the only stipulation being that she must be the best, if not the fastest, sailing vessel in the world. The merchants referred to were the well-known firm of N. L. & G. Griswold, of New York, and the builder, W. H. Webb, the man selected to construct this masterpiece of marine architecture, was at this time considered the leading shipbuilder of America and one well-fitted by experience and natural ability to carry out the order. Every piece of timber for the vessel was carefully selected, the spars were the finest money could buy and only the most skilful mechanics were employed in her construction. The *Challenge*, for so the vessel was named, was launched at New York, May 24, 1851, in the presence of the largest number of people that such an occasion had ever called out in this country. "I have seen," writes a spectator, "many launches, including that of the U.S. ship *Ohio*, but never have I witnessed such interest and excitement before, as attended this launch."

The *Challenge* was beautifully modeled and was the largest and longest merchant ship built to that date; 27 feet longer than our then largest war vessel, the *Pennsylvania*. Her dimensions were; length 224 feet; beam, 43 feet; depth of hold, 25 feet; tonnage, 2006. She had three decks, drew 20 feet of water when loaded, had 42 inches dead rise and 36 inches sheer. The hull was painted black with a gold stripe and her lower masts were also black. Her figurehead was a gilded eagle on the wing and each of her catheads bore the representation of an eye looking forwards. She was built of live oak, white oak and hard pine and the frame was strengthened by diagonal iron braces, placed five feet apart and intersecting. At light load line the vessel's sides were 20 inches thick and 11 feet of solid timber intervened between the lower part of the keel and the upper part of the keelson. Her mainmast was three feet in diameter, 97 feet in length, and, with the top- and sky-sail pole, towered to the height of 230 feet. The main yard was two feet in diameter, 88 feet in length and was a made-stick. The masts raked 1⅛, 1¼ and 1½ inches to the foot. The bowsprit was 30 inches in diameter and 20 feet outboard; the jibboom was divided at 20 and 15 feet for inner and outer jib; the spanker boom was 60 and the gaff 40 feet; she spread 12,700 yards of cotton duck, the mainsail alone taking 1273 yards. There was a large water tank, six feet square, extending from the floor to the upper deck. Cost of construction is said to have been $150,000.

The *Challenge*, as her name implied, was expected to be as fast as she was staunch and her admirers, if not her owners, boasted that after a record breaking voyage to California and China, she was to go to England and offer to race any British clipper ship, for any distance, the winner to take both vessels. Every effort was made to make her initial voyage a success and the first requisite, a competent commander, was secured in Capt. Robert H. Waterman. Among the many able captains of his day none stood higher than Captain Waterman in seamanship and the ability to drive his ship but he had the reputation of being a hard man to sail under. The crew, 60 in number, signing on the *Challenge* for her first voyage to California, were all foreigners, except two, and only six were able to take their trick at the helm. But poor crews had no terrors for Captain Waterman and on July 13, 1851, the *Challenge* sailed for San Francisco. With a freight list amounting to $60,000 and a promised bonus of $10,000 if he reached San Francisco in 90 days, Captain Waterman started on his voyage with every hope of making a record. Certainly in New York there was little doubt that the *Challenge* would eclipse all previous records and bets were freely offered that she would beat the Boston clipper *Telegraph* and Grinnell, Minturn & Co.'s new ship, the *Flying Cloud*.

The *Challenge* was not favored by winds and weather on her passage to San Francisco, which she reached Oct. 20, 1851, 108 days from New York, and, although her run was good for the season in which she sailed, still, her passage was not all her friends had expected and the news of her arrival at San Francisco was accompanied with intimation of serious trouble with the crew on the voyage. What had occurred is best told by Captain Waterman himself, in a letter to a friend in Boston: "The truth is, when in the neighborhood of Rio, about fifty of the crew fell on the mate with the intention of killing him and afterwards me, by their own confession. I was on the poop taking observations while the mate stood forward at the gallery. They stabbed him and had beaten him shockingly before I could get to him. I struck down three of them, rescued the mate and quelled the mutiny. I flogged eight of them. Off Cape Horn, three men fell from the mizzen topsail yard and were killed and after a few weeks more four more died of dysentery." In the opinion of those best qualified to judge, Captain Waterman was justified in the severe measures he took to suppress and punish the mutiny and the criticisms levelled against him seem to have been based on misconception of the facts. On this passage the *Challenge* had frequently logged 14 knots and on one occasion had run 336 miles in 24 hours; she had also beaten the *Telegraph*.

The mutiny, however, gave the *Challenge* a bad reputation and Captain Land, who relieved Captain Waterman at the termination of the voyage, was obliged to pay $200 advance money to each sailor before he could ship a crew at San Francisco for Shanghai; he finally secured 40 men, however, but they were a tough lot and mutinous, so that he was compelled to put into Hong Kong where Commodore Aulick sent a file of marines aboard and brought the men to reason. The passage had been a tedious one, 54 days. From Hong Kong she ran back to San Francisco with 553 Chinese coolies, in the very fast time of 34 days, one day longer than record; her best day, being 23½ hours, was 360 miles, and her best speed, 16 knots; her run of 18 days from opposite Japan to San Francisco has never been equaled by any sailing vessel. After a stay of but seven days in port, the *Challenge* was again on her way from the Golden Gate to Hong Kong and according to published accounts of the passage she did some extraordinary work. Was off Honolulu when eight days out and on her 23rd day was within 400 miles of Hong Kong,—most remarkable work,—and accomplished with only moderate winds. She was then headed off by adverse winds and took nearly three weeks to reach destination.

After the death of Captain Land, at Hong Kong, the command was given to the former mate of the *Witchcraft*, Mr. Pitts, and the *Challenge* left Whampoa, Aug. 5, 1852, with tea for London; her passage of 105 days to the Downs—65 days from Anjer and 39 days after passing the Cape, was the shortest made that season, eclipsing the runs of the *Surprise*, *Nightingale* and *Race Horse*, American clippers, and the *Chrysolite*, *Stornoway* and *Challenger*, British clippers. The *Challenge* attracted much attention and her lines were taken off for the Admiralty while she was in dock. She was im-

mediately taken up for a round voyage to China and again, on the
outward passage, led the fleet. On the return, however, she was unfortunate, being obliged to put into Fayal, leaking badly, with crew
and passengers working at the pumps. After discharging her damaged cargo at Fayal, she crossed to New York and then went out to
San Francisco under command of Capt. J. Kenney, being 114 days
to the Farallon's and 118 days to port of destination. Thence she went
to Shanghai in 58 days and from Manila to New York in 117 days,
75 days from Anjer. From New York she went out to Hong Kong,
thence with 800 coolies to Melbourne and after return to China,
sailed from Swatow with 900 coolies for Havana. She was again unfortunate and was obliged to put into port for water and medical
attendance; Captain Kenney, seven of the crew and 150 of the coolies
were sick, there had been a mutiny aboard and one man had committed suicide. She loaded at New York for San Francisco, going out
in 114 days, this being her last Cape Horn run. She was only 55 days
from the equator in the Atlantic to a similar crossing in the Pacific
but light winds in the northern part of both oceans, spoiled an otherwise fine passage.

From San Francisco she crossed to Hong Kong in 46 days, and returned to the Golden Gate in 46 days; then back to China in 49 days.
On the latter passage she lost all three topmasts with everything
above and the heads of the lower masts. Captain Fabens completed
the voyage under jury masts and after her arrival she was laid up
until sold to Captain Haskell for $9350. She showed up again at
San Francisco, on June 13, 1861, 51 days from Hong Kong, to
which port she returned. Under Captain Thorndike she sailed from
Hong Kong in October 1861; called at Singapore and Galle and arrived at Bombay, Dec. 21st, leaking badly. Was sold there for 78,-
000 rupees, docked and repaired.

The new owners of the *Challenge*, Thomas Hunt & Co., put Captain Hendee in charge, renamed her, *Golden City*, and employed
her in the Chinese and India trade, her hailing port being Hong
Kong. She continued to operate under the same ownership for sev-

eral years and some time in 1866 was bought by Wilson & Co., of South Shields, England, who employed her in the Java and Bombay trade, in which, for a time, she did well, but misfortune still followed her and on a voyage for Java, in a gale off the Cape of Good Hope, a heavy sea broke over the quarter, sweeping seven men off the deck and killing all the officers except the third mate. She finally reached port but on her next voyage was wrecked off the French coast, some time in 1876. Lloyd's Register of 1875 has her listed as *Golden City*, ex *Challenge*, owned by Wilson & Co., of South Shields, England, and commanded by Captain Jones.

At the time the ship was built the following description of her appeared in the *Boston Daily Atlas:*—

The New Clipper Ship Challenge, of New York

New York has long been famous on the ocean for the speed and beauty of her ships. Her central position as the great mart of American commerce, combined with the daring enterprise and more than princely liberality of her merchants have nursed and stimulated the genius of her mechanics; and hence, in every department of naval architecture, as well as other commercial pursuits, the capitalist can always find the genius and skill to give form and substance to his ideas. In no department of naval architecture has the desire to excel, to surpass, been more manifested than in the construction of clippers. No sooner had the short passages of the ships *Samuel Russell* and *Sea Witch* to San Francisco, demonstrated the advantages of clippers for that trade, than many of our enterprising merchants designed to build a class of ships that would surpass these in speed, as far as they surpassed other vessels. Ships of fifteen, sixteen, and as large as eighteen hundred tons, were called into existence in a few months, and still the desire to surpass had not abated. Determined to be first upon the "world of waters," Messrs. N. L. & G. Griswold, of New York, designed a ship to be named the *Challenge*. She was to be of 2000 tons register, of faultless beauty, matchless speed, and unquestionable strength; and Mr. Webb, the first of mechanics, was selected to build her. She is now afloat and rigged. The model and all the other details were left to the builder's skill, without reference to cost, the owners contracting only for the results. The *Challenge*, therefore, is the embodiment of her builder's idea of the perfect in naval architecture, and his reputation is thus practically pledged for her success. That nothing might be wanting on the part of the owners, they obtained the services of the first of sailors to command her. Capt. Robt. H. Waterman, whose name is associated with the shortest passages on record from China, superintended her construction and equipment, and to his skill as a sailor, without trenching upon the province of the builder, may be attributed her completeness aloft.—With a commander of such undoubted skill and daring, all that the *Challenge* can do she will be made to do.

She is 224 feet long on the keel, 240 feet 6 inches on deck, between perpendiculars, and 252 feet 6 inches from the chock over the bowsprit to the taffrail, and is the longest sailing ship in the world. She is 27 feet 7 inches longer between perpendiculars than the *Pennsylvania* line-of-battle-ship. The *Challenge's* extreme breadth of beam, which is forward of the centre, is 43 feet, breadth at the gunwales 41 feet; depth 25½ feet; her lines are concave forward and aft. A chord of 40 feet, drawn from the stem to the turn of the bow, shows the greatest concavity or hollow of the bow at the load line, to be 6 inches, and her run, from a chord of 20 feet in length, to be 7 inches. Below, of course, the lines are more concave, but along her sides they are boldly convex. There is not, strictly speaking, a straight line in her model. She has 42 inches dead rise at half-floor, 12 inches rounding of sides, and 3 feet sheer. Her sternpost is upright, and whole inclination or rake of her stem on deck, is about 12 feet.

The angles of her ends, and the rise of her floor show that she is the sharpest, as well as the longest sailing vessel in the world.

Her sheer is not sudden or marked by any peculiarity, but is truly graduated along her whole length, presenting an outline of perfect beauty. Her bow rises nobly, and although its lines are concave below, yet as they ascend they become gently modified, still preserving their angular form; and, on the rail, blend in perfect harmony with her general outline. A gilded eagle, represented on the wing, and an eye on each cat-head, are her only ornaments forward. The bow is plain to nudity, compared with other ships, but beautiful beyond the power of words to describe. It has neither head nor trail boards, not even chocks around the hawse-holes, nor is it lumbered with rigging. The head stays lead through the bows, and set up inboard; the bowsprit shrouds and bobstay, are therefore the only standing rigging secured to the bow, and these all set up to the bowsprit.

She has a narrow waist, defined between the mouldings of the upper wale and the planksheer. The moulding along the wale is gilded and extends from the talons of the eagle round the stern.

Her stern is elliptical, and slightly inclined aft, but is formed close to the rudder-case. Its outline at the moulding of the wale is apparently semi-circular, but as it rises it becomes clearly elliptical, to correspond with her outline on the rail.

Above the line of the planksheer it is ornamented with gilded branches, conspicuous among which are the arms of the United States, in bas-relief. Her name and port of hail—*Challenge*, New York—in gilded letters, are below.

The upper wale is continued round the stern, and the planking of the run is carried up to it.

She is sheathed with yellow metal up to 20 feet forward and 21 feet aft, and except the ornamental work, she is painted black up to the rail. Her sides are smooth as cabinet work, and every line and moulding is graduated to correspond with her sheer. End or broadside on, her appearance is truly beautiful; if cast in a mould she could not have been more perfect to the eye.

Her deck room is spacious and admirably arranged for working ship. The whole height of her bulwarks, including the monkey rail, is only 4½ feet and inside they are paneled and painted white, and the water-ways green. Their stanchions are of locust, bright on the outer square, and the rack rail, which is of oak, is also bright, and extends from the topgallant forecastle to the poop.

Her topgallant forecastle is the height of the main rail, has a capstan on it, and extends aft to the windlass. From the windlass to the poop her deck amidships may be briefly described as follows:— Companion which protects the entrance to the sailors' quarters below —fore hatchway—main stay bitts, before the foremast—hatchway abaft the foremast—a house, which contains the galley and a state-room fitted with berths—the launch—the main hatchway—the main-mast and pumps—hatchway—capstan—hatchway—mizzen mast, and abaft is another hatchway, and before the centre of the poop, the wheel. Her half poop is only 20 feet long, and has a skylight on it, amidships. Except the spanker sheets, vangs and signal halliards, all her running rigging leads on the same deck, so that, in working ship, there will be no running up or down stairs.

All the hatchways, except the main, have raised covers, with glass in the sides, which renders the deck below light, and if open, airy. The frames of the hatchways, the mast-partners on deck and the fife rails around the masts, are all of East India teak, and the combings of the hatchways, and gangway boards are of mahogany. She is fitted with winches for hauling the chain cables up, or for any other heavy work. Her chain lockers are abaft the foremast, on the lower deck, and the pipes through which the chains pass are covered by the fore part of the galley. She has three anchors, the total weight of which is 13,378 lbs., besides a stream anchor and chain. Her cables are each 120 fathoms in length, one of an inch and seven-eighths, and the other of two inches, and in each bow she has two hawse holes. Her ground tackle and the details connected therewith, have been made to surpass the strictest requirements of Lloyd's.

She has five boats, the first a launch 26 feet long, 9 wide and 3½ deep, double planked and modelled for sailing or rowing, having a jib and mainsail, and row-locks for 12 oars. The next are two cut-ters, carvel built, 27 feet long, 7 wide, and 2 feet 9 inches deep, also fitted for sailing and rowing, each have the same number of oars as the launch. The third cutter is 25 feet long, 5 feet 5 inches wide, and 2 feet 4 inches deep, to be rowed by 5 oars. The captain's gig is 30 feet long, 5 wide and 3 feet 3 inches deep, is clincher built, to be rowed with 6 oars. These boats are all built of white oak and cedar; are copper fastened, have brass row locks, and are furnished with sails, awnings, water breakers, etc.

Her pumps are of copper, have 8 inch chambers, and work with engine breaks, and throw their water on the upper deck. She has also a powerful force pump for washing decks and wetting sails, and may answer the purpose of an engine in case of fire.

Opposite the fore and main rigging on each side, she has powerful lever winches, secured to massive bitts, which extend through the deck below, and are secured there. These are well clear of the sides, leaving ample space for men to work around them.

The decks are of white pine, the planking uniform in width, and clear of knots or flaws. Of all the vessels which we have seen, not even excepting ships of war, we do not recollect one whose deck room for working ship is so spacious and well arranged as that of the *Challenge*. Her appearance on deck, as well as outside, is not surpassed in beauty by any vessel afloat.

The accommodations for her crew are forward on the main deck, and are fitted with berths for fifty men. The forecastle has four plate glass air ports, and is otherwise well lighted and ventilated.

She has two cabins, the first under the poop, with two doors in front, one on each side of the wheel. It is fitted for the accommodation of her officers, and forms an ante-room to the great cabin below. In the upper cabin her tiller traverses close to the beams, and her steering apparatus consists of a gun tackle purchase, on each side, brought to a roller on the end of the shaft which passes through the heart of the wheel outside.

The great cabin contains six staterooms, &c., and is wainscotted with oak and rose-wood, set off with elliptically arched panels, relieved with oak pillared pilasters, and enamelled cornices, ornamented with exquisite carving. The corners of the beams are also fringed with beautiful carving, and edged with gold. The transom forms a semi-circular sofa, and forward there is another sofa, both covered with rich green and gold brocatel. In the forward partition is a splendid mirror, which gives a reflected view of the cabin abaft it. In every stateroom there is a deck and side light, and the cabin furniture throughout is in perfect keeping with her other appointments. The pantry is before the cabin, and alongside of it is a door which leads into the main deck. This deck has plate glass airports and all the other means of light and ventilation now in use on board of passage ships. The paint-work of this deck is white, and the waterways blue; and the hanging knees, stanchions, the lower squares of the beams, carlines and ledges, are bright and varnished.

The waterways of the lower deck are painted lead color, and in the other details it is nearly the same as the main deck, excepting, of course, the side-lights, &c. Although designed for the California and China trade, yet the arrangements of her decks are as admirably designed for the accommodation of passengers, as those of a first class European packet.

These details will give some idea of the ship's outline, her accommodations, &c. We will now endeavor to give the leading particulars of her construction. Her keel is of white oak, in two depths, bolted together with copper, and sided 16 and moulded 38 inches. The floor timbers are sided from 12 to 14 inches, and moulded 17½, and every one is bolted through the keel with 1⅞ inch copper. Her first keelson is bolted with iron through the timbers, down into the first depth of the keel, and second keelson is equally well secured. Fifty feet of her keelsons forward, and sixty feet aft, are of live oak; the other parts are of hard pine. From the top of the keelson to the base of the keel is 8½ feet.

The stem is of white oak, all in one piece, sided 16 inches at the keel, and 18 at the head, and moulded from 3½ to 2½ feet. The apron is sided 34 inches, and moulded to correspond with the form of the bow. Both stem and apron are closely bolted with copper up to 24 feet, and above there with iron.

The stern-post is sided the same as the stem, and moulded in like proportion; and the false post, sternknee, &c., are bolted in the most substantial style.

All the frames forward of the foremast, all abaft the mizzenmast, all the top-timbers, and all the fourth futtocks amidships, and the dead-wood forward and aft, are of live oak. The frames are bolted together with 1 inch iron, and are made of uniform substance, dressed fair and smooth on all sides, and are braced diagonally with iron 4 inches wide, and ¾ of an inch thick. Those braces are 4 feet apart, and extend from the floor-heads to the gunwales, are rivetted together at every intersection, bolted through every timber, and form a complete network of iron, which binds the frame beyond the power of working. She is the first sailing vessel ever built in this country which has been braced with iron.

The ceiling on the floor is 4 inches thick, and on the bilge commences with 8 inches, which is graduated to 7 inches. Her lower deck clamps are also 8 inches thick, and all her thick work extends forward and aft, and is square bolted. Her beams are of hard pine, those under the lower deck sided from 15 to 17 inches, and moulded 14; the main deck beams are nearly the same, and the upper deck beams 2 inches smaller. The hold stanchions are kneed to the beams above and to the keelson below. She has three breast-hooks, of white oak, in the hold, but all her deck hooks are of live oak.

The hanging knees under the beams of all the decks are of white oak, sided in the body of the vessel from 10 to 12 inches, and moulded from 22 to 28 inches in the throats. Of course, towards the ends, the knees are diminished in size, for in every detail it has been the object of the builder to make the parts in correct proportions. A beam 15 feet long does not require as stout a knee to brace it to the side, as one double the length. The knees have from 16 to 18 bolts, driven from the outside and clinched on the inside.

The waterways of the lower and main decks are 15 inches square, the strake inside of them 8 inches thick, and that over them 10 by 12 inches, all closely cross-bolted. The clamps under the main deck are

7 inches thick, the ceiling below 6 inches, and the clamps and ceiling under the upper deck one inch less, but all square fastened. The stanchions in both decks are of locust turned, and are secured with iron rods through their centres, which bind all the decks together.

There are twenty-eight beams under the main deck, and a corresponding number in proportion to her length, under the other decks, and these have all hanging and lodging knees of white oak, well finished and strongly fastened.

The upper deck waterways are 11 by 12 inches, cross-bolted, and all her decks are of clear white pine, 3½ inches thick.

Her garboards are 8 inches thick, bolted with copper both through the timbers and the keel, and the strake outside of them 6 inches, also copper bolted. The planking outside of these is 4 inches, and on the bilge 4½ inches, which increases to 5, the substance of the wales. Her waist is of 4 inches; the planksheer or covering board 5 inches, and the main rail 6 inches, which is strengthened by an oak rack rail, already noticed; and her bulwark boarding is neatly tongued and grooved, and finished in the first style of workmanship.

All the outside above the garboards, which are bolted, is square fastened with copper spikes; and is also copper butt and bilge bolted, up to 24 feet draught. Her treenails are of choice locust, driven through and wedged in both ends. Her planking, ceiling and deck frames are all of selected hard pine. The details of her fastening and construction show her to be of excellent materials, well built, and neatly finished.

In ventilation, she has all the improvements of the day. Five of Emerson's patent ventilators are ranged along her decks, and communicate with the hold, and every deck below. In addition to these she has air ports in her ceiling, and brass ventilators along her planksheer, and in the ceiling of her bow, under the topgallant forecastle. Nothing has been omitted that experience could suggest to render her hull sound and durable.

She is a full rigged ship, and her masts rake, commencing with the fore, 1⅛, 1¼, and 1½ inches to the foot. The following are the dimensions of her masts and yards:

MASTS.

	Diameter, *Inches.*	Length, *Feet.*	Mast heads, *Feet.*
Fore	34	93	16½
Top	17⅜	52	8¾
Topgallant	12¾	34⅓	0
Royal	8¼	22⅔	0
Skysail	6½	17	pole.. 5
Main	36	97	17
Top	18½	54	9
Topgallant	13	36	0
Royal	8½	24	0
Skysail	7	19½	pole.. 6
Mizzen	29	84½	13
Top	14½	42¾	7⅙
Topgallant	9¾	28½	0
Royal	6½	19	0
Skysail	5¼	15	pole.. 4

YARDS.

	Diameter, *Inches.*	Length, *Feet.*	Yard arms, *Feet.*
Fore	22¾	84	yard arms.. 4⅔
Top	15¾	66	6¼
Topgallant	10¾	44	2⅔
Royal	6¾	33	1½
Skysail	5½	22	1¼
Main	24	90	5
Top	17	71	7
Topgallant	11½	47	3
Royal	7¼	35	1¾
Skysail	6½	23	1½
Crossjack	17½	70	3½
Mizzentopsail	13½	54½	4⅔
Topgallant	8½	36½	2
Royal	6	27⅔	1⅓
Skysail	5	18	1

Her bowsprit is 30 inches in diameter and 30 feet cutboard; jib-boom 17 inches in diameter, and is divided at 20 feet for the standing-jib, and 15 feet for the flying-jib, with 5 feet end; jib-a-jibboom 13 feet with 3 feet end; spanker-boom 13 inches in diameter, 60 feet long, including 3 feet 2 inches end; spanker-gaff 9 inches in diameter, and 40 feet long, including 6½ feet end; ring-tail boom 30 feet long, or 20 feet outboard; swinging [lower studding sail] booms 12 inches in diameter, and 60 feet long, and the other spars in proportion.

Her lower masts are made, fished on every square and filled in under the hoops, and her tops, like those of a ship of war, are solid, and fit close to the eyes of the lower rigging. The fore-top, in the wake of the after shrouds of the topmast rigging, is 16½ feet wide, the main 17, and the mizzen 13½. Her lower masts are painted black, her tops are bright, and also all above the doublings of the lower masts. The extremes of her mast-heads are ornamented with gilded balls; and all her yards are black.

The standing rigging is of Russia hemp, four stranded patent rope, without a heart, equal in size to that of a first class frigate,—and is wormed and served over the ends and eyes with marling. The lower rigging sets up through lignumvitae dead eyes, with lanyards which are also wormed, and the topmast rigging and stays on their ends. Her fore stays set up to the knight heads, entirely clear of the bowsprit, so that if the latter should be carried away, the foremast would not be affected by the loss. Her topmast stays, fore topgallant and jib stays pass through the bows and set up in-board, which leaves her bow outside uncommonly clear, and if possible adds to its beauty, besides possessing the great advantage of being set up in any weather, without exposure to the men. As the bowsprit is very short, and strongly secured between the knight-heads, it is not lumbered with rigging. It has only one bobstay and a single pair of shrouds, which are enough, considering that the foremast is not dependent upon it, and that her jib-boom is also very short. The bowsprit shrouds and bobstay, also the martingale guys and stays, are all of chain.

Her main stays set up to a massive pair of bitts before the foremast, and not to the windlass paul-bitt. This arrangement, aside from its manifest advantages in point of strength and snugness, leaves a clear forecastle for handling studdingsails, or performing any other work which may require the full scope of the deck.

Her maintopmast and topgallant stays lead into the fore top, man-of-war style; and the mizzen topmast and topgallant stays into the main top.

When carrying a press of sail by the wind, she will have topmast and topgallant breast-backstays. These however, will be shifting, not stationary like those in ships of war.

Her fore and main yards are scarphed in the bunts, as single spars of sufficient length and strength could not be procured. The slings of her lower yards are secured abaft the heels of the topmasts, to the lower mast-heads, and the yards have iron trusses of the most approved patent. She has chain topsail sheets, and double chain ties, with gins on the yards, and halliards on both sides. The other details of her rigging correspond in strength and neatness with those already enumerated.

A glance at the dimensions of her spars will show that she spreads a vast surface of canvas. With lower studdingsails set on both sides, the distance across from the outer leach of one studdingsail to that of the other will be over 160 feet. A single suit of her sails contains 12,780 yards of canvas—of course this includes studdingsails, staysails, &c.

The material of her sails is Colt's cotton duck, made to order, 16 inches wide. The drop of her main sail in the bunt is 47 feet 3 inches, and on the leach 49 feet 6 inches; its length on the foot is 100 feet, and it is made of 1273 yards of canvas. Her sails are so cut that their leaches form a continuous line from the head earings of the skysails to the clews of the courses. Her running rigging is of selected Manila hemp, hand spun, and her blocks and every other detail are designed for strength and hard service, but are at the same time neatly finished.

Her appearance aloft is truly grand. Notwithstanding the vast length of her masts and yards, they are so substantial, and correctly proportioned, and the rigging which supports them, so neat and snug, that the eye wanders in vain above her rail, to detect an unseamanlike detail. To our eye she is as completely perfect aloft, as she is faultlessly beautiful below.

She is owned by Messrs. N. L. & G. Griswold, of New York, was built by Mr. Wm. H. Webb, and is commanded by Captain Robert H. Waterman. Like the knights of old, who threw their gauntlets down to all comers, her owners send her forth, *to challenge the world afloat!*

CHALLENGER

EXTREME clipper ship, launched Dec. 19, 1853, by Robert E. Jackson, at East Boston. 206 x 38: 4 x 23; 1334 tons, old measurement. She had 20 inches dead rise with sharp ends and was of a beautiful model as well as rakish and neat aloft. A carved, full-length female in flowing garments was the figurehead while the graceful oval stern was ornamented with an arch of gilded carved work. Her lower masts were 80, 85 and 75 feet and the corresponding yards, 74, 78 and 59 feet. She was designed by Samuel H. Pook expressly for speed but her record does not show any very fast passages, although the average is good. It is noted that she was the subject of many mishaps. Her original owners were W. & F. H. Whittemore, who later sold her to Samuel G. Reed & Co., both Boston firms. Her first voyage was made under command of Capt. T. Hill; Capt. W. H. Burgess, formerly in the *Whirlwind*, succeeded and after his death aboard the ship at sea, Captain Winsor was in charge until she was sold in July 1863, to go under the Peruvian flag.

Leaving Boston, Feb. 17, 1854, she arrived at San Francisco, June 9th, a passage of 112 days. Was 60 days to the Horn and 88 days to the equator. Much of her cargo was light goods, so she was not deeply laden and Captain Hill was unable to carry a press of sail. From San Francisco she was 52 days to Manila and left that port Oct. 10th, arriving at Boston, Jan. 23, 1855, 104 days passage, 83 from Anjer. Sailed from Boston, June 2, 1855; arrived at San Francisco, Oct. 14th, a passage of 134 days; had head winds or calms nearly all the run; was 67 days to the Horn and 100 to the equator. Sailed from San Francisco, Nov. 9th and reached Hong Kong, Dec. 19th, claiming 34 days sailing time, but the dates give 39 days from port to port. Loaded at Shanghai with tea and silk valued at $2,000,000, the most valuable cargo laden in one bottom at that port up to that time. On July 31st, while bound to sea, got ashore at the mouth of the river and remained hard and fast for a time but got off without injury and proceeded to New York. Her third voyage was a round between New York and China but details are lacking. On her fourth voyage she left New York, Oct. 24, 1857, and reached San Francisco, Feb. 17, 1858, in 115 days; was 56 days to the Horn and 94 to the equator; in the Pacific had nothing but light winds with only a few days of trades. Sailed from San Francisco, Apr. 19th and arrived at New York, Oct. 17th, about 100 days from the Elide Island, where she had taken on a cargo of guano.

The fifth voyage of the *Challenger* started badly, she being obliged to return to New York, Feb. 16, 1859, partially dismasted. Repaired and sailed again Apr. 16th, arriving at San Francisco, Aug. 15th, in 121 days; was 20 days to the line, 56 to the Horn and off the Cape had 14 days of storms. This voyage was completed by her arrival at New York, Mar. 19, 1860, 96 days from Elide Island. On the following voyage she reached San Francisco, Oct. 4, 1860, Captain Winsor reporting 128 days from New York, 31 days to the line, 66 to the Cape, 97 to the equator. The second day at sea she passed the clipper ship *Neptune's Favorite*, also bound for San Francisco, and led her into destination eight days. Sailed from port, Nov. 3rd, and arrived at Liverpool, Feb. 21, 1861, in 109 days. Reached New York, May 5th, 25 days from Liverpool, with coal. When four days out a violent gale sprang up so suddenly that all her canvas was blown away. For three days thereafter she had no sail set and for five days had no main course, maintopgallant sail nor spanker.

The seventh voyage was from New York to San Francisco, arriving out Dec. 9, 1861, Captain Winsor reporting a passage of 118 days. She then went to Callao in 40 days, leaving there June 4, 1862, for Holland. While in Bremerhaven Roads, the night of Oct. 20th, she was in collision with the ship *Roswell Sprague,* during a gale, sustaining slight damage. She arrived at New York, Dec. 13, 1862, 42 days from Rotterdam, in ballast; had strong westerly gales throughout, with much ice east of the Banks. She left New York, sailing date reported as Feb. 7, 1863, and on arrival at San Francisco, June 20th, Captain Winsor reported his time as 128 days, although dates give 133 days. The *Mary L. Sutton,* which left New York 14 days after her, arrived at San Francisco five days before her, a beat of 19 days.

A few weeks after reaching San Francisco, the *Challenger* was sold to N. Larco, agent for the Peruvian Government's line of vessels used to transport coolies from China to the guano deposits. The price reported was $41,000 and she was renamed *Camille Cavour.* She afterwards, as practically all the other coolie ships did, became a lumber drogher, plying between Puget Sound and the West Coast of South America. In October 1875, while bound from Port Discovery to Peru, she was badly damaged in a gale and was abandoned off the coast of Mexico, her wreck finally drifting ashore near Manzanillo.

CHAMPION OF THE SEAS

EXTREME clipper ship, built by Donald McKay, at East Boston; launched Apr. 19, 1854. 238 (keel); 252 (between perpendiculars) x 45:6 x 29:2; 2447 tons, American measurement; 1947 tons, British measurement. Had three complete decks. Her sternpost was upright; fore rake, 14 feet; dead rise, 18 inches; shear, 4½ feet only. Her lines were not greatly different from those of the *Lightning* and *James Baines* but her ends were not quite so long and sharp and there was less concavity in the entrance. The masts raked ½, ⅝ and one inch to the foot and her working suit of sails consisted of 12,500 yards of canvas, 18 inches wide. Capt. Alexander Newlands had been sent over from Liverpool, by James Baines & Co., to superintend her construction and he was her first commander. By many she was considered a handsomer vessel than her predecessor, the *Lightning,* also built by McKay for the Messrs. Baines, her semi-elliptical stern, ornamented with the Australian coat-of-arms and a handsome carved life-sized shellback, as a figurehead, being particularly attractive. Her accommodations for carrying a large number of cabin and steerage passengers could not be surpassed.

From Boston she was towed to New York and loaded for Liverpool; sailed June 16, 1854, and arrived out July 15th, 29 days passage, having carried royals all the way, with very light winds. Left Liverpool, Oct. 11th, and reached Melbourne, Dec. 25th, 75 days, a run not quite up to expectations. The clipper ship *Swallow* reached Melbourne in company with the *Champion,* and Captain Tucker, in reporting his run as 73 days, 18 hours from Gravesend, was much elated in having beaten his larger and much-vaunted rival. The return passage of the *Champion* to Liverpool was made in 84 days. Her second voyage was 83 days out to Melbourne; 90 days return to Liverpool. Her third outward run was made in 85 days.

In 1857, the *James Baines, Lightning* and *Champion of the Seas* were chartered by the British Government to take troops from Portsmouth to India, on account of the mutiny there. The *Baines,* Captain McDonnell, and the *Champion,* Captain McKirdy, embarked troops Aug. 6th, and dropped out to Spithead the following day. Her Majesty the Queen, and the Royal Family had visited and inspected the two ships and had expressed themselves as never having seen any vessels approaching their dimensions or having their accommodations, nor having knowledge that such magnificent ships were in the British merchant service. Both ships sailed Aug. 8th; the *Lightning* got away on the 25th; all engaged in a competing trial not only between themselves but with seven screw transports. The *Lightning* and *Champion* arrived out together in 87 and 101 days respectively and their race up to the Sand Heads, as seen from the shore, is said to have been very exciting. The *Baines* arrived two days later, 102 days out. The season was the worst for navigation in the Bay of Bengal. Some of the clippers were obliged, when near Calcutta, to anchor all night to keep the headway they had made during the day and some of them lost as much as 11 days before they could get a pilot. Many of the transports were within 100 miles of each other for the greater part of the passage but were not aware of it until logs were compared. The average of the sailing transports, other than those named, was 120 days; of the full-powered screw steamers, 83 days; of the auxiliary screws, 96¾ days.

The *Champion* resumed her place in the Baines' "Black Ball Line" of Liverpool-Australian packets, and was a favorite ship for some years. Some time previous to 1870 she was sold at Liverpool, to T. Harrison & Co., of that city, for 9750 pounds sterling and became a general trader. In 1873, on a voyage from St. Johns, N. B., for England, with a cargo of deals, she put into Boston, Sept. 30th, leaky, and was obliged to discharge part of her cargo. Her timbers were found to be much rotted and the vessel was in bad shape; however, Capt. J. J. Josselyn, who had had her since 1871, refused to have her repaired but put aboard two steam pumps and an engine, took on some extra men and sailed for Liverpool, but was obliged to put into Queenstown, again leaky. She was sold at Liverpool, in July 1873, for 7500 pounds, to rate A 1 for four years.

She arrived at San Francisco, July 18, 1875, after a fast run of 39 days from Hong Kong, Captain Wilson in command; was chartered to load guano at the Peruvian deposits, for Cork, at 3 pounds, 12 and sixpence. Arrived at Callao, Oct. 5, 1875, 48 days from San Francisco. Loaded at Pabellon de Pica and was abandoned off Cape Horn, in a sinking condition, Jan. 3, 1876. The *Champion* had sprung a leak and the pumps choked. All hands were taken off by the British bark *Windsor,* whose second mate, Mr. Thompson, relates the following anecdote. Just as the captain of the *Windsor* was about to give the order to fill away the main-yard, he noticed someone standing on the poop of the *Champion,* and calling to the latter's captain, he said, "Captain, you have left one of your men on board the ship." The captain of the *Champion* took up the glass and then turned around and smiled, explaining that his ship had, for a binnacle stand, a life-sized wooden effigy of a sailor boy, holding the binnacle in his two hands; this was what had been seen, being quite lifelike with wide pants and flap collar and painted according to life.

At the time the ship was built the following description of her was printed in the May 20, 1854, issue of the *Boston Daily Atlas:*

The New Clipper Ship "Champion of the Seas."

This splendid vessel registers 2447 tons, and is the largest sailing merchant ship in the world. She was built at East Boston, by Mr. Donald McKay, and is intended for Messrs. James Baines & Co.'s Liverpool and Australian line of clippers. This enterprising firm own twenty sail of first class ships, and have under charter as many more, all employed in the Australian trade. The superior equipment of their clippers, their unrivalled passages, and the absence of disasters, have given them a world wide reputation which they are determined to maintain. They have, therefore, selected the first of mechanics to build for their line a class of clippers, which, for beauty, strength, speed, and completeness of accommodation, shall be peerless on the ocean. Mr. McKay has already built for them the celebrated clipper *Lightning,* which, on her first passage ran 436 miles in 24 hours, though drawing 22 feet water. The *Champion of the Seas,* in beauty of model, strength of construction, and all the other elements of perfection is a decided improvement upon the *Lightning.* Her ends are as long, though not so sharp or concave, and are even more beautiful in their form. She is 238 feet long on the keel, and 259 feet on deck, between perpendiculars, which as the sternpost is upright gives her a fore rake of 14 feet; her extreme breadth of beam is 45½ feet, and depth 29 feet; dead rise at half floor 18 inches, rounding or swell of sides 10 inches, and sheer 4½ feet. Her greatest breadth of beam is precisely at the centre of the load displacement line, and she is rather fuller aft on this line than she is forward. The concavity of her load line forward is about 2½ inches, but above there the form of the bow is decidedly convex, and flares above the outline of the upper wale. A full figure of a sailor, with his hat in his right hand, and his left hand extended, ornaments the bow. The ship has a waist of narrow strakes, defined between the mouldings of the upper wale and the planksheer, and this is continued round the stern, which is semi-elliptical in form, and is ornamented with the Australian coat of arms. The run is long and clean, and blends in perfect harmony with the general outline of the model. Broadside on she has all the imposing majesty of a ship of war, combined with the airy grace of a clipper. Outside, she is painted black, and inside white, relieved with blue waterways. Her bulwarks are 4½ feet high, built solid, and are surmounted by a monkey rail, which extends fore and aft. She has a spacious topgallant forecastle, fitted for the accommodation of the crew, and abaft the foremast a house 50 feet by 18 wide, and 6½ high, which contains the galleys, a cabin for second class passengers, and staterooms for the forward officers. Its forward part shelters a double staircase which leads to the deck below. Abaft the mainmast is a house 16 feet square, the forward part of which contains the chief mate's stateroom, and the rest of it shelters the staircase which leads to a vestibule below, from which the cabins are entered. There is another house aft, designed for a smoking room, and which also protects the helmsman, and shelters a staircase which leads to the captain's cabin. As all her cabins are below, she has very spacious deck room. Abaft the mainmast, we never saw a ship so perfectly beautiful on deck.

She has Crane's self-acting chain stoppers, a powerful patent windlass under the topgallant forecastle, Allyn's patent capstan on it, and on the spar deck two capstans forward and two aft, one on each side, and a patent steering apparatus.

Her cabins are on the main deck, and extend between 70 and 80 feet from the stern. The after one is 30 feet long, by 14 wide, and 7½ feet high; has two spacious recess sofas, and is beautifully wainscotted with mahogany, set off into Gothic arched panels, relieved with gilded carved work, and is furnished in the highest style of art. Its tables, mirrors, carpets and curtains are of the most costly materials, and are arranged with consummate taste.

Over the transom sofa are three panels, which contain daguerreotype pictures. The first is a representation of the ship *Great Republic*, under all sail by the wind; the second is the outline of the *Champion of the Seas*, as she now lies broadside on, and other objects in the background, and between the two ships is a picture of Mr. Donald McKay, their builder. These pictures were taken by Messrs. Southworth & Hawes, and are about the best of the kind we have seen.

The dining saloon is 40 feet long, is plain white, relieved with gilding, and is finished and furnished with the same taste as the cabin abaft it. The cabins have oblong square skylights over them nearly their whole length, and the frames of these lights are all of polished mahogany, protected with brass. All the staterooms have square sidelights or ports, which can be opened in fine weather, and deck-lights besides, and perforated ventilators between the beams.

The vestibule contains a pantry and a mess-room on the larboard side, and a bath-room and other apartments opposite, and before these there are several store-rooms. The deck before the cabins is also designed for the accommodation of passengers, has square ports along its sides, and will be fitted with staterooms. She will also carry passengers on her lower deck, which like that above it, is 7½ feet high. Every means of light and ventilation, consistent with the safety of the ship, has been applied to it. Along the sides of the houses, between the stanchions, around the water tanks, through the vestibule, through the dining saloon and cabins, and many other places, are ventilators and skylights; and besides these, she has Emerson's corresponding ventilators, forward and aft. She has in all 210 square feet of light and ventilation. Nothing that ingenuity could devise has been omitted to render her accommodations the most perfect in every particular.

A few of the leading details of her materials and construction will show that she is as good and well built as she is unquestionably beautiful. Her entire frame is of seasoned white oak, and all her hooks, pointers and knees are of the same wood, her planking and ceiling of hard pine, and she is square fastened throughout, and butt and bilge bolted with copper. The keel is of rock maple, in two depths, each 16 inches square, with 12 feet keyed scarphs, which are bolted with copper, and the parts of the keel, before the frames were raised, were also copper bolted. The floor timbers are moulded 21 inches on the keel, and sided from 12 to 13 inches, and over them are four tiers of midship keelsons, each 16 inches square, and on each side of them are two depths of sister-keelsons, of the same size, the whole scarphed and keyed, and fastened with 1¾ inch bolting, the bolts not more than eight inches apart. The whole frame, fore and aft, is diagonally cross braced with iron, five inches wide, seven-eighths of an inch thick, and thirty-eight feet long. These braces are bolted through every frame, and through every intersection; are let into the timbers and ceiling, and extend from the first futtocks to the top-timbers. The ceiling on the floor is five inches thick, and over the first futtocks there are two bilge keelsons, each 15 inches square, scarphed, keyed, square fastened and bolted edgeways. The rest of the ceiling in the hold, varies from 12 to 10 inches in thickness, and is also scarphed, keyed, and fastened in the same style as the keelsons, the bolting only diminished one-eighth of an inch. There are 32 beams under the lower deck, 34 under the main deck, and 35 under the upper deck, and their dimensions are as follows, commencing below; 15 by 16, 12 by 15, and 8 by 15 inches square, with oak lodging and hanging knees to those below, and hackmatack to the others. The lower and main deck waterways are 15 inches square, with thick work of ten by twelve inside and over them, and ceiling varying from seven to five inches in thickness, exclusive of a heavy clamp under the upper deck beams, and a lap strake under the lower deck knees. The upper deck waterways are 14 by 15 inches, with a thick strake inside of them, rounded off towards the deck. All the waterways, as well as the keelsons and ceiling, are scarphed and bolted in the most substantial style. The upper deck is of hackmatack, 3½ inches thick, and the others of hard pine, of the same substance. The stanchions in the hold are 10 by 22 inches, clasp the beams and extend to the deck beams above. Beside the midship stanchions, she has 12 wing stanchions fitted in the same style, and all of them are strongly kneed and bolted. Under the upper deck there is a tier of turned stanchions on each side, with iron rods through their centres, which set up with nuts and screws. Her ends are almost filled with massive hooks and pointers, which cross all the cants diagonally and fay to the beams. The hooks in the between decks are beamed and kneed and fastened through all.

Her garboards are 9 by 15 inches, the next strake 8 by 14, the third 7 by 14, the bottom planking 5 inches thick, the wale 6 by 7, and the waist 42 inches thick; the whole finished smooth as joiner's work, and strongly fastened. Every line and moulding is truly graduated her whole length, and presents a most beautiful combination of perfect workmanship. Her planksheer and main rail are each 7 inches thick, and as before remarked, her bulwarks are built solid, like those of a ship of war.

Her ground tackle, boats, &c., are of the best quality. She has below a water tank of 5000 gallons capacity, and upon her arrival in England will have other water tanks fitted alongside of the keelsons, and extending to the bilge.

She is a full rigged ship and has a noble set of spars. Her lower masts and bowsprit are built of hard pine, dowelled together, bolted and hooped over all with iron; and the topmasts and jibbooms are also of hard pine. The masts, commencing with the fore, rake ½, ⅝, and 1 inch to the foot, and are 74 and 63 feet apart. The lengths of the lower masts in the following table are above the deck:

Masts.

	Diameter. Inches.	Length. Feet.	Mast-heads. Feet.
Fore	40	65	17
Top	20	47	10
Topgallant	15	26	0
Royal	13	17	pole.. 8
Main	42	71	17
Top	20	50	10
Topgallant	15	27	0
Royal	13	17	pole.. 12
Mizzen	36	61	14
Top	16	42	9
Topgallant	12	24	0
Royal	10	15	pole.. 8

Yards.

Fore	24½	88	yard-arms.. 5
Top	19½	69	5½
Topgallant	13½	51	4
Royal	9	37	2
Main	24½	95	5
Top	19½	74	5½
Topgallant	13½	51	4
Royal	9	42	3
Crossjack	20	74	4½
Mizzentop	15	57½	5
Topgallant	9½	42	3½
Royal	7	30	2

The bowsprit is 40 inches in diameter, and 22 feet outboard; jib-boom 21 inches in diameter in the cap, and is divided at 16 and 15 feet for the two jibs, and 6 feet end; spanker boom 58 feet 2 inches long, and gaff 42 feet, main spencer gaff 22 feet long, and the other spars in proportion. Like a ship of war, royals are her highest sails

"BONITA," 1127 TONS, BUILT AT SOUTH BOSTON, IN 1853

"CHALLENGE," 2006 TONS, BUILT AT NEW YORK, IN 1851

From a lithograph by Endicott & Company, after a drawing by E. Brown

"Chariot of Fame," 2050 tons, built at East Boston, in 1853
From an oil painting formerly in the Williams Collection

"Chariot of Fame," 2050 tons, built at East Boston, in 1853
From a painting by S. Walters, showing the ship at Liverpool

fore and aft, consequently the harmony of her masts and yards is complete, making her a perfect picture to the eye. The caps are of wrought iron and the doublings of the masts are nearly wood-to-wood, or close together. Her rigging is of the best Russia hemp, very stout, and neatly fitted. She has all the chain and iron-work, aloft, and about the bowsprit, now in general use, such as bobstays, bowsprit shrouds, martingale stays and guys, topsail sheets and ties, patent trusses, iron futtock rigging, &c. The fore stays set up to the knight-heads, and the other head stays lead through the bow and set up inboard.

She has three backstays on each side to the fore and main topmasts, double topgallant backstays, with outriggers in the cross-trees double main topsail stays, which set up to the fore top, and a spring stay, which leads on deck. The mast-heads and yards are black, the lower masts white, and the studdingsail booms bright, with black ends. There are about 12,500 yards of canvas in a single suit of her sails. Aloft as well as below there is the same harmony of outline, and completeness of details which make her not only the most beautiful but the most perfect ship her talented builder has ever produced. But while we award Mr. McKay the highest praise for his genius and skill in the production of this noble ship, we must not forget her commander, Capt. Alexander Newlands, under whose superintendence she was built and equipped. Mr. McKay, with an openness worthy of his great reputation, nobly acknowledges his merits. He says, "At an early period of our intercourse I saw that Captain Newlands understood his business, and that he was worthy of my entire confidence, consequently he has been of the greatest service to me. Agreeably to his designs, the whole inside arrangements of the ship have been made, including the complicated and varied plan for light and ventilation.

"He designed the cabins and their details—had everything to do with the masting and rigging of the ship, in a word, has been always on hand, and has given me the most unqualified satisfaction. It is not saying too much to affirm that, of all the shipmasters who have from time to time been placed to superintend the outfits of my vessels, I do not know one who combines so many valuable qualities, and who, at the same time, makes less pretensions. He is calm but quick, reflective but earnest, and always displays that firm self-reliance peculiar to a thorough bred sailor, in every thing of consequence which he undertakes. Well educated, a perfect gentleman, and a sailor of the highest professional attainments, he is well worthy of commanding the finest merchant ship in the world."

Personally, we have sometimes enjoyed the pleasure of Capt. Newland's society, during the past three months, and we know that when he leaves here, we shall feel his absence as the loss of a friend.

The *Champion of the Seas* is now lying at the Grand Junction Wharf, East Boston, and in a few days will be towed to New York, and there load for Liverpool.

CHARGER

MEDIUM clipper ship, built by E. G. Pearce, at Portsmouth, N. H.; launched Oct. 25, 1856. 190 x 38: 1 x 23: 4; 1136 tons, old measurement and 1169 tons, new measurement. Owned by Henry Hastings of Boston. She had no figurehead, a billet substituting; her stern was ornamented with a carved, mounted charger, in full career. She was a handsome ship, well built and is said to have been the most costly ship of her size put afloat up to that time. Her model was adapted for both speed and capacity, and while a fast sailer, she could load dead weight cargo to nearly 50 per cent over her register.

Under command of Capt. Luther Hurd, the *Charger* left Boston on her maiden voyage, Jan. 4, 1857, the tug *Enoch Train* towing her and the extreme clipper *Stag Hound* down the Bay together. The *Charger* crossed the line 24 days out but did not weather Cape St. Roque until 10 days later. She arrived at San Francisco, May 8th, after a passage of 124 days, finding that the *Stag Hound* had been in port for 16 days, notwithstanding the fact that she had been seven days off the Californian coast. From San Francisco, the *Charger* went to Valparaiso in 44 days; thence home. Her second voyage was 121 days from Boston to San Francisco, arriving July 1, 1858; had crossed the equator 88 days out and been 10 days covering the last 300 miles of the run. From San Francisco she, in common with all other ships going over the route at the time, had a long run to Calcutta, some 100 days, but from that port to Boston she retrieved herself. Leaving the Sand Heads, Dec. 25, 1858, she reached Boston, Mar. 19, 1859, a passage of 84 days, which has been beaten only by the 81 days of the *Witch of the Wave* and the 83 days of the *Beverly*, and equalled only by the *Staffordshire* and *Dashing Wave*. On Jan. 31, 1859, his ship going 10 knots, Captain Hurd reported passing close to a shoal, but this proved to be imaginary. His position at the time was 110 miles west-south-west of Cape Agulhas, the *Charger* then being 37 days out, which run has never been beaten and very rarely equalled.

After arrival at Boston, Capt. James B. Hatch assumed command of the *Charger* and made the passage of 124 days to San Francisco, arriving Aug. 23, 1859; and generally light winds, being 30 days to the line and 30 days from the equator to destination. She then crossed to Hong Kong and after making a round voyage to Bangkok, returned home. On her fourth voyage, she reached San Francisco, Aug. 25, 1861, 126 days from Boston; had bad weather off the Horn, the after hatch-house being stove, the cabin filled, and some damage done on deck; had very light winds in the Pacific and was 30 days from the equator to destination. She then crossed to Hong Kong, in 41 days, returning to San Francisco, Feb. 27, 1862, in 49 days; then back to Hong Kong, in 48 days, and thence to Manila where she loaded for New York. Sailed July 10, 1862 and arrived at New York, Nov. 16th, 129 days from Manila, 88 days from Java Head, 67 days from the Cape, off which she had been detained 15 days by heavy gales. All other vessels making the voyage from the Orient, about this time, had similarly long passages down the China

Sea, some being 60 days to Anjer, with delays of 14 to 20 days off the Cape.

The command of the *Charger* was now given to Capt. Josiah N. Knowles, formerly in the *Wild Wave* and he arrived at San Francisco, May 18, 1863, in 125 days from New York. Was 25 days to the line and passed Cape Horn on the 56th day out; 10 days later was northbound in the Pacific and crossed the equator on the 94th day. Sailed from San Francisco, July 29, 1863, and was 107 days to Boston. Sailed from Boston, Jan. 28, 1864, and was 108 days to San Francisco, being off the Farallon Islands on the 105th day; in a calm with dense fog. Had crossed the line 18 days out; passed Cape Horn on the 53rd day and crossed the equator 85 days out. Returning to Boston she reached that port, Nov. 8, 1864, in 99 days. Sailed from Boston, Mar. 7, 1865, and at once ran into heavy weather. When three days out, while scudding in a gale, she shipped a sea which stove the after hatch, filled the cabin and carried overboard three seamen, besides injuring several others. She was 60 days to 50° South and 10 days off the Cape in rough weather; crossed the equator 107 days out and arrived at San Francisco, July 18th, 133 days from Boston. Sailed from San Francisco, Sept. 14th, and arrived at Boston, Dec. 19th, in 96 days, the fastest passage made about that time. She was within 50 miles of Boston, for five days, in very severe weather, losing one man overboard and having seven men badly frostbitten.

About this time Captain Knowles relinquished command of the *Charger*. He was subsequently in the *Glory of the Seas,* and after retiring from the sea became one of the most prominent and respected shipping merchants of San Francisco. Captain Lester, formerly in the clippers *Pampero* and *Invincible,* took the *Charger* and leaving Boston, May 24, 1867, arrived at San Francisco, Sept. 27th, a passage of 125 days. Was 30 days to the line; 70 days to 50° South; 15 days rounding the Horn. Sailed from San Francisco, Oct. 26th, and made the run to Liverpool in 97 days; beat the *Thatcher Magoun,* which had sailed in company, 20 days; reached Liverpool on the same day as the *Black Hawk* which had left San Francisco a week ahead of her. After crossing to New York, she went out to San Francisco in 127 days, arriving Nov. 21, 1869. In the Gulf Stream, the fore-royal mast was struck by lightning and shivered. Crossed the line 34 days out and passed Cape Horn on the 63rd day out; was thence 38 days to the equator. Sailed from San Francisco, Jan. 11, 1870; was 17 days to Honolulu and 28 days thence to Hong Kong. Arrived at San Francisco, Aug. 11, 1870, 37 days from Hiogo. Sailed Sept. 28, 1870, and was 108 days to Queenstown. She then went from England to Hong Kong and on Oct. 27, 1872, arrived at San Francisco, 54 days from the latter port, Captain Creelman being now in command. Sailed from San Francisco, Nov. 13, 1872, and was 114 days to Queenstown. Again went out from England to China and thence to Manila.

The *Charger* sailed from Manila, Dec. 10, 1873, with part cargo consisting of 1000 bales of hemp, bound for Cebu, where she was to complete her lading for Boston. Four days later she piled up on a reef, 10 miles from Cebu, and a week later had begun to break up. The wreck was sold for $7595 and a portion of the hemp was saved, damaged. Insurance was reported as only $25,000.

A second *Charger* was built at Boston, in 1874, for Henry Hastings and for a time Captain Creelman was her commander.

CHARIOT OF FAME

MEDIUM clipper ship, launched in April 1853, by Donald McKay, at East Boston, Mass., for Enoch Train & Co., of Boston, and intended for a packet between that port and Liverpool. She was a sister ship of the *Star of Empire*, both being large three-deckers, drawing 22 feet when loaded; their tonnage was 2050 34/95, old measurement. In 1868 the *Chariot* was listed as being 1573 tons and was owned by Wilson & Chambers of Liverpool. During her career as an American ship she was commanded by Capt. Allen

H. Knowles, who was later in the *Puritan* and the *Agenor*. Captain Knowles died at Hyannis, in July 1875.

Operating first as a packet, the *Chariot* made seven passages, back and forth, between Boston and Liverpool, which are said to have averaged about 17 days. One of her passages, in 1854, was a strenuous one. Leaving Liverpool, Jan. 11, 1854, with a cargo valued at 100,000 pounds sterling, the heaviest and most valuable cargo to leave that port for the United States up to that time, having 79 passengers in the steerage and others in the cabin, the first night out she came in contact with an unknown bark and lost her jibboom. Jan. 23rd, in a heavy gale with a high sea, the main topsail and main spencer were blown away and the main yard broken in the slings. Shortly after she shipped a heavy sea which smashed the bulwarks, flooded the cabin and washed away four boats. On the 24th, some of the furled sails were blown from the yards and the figurehead was washed away. On Feb. 2nd she got a new main yard up but five days later, on Feb. 7th, found herself in the same longitude as on Jan. 22nd. She reached Boston Bay, on Feb. 23rd, and again encountered a fierce northwest gale, during which she lost and split sails. With no more sails to bend and many of the crew frostbitten, she put into Provincetown in a blinding snowstorm and later was towed to Boston, by the *R. B. Forbes*, arriving Feb. 26, 1854.

After completing her operations as a packet the *Chariot* was chartered by the "White Star Line" of Australian packets and is said to have made a number of good passages. After 1855 she was engaged in general trade and on May 27, 1856, sailed from New York for Acapulco; had a series of light winds and unfavorable weather on the passage, which occupied 145 days; was 41 days from New York to the line but others at the same time had similar experiences. From Acapulco she went to Callao and later loaded guano at the Chincha Islands for Hampton Roads. On arrival at New York, she loaded for San Francisco and arrived out May 13, 1858, after a passage of 126 days, 4 hours; her cargo, 3600 tons, was the largest to be laden for San Francisco up to that time, except that of the *Great Republic*.

Captain Knowles reported being 22 days to the line; 60 days to 50° South; 14 days rounding the Horn; 94 days to the equator; 12 days thence to eight degrees north; after losing the trades in 37° North, she was becalmed two days, making her time from the equator to port, 32 days. Off Cape Horn she was in company with the *Ocean Express* and they arrived out in company, the passage of the *Express* being 122 days, 21 hours. From San Francisco, the *Chariot* went to Callao, loaded guano at the Chinchas and arrived at Hampton Roads in January 1859, having on board the crew of the ship *Oxnard* of Boston, abandoned off Cape Horn on her voyage from Cardiff for San Francisco.

On Aug. 3, 1859, the *Chariot* arrived at San Francisco, 117 days from New York. Was 23 days to the line; 63 days to the Horn and crossed the equator 86 days out. On Aug. 1st, 115 days out, she was obliged to drop anchor close to shore, 20 miles south of the Golden Gate, the wind being too light to wear off. Hove up her anchor the morning of Aug. 3rd. Sailed from San Francisco, Sept. 22nd, and arrived at Valparaiso, Nov. 5th, 44 days passage. Was chartered for guano, Chinchas Islands to Hampton Roads, at $15 a ton and sailed from Callao, Mar. 10, 1860, arriving at Baltimore, June 19th. Loaded at that port for San Francisco and arrived out, Dec. 27, 1860, 143 days' passage. Captain Knowles reported being 44 days to the line from Cape Henry; thence 28 days to 50° South; was 23 days rounding the Horn and 24 days thence to the equator, crossing 119 days out, and thence 24 days to destination. Near the Cape, three immense icebergs were seen, while fields of ice were visible from the topgallantmast as far as the eye could reach. During subsequent gales the crossjack yard was carried away, a portion of the cargo shifted and the ship lay for a time with head rail under water. Sailed from San Francisco, Feb. 20, 1861, and arrived at Liverpool, July 11th, in 141 days. She then went out to Melbourne; thence to New Zealand and back to London where she was sold. The command was given to Captain Kerr and for a time she continued in trade between England and Australia or New Zealand. Her name was dropped from Lloyd's, prior to 1874.

CHARLES MALLORY

MEDIUM clipper ship, built in 1851, by Charles Mallory, at Mystic, Conn., and owned by the builder. 155 x 33 x 18 feet; 698 tons register; dead weight capacity, 1000 tons. Had good lines and during her short existence showed up as a fast sailer. Under Capt. Charles Hull she left New York, on her first voyage, Sept. 15, 1852, and arrived at San Francisco, Jan. 8, 1853, a passage of 115 days. She had poor luck in the North Atlantic, being 33 days from Sandy Hook to the line, but thereafter retrieved herself, and her run of 37 days thence to 50° South, Pacific, was excellent, as was also her time of 45 days from there to destination. From equator to equator crossings she was but 60 days and from the Atlantic Line to the Golden Gate, 82 days, fast runs even for large, powerful clippers.

Sailing from San Francisco, Jan. 27, 1853, she went to Honolulu, in ballast, in something over 13 days, and there loaded about 4500 barrels of oil, the partial catch of several whalers. Taking her departure for New London, about Apr. 1st, she made good progress and was some 65 days out when she ran ashore, prior to June 9th, on Cape St. Augustine, the extreme easterly headland of Brazil. About 3000 barrels of oil were saved but salvage operations were difficult, it being possible to work only four or five hours daily, besides which the barrels had to be rolled two miles along a rough beach. At the end of July she was reported as lying in a bad position and probably would soon break up, so was sold as she lay for 210 milreis (about $115). Captain Hull was then reported as being very sick.

CHARMER

MEDIUM clipper ship, launched Oct. 28, 1854, from the yard of George W. Jackman, at Newburyport, Mass. 203 over all x 37 beam x 23: 3 depth of hold; 1055 tons, old measurement and 1024, new measurement. Dead rise, 12 inches; sheer, 3½ feet. Her figurehead was described by the reporter who attended her launch as that of a snake with the tongue hanging out of its mouth, as if it had had a drink of Cochituate water and did not like it. Her original owners were Bush & Wildes of Boston. She was a good carrier and sister ship to the *Daring* and *War Hawk*. The *Charmer* remained the property of Bush & Wildes until she was sold to sail under British colors, and during their ownership was commanded by Capt. J. S. Lucas.

She arrived at San Francisco, Apr. 12, 1855, Captain Lucas reporting his passage as 114 days from Boston; 25 days to the line; 51 to Cape Horn and off it 18 days, losing jibboom and gear attached; crossing the equator in the Pacific, Mar. 16, 1855, and being within 500 miles of the Golden Gate for seven days. Returned to New York in 104 days. She again arrived at San Francisco, Mar. 8, 1856, in 143 days from New York. She got to leeward of St. Roque and was obliged to beat to the eastward. As it was she crossed the line four times, taking nearly a month altogether and was not in south latitude until nearly 50 days out. She was 80 days to the Horn and off it seven days in light winds; crossed the equator, Feb. 8th, and was within 800 miles of San Francisco for 11 days. Sailed from San Francisco, Mar. 22, 1856, and was 53 days to Hong Kong. Arrived at New York, Jan. 28, 1857, from Whampoa.

She arrived at San Francisco, Sept. 2, 1857, 136 days from New York; 23 days to the line; 64 to the Horn; crossed the equator, Aug. 2nd, and thence light winds. Sailed from port, Sept. 18, 1857, for Calcutta. Arrived at Manila, Oct. 19, 1860, from Whampoa and sailed Nov. 14th for New York; got ashore on a reef off the Island of Banka; jettisoned a quantity of hemp and got off; passed Anjer, Dec. 4th and arrived at New York, Mar. 22, 1861.

The *Charmer* was at Key West, June 3, 1861, from New York, arriving back July 7, 1861, eight days from Key West in ballast. Captain Freeman was in command for this brief round voyage. Arrived at San Francisco, Mar. 12, 1862, 131 days from New York. Sailed from San Francisco, Apr. 3rd; hove to off Honolulu the 17th, and proceeded the same day; arrived at Hong Kong, May 23rd, and sailed for Manila, May 30th, arriving off that port, June 4th. Thence to Liverpool. Sailed from Liverpool, Jan. 17, 1863, for Boston, but returned to port two days later and soon, thereafter, was purchased by W. H. Daunt of Liverpool and operated as a British vessel with Captain Cole in command. In 1870 she was the British ship *Charmer*, Captain Harrington, owned in Liverpool by C. Morrison & Co. In 1875 she was listed as the Glasgow ship *Charmer*, Captain Hogg, owned by J. D. Clinch & Co., of that city.

CHERUBIM

MEDIUM clipper ship, built by J. Abraham, at Baltimore, in 1855. 217 x 43 x 24; 1796 tons, old measurement. Owned by D. Currie and others, of Richmond, Virginia. She was commanded by Captain Smith and later by Captain Skinner.

Most of the operations of the *Cherubim* were between the west coast of South America and England. On Sept. 5, 1856, she ran down and sunk the emigrant ship *Ocean Home*, off the Lizard, causing a great loss of life. On Jan. 16, 1857, she arrived at Callao, in ballast, from London, Captain Smith reporting his passage as 78 days.

She made but one passage to San Francisco, arriving at that port Nov. 19, 1859, 193 days from New York, via Valparaiso, 43 days. Captain Skinner reported being 46 days to the line and 56 days off the Horn in very heavy weather; lost a number of sails, etc. Forty thousand gallons of water, practically their whole supply, was lost through the mischievousness of one of the crew who allowed salt to get in and for forty days thereafter all hands were on an allowance of one pint per day per man. Put into Valparaiso, Sept. 30th, to replenish their supply and were in port one week. Sailed from San Francisco, Dec. 27, 1859, with a cargo of lumber for Valparaiso and made the passage down in 45 days. Went from the West Coast to London.

The *Cherubim* was laid up at London on account of the Civil War, she being still owned in the South, until October 1863, when she was sold for £12,500, to Cox Brothers. She was renamed *Lochee,* her hailing port being Dundee. Her name was dropped from registers about 1870.

CLEOPATRA

MEDIUM clipper ship, launched from the yard of Paul Curtis, at East Boston, Mass., Mar. 28, 1853. 220 feet over all, x 41: 6 x 23: 3; 1562 tons. Dead rise 15 inches; swell of sides six inches and sheer four feet. Her lines were rounded with long sharp ends. The full length figure of Cleopatra, in robes of white fringed with gold, ornamented her bow. The stern was oval. Her owner was Benjamin Bangs of Boston and her command was given to Capt. Samuel V. Shreve.

Sailing from Boston, Apr. 23, 1853, she was 24 days to the line; 53 days to 50° South; thence 16 days to same latitude in the Pacific; thence 34 days to the equator, 103 days out; thence 28 days to port; total 131 days. Captain Shreve reported having light winds and pleasant weather throughout the passage and was only able to make any kind of a showing towards its end, when the final 1200 miles, from 41° 29″ North, 149° West, was made in five days. From San Francisco she had a slow run of 71 days to Callao; was 27 days to the line; thence 17 days to 41° South, her highest latitude; thence 27 days getting north to destination. Sailed from Callao, guano laden, March 15, 1854 and was 86 days to Hampton Roads; thence four days to New York.

Left New York, Nov. 14, 1854, under Captain Thayer; was 35 days to the line; 58 days to 50° South; came round Cape Horn under skysails, 63 days out; was 12 days from 50° to 50°; thence 22 days to the equator, 92 days out; thence had fine winds and made the run to the Golden Gate in less than 19 days, of which the final 36 hours were spent in fog off the port. Only once on the whole passage had topsails been close reefed. On the same day she arrived, there also reached port, the *Electric,* which had left New York in company, the passages of both ships being 110 days.

The *Cleopatra* sailed from San Francisco, Mar. 26th and arrived at Callao, May 15th, loaded 1600 tons of guano at the Chincha Islands and sailed from Callao, Aug. 13th, bound for New York. On Sept. 23rd she struck a submerged wreck in 23° 31″ South, 31° 19″ West, while going 15 knots and foundered two days later. Captain Thayer and his crew, 25 in number, in two boats, reached Rio nine days later. She was insured for $90,000.

CLIMAX

CLIPPER ship, built in 1853 by Hayden & Cudworth, at Medford, Mass., for Howes and Crowell, of Boston. Deck 180 x 36 x 22: 9; 1051 15/95 tons. Dead rise 17 inches, swell of sides four inches and sheer 26 inches. She was said to have given the effect of a pilot boat build, her bow having the same easy rake and graceful rise. Her figurehead was a gilded eagle on the wing and her stern oval. She had a small topgallant forecastle and large house amidship for the crew; her cabin was under a half poop deck with house in front; the cabin contained seven staterooms beautifully furnished. Her lower masts were 74, 79 and 70 feet and she carried double topsails, an adaptation and improvement on the Forbes rig, where the topmasts were fidded abaft the lower mastheads. This rig was the invention of Capt. William F. Howes, who had superintended her construction and was to command her, and received its first trial on the *Climax*. In her case, a crew of only 14 men and two boys was required, about half of what the complement would otherwise have been. Captain Howes' plan soon replaced the old style single topsails.

After loading 1785 tons of cargo for San Francisco, freight list $56,000, the *Climax* sailed from Boston, Mar. 28, 1853, the day before the clipper ship *Competitor*, also a Medford-built ship and some 200 tons smaller, had taken her departure for the same destination, and it was reported that considerable money was wagered on the result of the race. The *Climax*, with good trades in the North Atlantic, was but 19 days, 17 hours to the line against the *Competitor's* 24 days and this lead the *Climax* held until getting into the Pacific, being 12 days only from 50° South to 50° South. When off Cape Horn, 54 days out, the *Competitor* had her stem split, starting a bad leak, and had to be kept before the wind while her bows were being strapped together. Although she got into the Pacific six days after the *Climax*, she overhauled her, crossed the line one day ahead and reached San Francisco on July 20th, her rival reaching port the following day. The time of passage for both was 115 days although the *Competitor's* backers claimed she had done better work and had actually beaten by a few hours. The *Climax* sailed 3600 miles to the line in something under 20 days; 7730 miles to the Horn in 52 days; 12,550 miles to the Pacific equator crossing in 88 days; 15,976 miles to destination. After discharging cargo she went to Callao in 60 days and was thence 66 days, 16½ hours, to Hampton Roads, guano laden.

On her second and last voyage as an American ship, she reached San Francisco, Nov. 8, 1854, Capt. Benjamin Freeman in command, 132 days from New York. Reported being 75 days to the Horn, coming around in fine weather. Had a continuation of light winds and calms from the Cape to port, not having to furl royals once; was 35 days from the line to the Golden Gate. Her former rival, the *Competitor*, had reached port some time previously in 122 days from New York.

From San Francisco, the *Climax* again went to Callao and loaded guano at the Chincha Islands. Leaving the islands, Mar. 28, 1855, for Callao, to get her clearance, a leak was discovered when she was 30 hours out. On arrival at Callao there was eight feet of water in her and the crew were exhausted from pumping. Every effort was made to free her, 100 tons of guano being transferred to the ship *Osborne Howes*, but her pumps choked and she sank in 21 fathoms with about 700 tons of her cargo aboard, She was sold as she lay, to Antonio Terry, for $13,000, and through the aid of state prisoners, working day and night, she was floated and subsequently repaired.

She was renamed *Antonio Terry* and under the Peruvian flag, hailed from Callao. For a time she was engaged in transporting coolies from China, for the guano deposits, but later went into the general carrying trade. While at anchor in the harbor of Callao, with 500 coolies aboard, Jan. 1, 1857, she was injured by cross fire from the Government forces on the mole shooting at the Revolutionary fleet. The latter had previously boarded her, intending to "cut her out," but had to desist on account of being too close inshore and under the batteries.

While under Peruvian ownership, the *Antonio Terry* arrived at New York, Jan. 15, 1864, from Manila, Aug. 18, 1863, reporting that in very heavy weather off the Cape, she had her mainmast sprung. She cleared at New York, Mar. 30, 1864, for Shanghai and the following year was sold at Hong Kong for $19,000. Captain Frederick gave up the sea after making one voyage in the *Climax* and thereafter gave his attention to installing his double-topsail rig on square-rigged vessels. He died at Yarmouth, Mass., June 26, 1882. Capt. Benjamin Freeman retired from the sea after the *Climax* was abandoned to the underwriters at Callao, in 1855, and died at Brewster in 1884.

COEUR DE LION

MEDIUM clipper ship, launched from the yard of George Raynes, Portsmouth, N. H., in January 1854, and built for the account of W. F. Parrott of Boston, and Captain Tucker of Portsmouth. Length between perpendiculars, 178: 4; over all, 198 x 36: 2 x 21: 6; tonnage, 1098 old measurement, 915 new measurement. Dead rise, 15 inches; swell of sides, seven inches, and sheer, three feet. Her figurehead was a representation of King Richard and on her semi-circular stern there appeared the escutcheon of that monarch. Her entrance lines were slightly concave and quite sharp; she was designed to sail fast and yet carry a fair cargo. Her lower masts, counting from the foremast, were 80, 82 and 76 feet long, and the corresponding yards 69, 73 and 56 feet. Capt. George W.

Tucker was in command until she was sold to go under a foreign flag.

On her maiden voyage, the *Coeur de Lion* left Boston, Feb. 5, 1854, and had a light weather passage of 133 days to San Francisco. Was 26 days to the line and 32 days in the South Pacific, not being up with the equator until 104 days out. From San Francisco she was 48 days to Hong Kong, thence proceeding to Shanghai where she loaded for New York. Sailed September 24th and was 42 days to Anjer; passed the Cape, 78 days out, and was 50 days thence to New York. Sailed from New York, Apr. 4, 1855, and was 119 days to San Francisco, not having reefed a sail on the whole passage. Was 24½ days to the line; 53 days to 50° South; 11 days rounding the Horn; 88 days to the equator crossing and 31 days thence to destination. From San Francisco, she was 57 days to Hong Kong. Left Whampoa, Nov. 5, 1855; cleared the Straits of Sunda, 24 days out; crossed the meridian of the Cape, 63 days out, and was 45 days thence to New York, arriving Feb. 21, 1856, 108 days from Whampoa, 84 from Anjer and 45 from the Cape.

On her last Cape Horn voyage, the *Coeur de Lion* sailed from New York, Apr. 18, 1856, and was 130 days to San Francisco. Crossed the line 27 days out and was in latitude 50° South on the 58th day; had very heavy weather off the Horn, encountering large quantities of snow and ice; crossed the equator 103 days out. From San Francisco she went to Hong Kong in 54 days and thence took British troops to Calcutta, arriving Dec. 8, 1856. Her passage was reported as 26 days, which is phenomenally fast. From Calcutta she proceeded to Rangoon, and was 99 days thence to Falmouth, England. Shortly after leaving port she came up with the Dutch bark *Henrietta Maria*, flying distress signals. On being boarded it was found that she had been bound to Havana with coolies, who had taken possession of the ship and secured all the arms aboard. The captain and a portion of the crew then deserted the vessel, leaving in the gig; the cook jumped overboard and was drowned; and the coolies escaped to the shore. Mr. Crawford, mate of the *Coeur de*

Lion, with four of his crew and those left on the bark, then worked her into Singapore.

In the autumn of 1857, the *Coeur de Lion* was reported at Singapore, disengaged. Not long after she is said to have been sold to merchants of Hamburg. In May 1860, she was at San Francisco, as the Russian ship *Zaritza,* Captain Riedell, 16 days from Sitka, Alaska. Her owners were The Russian American Fur Company and she was operated between their northern posts and St. Petersburg. After the purchase of Alaska by the United States, she engaged in general trading. In 1869 she left Newcastle, N. S. W., Oct. 24th, and arrived at Hong Kong, Dec. 2nd, in a 39 days' passage. She took the "middle route" course, covering about 5500 miles and during the ensuing five years her run was beaten only once and equalled only once, both performances being to the credit of the British clipper ship *Thermopylae,* Newcastle to Shanghai.

About 1874, the *Zaritza* went under the Swedish flag, without change of name, but in later years she was rigged as a bark. Registers of 1913 give her hailing port as Simrishamm, and owner, S. M. L. Bjorkegren. Her last operations are said to have been in the split wood trade between the Baltic and England. About August 1915, she was reported to have become a wreck after collision off the Skag, in the Baltic Sea.

COMET

EXTREME clipper ship, built by William H. Webb, at New York; launched July 10, 1851. Length of deck, 229 feet; over all, 241 x 41: 4 x 22: 2; 1836 tons, old measurement. Dead rise, 27 inches; she had long, hollow entrance lines and a fine run aft. She was very strongly built, her frame being diagonally iron strapped. The poop deck extended forwards to the mainmast and the cabins were large and elegantly furnished; she was provided with toilet, smoking and bath rooms as well as a fine library. She was a particularly handsome ship in every way and was afterwards conceded to

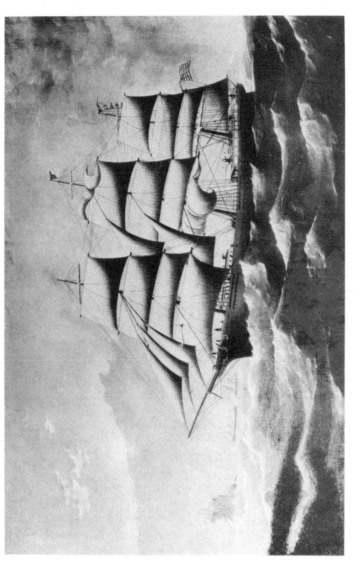

"CHARMER," 1055 TONS, BUILT AT NEWBURYPORT, MASS, IN 1854
From a painting by an English artist, showing the ship off Fastnet Light

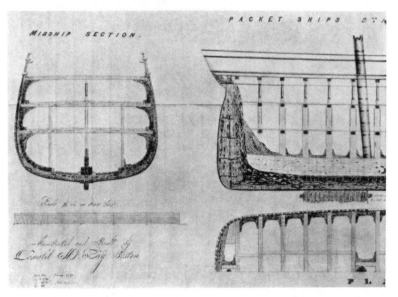

SECTIONAL DRAWING OF THE "CHARIOT OF FAME," BUILT BY DONALD MCKAY,
IN 1853
From the original at the Peabody Museum, Salem

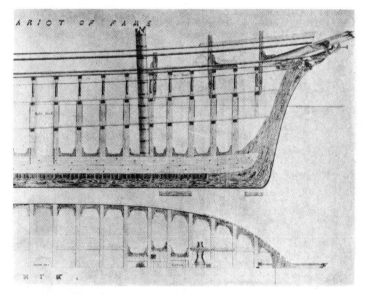

SECTIONAL DRAWING OF THE "CHARIOT OF FAME," BUILT BY DONALD McKAY,
IN 1853
From the original at the Peabody Museum, Salem

"Coeur De Lion," 1098 tons, built at Portsmouth, N. H., in 1854

be one of the fastest sailers as also one of the most successful sailing ships ever launched from any shipyard. Her command was given to Capt. E. C. Gardner, who had made a fine record in the clipper ship *Celestial*, and the owners of the *Comet*, Bucklin & Crane of New York, anticipated and realized a still better record with their new ship.

Leaving New York on Oct. 1, 1851, the *Comet* arrived at San Francisco on Jan. 12, 1852, in a passage of 103 days. The run from Sandy Hook to the line, 26 days, was not up to expectations but from there to the crossing of the parallel 50° South, in the Pacific, she was only 32 days. The run up the South Pacific was long, nearly 30 days, but from the line to port it was very fast; between 15 and 16 days. From San Francisco she went to Hong Kong in the fast time of 37 days. Sailed from Whampoa, May 6, 1852, during the unfavorable season, yet in 14 days she was up with Anjer; 83 days later she arrived at New York. She had experienced much light weather, her skysails being set for all except 12 days of the whole passage. Her cargo of tea and silk was the largest and most valuable imported into the United States to that date.

The *Comet* sailed from New York, Sept. 27, 1852, and reached San Francisco after a passage of 112 days, which was remarkably short considering the very large amount of severe weather she encountered. When five days out she had a heavy southwest gale and while lying to the wind suddenly shifted and blew with terrific force; over the side went the fore topmast and everything attached, and the main royalmast; both topsails were lost and other damage done; repairs could not be made until the weather moderated. She did not cross the line until the 33rd day out but her run thence to San Francisco, 79 days only, was excellent. On her return voyage to New York from San Francisco, the *Comet* had an interesting race with another Webb-built clipper, the *Flying Dutchman*. The *Comet* left San Francisco, Feb. 12, 1853, and on Mar. 17th, overtook the *Dutchman*, which had sailed one day before her, and passed her; both were in ballast. On Apr. 30th, the two clippers again met and were all day in company, often in pistol shot distance, now one gaining and then the other, but the wind increasing, the *Comet* drew ahead and the next morning the *Dutchman* was barely visible astern. On May 3rd, in a strong breeze, the *Comet's* mainsail split and had to come down; the *Dutchman* passed ahead in the night and was not seen afterwards. The *Comet* arrived in New York, May 7th, 83 days and 18 hours from San Francisco; the *Dutchman* arrived the following day, being 85 days.

According to Lieutenant Maury's official report on this voyage, the whole distance logged by the *Comet* was 15,541 nautical miles, an average of 185½ daily. The log showed a run of 1238 nautical miles on four consecutive days, an average of 309½. Her run from San Francisco to the equator, 12 days, is believed to have been beaten only twice up to the present time and then by some 12 hours only. She was up with the Cape on her 38th day at sea.

On her third voyage the *Comet* arrived at San Francisco, Dec. 10, 1853, in 128 days from New York. Five other first-class clippers reached the same port from New York or Boston within a few hours of the time of the *Comet's* arrival, these being the *Trade Wind, Witch of the Wave, Raven, Mandarin* and *Hurricane*. The length of their passages differed but slightly, the *Comet's* 128 days being the longest and the 117 days of the *Witch of the Wave* the shortest. All reported having unfavorable weather conditions off the Horn. Sailing from San Francisco on Dec. 27, 1853, the *Comet* reached New York, Mar. 14, 1854; passage, 76 days and 7 hours, anchor to anchor, the record from San Francisco to any North Atlantic port to this day. She was 13½ days from San Francisco harbor to the equator; thence 22 days to Cape Horn, which was passed when she was 35 days and 7 hours out, which time has never been beaten. From the Horn to the line in the Atlantic, she was 26 days and when 73 days, 18 hours out she was within 220 miles of Sandy Hook but here the wind came out dead ahead. She took her New York pilot exactly 76 days after having discharged her 'Frisco pilot off the

Heads. This passage stands as a classic in the annals of commercial navigation.

In 1854, freight rates to California were low and the *Comet* was sent to Liverpool where she loaded for Hong Kong, sailing June 17th and arriving at destination Sept. 9th; passage from anchor to anchor, 84 days and 16 hours; from pilot to pilot, 83 days and 21 hours, a record which is believed to stand as the fastest for that run to this day. Her best day's run was 350 nautical miles. Continuing her good work and favored by the northeast monsoon of December, she flew down the China Sea from Hong Kong and arrived at Batavia in seven days, called another record passage. From that port she went to Bremen in 91 days and arrived back at New York, Aug. 19, 1855.

Captain Gardner now gave up the command of the *Comet* to take the new ship *Intrepid,* and Captain Arquit, her new master, took the *Comet* into San Francisco harbor on Feb. 25, 1856, after a passage of 123 days from New York; continuing the voyage she crossed the Pacific to Shanghai in 43 days and thence to Whampoa where she loaded for New York. Arrived out, Oct. 23, 1856, in 130 days, the slow run being due to an adverse monsoon and generally unfavorable weather conditions throughout. Sailed from New York, Jan. 31, 1857, and was 142 days to San Francisco. Went back to New York, via Elide Island, where she loaded guano and made the whole run from the Golden Gate to Sandy Hook in 98 sailing days.

There is little positive information about the operations of the *Comet* in 1858; it is reported that she made a run out to Australia in 75 days but no confirmation is obtainable. In 1859, under Captain Todd, she was 113 days from New York to San Francisco; thence 47 days to Hong Kong, later proceeding to Manila. Left that port Sept. 24, 1859; arrived at New York, Jan. 17, 1860, 115 days' passage, 77 days from Anjer and 41 days from the Cape. Her seventh passage from New York to San Francisco, being her ninth voyage, was made in 139 days, her arrival out being July 26, 1860. In her stormy passage of 25 days around the Cape, she lost a number of sails and while in a hurricane, north of the line in the Pacific, the mainmast was sprung and sails were blown from the gaskets. Crossing to Hong Kong, she left there March 16, 1861, and was 101 days to New York, being 47 days from the Cape and 28 days from St. Helena. In heavy gales lasting seven days, off the Cape, she lost a number of sails and had to heave to and later had the mainmast sprung in a sudden shift of wind. On her last round-the-world voyage she arrived at San Francisco, Feb. 20, 1862, 141 days from New York, having been 26 days rounding the Cape, having the bowsprit sprung so badly that thereafter she could carry but little head sail. From San Francisco she was 41 days to Hong Kong; left Macao, Aug. 6th, and in the China Sea had the rudder-head sprung in a typhoon, necessitating the ship being hove to until repairs could be made. Arrived at New York, Dec. 19, 1862. Sailed thence Mar. 11, 1863, and was 19 days to London.

Shortly after arrival at London, the *Comet* was sold through George Croshaw & Co., for £8100 sterling, and was renamed *Fiery Star*. Being well adapted for carrying passengers she was put on the run between England and Australia and on her first passage as the *Fiery Star*, she arrived at Moreton Bay, Queensland, in November 1863, after a passage of 93 days from Queenstown. Captain Yule was in command and besides first and second class passengers, she took out about 500 emigrants. Her second outward run was to Brisbane and on the return she left Moreton Bay, Apr. 1, 1865, bound for London. When three weeks out she was discovered to be on fire; everything was battened down and water pumped into the hold but without avail. All the passengers and a part of the crew, in all, some 80 persons, took to the boats, leaving the mate, Mr. Sargeant and 17 of the crew aboard, there not being room for them in the boats. Captain Yule and the officers in command of the three boats intended to stand by the ship but the morning after they left her they were not to be seen and none of the boats were ever heard of thereafter. The ship, when about ready to sink, was fallen in with by the bark *Daunt-*

less, from Kingston for Auckland, and those aboard and who had originally volunteered to stay by her, were rescued.

COMPETITOR

CLIPPER ship, built by J. O. Curtis, at Medford, Mass., and launched in February 1853; owned by W. F. Weld & Co., of Boston. 175 feet long, over all, x 33: 5 x 20: 2; 871 tons, old measurement; 690 tons, new measurement. For a figurehead she had an eagle on the wing and her neat, round stern was ornamented with a carved sporting dog, surrounded by scroll work. She was of sharp model and a handsome ship in every way, alow and aloft. Capt. Moses Howes, Jr., was appointed her commander.

On her maiden voyage she left Boston, Mar. 27, 1853, for San Francisco. The following day the *Climax,* also a Medford-built ship on her first voyage, left Boston for the same port and considerable money was wagered on the result of the race. The *Competitor* arrived out, July 20th, in 115 days, and the *Climax* reached port the next day, also in 115 days. Both had the same length of passage to Cape Horn, 53 days, but the *Competitor* was then hove to for five days to chain-strap her bows together in an effort to stop a leak caused by a split stem. The *Climax* in the meantime was bowling along before a fresh westerly breeze and when they were 67 days out, she was leading by 14 degrees of latitude. The *Competitor,* however, retrieved herself in the South Pacific and crossed the equator two days before her rival and when 100 days out, she was within 900 miles of the Golden Gate. Continuing her voyage, she crossed the Pacific and was 111 days from Whampoa to New York, arriving at that port Apr. 2, 1854.

On her second voyage the *Competitor* was 122 days from New York to San Francisco, arriving Sept. 23, 1854; was 51 days to 50° South, and 18 days rounding the Horn; when 99 days out, was within 800 miles of the Golden Gate. Passed Staten Island in company with the *Bonita* and led her to port by three days. Then crossed to Shanghai in 50 days; thence to Boston, arriving Apr. 22, 1855. Sailed from Boston, May 28th, Capt. Otis White in command, and was 139 days to San Francisco; lost her figurehead in a pampero off the Platte but otherwise had nothing but light winds, including the 15 days spent in rounding the Horn. From San Francisco she went to Manila in the fast time of 36 days; thence going to Boston. Returned to San Francisco in 139 days, arriving Sept. 13, 1856; had nothing but light or head winds throughout. Returned to Boston via Shanghai and then went out to Shanghai in 131 days from London. Left Swatow, Jan. 30, 1858, with 380 coolies for Havana; had a long passage and 127 of her passengers died en route. Captain White then took the ship *Renown* and was succeeded in the *Competitor* by Capt. J. B. Hildreth, who took his ship to San Francisco in 118 days from Richmond, Va., arriving Feb. 10, 1859. Reached port in company with the fast clipper *Archer*, 119 days from New York, both ships reporting only 15 days from the Pacific equator crossing to destination. The *Competitor* then crossed to Hong Kong in 35 days, beating the *Sea Serpent*, two days and the *Boston Light*, three days. Went to New York in 112 days from Foo Chow, beating the *Charmer*, eight days, and the *Eagle*, 10 days, on the run from Java Head home. In 1861 she went out to Sydney in 96 days from New York and thereafter, until May 1863, was trading on the Asiatic coast with the exception of one voyage from Hong Kong to San Francisco, in May-June 1862, 53 days, returning to Hong Kong in 59 days; Captain Leckie in command at this period. Sailed from Manila, July 27, 1863, and was 116 days to New York. Shortly after her arrival she was sold by Weld & Co., for $31,100.

On Feb. 11, 1864, as the Hanoverian ship *Loreley*, owned by Ruger Bros., she left New York for Liverpool, but on Mar. 5th put into Fayal, leaking so badly that she was forced to discharge her cargo. For a few years she operated on the Atlantic, but in July 1869 she was at Hong Kong, from Baltimore, known then as the British ship *Competitor*, of Hong Kong, Captain Matthews. For some four years she ran between New York and Australia or the

This victory of a Boston vessel over two fast New York clippers was made much of in the Boston papers and the owners of the *Contest* replied by claiming that on the round trip, out and back, the *Contest* had beaten the *Northern Light*, which was true. The article concludes as follows: "The *Contest* claims to have beaten on this voyage the clippers *Game Cock*, *Telegraph*, *Meteor* and *Queen of the Seas*, all Boston ships, which sailed on or about the same time, by 8 to 11 days. If the owners of the *Northern Light* feel inclined to bet on a race with the *Contest*, we will accommodate them."

The second appearance of the *Contest* at San Francisco was on Oct. 24, 1853, exactly 10 months after the date of her first arrival and only seven months and 13 days on the round to New York and return. Her passage on this trip was 108 days and on the day of her arrival there also entered port the extreme clipper *White Swallow*, 158 days from Boston, the Boston clipper *John Bertram*, after a run of 114 days, the New York clipper *Atalanta*, in 124 days, while on the following day the Boston clipper *Wild Ranger* showed up in 125 days. The *Contest* was the least sharp of these vessels yet made the fastest run; her best work was in the South Pacific where for a number of days in succession she averaged 275 miles. From San Francisco she went to Honolulu and thence to Tahiti where she loaded for New York, arriving home May 5, 1854, in 85 days from the South Seas. Her third voyage, New York to San Francisco, was made in 126 days, her arrival out being Nov. 17, 1854. Off the Horn, while lying to in a gale, she shipped a heavy sea which washed overboard three men and did considerable damage; was 15 days from passing the Horn to 50° South in the Pacific. From San Francisco she went to Shanghai and was thence 99 days to New York.

From the summer of 1855 until the end of 1860, the *Contest* was engaged in trade between New York and the Far East. On July 10, 1855, she left New York and was 90 days to Bombay. Sailed thence, Nov. 23rd, for Hong Kong and took her departure from Whampoa, Apr. 4, 1856, for New York, arriving Aug. 21st. Then loaded for Shanghai where she arrived Feb. 7, 1857. Was on the China coast until December 1857, when she sailed from Whampoa and was 102 days to New York. In December 1858 she was at Hong Kong and in August 1859 at Shanghai.

On Mar. 1, 1861, the *Contest* again sailed from New York for San Francisco and experienced very heavy weather in the North Atlantic, being obliged to jettison 200 tons of cargo and put into St. Thomas, leaking 18 inches an hour. Having discharged her cargo at St. Thomas she put back to New York, in ballast, for repairs and two weeks later resumed her voyage, reloading at St. Thomas, and reached San Francisco, Nov. 4, 1861. From San Francisco she crossed to China, loaded tea at Foo Chow for New York and made the run home in 107 days, via St. Helena, 44 days. This was the fastest run from China to an Atlantic port for quite a long time. Captain Steele, who had had the *Contest* on this voyage, was now relieved by his predecessor Captain Lucas.

Leaving New York on what was to be her final voyage, in February 1863, the *Contest* ran out to Hong Kong in 99 days; thence to Yokohama, where she loaded for New York; sailed Oct. 15, 1863, and on Nov. 11th was captured and burnt by the Confederate privateer *Alabama*, near the Straits of Sunda. The following is a copy of the statement of James D. Babcock of New Bedford, to the U. S. Consul at Singapore, forwarded to Secretary of the Navy, Gideon Welles, by D. McDougal, commanding U. S. *Wyoming*, cruising in search of the *Alabama*.

"Was chief officer of the ship *Contest* of New York. Left Yokohama, 13th of Oct., bound for New York. On the morning of the 11th Nov., about 70 miles east of Batavia, at 10 A.M. saw a steamer abeam, bearing right down on us; about 20 minutes after, she hoisted American ensign. We ran up our colors and kept on our course. In about 20 minutes more she fired a blank shot, we still keeping on our course. About 11:45, being then about three miles off, she hauled down the ensign, ran up the Confederate flag and gave us a shot. We crammed on every sail we could carry, 14 knot breeze blowing, and dropped her until she got about a point on our quarter. She crammed on everything, full steam and all hands aft to trim her. Finding us gaining, she headed up and gave us a 110 pound shot which fell about one-half mile astern. About 12: 30 the wind died away to a six knot breeze when she rapidly overhauled us. From about one-fourth mile astern she fired a shot which passed between fore and mainmast, doing no harm but we thought it time to lay to. An armed boat came off and declared us a prize to the Confederate steamer *Alabama* and our captain was ordered to report himself on board thereof with his papers. I, with my crew, was ordered to break out stores and provisions. We were anchored in 17 fathoms. The ship was plundered of every thing valuable and we were sent aboard the privateer about 7: 30 o'clock, P.M. They fired our ship about 9: 30 P.M., and then hoisting the propeller sailed N. E. Our officers got a waist boat to sleep in; the crew being kept on deck under guard. We had one sick passenger, Mr. Nevis of New York; he got a cabin aft and messed in the wardroom. Our captain, Lucas, remained on deck the first night; afterwards had berth and mess in the steerage. Next morning our baggage was overhauled; captain was allowed one small trunk and bag; Mr. Nevis, all luggage; officers and crew, one small bag; all our money and knives taken away. Under sail until evening of 16th, when anchored off Serutu Island. Noon, 18th, sighted ship; hoisted Dutch ensign; thought the ship American. When about two miles off sent a boat on board; turned out to be English; captain agreed to take us and land us in nearest port; arrived in Batavia, 28th. The ship was *Avalanche* of Liverpool, bound to London. During the 10 days we were aboard her, were treated with the greatest kindness by captain and crew."

It is to the credit of the *Contest's* sailing qualities that so long as the wind held she outsailed the *Alabama,* though that vessel was under sail and steam both and Captain Semmes himself allowed that had the breeze been stronger the *Contest* would have escaped. The claim filed for her loss was $158,465.97 of which $45,000 was for vessel; $61,500 for freight money; $30,522 for cargo; $10,650 for wages of 40 men for ten months.

CORINGA

A FINELY modeled ship launched from the yard of Jotham Stetson, at Medford, Mass., Aug. 9, 1851, for account of N. B. Goddard & Co., of Boston. 153 x 36 x 22; 777 tons, new measurement. Although advertised at times as a clipper she is classed by Lloyds as full built. During her career the *Coringa* was engaged principally in trade between Boston and the Far East, mainly with Calcutta. She made three passages from Boston to San Francisco, between 1852 and 1855, but all were slow runs,—132, 150 and 148 days, respectively. On the last passage she arrived out in company with the clipper *Meteor* which had left Boston 38 days after the *Coringa*. Her runs home from Calcutta were usually in the neighborhood of 120 days. On the occasion of her first passage to San Francisco, she left Boston on Aug. 17, 1852, and the same day, when 40 miles off Cape Ann, collided with a schooner, sinking her and losing her own cut-water and head gear. She returned to Boston, repaired and sailed again Aug. 22nd, under Captain Mason who had replaced Capt. Symmes Potter. She arrived at San Francisco, Jan. 8, 1853, making the passage in 132 days. From San Francisco she was 54 days to Singapore, thence to Calcutta and back to Boston. Her next voyage was made under command of Captain Bates and Capt. Joseph H. Hallet had her the following year. On July 30, 1857, she left Manila, homeward bound, but returned in distress five days later, having been aground on the Apo Shoal. Captain Bogart was master for a number of years during the 60's. Under command of Captain Ropes she left Enderbury's Island, July 9, 1873, with guano for Hamburg and soon started a leak which compelled her to put into Honolulu on Aug. 3rd. She discharged her cargo of 930 tons of guano, was surveyed and repaired at a cost of about $20,-000. On her return to Boston, in 1874, she was opened and found perfectly sound and classed A 1½ for three years, being rerigged as a bark. She was chartered by the Tudor Co., for a round voyage to Calcutta, the outward cargo being ice.

COURSER

MEDIUM clipper ship, built in 1851, at Medford, Mass., by Paul Curtis. 176 x 35 x 24; 1024 tons. Richardson & Company of Boston original owners; when lost she was owned by William Appleton of same city.

The *Courser* made one passage from Boston and three from New York, to San Francisco in 108, 137, 136 and 145 days respectively, an average of 134 days. Her maiden voyage was the fastest; 108 days out; 44 days from San Francisco to Hong Kong and 120 days home, her departure from China being in August, the bad season for a fast run in the China Sea and the Indian Ocean. On this passage, however, Captain Cole reported his run from the Cape of Good Hope to Sandy Hook as being only 38 days, the record to that time, and which, indeed, has seldom since been equalled. On the passage out to San Francisco, this voyage, she was 19 days from latitude 50° South in the Pacific to the line,—very good time. Her best run home from China was in 1853, on completing her second round, being 102 days. In 1854, her east-bound passage was from Callao to Liverpool, 101 days; the following voyage was out to China direct and return to New York.

She sailed from Foo Chow, Apr. 2, 1858, for New York and at 9: 30 on the 4th, when Captain Cole supposed he was in mid-channel between the Pratas Shoal and the mainland, breakers were heard ahead and before the ship could be put about, she struck heavily near the forechains and instantly began to fill, so that in two hours she had six feet of water in her. All hands got into three boats and made for Hong Kong but fell in with some junks which the ship's party took to be fishermen, until the boats were fired upon. Being well armed, the mate dashed alongside a junk from which stink-pots were thrown into the boat and as the crew endeavored to avoid them, the boat was capsized and two seamen drowned. The mate and nine men after being stripped of everything, righted the boat, baled her out and arrived at Hong Kong the following morning; the other two boats were reported to have gone to Macao. Some of the cargo of the *Courser* floated and was picked up on May 9th, by the *Flying Fish*, two days out from Hong Kong. The *Courser* was insured for $80,-000 in Boston and other insurance in New York.

Captain Cole was commander on the initial voyage of the *Courser*, and was succeeded by Captain Berry; but Cole subsequently took charge and was in command when she was lost. Anxiety and vexation resulting from the disaster brought on a fever from which he died.

CREST OF THE WAVE

MEDIUM clipper ship, built at Thomaston, Me., in 1854. 175 x 34 x 21; 942 tons, new measurement. For some time prior to 1861 she was owned by M. R. Ludwig of Baltimore, and in that year, she was seized by the United States Government as the property of a rebel. In 1863 she was purchased by Jones & Co., of Baltimore, who continued ownership until she was lost. She is reported to have made a passage from an Eastern port to New Orleans in 8 days and 19 hours. Her sea life appears to have been an unfortunate one.

The *Crest* arrived at San Francisco, Apr. 8, 1859, under Capt. William S. Colley, 163 days from New York; thence to Puget Sound for a lumber cargo, returning to San Francisco and taking departure therefrom, Sept. 17th, for Callao. Sailed from that port, Feb. 7, 1860, for Hampton Roads. Made a voyage to the West Coast of South America and arrived back at New York, July 11, 1861, 80 days from Tomé. Sailed from New York, Sept. 12, 1861, under Captain Johnston and arrived at Valparaiso, Dec. 7th; passage 87 days. Under Captain Watts, sailed from Tomé, Mar. 1, 1862, and was 81 days to New York. Under Captain Price, left New York, July 26th, and put into Port Stanley prior to Nov. 11th with loss of rudder and other damage; arrived at Valparaiso, Dec. 21st. Sailed from Caldera, prior to Mar. 20, 1863, and arrived at Baltimore June 15th.

The *Crest of the Wave*, Captain Woodburn, arrived at Valparaiso from Acapulco, Nov. 6, 1864. On the passage, the captain's wife, the mate, Mr. Heaps, and 13 of the crew had died of yellow fever and the few remaining on the vessel, except the captain, were sick. The *Crest of the Wave*, under command of Captain Jones, cleared from Liverpool for Baltimore, Mar. 8, 1870, with a cargo consisting of 600 tons of salt and 400 tons of merchandise. Sometime prior to Apr. 14th, during a severe gale, she struck Wreck Island, 15 miles north of Cape Charles. How it occurred will never be known as no one lived to tell the story, but two boats were washed ashore, one containing three dead bodies and the other, the body of Captain Jones. A little later her flag and a portion of her quarter board, with name inscribed, were found floating near the beach. Besides her captain she carried a crew of 14 seamen, two mates, a cook, steward and carpenter. She was insured in Baltimore for $25,000 on the vessel and $5000 on the freight. Captain Jones was only 32 years of age and in 1867, while in command of the bark *Isabella*, had been wrecked near St. Thomas and was the only person aboard who escaped death.

CRITERION

BUILT by Wm. Hitchcock & Co., at Damariscotta, Me., in 1855. 200 x 38 x 28; 1546 tons. F. Nickerson & Co., of Boston, owners. Sold to Moravia, in 1882.

CYCLONE

MEDIUM clipper ship, launched Aug. 18, 1853, by E. & H. O. Briggs, at South Boston, Mass., for Curtis & Peabody of Boston. 173: 3 x 35: 7 x 22: 6; 1109 tons, old measurement; 840 tons, new measurement. She is said to have closely resembled the *Meteor*, a prior product of the same yard, for the same owners, and after their sale of the original, they had a second *Cyclone* built in 1864, on nearly the same lines. The latter was wrecked in 1886. The first captain of the original *Cyclone* was Nathaniel Ingersoll, Jr. After the first round voyage, Captains Osgood and Millett were successively in command until the summer of 1860, when Ingersoll returned to her, continuing in charge until she was sold and even a few years after, when she was known as the British ship *Avon*.

The first voyage of the *Cyclone*, 1853/55, was 114 days from Boston to San Francisco; 87 days thence to Anjer; 18 days more to Calcutta; 67 days from there to Sydney; 54 days returning to Calcutta and 118 days thence to Boston, arrival home, Aug. 14, 1855, 21 months and 12 days from the date of her departure. The second voyage was a round between Boston and Calcutta; 112 days outward; 110 days homeward. On her third voyage she left Boston, Aug. 22, 1856, and was 48 days to the line, some 10 days longer than the average for even that unfavorable season of the year. She was 20 days off the Horn and 26 days running up the Pacific, to the line, in light winds; total time from Boston to San Francisco, 140 days. Went to Manila in 43 days and was 128 days from there to Boston. She then crossed to London and went out to Calcutta in 99 days; thence to Boston in 108 days. Went again to San Francisco, 122 days' passage; thence 65 days to Melbourne and from that port to Singapore and was 95 days thence to Boston. Her sixth outward passage was to the East Indies direct, time not ascertained; returned from Padang to New York in 82 days, arriving Mar. 31, 1861. Then out to San Francisco in 147 days, 50 days thence to Manila and 106 days from there to New York. Her eighth and last voyage under the American flag was 123 days from New York to San Francisco, arriving out Nov. 9, 1862; sailed Dec. 4th for Hong Kong; stopped off at Honolulu, the 16th, 11 days and 18 hours' passage; arrived at Hong Kong, Jan. 14th, 27½ days from Honolulu and 39 days from San Francisco; a fine passage. Loaded at Manila for New York; sailed Mar. 1, 1863, passed the Cape, 56 days out, and was 49 days thence to New York, arriving June 14, 1863; passage 105 days. On July 28th she reached Boston from New York and was soon reported as sold for $24,000, going under the British flag as

"COMET," 1836 TONS, BUILT AT MYSTIC, CONN., IN 1851

From a lithograph by Currier showing the ship in a hurricane off Bermuda, in October, 1852

"COMPETITOR," 871 TONS, BUILT AT MEDFORD, MASS., IN 1853

From a photograph made at Stavanger, Sweden, in 1904, when she was the Swedish bark "Edward"

"CONTEST," 1098 TONS, BUILT AT NEW YORK, IN 1852
Burned by the Confederate cruiser "Alabama," Nov. 11, 1863

"DASHING WAVE," 1180 TONS, BUILT AT PORTSMOUTH, N. H., IN 1853

From an oil painting showing the ship off Boston Light

the *Avon*. As the British ship *Avon,* Captain Ingersoll, she cleared from Boston, Aug. 25, 1863, for a port in New Brunswick; then went to China and on May 16, 1864, arrived at San Francisco, 49 days from Hong Kong, with Captain Ingersoll still in command. Sailed from San Francisco, June 24, 1864, and arrived at Honolulu in 12½ days; had a long passage, some 50 days, thence to Hong Kong. The *Avon* remained registered as owned by Curtis & Peabody of Boston, with hailing port, Hong Kong, up to 1866, when she was registered as owned by M. Nolan of London. Her name does not appear in the registers of 1874.

DARING

MEDIUM clipper ship, launched Oct. 8, 1855, from the yard of George W. Jackman, at Newburyport, Mass. 181 x 36 x 23; 1094 tons, old measurement. She is described as a fine ship, of excellent workmanship, beautiful model, handsome in spars and rigging; was a sister ship to the first *Charmer,* a product of the same builder, the previous year, for the same owners, Bush & Comstock of Boston. She carried as a figurehead the representation of a pirate.

Under command of Captain Simonson, the *Daring* sailed from Boston, Nov. 22, 1855, and arrived at San Francisco, Mar. 13, 1856, in a passage of 112 days, her cargo being 2130 tons, weight and measurement. She was 23 days to the line and 52 days to 50° South; was 22 days from the equator crossing to destination but covered all except the final 200 miles in 17 days. From San Francisco she went to Hong Kong in 47 days; thence to Shanghai and 112 days from that port to New York. On her second voyage she arrived at San Francisco, Aug. 22, 1857, in 131 days from New York; was 27 days to the line and 65 days to 50° South; had light winds in the North Pacific, being 37 days from the equator to port. Then crossed to Hong Kong in 45 days; returned to San Francisco in 45 days, thence back to Hong Kong in 52 days; thence 101 days from Whampoa to New York. Loaded for San Francisco and made the passage out in

147 days, arriving Nov. 5, 1859; was 30 days to the line; 60 days to 50° South and 35 days rounding the Horn in strong gales; from the equator to port was 33 days, taking 14 days to cover the final 400 miles. From San Francisco she went to Baker's Island and after loading a cargo of guano was 110 days to Hampton Roads; arrived at New York, Aug. 12, 1860.

The *Daring* left New York, Feb. 9, 1861, and was 17 days to Liverpool; returned to New York in 19 days; thence went back to Liverpool and from there was 127 days to Calcutta. Arrived at Boston, July 13, 1862, from Calcutta. Then went to New York in ballast and in January 1863 was sold to Henry Hastings, of Boston, for $50,000, having in the interim made a round voyage between New York and Liverpool. After returning to New York, in December 1862 in 55 days from Liverpool, she loaded for San Francisco and arrived out Aug. 17, 1863, her passage being 129 days. After the change in ownership, Captain Henry had been put in command as successor to Captain Simonson. Included in her cargo was a shipment of ordnance stores for the United States Government; cannon, powder, etc. From San Francisco she crossed to Hong Kong, via Honolulu, in 60 sailing days.

On her last voyage as an American ship, the *Daring* arrived at San Francisco, Nov. 21, 1864, 129 days from Boston. Thence went to Baker's Island and loaded guano for Liverpool. Sailed Apr. 20, 1865, and in very heavy weather was partially dismasted and obliged to jettison a portion of her cargo. Put into Valparaiso where she was condemned and sold for $1090. She was repaired and went under British colors, retaining her original name. In 1868 she is listed as owned by C. Finley, hailing port London. In 1870, H. Holmes was owner. Her name does not appear in registers of 1874.

DASHAWAY

B UILT by J. Rideout, at Hallowell, Me., in 1854. 177 x 35 x 23; 1012 tons. Read, Page & Co., Hallowell, owners. Sold to go under British flag in 1863. Renamed *Mauritius Merchant*.

DASHING WAVE

M EDIUM clipper ship, launched from the yard of Fernald & Pettigrew, Portsmouth, N. H., July 15, 1853. 181: 8 x 39: 6 x 21: 3; 1180 tons, old measurement; 1054 tons, new measurement. A billet took the place of a figurehead and unlike most of the clippers of her day, her stern was square, though graceful. Originally rigged with single topsails and crossing three skysail yards, she was very neat and trim in appearance and of a fairly sharp model. She was built to the order of Samuel Tilton & Co., of Boston, who, in April 1866, sold her to Washington Libby and others. In 1870 she appears registered in the name of G. D. S. Trask; hailing port, New York. Her last work as a Cape Horner, or Indiaman, was in 1870, as after her arrival at San Francisco in that year she was remodeled somewhat to adapt her to the lumber trade and thereafter her outward cargoes were laden at Puget Sound, occasionally for foreign ports on the Pacific, but mainly to San Francisco and coastwise until her conversion into a barge in 1901. For many years she was owned by Hanson Ackerson & Co., of San Francisco, proprietors of the Tacoma Mills. In February 1894, her port of registry was changed from Port Townsend to Tacoma, and she is said to have the distinction of being the first, and for a time the only, deep sea vessel showing Tacoma on her stern.

The first two voyages of the *Dashing Wave* were made under Capt. J. B. Fisk, who had been the original commander of the celebrated *Nightingale*. Fisk was succeeded by Captain Young who was in the ship two voyages. Capt. David R. Lecraw took her in 1859, continuing until 1866 when he turned her over to Captain Carlton. After making one voyage the latter gave way to Captain Mayhew who died at Valparaiso in 1869, the ship being then on her last run from New York to San Francisco, and the mate, Mr. Norton, completed the passage. In later years, while operating in the Pacific, she had many masters, among the earliest of whom were Captains Lawrence, Nickels, Marshall and Conner; the latter and his ship, were, for a number of years, the most prominent figures in the coastwise fleet.

On her maiden voyage the *Dashing Wave* left Boston, Oct. 4th and Philadelphia, Nov. 27, 1853, and was 118 sailing days to San Francisco, via Valparaiso, 40 days. Between that date and Feb. 15, 1870, she made 10 passages from New York or Boston to the Golden Gate, on her last one being obliged to put into Rio, and later, Valparaiso, in both instances being in distress, leaking. Eliminating this run, her average for the other 10 is 127 days. In 1860, her time was 143 days and in 1863, 155 days. In the first instance she was 31 days to the line, 22 days off the Horn and 42 days in the South Pacific. In 1863 she was 34 days to the line, 79 days to the Horn and 42 days in the stormy regions in that vicinity; was twice driven back through the Straits of LeMaire by furious gales. Her average for the other eight passages is 122 days; fastest, 107 days, in 1858; slowest, 133 days, in 1868. Her passages out of San Francisco were as follows: in 1854, 76 days to Calcutta; in 1855, 55 days to Melbourne; in 1856, 48 days to Singapore, 71 to Calcutta; in 1858, 92 days to Calcutta; in 1859, 46 days to Shanghai; in 1861, 115 days to New York; in 1862, 41 days to Manila; in 1863, 46 days to Sydney; in 1866-67, 99 days to New York; in 1868, 116 days to New York. From the East Indies, homeward bound, her runs were: in 1854, Calcutta to Boston, 115 days, which was practically the same time as was made by the *Gray Feather* and *Syren;* in 1856, she was 88 days from Batavia to Bremen; in 1857, '59 and '60 she was 84, 93 and 109 days respectively from Calcutta to Boston; in 1862, 141 days, Manila to Boston, being 33 days to Anjer and 30 days off Good Hope in heavy gales; all other arrivals from the Far East that season reported similarly unfavorable conditions, some ships being six to eight weeks working down the China Sea and two to four weeks off the Cape in storms.

In 1865-66, she was about 95 days from Calcutta to Boston; off East London was in company with the *Sea Serpent*, from China for New York, but the latter reached her port five days ahead. Conspicuous among the fine passages made by the *Wave* may be mentioned: 76 days from San Francisco to Calcutta (1854) which, while not particularly fast, was yet the best made about that time, she beating, among others, the *Syren, Polynesia* and *Westward Ho*, the latter by 11 days. In 1856 she was 26 days from Melbourne to Batavia and George Francis Train, who was a passenger, spoke highly of her performances. Her run of 84 days and some hours from the Sand Heads, Sept. 3, 1857, to Boston, Nov. 27th, is said to have been beaten only by the *Witch of the Wave*, 81 days and by the *Beverly*, 83 days and equalled only by the *Staffordshire* and *Charger*. Her passage of 107 days from Boston to San Francisco in 1858, was the fastest over that course that year. She crossed the equator in the Pacific, 79 days out, and on her 90th day was only 800 miles from destination. The next year, her run being 121 days from New York, she was, according to Captain Lecraw's report, only 15 days and 16 hours from 50° South, Pacific, to the equator, which time has rarely been equalled. She crossed the equator 88 days out and 15 days later was 500 miles from the Golden Gate, but then encountered light winds and fogs for 18 days. On her passage from San Francisco to New York in 1861 (115 days) she had no westerly winds in the Pacific and was off Cape Horn 20 days in stormy weather, but from a position off the Falkland Islands made the run into New York harbor in 48 days and 20 hours. Outward bound on the following voyage, she was 18 days from the equator crossing to San Francisco. In 1869 she was 42 days from New York to latitude 50° South. In 1871, after delivering a cargo of lumber at Shanghai, she loaded at Hong Kong for San Francisco, sailing Jan. 14, 1872; had a strong northeast monsoon to the Loo Choo Islands, but thereafter fine westerly winds to port, arriving at San Francisco, Mar. 5th, in 51 days' passage; was 21 days from a position opposite Yokohama and 11 days from the 180th meridian to port. As a lumber drogher she was considered the fastest of the coastwise fleet, which included many smart ships and former Cape Horn clippers. Her particularly strong competitors were the Newburyport-built *War Hawk* and the Pacific-coast production *Forest Queen,* a bark. On several occasions she made the voyage from San Francisco to Tacoma and return, including about eight days loading at the mills, in 20 days; her run of 54 hours from San Francisco to Cape Flattery was said to be the record for a sailing vessel; distance sailed, 676 miles; average 12.5 knots.

The *Dashing Wave* had many mishaps, some of which were very serious. After leaving Calcutta, June 1, 1857, she grounded in the river and had to put back with four feet of water in the hold; the cargo was discharged and she was in port two months before resuming the voyage. In December 1864, she was at Singapore repairing damages sustained on her passage from Hong Kong and remained in port until April. Having left San Francisco, Nov. 1, 1866, for New York, she was up at Barnegat, the night of Feb. 8, 1867, and struck on the shoals and came off leaking badly. Off Woodlands received her pilot, the pilot boat standing by, all hands at the pumps but the leak gaining, when up to the point of Sandy Hook, a tug hooked on but at 1 P.M. had to leave her. At 7 A.M. she sank in five fathoms, the main deck being five feet under water. The officers and crew were taken off by the tug. She remained under water until Sept. 12th, when she was raised and towed to New York. She was then valued at $76,000. The insurance paid on vessel and cargo of grain was $122,000. On her last passage from New York she sailed Mar. 11, 1869, and was 42 days to 50° South, Atlantic; then had a succession of gales, during which she lost spars, split sails and started a bad leak. Captain Mayhew was taken sick and the ship was put about for Rio, arriving July 6th. There she discharged part of her cargo and repaired at a cost of $37,000, left port Oct. 11th and when again off Cape Horn encountered heavy gales and started a new leak.

Steered for Valparaiso, arriving there Dec. 5th, Captain Mayhew being very sick; the mate, Morton, in charge and the crew mutinous. The captain was taken ashore and died Dec. 10th. The leak was found to be in bottom of vessel and was repaired by divers; insurance loss, $7000. Sailed from Valparaiso, Jan. 2, 1870, and reached San Francisco, Feb. 15th, 341 days from New York, 44 days from Valparaiso. On Dec. 11, 1871, at Hong Kong from Shanghai, with a cargo of rice, she went into dry dock, having been ashore on the Brunswick Rocks, Canton River.

On Mar. 1, 1920, the barge *Dashing Wave* was on dry dock at Seattle, for examination, when it was found that her hull was in first-class condition from stem to stern. She later loaded 1200 tons of cannery supplies for the Taku, southeastern Alaska, plant of her owners, Libby, McNeil & Libby. Some two weeks later, when on her trip north in tow of the tug *San Juan*, she stranded on the mud flats of Seymour Narrows and became a total loss.

DAUNTLESS

EXTREME clipper ship, built in 1852, by Benjamin F. Delano, at Medford, Mass. Keel, 172; deck, 175; over all, 185 x 33 x 21½; 791 tons. She was designed, modelled and owned by W. N. Goddard of Boston, who also superintended her construction. She was called the most expensive ship of her size built in Boston, up to the date of her launch, and beautiful beyond comparison. She was very narrow and her ends were sharp and had great length for her tonnage; sheer bold and lively and stem upright; lines concave; dead rise, 15 inches; swell of sides, 12 inches and sheer, three feet. Her figurehead was a nymph with outstretched wings, in flowing white garments, with a golden girdle, and on its head was a chaplet of flowers blazoned in gold. Her stern was ornamented with gilded work and the catheads were carved and gilded. The cabins were finished in fancy woods and stained glass windows presented pictures of the *Sovereign of the Seas,* the yacht *America* and the counting house of Enoch Train.

She arrived at San Francisco, Feb. 12, 1853, under command of Capt. James Miller, in 116 days from Boston, via Valparaiso, 39 days. Was off the Horn 15 days in heavy weather, crossing the equator in the Pacific, Jan. 22nd, and had mostly light winds the remaining 21 days of her passage. Sailed from San Francisco, Mar. 3rd, and arrived at Callao, Apr. 16th. Left there Apr. 19th and arrived at Valparaiso, May 14th; thence 64 days to Boston. Sailed from Boston, Oct. 23, 1853, for Valparaiso, and was never heard from, Captain Miller still in command.

DAVID BROWN

EXTREME clipper ship, launched Oct. 8, 1853, at New York, from the yard of Roosevelt & Joyce, successors to Jacob Bell (formerly Brown & Bell), for account of A. A. Low & Brother, New York. Messrs. Low had been so well satisfied with the performances of their ships *Houqua, Samuel Russell* and *Oriental,* all Brown & Bell productions, that they named their next clipper *Jacob Bell,* which was built by him, and the following one after his old partner, David Brown. The *Brown* measured 225 feet on deck, by 41 x 22: 6 feet; 1717 tons. She was in every way a beautiful ship and in the opinion of the crowds who visited her on the occasion of her first call at London, her model was faultless. She was heavily sparred and realized the expectations of her admirers as to ability for speed.

On her maiden voyage, under command of Capt. George S. Brewster, she left New York, Dec. 13, 1853, and three days later the new McKay clipper *Romance of the Seas,* Capt. Philip Dumaresq, left Boston, both bound for San Francisco. The *Romance* was considered McKay's masterpiece; was slightly larger (1782 tons) and longer, but narrower and shallower than the *Brown* and much interest was taken in the initial performances of the two thoroughbreds. Both reached their common destination Mar. 23, 1854, the *Romance* a few hours in the lead. Much matter was published about how the *Romance* came up with and passed her rival off the coast of Brazil and of the two ships being frequently in company at various times on the long passage, but a comparison of their logs disproves these statements. The *Brown* was in the lead four days to the line, one day to the Horn and one day to the Pacific equator crossing and was only caught up with six days before arrival, when at noon both were in the same latitude, but the *Romance* was 40 miles to the good in longitude. The total distance logged by the *Brown* was 16,167 miles; average, 161.1 daily; passage, 99 days, 20 hours. Total distance logged by the *Romance*, 15,154 miles; average, 156.6 daily; passage, 96 days, 18 hours. From New York to the line, the *Brown* was 21 days, sailing 4205 miles, averaging slightly over 200. The *Romance* was 22 days from Boston, 3784 miles, averaging 172. The *Brown* fell to leeward of St. Roque and had to beat around, on one day tacking five times, in consequence of which she lost nearly three days, making 30 days from the line to the Horn, sailing 4203 miles and being within 10 miles of the Cape when 51 days out. The *Romance* was within three miles of the Cape in 27 days from the line, sailing 4123 miles, when 49 days out. Both ships had 13 days between the two crossings of 50° South and both had 29 days from Cape Horn to the line; both crossed in 111° West, the *Brown* being 80 days out against the *Romance's* 78 days. Coming up to the Golden Gate, the *Brown* stood out further to the westward, taking 15 days to latitude 33° North, 2656 miles, while the *Romance* was but 12 days to the same latitude, covering but 2322 miles. From that position to port, the *Brown* was five days covering 452 miles while the *Romance* was six days doing 436 miles. The latter, when 89 days out, was 540 miles distant from the Golden Gate. Each ship, on the whole passage, had eight days of over 250 miles, the *Brown's* total for the eight being 2104; best, 284; the *Romance's* total being 2187, best 322. The *Brown* had her jibboom carried away 10 days before entering port and the *Romance* had her jibboom carried away twice, once when 16 days out and again 17 days before arrival; she also had her foretopmast carried away in the North Atlantic and again in the South Pacific.

This remarkable instance of close sailing between two ships, neither apparently having any advantage over the other as to speed, over the longest and most difficult course in ocean transportation, was further exemplified by the passages of the two rivals from San Francisco to Hong Kong. Both sailed on Mar. 31st, the *Brown* hauling out into the stream first and saluting her rival with several guns. They towed to sea in company at 3: 30 P.M. Many bets were made, the *Romance* being the favorite. They arrived at Hong Kong, May 16th, the *Romance* about one hour in the lead; passages, 45 days; average, 171 daily. The *Romance* loaded at Whampoa and was 102 days to London, 79 days from Anjer. The *Brown* went up the coast to Shanghai and was thence 111 days to London, 72 days from Anjer. It is to be regretted that they had no further opportunity to test their merits together.

The *Brown* left London, Jan. 30, 1855, for Bombay; was 23 days to the line and 46 days to the Cape of Good Hope; arrived out May 8th, passage 98 days. From Bombay she went to Liverpool, in 90 days, and from that port to New York, in 25 days. Had been absent 23 months during which she had given a good account of herself.

At New York she loaded for San Francisco and under command of Captain Bradbury, took her departure, Jan. 16, 1856; was 22 days to the line and 54 days thereafter crossed the equator in the Pacific, being then only 76 days out from New York and having excellent prospects for at least equalling the passage of her rival on the previous run out. Fate was against her, however, for calms and light and head winds succeeding each other in the North Pacific and she did not make port until 27 days from the line; 103 days from New York. This was a fine performance but under the circumstances quite disappointing to Captain Bradbury. From San Francisco she went to Hong Kong and operated between Batavia, Manila and China for over a year, finally arriving at New York, Dec. 28, 1857. While on the coast of Asia, she was forced to put into port in distress on two occasions on account of leaking, in one instance her cargo being forwarded to Hong Kong by the *Eagle Wing*. In March 1858 she sailed from New York, under Captain Behm, for Singapore; was at Bangkok in October, loading rice for Hong Kong. May 5, 1859, she arrived at Shanghai from Bangkok, with a cargo of rice. May 17th, in shifting her berth, in charge of a pilot, she collided with the bark *Syrian* and drifted ashore but got off May 21st, after discharging a large part of her cargo. Sailed from Whampoa, Dec. 20, 1859, and arrived at New York, Mar. 2, 1860, 103 days from Whampoa and 82 days from Anjer. Had light winds almost all the passage and carried her three skysails 91 days on the trip. She had come through the Straits of Sunda in company with the *Panama* and both took their Sandy Hook pilots the same day.

She arrived at San Francisco, Aug. 30, 1860, under Captain Berry, 121 days from New York; had 28 days to the line; passed the Horn, 61 days out; crossed the equator, 95 days out; had no trades and was becalmed seven days north of the line. At San Francisco she was chartered to load wheat for Liverpool, for the lump sum of £5700 sterling; took on 1854 short tons and sailed Oct. 11, 1860, with a crew of 22 men and 24 passengers, of whom 19 were women and children. In latitude 45° South, in the Atlantic, she had a very heavy gale from the southwest and a head sea, starting everything about decks. Was found to have sprung a leak but it was controlled with the forward pumps. Early in January she had continuous strong northeast winds and a head sea, causing the leak to increase. Finally, at noon, Jan. 6, 1861, in latitude 22° 16″ North, 39° 50″ West, she was abandoned, having then 7½ feet of water in her. Captain Berry took 18 of the crew and the women and children in his boat; the balance of the crew and the male passengers were under charge of the mate, Mr. Daly, in his boat. After three days the boats parted company and the occupants of both are said to have suffered greatly from hunger, thirst and exposure. Jan. 16th, those in the captain's boat were picked up by the Spanish bark *Observador* and taken to Havana. Mr. Daly and his party were taken aboard the bark *Sea Wave* and carried to Liverpool. The insurance carried on the *Brown* and her cargo totalled $170,000.

DAVID CROCKETT

THE *David Crockett* was one of the longest lived of the American clipper fleet, having a career of nearly forty years, during all of which time she was driven hard, and the fact that some of her fastest passages were made after she had passed the quarter-century mark is ample evidence of the superiority of her construction. From 1857 until 1882 she was operated in trade between New York, San Francisco and Liverpool, her principal competitor being the equally celebrated clipper *Young America* and many a close race was run between the two. She was launched on Oct. 18, 1853, from the yards of Greenman & Company of Mystic, Connecticut, for the account of Handy & Everett of New York and was originally intended to run as a packet between New York and Liverpool. The result of a brief packet experience was her withdrawal from the trans-Atlantic route and transference to the California trade where she rightly belonged.

The model of the *Crockett* proved to be one of the most successful combinations of speed and cargo capacity and in this respect connoisseurs of marine matters regarded her as almost perfect. The builders' measurements were: length, 215: 10; breadth of beam, 40: 10; depth of hold, 27 feet; tonnage, old style, 1679. Under the new system of measurement her dimensions were given as 218: 8 x 41 x 27; 1547 tons. Her capacity for California cargo was 2800, weight and measurement tons; when carrying wheat from San Francisco to Liverpool she was deeply laden with 2200 short tons. While heavily sparred she was not as lofty as some of her clipper competitors, notably the *Young America,* nor was her general appearance quite so handsome, but she was decidedly distinctive. She crossed three skysail yards and through all her Cape Horn passages retained the old style single topsail on the mizzen mast. A life-sized image of the eccentric backwoodsman for whom she was named was carved for use as her figurehead. The coonskin and long rifle were in evidence and the whole figure was as natural as life. Strange to say, the figure, although carried aboard the ship was, for some reason, not mounted, and in perfect condition it now decorates the rooms of the San Francisco Chamber of Commerce.

Throughout her career the *Crockett* was a phenomenally successful ship and, up to the time of her sale in 1883, is said never to have cost the underwriters one dollar. She also proved to be a mint for her owners. Her original cost was $93,000, and up to 1876 she is said to have returned a net profit of $500,000, including allowance for a thorough overhauling in 1869. In 1866, her freight list from New York to San Francisco was $46,872, gold, and for her return cargo of wheat and barley to Philadelphia, she received $30,000 in currency. The total time on the round voyage was 234 days, including 26 days in port in San Francisco. In 1872-1873, her total time on the voyage from New York to San Francisco and thence to Liverpool, was 261 days of which 55 days were spent in port. Her net profit was $37,000 on the trip and for her grain cargo to Liverpool she received £4.6.2 for each 2000 pounds.

During 1854, the *Crockett* was operated in the Handy & Everett line of New York-Liverpool packets. In January 1855 she left Liverpool for Aden and made the passage out in 85 days. Proceeding thence to Bombay she made the run from that port to Liverpool in 104 days. She then returned to trans-Atlantic trade and was so operated for something over a year, during which time her fastest voyage was 19 days from New York to Liverpool and 25 days back to New York. She was then put on the berth for San Francisco, arriving out July 19, 1857, in 122 days' passage. Captain Spencer reported being 15 days off the Horn in heavy gales, during which time the deckhouse and everything movable were washed overboard. She crossed the line in the Pacific on June 28th, and the run thence to port in 21 days was made in the face of strong northerly winds. She sailed from San Francisco, Oct. 6th, and anchored off Sandy Hook, Jan. 9, 1858, in 95 days, having made the run from the equator in 18 days.

On her second passage from New York to San Francisco, the *Crockett* was 19 days to the line; 64 to Cape Horn; 11 days from 50° to 50°, in moderate weather; crossed the equator 90 days out and arrived at destination July 19, 1858, in 117 days. She sailed from San Francisco, Oct. 17th and arrived at New York, Jan. 15, 1859, some hours under 89 days. She again sailed from New York, Mar. 16, 1859, making the run to San Francisco in 131 days. Captain Rowland reported very severe weather throughout the passage. On June 14th, while lying to in a heavy gale, latitude 40° South, Pacific, the vessel shipped a sea which stove the monkey rail and the doors of the forward deck house and so severely injured the carpenter that he died three days later. She sailed from San Francisco, Oct. 15th and on Dec. 2nd, 48 days out, was off the Straits of LeMaire; arrived at New York, Jan. 16, 1860, 93 days from the Golden Gate.

The command of the *Crockett* was now given to John A. Burgess of Somerset, Mass., who had been educated at Brown University and had taken up sea life on account of ill health. He had become a navigator of national reputation and had held command of the *Governor Morton* and *Monarch of the Seas*. In 1874 he had decided to retire from a sea life and was homeward bound from San Francisco when he was washed overboard from the deck of the *Crockett* and drowned. On his first passage in the *David Crockett*, Captain Burgess brought his ship into San Francisco harbor, July 3, 1860, 123 days from New York; was 29 days to the line, 64 days to Cape Horn and off it 14 days in heavy weather. On the return trip he sailed from San Francisco, July 24th, and arrived at Callao in 47 days; loaded with guano and was 72 days thence to Hampton Roads.

The following voyage the *Crockett* was 113 days from New York to San Francisco and returned to New York direct in 88 days. On her sixth Cape Horn voyage she left New York, May 8, 1862, was 29 days to the line; 56 days to the Cape and 11 days off it; crossed the equator 84 days out and was within 400 miles of San Francisco, 110 days out, reaching port seven days later. Returning she sailed from San Francisco, Nov. 1st, and arrived at Liverpool, Feb. 17, 1863, in a passage of 108 days. She then crossed to New York and went out to San Francisco in 110 days; loaded grain and arrived at Liverpool, Mar. 14, 1864, 100 days out. On her eighth passage to San Francisco she arrived out, Jan. 27, 1865, after the fine run of 107 days from New York. She then went to Valparaiso in ballast and loaded guano at Paquica for Liverpool, arriving back at New York, Feb. 11, 1866, with merchandise consigned to Lawrence Giles & Co., who were then her owners.

Her ninth run out to San Francisco occupied 114 days. She then loaded with 1980 tons of wheat and 110 tons of barley and arrived at Philadelphia on Dec. 25, 1866, in 94 days from San Francisco. The tenth westward Cape Horn passage was made in 110 days, arriving at San Francisco, July 22, 1867. She had crossed the line 20 days out and made the fine run of eight days from 50° to 50° but had 36 days of light northerly winds in the North Pacific. She returned to New York in 114 days and sailed again for San Francisco, making a slow passage of 137 days with unfavorable conditions throughout. On her return passage she reached New York, Nov. 27, 1868, in 95 days. Her receipts were $34,500, currency, for the homeward charter as against $30,000 the previous year. In 1869, her outward passage was 106 days; return, to Liverpool, in 114 days with wheat at £3 per ton. Her next voyage followed the same course and she again loaded wheat but this time at £2 per ton. Was 118 days on the outward and 111 days on the return passage.

The fourteenth passage of the *Crockett* from New York to San Francisco was made in 103 days and this was the fastest westward run in her career. She sailed from New York, Nov. 6, 1871; crossed the line in 20 days; had 30 days thence to 50° South and 12 days later was northbound in the Pacific. On the 82nd day she crossed the equator and was 21 days to anchorage, arriving Feb. 17, 1872. The return voyage to New York was made in 102 days. The following run out to San Francisco occupied 108 days but that portion from 50° South, in the Atlantic, to 30° North, in the Pacific, occupied only 50 days,—remarkably fast time. She was 11 days from 50° to 50°; thence 25 days to the equator crossing and nine days from 30° North to port. Arrived Jan. 26, 1873, and sailed Mar. 22nd, for Liverpool, which she reached after a passage of 98 days.

The sixteenth passage of the *Crockett* from New York to San Francisco was made in 113 days. She again loaded wheat for Liverpool and was in the stream ready to sail on Apr. 20, 1874, when the crew mutinied and detained her five days. She reached Liverpool, Aug. 10th, in a passage of 107 days. On June 25th, in a heavy gale off the Platte, Captain Burgess, while clearing away some tackle which had jammed, was washed overboard and drowned. The mate, John Anderson, took the ship into port and was appointed to the command, in which he continued while she was operated as a sailing ship. From Liverpool she crossed to New York, loaded for San Francisco and had a rough passage to the Horn, which she passed Jan. 13, 1875, 52 days out; crossed the equator Feb. 15th, and after a fine run of 18 days hove to in a thick fog seven miles southwest of the Farallon Islands, 103 days from Sandy Hook; entered port the next day; passage 104 days. The mate was off duty the best part of the run and considerable annoyance was had from the crew. From San Francisco she went to Liverpool in 116 days.

On the next three passages of the *Crockett*, from 1875 to 1878, inclusive, from New York to San Francisco, the outward runs were made in 109, 113, and 116 days respectively. The passage out in 1877 would have been a fast one for when 100 days out the ship was within 800 miles of the Golden Gate. Because of light and baffling winds it took 13 days to cover the 800 miles. The return passages from San Francisco were respectively, 120 days to Cork, 104 days to New York direct, and 100 days to New York, also direct.

On her twenty-first outward passage to San Francisco, the *Crockett* left New York, Mar. 26, 1879, and on Aug. 7th, at 9 A.M., was close enough to Point Reyes to hear the fog horn, but calms and a

"Derby," 1062 tons, built at Chelsea, Mass., in 1855

From a painting by a Chinese artist showing the ship "entering Hong Kong, Mar. 13, 1864"

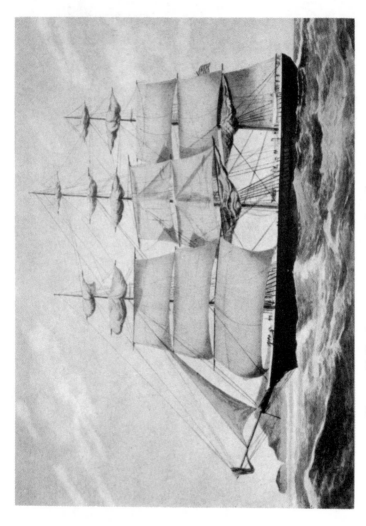

"Donald McKay," 2598 tons, built at East Boston, in 1855
From a watercolor by J. Rogers, 1855, in the Macpherson Collection, showing the ship off "Anglesey, in 18 days out of Boston"

"Donald McKay," 2598 tons, built at East Boston, in 1855
From a watercolor by Thomas Chisman, mate, dated May 23, 1857

"DONALD McKay," 2598 TONS, BUILT AT EAST BOSTON, IN 1855
From an oil painting showing her narrow escape from shipwreck

dense fog delayed her arrival for two days, making her run 136 days. When five days out she encountered a fearful gale lasting 48 hours; crossed the line 28 days out; passed the Horn 63 days out, and then took a terrible gale which lasted 12 days with awful squalls of hail and snow. On June 9th, 11 days later, she had drifted back to Cape St. John, with damage to sails and rigging. Captain Anderson stated that in his 14 passages round the Cape he had never seen such fearful weather before; got past the Cape for the second time, 14 days after the first crossing and was within 600 miles of the Golden Gate for 15 days. The return trip was direct to New York in 100 days. Sailed from New York, Mar. 22, 1880, and arrived at San Francisco, July 28th, in a passage of 128 days. Arrived at New York, direct, Feb. 11, 1881, in 116 days.

On her twenty-third run out to San Francisco she left New York, Mar. 22, 1881, was 22 days to the line; passed in sight of the Cape, 60 days out, then took a violent gale from the west and for six days was hove to under lower topsails, drifting to the eastward; passed the Horn, May 28th, for the second time and arrived at destination July 23rd, in 124 days' passage. Returned to New York in 99 days. The following westward run was the poorest showing the *Crockett* ever made, due to continued adverse winds and a succession of heavy gales. She arrived at San Francisco, July 27, 1882, in 157 days from New York and returned to New York, direct, in 102 days.

On her twenty-fifth and last passage out to San Francisco, the *Crockett* left New York, Feb. 10, 1883; had light trades and was 36 days to the line; passed Cape Horn, 78 days out; crossed the equator, 104 days out, and then had light winds and calms to port, arriving June 28, 1883, in 138 days' passage. Returned to New York in 92 days.

Early in the career of the *Crockett*, probably about the time she became a regular packet between New York and San Francisco, she had been purchased by Lawrence Giles & Co., of New York. That firm subsequently sold her to George Howes & Co., of New York and San Francisco, who retired from business in the summer of 1880 and were succeeded by John Rosenfeld, of San Francisco, who took over the Howes' fleet, which included such other well-known ships as *Young America, Black Hawk* and *Valparaiso.* In 1883, after her arrival at New York on her last passage from the Pacific, the *Crockett* was sold to Thomas Dunhams Nephew & Co., who later sold her to S. W. Carey and she was operated in the Atlantic, latterly rigged as a bark. In May 1890, she was purchased by Peter Wright & Son and after being towed to Philadelphia was converted into a barge. At the time, referring to a famous maxim of the quaint character after whom she was named, the comment was made, "The Crockett was always right, and always went ahead, but ships, like men, cannot go on forever." In September 1890, a correspondent of the *New York Times* wrote "The pride of the California fleet is being converted into a coal barge, divested of her tall masts and spars and fitted with leg-of-mutton sails. She will carry coal for Eastern ports between Gay Head and Cape Elizabeth, to any port where there is water enough to float her. She will earn her future livelihood with the matter of fact assistance of a steam tug. Her sailing days are over." She was ultimately lost but details are not available.

DEFENDER

BUILT by Donald McKay, at East Boston, in 1855. 184 x 38 x 23; 1413 tons. Kendall & Plimpton, Boston, owners. Wrecked on Elizabeth Reef, South Pacific, Feb. 27, 1859, while on voyage from Puget Sound to Sydney, Australia, with lumber.

DEFIANCE

EXTREME clipper ship, launched from the yard of George Thomas, at Rockland, Maine, Mar. 8, 1852; built under the direction of Capt. Isaac Taylor of Boston. Length over all, 240 x 43: 6 x 29 feet; 1900 tons. At a later period, when owned in Spain, her tonnage was given as 1695. She was designed by Samuel H.

Pook and had three complete decks. Her ends were long and sharp, more so than those of the *Flying Cloud*, and her lines were concave. In model she was in many respects unlike other early ships of her class, one peculiarity being a comparatively flat floor, with only 10 inches dead rise. She was an unusually handsome ship and intended, as her name implied, to excel all others. Her original owner was William T. Dugan, who sold her, in 1854, to McCreedy, Mott & Co., of New York; reported price $85,000.

From Rockland she went to New York and on the run to Fire Island Light she traveled at the rate of 18 knots and from Fire Island to Sandy Hook, 20 knots were made. On her only passage to San Francisco she arrived out, Dec. 2, 1852, Captain McCerren reporting 136 days from New York and 83 days from Rio. Had a continuation of calms and storms, with head winds practically the whole run. Had very heavy weather off the Horn and was off San Francisco for several days. Had put into Rio and remained there for 23 days. Sailed from San Francisco, Feb. 17, 1853, and arrived at Callao, Apr. 13th, in a 54-day passage. Left Callao, Oct. 10th, and arrived at New York, Jan. 10, 1854. Sailed from New York, Aug. 17, 1854, for the West Coast of South America. Left Callao, Jan. 31, 1855, and was 78 days to Hampton Roads.

On the 14th of August 1853, the *Defiance* was at the Chincha Islands, loaded and almost ready to sail, when an event of some international importance occurred. One of the crew, on shore leave, was arrested and placed in jail on the charge of having shot a pelican. Captain McCerren went to the authorities and asked for the release of the man, as he was about to sail, at the same time offering to pay the fixed penalty for the offence, which was only one dollar. The authorities, however, refused to release the man or receive the fine. Captain McCerren then sent for the Commandante of the port and again requested the release of the man and was again refused. This uncalled for and unjust treatment excited great indignation among the American captains in port and on the day she was to sail, some thirty captains and officers of American vessels, then lying at the

Chinchas, came on board the *Defiance* to see her off. One of the ship's guns was fired as the usual signal for sailing and immediately three boats put off from the Peruvian War Steamer *Rimac*, and came alongside the *Defiance*. The officer in command of the boats boarded the ship and demanded of Captain McCerren a fine of 25 dollars as penalty for firing a gun in port. This the captain paid, at the same time remarking that if the officer staid in the vicinity of the ship fifteen minutes longer, there would be another fine to collect. The Peruvian officer then called his men aboard and a fight ensued during which several of the Americans were badly wounded and Captain McCerren, with his scalp cut to the bone from a blow of a carbine, was finally ironed and carried off to jail. The *Defiance* was abandoned to the Peruvian Government and her mate went to Callao and put the case in the hands of Mr. Clay, our Minister at the time, at Callao. The Peruvian Government afterwards disavowed the act of the Commandante; promised redress and the removal of the offending official.

The *Defiance*, under command of Capt. John Kendrick, left Liverpool, Oct. 25, 1856, for Bombay and put into Santa Cruz, Canary Isles, in November, leaky. She had encountered a severe gale on Nov. 2nd, during which she was thrown on her beam ends, bursting her water tank and shifting the cargo. The 1st officer, who went down into the hold to examine her condition, had both legs crushed and the 2nd mate, who accompanied him, received a fractured arm, both being caught by the shifting cargo. The *Defiance* was condemned and sold, going under the Spanish flag as the *Teide*, of Cadiz, J. Matia, owner.

DERBY

MEDIUM clipper ship, built by John Taylor, at Chelsea, Mass., in 1855, for Pickman, Silsbee, and others, of Salem, Mass. 180 x 36: 9 x 23: 5; 1062 tons, old measurement; 1094 tons, measurement rules of 1865; 1085 tons in 1885. Purchased at San Francisco in April 1865, by George Howes & Co., for $30,000 cash. Sold about 1876 to go under the German flag, without change of name. In 1890 was under the Norwegian flag, still named *Derby*. The *Sumatra*, built by Taylor in 1856 for the same owners was a sister ship.

The *Derby* arrived at San Francisco, May 21, 1856, 120 days from Boston. Her captain, Hutchinson, reported 23 days to the line; much calm weather from 30° to 50° South; passed Cape Horn, Mar. 22nd, 60 days out; was 20 days from 50° South, Pacific, to the line, crossing Apr. 23rd, 92 days out; thence light and calm to port. Sailed from San Francisco, June 11th, and arrived at Hong Kong, July 25th, in 43 days. Went on to Calcutta and left the Sand Heads, Mar. 29, 1857; was 53 days to the Cape; thence 24 days to the line and 23 days from there to Boston, arriving July 7th, in 100 days' passage.

Her second voyage was out to Hong Kong, arriving Mar. 2, 1858; went home from Calcutta. Arrived at San Francisco, May 18, 1859, 133 days from New York. Sailed from San Francisco, June 9th, and arrived at Manila, Aug. 6, 1859. Arrived at San Francisco, Oct. 19, 1860, 155 days from New York. Sailed Nov. 29th, and arrived at New York, Mar. 27, 1861, in 119 days. Had much calm weather on the passage. Was 24 days from the equator to New York. Arrived at San Francisco, Jan. 2, 1862, in 144 days from New York. Sailed Feb. 8th and arrived at Manila, Mar. 31st, in 50 days, being beaten nine days by the *Dashing Wave*, sailing five days after her and arriving four days ahead. Left Manila, May 18th, for Boston.

Arrived at San Francisco, Apr. 28, 1863, under Captain Allen, who had succeeded Captain Hutchinson, in 150 days from Boston. Sailed May 26th and arrived at Hong Kong, Aug. 4th, in 69 days. All others about this time had also slow passages. Returned to San Francisco arriving Dec. 7th, 59 days from Hong Kong. Sailed Jan. 15, 1864, for Hong Kong and arrived at Honolulu, Feb. 2nd; sailed the 5th and arrived at Hong Kong ———. Arrived at San Francisco, July 5, 1864, in 59 days from Hong Kong. Sailed July 29th, under Captain Lord, and arrived at Hong Kong, Oct. 1st, in 62 days. Arrived at San Francisco, Mar. 21, 1865, in 54 days from

Hong Kong. Then made a round voyage to Puget Sound and under Captain Manson sailed from San Francisco, Aug. 8th, for Swansea; arrived Dec. 8th, in 122 days' passage.

Arrived at San Francisco, Nov. 21, 1866, in 125 days from New York. Captain Manson reported sailing July 17th; 34 days to the line; 62 days to 50° South; 20 days rounding the Horn; 24 days thence to the equator, 106 days out, and 19 days from there to destination. Sailed Dec. 17th and arrived at Liverpool, Apr. 17, 1867, in 121 days.

Arrived at San Francisco, Dec. 26, 1867, in 139 days from New York. Captain Goff then took her and sailed Jan. 22, 1868; arrived at Liverpool, May 21st, in 120 days' passage. Arrived at San Francisco, Jan. 20, 1869, in 139 days from New York. Sailed Feb. 11th for Mazatlan; left there May 11th; arrived at Liverpool, Sept. 7th, in 99 days' passage. Arrived at New York, Nov. 6th, in 33 days from Liverpool.

Arrived at San Francisco Apr. 30, 1870, in 117 days from New York. Had sailed Jan. 3rd; was 27 days to the line; thence 20 days to 50° South, 47 days out; thence 13 days to 50°, Pacific, very good time; had a poor time in the South Pacific, 33 days from 50° South, to the equator; thence 24 days to port; had moderate weather throughout. Sailed from San Francisco, June 25th and arrived at New York, Oct. 4th, in 101 days' passage. This voyage of the *Derby* was the fastest in her career.

Arrived at San Francisco, Apr. 4, 1871, in 132 days from New York; sailed May 5th for Manila. Arrived back at San Francisco, Sept. 29th, in 52 days from Manila. Sailed Oct. 19th and arrived at Manila, Dec. 7th, 48 days. Was back at San Francisco, Mar. 12, 1872, in 52 days from Manila. The British ship *Tamesa*, Captain Jones, arrived the day before in 67 days from Manila. Under Captain Sprague, the *Derby* left San Francisco, Apr. 18th, for Manila and was back at San Francisco, Sept. 18th, in 71 days from Manila. Sailed Oct. 17th; arrived at Liverpool, Feb. 6, 1873, in 112 days. The *Derby* did not again visit San Francisco.

The German ship *Derby* arrived at New York, Sept. 23, 1881, in 123 days from Bremen; sailed from New York, Oct. 26, 1881, and arrived at Bremen, Nov. 18th, in 23 days' passage.

DICTATOR

BUILT by Jas. W. Cox at Robbinston, Me., in 1855. 1293 tons, for Samuel Train of Medford; sold to Charles R. Green of New York. Captured and burned by the *Georgia*, April 1863.

DONALD McKAY

CLIPPER ship, built by Donald McKay, at East Boston, Mass.; launched in January 1855. Length of keel, 257: 9; between perpendiculars, 266; beam, 46: 3; depth of hold, 29: 5; 2598 tons, American old measurement; 2614 tons gross and 2449 tons net, British measurement. Dead rise, 18 inches. A Highlander dressed in the tartan of the MacKays was her figurehead. She was the last of the famous quartette built by Donald McKay for James Baines & Company's "Black Ball Line" of Liverpool-Australian packets and except for the *Great Republic*, was for years the largest sailing ship afloat. Her model closely resembled that of the *Champion of the Seas*, neither being so sharp ended as the *Lightning* or *James Baines*. She swung a main-yard of 100 feet, had Howes' double topsails, a skysail yard, and her sail area on the mainmast was 17,000 yards, which was somewhat in excess of that of the *Great Republic* after her reconstruction. Her actual dead weight carrying capacity is said to have been slightly more than that of the *Republic*. She had three decks. The after cabin contained 12 large staterooms and below were 24 staterooms designed for gentlemen passengers. All the cabins were profusely decorated according to the taste of the day.

The *Donald McKay*, under command of Captain Warner, formerly of the *Sovereign of the Seas*, sailed from Boston, Feb. 21, 1855, and was 17 days to Liverpool. She made Cape Clear, Mar.

5th, 12 days out, and the next day made Fastnet Rock. In the Channel, her passage was spoiled by easterly winds and she did not receive her pilot off Point Lynas until Mar. 10th. On Feb. 27th, she ran 421 nautical miles, the log showing,—"First part, a strong gale from N.W.; middle part, blowing a hurricane from W.N.W., ship scudding under topsails and foresail at the rate of 18 knots; latter part, still blowing from W.N.W., with heavy rain squalls and very heavy sea running." Donald McKay, himself, went over in the ship and expressed himself well satisfied with her. She immediately took her place in the "Black Ball Line" and from Liverpool went out to Melbourne in 81 days, returning in 86 days.

For some 12 or 13 years the *McKay* continued running as a "Black Ball" packet and became very popular. Her passages, while never remarkably fast nor up to those of the *Lightning* or *James Baines*, were consistently good; her average for six consecutive outward runs is 83 days, and homeward bound, is said to be 85 days. After ending her career in this service, she was engaged in general trade and from 1868 to 1874 she is registered as owned by Thomas J. Harrison, hailing port, Liverpool. In 1874 she was sold at auction, in London, for £8750 to J. S. DeWolfe of Liverpool. In 1875, under command of Captain Richards, she conveyed the "Connaught Rangers" to Bombay and took home from there another regiment without losing a man. Captain Richards received from the Government a handsome testimonial and a vote of thanks for his services. On another occasion she is said to have taken 1000 troops from Portsmouth to Mauritius in 70 days.

On Sept. 13, 1879, the *McKay* was sold at Bremen to sail under German colors, without change of name, her hailing port becoming Bremerhaven. As a German ship she made a number of trips between Bremen and New York, and eventually went to Madeira as a coal hulk. In November 1878, she was at Philadelphia, taking in the largest cargo of petroleum ever loaded at that or any other port. She had not, theretofore, been in American waters since leaving Boston on her maiden voyage.

DON QUIXOTE

MEDIUM clipper ship, launched in September 1853, from the yard of Samuel Lapham, at Medford, Mass. Keel, 192; deck, 200; over all, 207 x 38: 5 x 23: 9; 1429 tons, old measurement. She had no figurehead, a billet substituting. Her ends were quite sharp, being slightly concave below the water-line, her bow raking boldly forwards. She was, however, a large carrier, being able to stow 2400 tons cargo, weight and measurement, for the California trade. Her model was also adapted for speed and on her maiden voyage she established a good name in that respect which was thereafter consistently maintained. Her spread of canvas was about 9000 yards. She was built for John Ellerton Lodge of Boston, her construction being superintended by Capt. William Nott, formerly of the *Argonaut*, belonging to the same owner. Captain Nott was the first captain of the *Quixote* and in 1864 he and his friends bought her. Captain Nott referred to her as being as good as she was beautiful.

The *Quixote* made seven passages from Eastern ports to San Francisco, the first four being from Boston and the last three from New York. The runs were, in order: 126, 107, 109, 111, 139, 119 and 139 days. On her maiden trip head winds or adverse gales prevailed nearly all the passage: best day's run, 301 miles; poorest, seven miles. On her second run, she doubled the Cape on the 47th day out; crossed the equator on the 84th day and on the 97th day was only 300 miles from the Golden Gate. On the following passage she was in 50° South, Atlantic, on the 41st day out and crossed the equator on the 80th day. The fourth run started poorly. On the third day out she carried away the spritsail yard and lost three topsails, being without these sails for over two days thereafter; also fell to leeward of Cape St. Roque. She was reported, however, to have been up with the latitude of Valparaiso when 69 days out and crossed the equator on the 85th day. When 102 days out she was close to the Heads, San Francisco, fog bound. Captain Hall claimed that she was actually under sail only 108½ days, which was the shortest run that had been made for the previous six months. On one day she made 312 miles. On her fifth passage, arriving at San Francisco, Jan. 4, 1860, she had no opportunity to make good, yet her run was faster than had been made during the previous two months by some 15 other ships, including some particularly noted for speed. In 1861 she left New York, very deeply laden, and on one occasion, on the passage, Captain Ellery feared for her safety. However, she weathered all storms and was up with the equator in the Pacific when 91 days out and on the 104th day was within 900 miles of the Golden Gate. On her last westward Cape Horn passage she was 41 days to the line, 78 days to the Cape and 300 miles from San Francisco when 123 days out.

The second section of the seven voyages mentioned, was in each instance from San Francisco to Hong Kong, her time being 40, 40, 45, 45, 41, 56 and 53 days respectively, an excellent average of 45 5/7 days. In 1854 she was 107 days from Whampoa, 76 days from Anjer, to New York, the season being unfavorable. In 1855, leaving Foo Chow at about the poorest season, she led the fleet of British and American ships to London, her time being 106 days. From London she was 22 days to Boston. During a portion of 1856 she was engaged in carrying rice from Bangkok to China. Finally loaded at Foo Chow for New York and made the passage in 104 days, 76 days from Anjer; season unfavorable. In 1858/59 she was 112 days from Whampoa to New York, season favorable. In 1860 her time from Manila to New York was 112 days, season being fair. Her last run from the Far East, homeward bound, was in 1862, when Captain Nott, who had resumed command, reported on arrival at New York, Aug. 16th, that he had sailed from Foo Chow, Mar. 29th; had constant, faint southwest winds and calms down the China Sea; passed Anjer, Apr. 28th and had very light southeast trades across the Indian Ocean, interrupted every three or four days by westerly winds; was off the Cape of Good Hope the whole month of June; passed St. Helena, July 13th, and the line, July 22nd.

The *Quixote* left San Francisco, Apr. 6, 1863, and was 17 days to Honolulu and 36 days thence to Hong Kong. Sailed from the latter port, July 14th, in ballast; put in at the Island of Formosa and received aboard the Chinese passengers from the wrecked ship *Ringleader;* then proceeded to Simoda, Japan, and took on the Chinese passengers from wrecked ship *Viking.* Arrived at San Francisco, Sept. 15, 1863, 30 days from Simoda, with 600 coolies. She sailed from San Francisco, Oct. 24, 1863, and arrived at Liverpool, Mar. 15, 1864. This was a long passage of 142 days but was faster than any others making the run about that time except the clipper *Young America,* which had, for her, the long time of 125 days.

After arrival at Boston from Liverpool, in 1864, the *Quixote* was sold and Aug. 31, 1864, cleared from Boston for the Gulf of St. Lawrence, as the French ship *St. Aubin,* under command of Capt. Isaac C. Knapp, sailing Sept. 5th. The registers of 1866/68 give the owners of the *St. Aubin* as F. Couisinary & Co., hailing port, Havre. In 1874 she was owned by H. Deglaires, hailing port, Havre. That she was well and strongly built is evidenced by the fact that in 1874 she was classed A 1, in British Lloyds, although over 20 years old.

On three different occasions Captain Nott had command of the *Don Quixote;* in the interim her masters were Elwell, Hall and Ellery. From the autumn of 1862 until she was sold, in 1864, Captain Johnson had her.

DREADNOUGHT

MEDIUM clipper ship, launched Oct. 6, 1853, from the yard of Currier & Townsend, at Newburyport, Mass., and built for account of E. D. Morgan, F. B. Cutting, David Ogden and associates, of New York, especially to be commanded by Capt. Samuel Samuels. The captain, a young man of great push and energy, a thorough seaman and navigator, formerly master of the ships *Manhattan* and *Angelique,* was given an interest and he superintended her construction, she being built to be operated in the "Red Cross

Line" of New York and Liverpool packets, of which Mr. Ogden was the agent. Her dimensions were: keel, 200 feet; deck, 212; extreme beam, 41: 6; depth of hold, 26: 6; tonnage, 1413, old measurement; 1227, new measurement; capacity for cargo, about 2000 tons weight. While not of a sharp model she had good lines. She was very carefully built of the best materials and in hull, spars and rigging could not have been made stronger and she was always well kept up. As Captain Samuels puts it, "She was built for hard usage and to make a reputation for herself and me and I intended that she should do her duty, or that we both should sink." Up to her accident in January 1863, the least sail that she had ever carried at sea was double-reefed topsails and she had never been hove to. She was nicknamed by sailors "The wild boat of the Atlantic" and "The Flying Dutchman." Due to the unceasing vigilance and splendid seamanship of her captain, who was particularly active during the nighttime, and his confidence in the ability of his ship to stand driving in the worst weather, the *Dreadnought* maintained a high average of speed. During the nine years that Captain Samuels was in command, she was never passed in anything over a four knot breeze. It is safe to say that she had greater renown than any other merchant ship ever built and tales of her performances have often appeared in song and story.

The *Dreadnought* left Newburyport, Nov. 3, 1853, in tow of the tug *Leviathan*, for New York, and in commencing her first voyage, sailed from that port Dec. 6th. Between that date and Feb. 26, 1864, she completed 31 round voyages between New York and Liverpool, as a Red Cross packet. Records are available of 20 of her passages to the eastward, these showing an average of exactly 19 days. There were seven of 20 days or over, the longest being 30 days in the summer of 1854. Nine were of 16 days or under, of which six were consecutive runs. In November 1854, her time from Sandy Hook to anchorage in the Mersey, was 13 days, 11 hours; distance sailed, 3071 miles; best day, 320 miles. On Jan. 24, 1856, she passed Sandy Hook and in 14 days was hove to off Point Lynas waiting for the tide, daylight and a pilot. She had covered 3116 miles at an average of 222 per day; best day, 312; when five days out, was forced backward 90 miles by a violent gale. Leaving New York, Feb. 27, 1859, she was 13 days, 8 hours, from the Sandy Hook pilot to the Northwest Lightship, Liverpool; distance sailed, 3018 miles; best days, 313 and 308 miles; poorest days, 133 and 150 miles. This is her fastest eastward passage, port to port. A remarkable run of 9 days, 17 hours, from Sandy Hook to Cape Clear, which she is believed to have made in June 1859, is referred to later.

Records are available of 22 of her passages to the westward, on two of which she was forced to put into Fayal, due to loss of her rudder. The average of the other 20 is 26½ days, there being five of 30 days or over, made during late summer or autumn months. Her shortest run was 19 days, this being in February 1854, in completion of her maiden voyage. This run was remarkable from the fact that the weather was and had been very severe, and all other vessels, steamers included, had been making long passages. In February 1857, her passage was 21 days from Liverpool, the run from land to land being given as 15 days. Her fastest round voyage is believed to have been that made in the autumn of 1861. She left New York, Sept. 16th and arrived back Nov. 14th, 58 days, gross; 21 days outward; 15 days at Liverpool; 22 days homeward.

On Jan. 16, 1863, the *Dreadnought* sailed from Liverpool and when five days out was in the grip of a furious gale, sail being finally reduced to a close-reefed maintopsail, the least canvas she had ever shown. In an attempt to heave her to, the approach of a mountainous sea unnerved the men at the wheel, who put it the wrong way. The sea carried away the rudder, with its braces, smashed the skylight, flooded the cabin, and stove the hatches, thus allowing great quantities of water to get below. Captain Samuels received a compound fracture of the right leg, besides which the femoral artery was punctured. His escape from being lost overboard was miraculous. The sea, in the trough of which the ship lay with topsail aback, swept over the decks as it does over a half-tide rock, and with the passengers in a panic, the first officer incompetent, the carpenter killed and her captain in a pitiable condition in his cabin, whither he had been carried, the position of the *Dreadnought* was desperate.

After the storm lulled, the second officer contrived a jury rudder but it was lost overboard. On the fifth day after the disaster, a passing ship spent a whole day in a vain attempt to get the bow of the *Dreadnought* turned towards Fayal, which was distant some 350 miles, but was forced to abandon the attempt, finally proceeding on her voyage to Bordeaux. The following day Captain Samuels instructed his second officer to attempt to sail the ship backwards to Fayal, and this was done so successfully that during the ensuing 52 hours they covered 183 miles. The wind then fell calm and a smooth sea allowed a new jury rudder to be shipped. In the evening of the fourteenth day after the accident, the ship anchored in the roadstead of Fayal with the captain more dead than alive. He was taken ashore where he received temporary relief and 52 days later was returned to his ship. After a survey, it had been recommended that the ship be discharged and hove down, but as this meant her practical confiscation, the captain had rejected the plan and under his instructions, a short rudder, with new braces, was finally fitted and the ship got ready to resume her voyage. She left Fayal, Apr. 6th, and reached New York 19 days later. Captain Samuels was long in recovering and did not again resume command of the *Dreadnought,* or other sailing vessels, going into steam navigation. After a few years he gave up the sea. In 1878, he was general superintendent of the Pacific Mail Steamship Company, at San Francisco. He passed away at Brooklyn, N. Y., in May 1908, aged 85 years.

After repairs had been made to the *Dreadnought,* she sailed from New York, June 9, 1863, for Liverpool and arrived back Aug. 22nd, having been 18 days on the outward, and 30 days on the homeward passage. On returning from the following voyage, she put into Fayal, Dec. 26, 1863, partially dismasted and with her rudder completely gone. While on his quarterdeck, Captain Lytle had been struck by a sea, receiving injuries from which he died. The ship arrived at New York, Feb. 26, 1864, 25 days from Fayal, under command of her mate, Mr. Rockwell. This was her last trans-Atlantic voyage.

In the summer of 1864, the *Dreadnought* was put on the berth at New York for San Francisco, under command of Captain Cushing, and arrived at her destination, Oct. 1st, after a passage of 134 days. She then went to Honolulu, being 13 days on the run, and sailed from that port Dec. 17th, for New Bedford. On Mar. 11, 1865, she anchored in New Bedford bay, 43 days after passing Cape Horn, 84 days out from Honolulu; distance sailed, 12,570 miles; best day, 272. She again went out to San Francisco, arriving Jan. 18, 1886, 127 days from New York, and returned east via Callao. Captain Cushing was then succeeded by Captain Callaghan who took his charge to San Francisco in 149 days from New York, arriving July 29, 1868. From San Francisco she went to Queenstown in 121 days, proceeding to Liverpool to discharge. Then loaded for San Francisco, with iron, crockery and hardware, principally, and sailed, Apr. 28, 1869, under command of Capt. P. N. Mayhew, well known in connection with his former command, the clipper *Wild Pigeon*. The following is Captain Mayhew's account of her loss.

"We were 29 days from Liverpool to the equator and nothing unusual happened until daylight, July 4th, when the ship was discovered to be amongst the breakers, and seeing no chance to save her we put the boats into the water and after much trouble the crew got into them, but not before the ship struck, the sea making a complete breach over her. She soon became a complete wreck. We then landed on the beach after much trouble, the place being Cape Penas, to the northeast of the island of Tierra del Fuego. After consulting with my officers, it was decided to try to reach the Straits of Le Maire to intercept some passing vessel. After 17 days of severe hardship, sleeping on shore nights and living on mussels and limpets and such things as we could pick up on the beach, and being more or less frostbitten, we arrived on July 20 at Cape San Diego and at daylight saw a sail going through the Straits of Le Maire. Made all the signals we were able to and fortunately were seen by a barque, which hove to. On getting on board, found her to be the Norwegian barque *General Birch*, Captain Amuseden, from Hamburg for San Francisco, who kindly received our party of 34 persons, including the stewardess and a boy of 12 years, and treated us with true sailor's liberality. We then encountered severe head winds, and having so many extra persons on board, the ship getting short of water and provisions, and the rescued crew suffering from frost, the captain deemed it best to get to the nearest port as soon as possible and on August 17, we arrived at Talcahuano, Chile, and were kindly received and cared for by Mr. Randall, United States Consul."

The loss of the *Dreadnought* is said to have been occasioned through her having been becalmed and then carried by the strong current into the breakers. While ashore at different times, the party fell in with many Indians who, however, treated them well, not offering them the slightest violence. Captain Mayhew and his mates, William Taylor and William Sawyer, with 22 members of the crew, reached Valparaiso, Sept. 2nd, on the steamer *Bio Bio*, leaving the remainder of the crew in the hospital, at Talcahuano, suffering greatly from frost bites and with the certainty that they would lose fingers and toes. All hands signed a card, which was published, expressing appreciation and thanks to Captain Amuseden for his attention and his putting out of his course to land them.

The following is from the memorandum of the passage of the barque *General Birch*, at San Francisco, Oct. 12, 1869, 166 days from Hamburg, via Talcahuano, 53 days;—"On July 20, at the entrance to the Straits of Le Maire, fell in with two boats containing 34 persons, being the officers and crew of the ship *Dreadnought*, which vessel was wrecked July 4th on Cape Penas. Took them on board and landed them at Talcahuano August 17th."

At the time of her loss the *Dreadnought* was owned by John Parrott of San Francisco, who had bought her about a year previously. The insurance paid on vessel and cargo, by American underwriters, was $83,000.

The passage of the *Dreadnought* from Sandy Hook to Cape Clear, in 1859, was listed for many years as being 9 days, 17 hours, in tables of fast passages contained in publications of good repute, besides being quoted in encyclopaedias of unquestioned reliability; yet its actual accomplishment was not brought into question until some years after the death of Captain Samuels. Following the first announcement that it was "mythical" it has been assailed by various alleged authorities, some going so far as to say that they knew the run never was made, yet they advance nothing to show in favor of their contention, nor has indication been given that any proper investigation has been made. That which follows may be considered conclusive evidence that the authenticity of the alleged record trans-Atlantic passage is doubtful, but the facts here given seem to be all the data that is available.

It appears that the *Dreadnought* cleared at the New York Custom House on June 16, 1859, but unfortunately the date of her sailing was not published. It has always been the general custom to get out clearance papers a day or so in advance of the date of sailing. The *Dreadnought* arrived at Liverpool, July 2nd. In its issue of July 9, 1859, the "Illustrated London News" published this item;—"The packet ship *Dreadnought*, Captain Samuels, famed for her rapid passages across the Atlantic, arrived off Cape Clear on the 27th ultimo, in 9 days from New York." Had she passed Sandy Hook the day following her clearance, she would have been, on the 27th, off Cape Clear, in the neighborhood of 10 days, a few hours more or less, depending on the exact time of her being up with the Cape. The "Illustrated News," for many years had made a specialty of recording fast passages, with illustrations of noteworthy vessels of all descriptions, its statements being always accepted as authoritative by parties engaged in particular research work. That it would have invented the figures it quoted, is not to be thought of and it is impossible now to trace its source of information, but in view of the fact that the extra hours over the nine days were not given, there is no doubt but that the run was elsewhere published and commented on. In Captain Samuel's book, "From Forecastle to Cabin," the run is not referred to but it is noted that in quoting passages, only those from port-to-port are mentioned. His active career in the *Dreadnought* furnished so great an amount of material to be condensed into the small part of one book, that he could not cover everything. For example, he neglected to even mention the fact of having been in collision with and sinking the ship *John Evans* in February 1862, when two days out from New York bound for Liverpool. Shortly before his death, the Captain was very positive in his statements to interested inquirers that the passage was actually made, although having no documents to refer to, and relying on his memory, he did confuse the date with the voyage just previous. Mr. C. F. Ogden, son of the former New York agent of the "Red Cross Line," has also asserted that he remembers the passage having been made in the time stated. That it could have been performed, cannot be questioned. In his book, Captain Samuels recounts that on leaving New York in the middle of a certain February (believed to be 1855), the *Dreadnought* logged 1080 miles during the first 72 hours from Sandy Hook. He figured that had the wind continued, he would have landed his passengers in Liverpool in under nine days from New York. However, later encountering large quantities of ice and then being in collision with the British ship *Eugenie*, the passage was prolonged to 14 days.

There appears to be but little chance of any additional facts ever being brought to light regarding the run in question.

EAGLE

EXTREME clipper ship, launched from the yard of Perine, Patterson & Stack, at Williamsburg, N. Y., May 3, 1851, for Harbeck & Co., of New York. 192 x 38: 10 x 22; 1296 tons, old measurement. Dead rise, 30 inches. She had a long, sharp entrance, with concave lines. The figure of an eagle ornamented her bow.

On her initial voyage she left New York, July 10, 1851, and arrived at San Francisco, Nov. 18th, in 131 days' passage. Capt. J. S. Farran reported having had a succession of light winds, with no opportunity of making a showing. The passage around Cape Horn occupied 19 days and she was three days off the Golden Gate in a dense fog. The voyage was completed by her return to the Atlantic via Calcutta.

On her second voyage she arrived at San Francisco, Apr. 30, 1853, in 111 days from New York. Crossed the line 24 days out and on the 40th day was off the Platte; was 16 days rounding the Horn, which was passed 54 days out; had to go as far south as latitude 59° 20″, and had bad weather to 30° South, Pacific; crossed the equator 91 days out. She came through the Straits of Le Maire in company with the clipper ship *Celestial* and off the Cape spoke the *John Stuart;* led these ships eight days and four days, respectively, into San Francisco. Sailed thence May 20th and was 113 days to New York, including a stop at Rio.

On Feb. 16, 1854, she was again at San Francisco from New York, her passage being 104 days. She was 10 days from 50° to 50°, passing the Cape 56 days out; thence 48 days to destination. On Feb. 12th, 100 days out and 15 days from the equator, she was 170 miles from the Golden Gate. Her time between the two equatorial crossings was 54 days. Sailed from San Francisco, Mar. 29th, and was 101 days to New York.

Sailed from New York, Mar. 16, 1855, and on arrival at San Francisco, July 15th, Captain Farran reported his passage as being 115 days; 75 days from Rio. He had made land 30 miles south of the Golden Gate, on July 13th, but had been obliged to come to an anchor 1½ miles from shore. This voyage was completed by the ship going to England, via the West Coast of South America.

On Nov. 15, 1856, the *Eagle* arrived at Shanghai with a heavy cargo from London and in April 1857, she was reported as putting into Manila to bury her captain. From Manila she went to London, in 116 days, thence going out to Hong Kong in 115 days. For a time, thereafter, she operated on the coast of Asia. In October 1860 she was at Manila from Hong Kong. Sailed from that Philippine port, Nov. 13, 1860, and arrived at New York, Mar. 24, 1861, via Cape Town, Jan. 27th, Captain Williams being then in command.

During the fall of 1862, the *Eagle* was thoroughly overhauled at New York, also receiving new masts and rigging. She then went out to Calcutta and was sold there to H. J. B. Johar, a Parsee merchant, who had her name changed to *Turkey*. The consideration reported was 94,750 rupees.

EAGLE WING

MEDIUM clipper ship, launched from the yard of James O. Curtis, at Medford, Mass., Oct. 4, 1853, for Chase & Tappan of Boston. 198 x 39 x 23; 1174 tons. She was a beautiful ship with a very graceful bow, a good sheer and long sharp entrance and clearance lines. Her bottom was sharp and when anchored in the stream, without cargo, some 600 tons of ballast were required to keep her upright. Her lower masts, commencing with the foremast, were 75, 80 and 72 feet; fore and main topmasts, alike, 45 feet; mizzen topmast, 37 feet; fore and main topgallant masts, 25 feet; mizzen, 19 feet; other spars in proportion. She carried a main skysail but nothing higher than royals on fore and mizzen masts. The yards on fore and mainmast were alike, 74, 59, 43 and 32 feet; main skysail yard, 25 feet; mizzen yards, 55, 44, 32 and 25 feet.

The *Eagle Wing* closely approached the model of an extreme clipper, developed great speed and made some remarkably fast passages, as follows:—Boston to San Francisco, on her first run, 105 days, being 82 days to the Pacific equator crossing and when in 18° North latitude, had good chances of completing the trip in 95 days; thereafter, however, had light winds only. Leaving London, in April 1855, she was 84 days to pilot off Hong Kong or 84 days, 22 hours from anchor to anchor. Completing this voyage, she left Shanghai, Nov. 21, 1855; got away from the river two days later and was 86½ days to New York, crossing the line 66½ days out. In 1860 she was 90 days from San Francisco to New York and in 1864

ECLIPSE

EXTREME clipper ship, built in 1850, at Williamsburg, N. Y., by Jabez Williams. Owned by Thomas Wardle and Booth & Edgar of New York. 200 x 37 x 22; 1225 tons; Captain Joseph Hamilton. Her cabins were elegantly fitted up and decorated. She was launched Nov. 30, 1850; sailed from New York, Jan. 15, 1851, and arrived at San Francisco, May 20th. Captain Hamilton reported an uneventful passage of 124 days, with much light winds and fine weather, the ship being practically becalmed for 31 days. She left San Francisco, June 24th; arrived at Valparaiso, Aug. 6th, in 42 days; sailed the 10th; touched at Rio, Sept. 16th; sailed following day and crossed the equator in 7 days and 10 hours from Rio, the record to that date; arrived at New York, Oct. 20th, 33 days from Rio, 71 days net from Valparaiso and 113 days net from San Francisco.

On her second voyage, the *Eclipse* left New York, Jan. 3, 1852; the first night out, carried away jibboom; arrived at Valparaiso, Mar. 13th, 70 days out; sailed the following day; arrived at San Francisco, Apr. 22nd, 39 days from Valparaiso and 109 sailing days from New York. Had not seen nor spoken a single ship on the passage. From San Francisco she crossed to Shanghai in 60 days; loaded for London; passed Anjer, Oct. 9th, and put into St. Helena, Dec. 3rd, a very slow run that far.

Her third and last voyage began at New York, Apr. 18, 1853, she being thence 121 days to San Francisco, arriving Aug. 17th. Had 30 days to the line, 59 days to the Horn, off which was 10 days in moderate weather; was 23 days from equator crossing to destination with light winds, and for three days was within 300 miles of the Golden Gate. From San Francisco she went to the open roadstead of Ypala, between San Blas and Manzanillo, Mexico, to load Brazil wood. On Oct. 11, 1853, the wind suddenly shifted and blew a hurricane, driving the ship ashore when she immediately broke in two and went to pieces. She was valued at $90,000 and well insured. She was partially loaded, having been off the port 11 days, riding in 70 fathoms to her best bower.

EDWIN FORREST

MEDIUM clipper ship, built by Daniel D. Kelly, at East Boston, Mass.; launched Oct. 5, 1853. 186: 6 x 36: 4 x 23; 1141 tons, old measurement. Her entrance lines were long and sharp; dead rise, 13 inches. For a figurehead she had a full-length representation of the celebrated actor for whom she was named, in the character of Spartacus. She was a splendid ship in all respects. Her owners, Crosby, Crocker & Co., of New York, appointed as her master, Captain Crocker.

On her initial voyage the *Forrest* left New York, Dec. 4, 1853, and was 28 days to Havre; returned to New York in 29 days. She then went out to Australia and Calcutta and was 106 days from the latter port to London. Then followed a round voyage to Calcutta, on the return of which she sailed Feb. 5, 1856, and arrived at London, May 13th, in 98 days' passage. Crossed to New York and loaded for San Francisco, which port was reached Feb. 25, 1857, in 132 days. She had generally light winds on the whole run; was 27 days to the line; 14 days rounding the Horn, and 21 days from the equator crossing to destination. From San Francisco she went to Valparaiso in 50 days; thence to the Chincha Islands for guano and made the fine run of 64 days from Callao to Hampton Roads. Arrived at San Francisco, June 8, 1858, in 133 days from New York. Was 21 days to the line; 49 days to 50° South, and 10 days rounding the Horn; from 50° South, Pacific, to 35° South, she experienced a succession of heavy westerly gales and her prospects for making a fast passage were spoiled. The equator was not crossed until 99 days out and from latitude 28° North, to port, light winds and calms were met with and she was off port four days in a dense fog. From San Francisco she was 57 days to Melbourne, later proceeding to Calcutta; was 102 days from Calcutta to New York.

In 1859/60, the *Forrest* made a round voyage from New York to China, on return from which she sailed from New York, Aug. 1, 1860, for Hong Kong and was never thereafter heard from.

ELECTRIC

MEDIUM clipper ship, built in 1853, by Irons & Grinnell, at Mystic, Conn., and launched Sept. 5th. 181 x 38 x 21; 1046 tons. Her first owner is said to have been G. Adams of New York, but she is reported to have later been the property of the Gerry family of the same place. About 1860 she was sold to R. M. Sloman & Edye of Hamburg, going under the North German flag without change of name.

The *Electric* was first operated in the trans-Atlantic trade between New York and Havre. On Nov. 15, 1854, she left New York for San Francisco under command of Captain Gates; had the long run, for that season, of 34½ days to the line but thereafter did well; from the line to 50° South she was only 19 days; passed Cape Horn, Jan. 12, 1855, 57½ days out; was 17 days between the 50's, with nine days of heavy westerly gales; from 50°, in the Pacific, she was 20 days to the equator and 16 days thereafter, 107 days out. She made the Farallon Islands in a dense fog and had to stand off shore; the following day she took a pilot but did not enter port until Mar. 4th, 109 days from New York. Her run of 49 days from Cape Horn to landfall was particularly good, as was also her 56 days between the two equator crossings, considering the 17 days rounding the Cape. The clipper ship *Flyaway* also made the run from New York in 109 days and both ships left San Francisco on Mar. 24, 1855, for Hong Kong. The *Electric's* passage across was 48 days while the *Flyaway* was 43 days. The *Electric* went up the coast to Shanghai and was thence 106 days to New York, while her competitor was 106 days from Manila to the same destination.

The above was the only passage made by the *Electric* to San Francisco and on her return from the voyage she resumed her place in trans-Atlantic trade and after her sale to Hamburg parties ran as a packet between that city and New York. In 1868 she left Hamburg, Nov. 2nd, with 350 passengers and a general cargo and Dec. 21st, went ashore at Great Egg harbor, N. J. Her passengers were landed on the beach, her cargo was lightered, and she was towed to New York where extensive repairs were made. She was abandoned leaky and nearly full of water on Nov. 7, 1872, while bound from Hamburg to New York, in latitude 40° North, longitude 55° West. Her crew were picked up by the *Helmesbrand,* Captain Kjaer, and landed at Queenstown. Prior to her disaster the *Electric* had taken off the crew of British bark *Chase,* which was in a sinking condition.

ELECTRIC SPARK

MEDIUM clipper ship, built at Medford, Mass., by Hayden and Cudworth; launched Nov. 17, 1855. 184 x 40 x 24; 1216, old measurement; 1204 tons, new measurement. She was highly spoken of for symmetry of model and proportions as also for thoroughness of construction and is said to have so closely resembled the *Thatcher Magoun,* in hull and rigging, as to be called a sister-ship. During her whole career she was owned by T. Magoun & Son of Boston, who also owned the *Thatcher Magoun.*

The *Electric Spark* was engaged in trade, principally with San Francisco; in fact, the only other outward long voyage she made from an Atlantic port was in 1858/59 when, after discharging a guano cargo at London, she sailed from that port Aug. 23rd and went out to Sydney in 105 days. Captain Lothrop was in command. From Sydney she went to Hong Kong; sailed from Whampoa, Dec. 11, 1859, and arrived in New York, Mar. 5, 1860, after a very fast run of 84 days.

On her maiden voyage she left Boston, Dec. 24, 1855, and thereafter made seven passages from that port and one from New York, her second, to San Francisco. Her first run, 106 days, was the only one in which she did not meet with unfavorable conditions on one or more particular sections of the passage. On that occasion she had 21 days to the line; passed through the Straits of Le Maire, 44 days out; sighted the Horn the next day; crossed the equator on the 81st day, and then had 25 days of light winds to port. On her second passage, 118 days from New York, in 1857, she was again 21 days to the line and 67 days thereafter was on the line in the Pacific; then had 30 days to port with light winds and calms, with no trades. In 1860, her run from Boston was 142 days; 32 days to the line and throughout the whole passage, either gales, head winds or calms were encountered. On Sept. 16, 1862, when seven days out from Boston, on the third passage, a hurricane in the Gulf Stream took off the jib-boom, foresail, two lower topsails and two head sails. The decks were swept, two of the crew were carried overboard and lost and everything movable washed away. Later, while scudding in 35° South, she shipped a sea which stove boats, damaged decks and carried a sailor overboard. On the 72nd day out she crossed 50° South; 17 days later was in 50° Pacific, and 32 days thence was on the equator. Had no winds on the passage that would allow of a 200 mile run in any one day. In the Pacific, the three skysails were set for 44 days at one time without the halliards being even started. This passage occupied 145 days. In 1863/64, her run being 128 days, she had light winds and calms throughout, even while rounding the Horn; there, however, they were favorable enabling her to cover the distance between the 50's in nine days, with a smooth sea. In 1866, her time was 155 days, Captain Eastman reporting 42 days to the line and 40 days from the Pacific equator to port, she being within 90 miles of the Golden Gate for 18 days. Her passage in 1867 started well, the line being crossed on the 22nd day, but thereafter light winds and lack of trades prevailed, excepting off the Horn where 18 days were spent fighting heavy gales. She was 33 days from the Pacific equator to port, the whole passage being 139 days. On her last westward Cape Horn run, in 1868, there were 57 days which averaged under 100 miles. She was 33 days to the line; 70 days to the Horn; thence 39 days to the equator; had strong head winds from 24° South to 12° North. In 45° South, Atlantic, had a terrific gale in which sails were blown away, boats stove and decks damaged. The whole passage was 144 days.

From San Francisco she returned east, on four occasions, via Callao. In 1856, her time was 80 days thence to Hampton Roads. In 1864 she left Callao, Aug. 6th, for Queenstown; went thence to London and Shields; sailed from the latter port, Feb. 22, 1865, for Portland, Maine, and passed the Needles, Feb. 26th. On Apr. 3rd she went ashore on Hog Island, near Portland, but got off at high tide. The next day she stranded in the mud; was hauled off on the 6th and arrived at Boston, Apr. 29th. In 1860 she loaded at Baker's Island for Hampton Roads and made the passage in 94 days; thence to New York and continued on to Havre; arrived at Boston, July 3, 1861, from Havre. In 1862 she took a cargo of lumber from Puget Sound to Melbourne; went thence to Callao, in ballast, in the fast time of 44 days; sailed Jan. 18, 1863, for Queenstown, and made the run in 107 days; thence was ordered to London and arrived at Boston, Aug. 15th, in 37 days from London and 34 days from Deal. On her last two visits to San Francisco she loaded grain for Liverpool and made the runs in 119 and 144 days respectively.

On her passage from San Francisco to Callao, in 1857, the crew mutinied and on arrival out had had possession of the ship for two weeks. Captain Titcomb was locked in his cabin and would have starved but for a supply of preserved food, the existence of which was unknown to the cook and steward who were parties to the mutiny.

After her arrival at Liverpool, June 11, 1869, from San Francisco, the *Electric Spark* loaded back for the Pacific Coast port and sailed Sept. 22nd. On the night of the 26th she stranded at Blackwater Head, near Wexford, Ireland, due to the pilot mistaking lights, and on the night of the 28th she broke up during a southwesterly gale. All the crew had been taken off by a lifeboat. A small portion of the cargo and some stores were saved. The hull, sails and rigging were sold for £720 sterling. The loss to insurance companies was $100,000.

Capt. Laban Howes, Captain Titcomb and Capt. Asa Lothrop were, in turn, in command for the first three voyages; then Captain Candage for three voyages; Captain Eastman one and Capt. S. K. Leach from January 1867 until she was lost.

ELIZA F. MASON

BUILT at Baltimore in 1851. 127 x 30 x 15; 582 tons. Owned in Philadelphia. Sold at Hong Kong to go under the Chilian flag, June 1863. Later was Chilian bark *Emanuela*.

ELIZABETH F. WILLETS

CLIPPER ship, built by Charles Mallory, at Mystic, Conn., in 1854. 156 x 34 x 19; 825 tons. Owned by the builder as late as 1861. Sold at Shanghai in 1864. Like most of Mr. Mallory's productions she was a good sailer and a handsome craft.

She arrived at San Francisco, May 10, 1855, under command of Captain Sisson, 118 days from New York. Was 28 days to the line; 57 days to 50° South; 11 days from 50° to 50°; crossed the equator 90 days out and then had seven days of calms close to the California coast, being within 800 miles of the Golden Gate for 11 days. She then went to Callao in 62 days and took guano to England. Left Cardiff, Mar. 25, 1856, and went to Hong Kong. Sailed from Foo Chow, Oct. 25, 1856, and arrived at New York, Feb. 14, 1857, in 111 days from Foo Chow and 89 from Anjer. Arrived at San Francisco, Aug. 1, 1857, Capt. J. Warren Holmes of Mystic, in command, in 130 days from New York. Crossed the Pacific equator, 93 days out and was within 100 miles of destination for seven days. Sailed from San Francisco, Aug. 31st and was 94 days to New York. The *Ringleader*, which left San Francisco one day after her, reached New York 31 days later. Arrived at San Francisco, June 11, 1858, in 122 days from New York. Crossed the Pacific equator 97 days out and was thence 25 days to port. From San Francisco she took gold seekers to Fraser River, B. C., and returned to port of departure in six days from Victoria, Captain Holmes reporting the remarkable run of three days from Cape Flattery.

The *Willets* crossed the bar, outward bound from San Francisco, Sept. 1, 1858, in company with the *Skylark* and the *Raduga*, all bound for Honolulu and having an even start. At 2 P.M., Sept. 16th, the

Willets showed up rounding Diamond Head, followed at 3 o'clock by the *Skylark* and at 4 o'clock by the *Raduga*. At 5 P.M., the *West Wind* appeared, she having left San Francisco two days after the others. It was one of the finest marine scenes ever witnessed at Honolulu. From Honolulu the *Willets* went to New London. The *Willets*, Captain Gates, arrived at San Francisco, July 27, 1859, 111 days from New York. Was 21 days to the line; passed the Horn on the 64th day; was 11 days, 50° to 50° and only 17 days from 50° South, Pacific, to the equator, which she crossed 87 days out; and was only 48 days from Cape Horn to San Francisco. From San Francisco she went to the Sandwich Islands, thence to New Bedford, where she arrived Mar. 2, 1860, making the fast passage of 87 days.

At New York, Captain Barrett took her and was 163 days to San Francisco, thence 111 days back to New York, arriving Feb. 11, 1861. She then went out to China under Captain Henderson. She arrived at New York, Feb. 9, 1863, under command of Captain Williams, 96 days from Whampoa. Sailed from New York, Apr. 1, 1863; went to Shanghai and there was sold.

ELIZABETH KIMBALL

BUILT by Edward Dutton, at Marblehead, Mass., in 1853, for Edward Kimball of Salem. The *Kimball* was one of seven ships built at Marblehead, the first being the *Robert Hooper*, in 1849, and the last, the *Belle of the Sea*, in 1857. The *Kimball* was 998 tons, old measurement, a finely modeled medium clipper, crossing three skysail yards and was considered to be a fast sailer under ordinary conditions. Until 1863 she was engaged in trade, principally with the Orient.

The maiden voyage of the *Kimball* was a round between Boston and Calcutta. The outward cargo was ice, with barrels of apples stowed in sawdust, interspersed. Her mate, John D. Whidden, afterwards one of the best known American ship captains, recounts how the apples found a ready sale at Calcutta for fifty to seventy-five cents each. On the homeward passage, strong southwest monsoons, with accompanying bad weather, so prolonged her run down the Bay of Bengal that she did not pass Ceylon until the 24th day out. Off the southern end of that island, the headway of the ship was momentarily stopped as though she had struck a reef. The cause was actually a submarine earthquake. Off Madagascar, a leak of 2000 strokes per hour developed but on coming to anchor off Port Louis, Mauritius, and shifting stores aft, the leak, which was near the stem, was stopped. The voyage was not to terminate without another experience which came near being the end of the ship. She made the American coast in a dense fog and struck on the south shoal of Nantucket, but fortunately just scraped the outer edge and dragged through the sand. It was a close shave but the ship suffered no damage and arrived at Boston, 122 days from Calcutta.

She then loaded for San Francisco, sailing Dec. 10, 1855; was 25 days to the line; 37 days rounding the Horn, in heavy gales; 21 days from 50° South to the equator and 27 days thence to port; was within three days' sail of the Golden Gate for 15 days. Time of passage, 140 days. She then went to Calcutta in 90 days and left that port Sept. 11, 1856; was off the Cape, 52 days out; thence 27 days to the line; thence 24 days to Boston; a total of 103 days.

On June 9, 1863, the *Kimball* arrived at San Francisco in 52 days from Hong Kong and later was sold to Pope and Talbot. Thereafter, her operations were entirely in the Pacific, outward cargoes being lumber from Puget Sound for overseas ports or for San Francisco. Her passages were consistently better than average, frequent runs from San Francisco to the Sound being six or seven days. In 1872 she reached Port Gamble in four days and seven hours from the Golden Gate.

The mishaps attending the career of the *Kimball* were many. In addition to those heretofore referred to, may be mentioned the following. In May 1861, while bound to Cork from Callao, she put into Valparaiso in distress, leaking badly. In January 1865 she got ashore on Trial Island, near Victoria, B. C. The repairs at San Francisco cost $18,000. In May 1866 she arrived at San Francisco, 77 days from Newcastle, N. S. W. Had sprung a leak, due to defective caulking, and been forced to jettison part of her coal cargo; loss and damage $1000. In December, of the same year, she sprung a leak after leaving Coronel for San Francisco and was forced to put into Valparaiso; cause given again as defective caulking and repairs cost $4300. In December 1867, while beating out of San Francisco Bay, she got ashore off Black Point, but received no damage. In 1865 she was in difficulties off Dungeness, Puget Sound, and lost an anchor and chain.

On Mar. 24, 1873, the *Kimball* left Port Gamble for Iquique and on Apr. 20th, in 28° South, 122° West, about 600 miles from Easter Island, she sprung a leak and the deck load of lumber was jettisoned. Every effort was made to free her, but unsuccessfully, and it was determined to beach her on Easter Island. She was run ashore with 15 feet of water in the hold, which was 18 feet deep. The population of the island was found to be a Frenchman and about 75 Kanakas. All the provisions in the ship and part of the rigging and sails were saved. A ten-ton schooner was built of materials saved from the wreck and on July 29th, Captain Keller, his wife and eight others, left for Tahiti. They made the distance, 2550 miles, in 24 days. The two mates, with eight of the crew, remained on Easter Island with plenty of provisions and were finally taken off by a French steamer sent to their assistance. The *Kimball* was valued at $15,000; cargo, $8000. Captain Freeman was in command of the *Kimball* on her first voyage, and was succeeded by Captain Condon. In 1861, Captain Wilson had her, and in 1863-1865, Captain Grindle. Captain Frost was master in 1866, being followed by Captain Bunker. Captain Keller had been in command for several years prior to her loss.

"Don Quixote," 1470 tons, built at Medford, Mass, in 1853
From a copy of a daguerreotype showing her on the stocks

"DREADNOUGHT," 1413 TONS, BUILT AT NEWBURYPORT, MASS., IN 1853

From a lithograph by Currier, after the painting by J. E. Butterworth, showing the ship off Sandy Hook, Feb. 23, 1854, in 19 days from Liverpool

"Dreadnought," 1413 tons, built at Newburyport, Mass., in 1853

From a painting in the Macpherson Collection

"ELECTRIC," 1046 TONS, BUILT AT MYSTIC, CONN, IN 1853
From a lithograph by Lemercier, Paris, showing the ship off Sandy Hook

ELLEN FOSTER

MEDIUM clipper ship, built in 1852, by Joshua T. Foster, at Medford, Mass. 180 x 37 x 24; 996 tons. Owned by J. & A. Tirrell of Boston. For a figurehead she had a representation of the wife of the builder. Captain Scudder took command.

So far as available records show, the *Foster* has no remarkable sailing records to her credit and she appears to have met with more than a fair share of unfavorable weather conditions on many voyages. The first three years of her career were spent in the East India trade and in 1853 she appears to have been over 150 days from Calcutta to Boston. Between 1855 and 1862 she made three passages from Boston to San Francisco, being 147, 167 and 165 days respectively. On only one of these runs did she have any favorable weather and that was in 1857, when Captain Robinson reported being 22½ days to the equator and 53 days to Staten Island. But there good fortune ceased for she battled heavy gales and storms off Cape Horn for 42 successive days. In 1855-1856 she made three passages back and forth between San Francisco and Hong Kong; was 53 days on each of the two outward runs and 49 days on the one return. Of her homeward passages from Callao, with guano, none appear to have been better than average.

In July 1867 she sailed from Callao for Hampton Roads, but was forced to return to port in distress. The Belgium ship *Frederich*, formerly the American ship *Gosport*, was chartered to take her cargo to destination. The *Foster* was condemned and sold. After some repairs were made she left Callao for Puget Sound, to load a cargo of lumber. When close to her destination, in December 1867, she went ashore at Neah Bay and broke up. She was in ballast and was insured for $20,000. At the time of her loss she was commanded by Captain Anderson and owned by Charles Parker of Callao, who had purchased her from Howes & Crowell of Boston, her owners for several years.

EMILY FARNUM

BUILT by George Raynes, at Portsmouth, N. H., in 1854. 194 x 35 x 23; 1119 tons. W. Jones & Co., Portsmouth, owners. Wrecked near Cape Flattery, November 1875.

EMPRESS

BUILT by Paul Curtis, at East Boston, in 1856. 193 x 38 x 23; 1293 tons. H. Harbeck & Co., New York, owners. Sold to go under British flag, in 1863. In 1886, was the German ship *Elisabeth*.

EMPRESS OF THE SEAS

CLIPPER ship, built by Donald McKay, at East Boston, Mass.; launched Jan. 14, 1853. Length of deck, 230 feet; from knightheads to taffrail, 240 x 43 x 27; 2197 tons, American measurement, old style; 1647 tons, British measurement. Dead rise, 27 inches; sheer, 36 inches. She had three laid decks; was yellow metaled to 20½ feet forward, and 21½ feet aft; draft, fully loaded, 24 feet. The bow was ornamented with a full-length female figure in white garments, the left hand extended, grasping a globe, while the right hand, reposing by the side, held the sceptre of the seas. Her ends were long and quite sharp, although not to the extent of many of her contemporaries; the lines, concave below, merged into convex at the water-line. The stern was semi-elliptical and exceedingly graceful. The dimensions of the spars on the mainmast were: lower mast, 91¾ feet long by 38 inches in diameter; topmast, 53 feet by 19 inches; topgallant, 28, by 14½; royal, 18, by 12; skysail mast, 14, by 10, with a 12-foot pole. The corresponding yards measured; 90 feet by 24 inches; 70, by 19; 53½, by 14; 42½, by 10; 31, by 7½. The lower masts were of hard pine, hooped; she carried single topsails and crossed a skysail yard on the mainmast only. A topgallant forecastle accommodated a portion of the crew and a large house on deck took care of the remainder. The trunk cabin was built into a long, half-poop deck.

The original intention of her builder was to operate her on his own account, but when she was about half completed, he accepted the offer of purchase made by William Wilson & Son, of Baltimore, at the price of $125,000, which netted a good profit. Her new owners sent her to New York to load in Oakford's line of California clippers.

The *Empress* left New York, Mar. 13, 1853, with 3100 tons, weight and measurement, general merchandise, on which her freight list was $104,000 and arrived at San Francisco, July 12th, in a passage of 121 days. Her captain, Putnam, reported being 25 days to the line and nine miles east of Cape Horn on the 59th day out; crossed the equator 30 days later. The clipper ship *Surprise*, which had left New York in company with her, reached their common destination three days in advance. The *Empress* then went from San Francisco to Callao, in 49 days, and from the latter port was 75 days to New York. Captain Oakford then assumed command, and took his ship to London via Quebec. Sailed from London, Nov. 28, 1854, and was 97 days to Bombay. Returned to England and thence to New York.

On June 3, 1856, the *Empress* arrived at San Francisco, 115 days from New York. Captain Wilson, formerly her chief mate, was in command and reported being 26 days to the line; passed through the Straits of Le Maire, 54 days out; was 11 days off the Horn, in heavy gales; and crossed the equator, 89 days out. Made 1200 miles in one stretch of four consecutive days and on one day covered 295 miles under single reefs. From San Francisco she went to Callao, in 49 days; thence in 76 days to Hampton Roads; arrived at New York, Jan. 17, 1857, and while at anchor in the North River, was somewhat damaged by ice. Sailed from New York, July 13th, under command of Captain Haley, and was 124 days to San Francisco. Was 27 days to the line; passed Staten Island on the 60th day out and was 18 days thence to Cape Pillar; crossed the equator, 104 days out.

Sailed from San Francisco, Dec. 17th, for Elide Island, to load guano for Baltimore. Arrived at the latter port, Aug. 8, 1858.

The *Empress* made no further passages to California. For a time she was commanded by Capt. William B. Cobb, of Brewster, Mass., who had formerly been master of the bark *J. Godfrey* and who subsequently was in different steamships plying across the Pacific. Eventually the *Empress* was operated between England and Australia. On June 1, 1861, she sailed from Liverpool for Melbourne and arrived out, Aug. 6th, in a remarkably fast passage of 66½ days. On Dec. 19th, following, she was burned at Queenscliff Bight, Port Phillip, becoming a total loss.

ENDEAVOR

MEDIUM clipper ship, built at East Boston, in 1856, by Robert E. Jackson. Length over all, 192 feet; deck, 184: 6 x 36: 6 x 22: 2; 1137 tons, old measurement; 960 tons, new measurement. Dead rise, 12 inches; swell of sides, 6 inches; sheer, 4 feet. Her original owners were Cunningham Brothers of Boston; later she belonged to Frank Hathaway of New Bedford and New York. She had quite sharp ends for a medium clipper and bore the reputation of being a good sailer. Capt. Alfred Doane of Orleans, Mass., was in command until 1868, when he took the new ship *Cleopatra*. He was succeeded by Capt. W. C. Warland, who, after the loss of the *Endeavor*, was in the *Annie M. Smull*.

The *Endeavor* was built for the California and China trade and operated out of New York. She reached New York from Boston on Apr. 21, 1856, in tow of the *Enoch Train*, and sailed for San Francisco, May 18th and reached her destination in 131 days. Over this course she made in all eight runs, the last being in 1869. In all, except two instances, her departure from New York was taken during the unfavorable season and the memoranda of her various passages show generally light weather voyages. On this route her average is 133 days, the longest being 146 days. On the shortest, 122 days, in

1858, she was 33 days to the line, and made the Cape Horn passage in eight days; was off the pitch of the Cape, 64 days out; crossed the line on the 93rd day and was then 11 days making 10 degrees of latitude. On her passage of 128 days, in 1869, she was 48 days from 50° South, to San Francisco, being within 600 miles of the Golden Gate for 12 days. On another occasion she did not furl a royal from latitude 46° South, to port.

Her record in trade with the Far East shows up more favorably. Leaving Manila, in February 1866, she was 101 days to New York. In September 1862 she left Foo Chow and was 100 days to New York, being 75 days from Anjer and 47 from the Cape. The following year she left Foo Chow, also in September, and was 104 days to New York, being 48 days from the Cape. In 1856 she was 103 days from Shanghai to New York. She made one run from San Francisco to New York, 103 days, in 1861. The previous year she had been 89 days from Manzanillo, Mexico, to New York.

Towards the close of her career the *Endeavor* made several voyages to Japan and was there destroyed by fire in 1875.

EUREKA

EXTREME clipper ship, launched Feb. 9, 1851, from the yard of Jacob A. Westervelt, New York, and built for the account of Chambers & Heiser of that city. 171 x 36: 5 x 21: 6; 1041 tons, old measurement. She was very sharp and much was expected of her but she appears to have been very unfortunate and not successful and is said to have never been a popular vessel in any trade. Her original owners sold her in June 1859 to N. L. & G. Griswold of New York, for the low price of $25,000 and she was thoroughly overhauled. In 1863 she was sold to J. Stanwood of St. John, New Brunswick, and went under the British flag without change of name. In June 1866 she was condemned at Calcutta and her cargo forwarded by the ship *Richard Busteed*.

In April 1851 she, with other clippers, was "up" at New York for

San Francisco. Competent authorities predicted that she and the new clipper, *Witchcraft,* would make the passage in 115 days, while the time allowed the *Flying Cloud* and the *N. B. Palmer,* also new ships, was 95 days each. By a singular coincidence both the *Eureka* and *Witchcraft* lost spars or masts and put into ports en route, the *Witchcraft* into Rio and the *Eureka* into Valparaiso. The former was 127 days gross, 107 days net, from New York to the Pacific coast port, her time from Rio being only 62 days. The *Eureka* arrived out after a passage of 174 days gross, being 45 days from Valparaiso to destination, but Captain Auchincloss did not report the number of days she was actually under sail. The time of the *Flying Cloud* was 89 days and 21 hours, and of the *N. B. Palmer,* 106 days. From San Francisco the *Eureka* went to Hong Kong in 52 days, and leaving that port, Feb. 9, 1852, made the run to New York in 101 days.

Captain Welch then took command of the *Eureka* and arrived at San Francisco, Sept. 7, 1852, in 138 days from New York. She then took some 250 Chinese passengers to Hong Kong, via Honolulu, having a fair passage of about 48 sailing days. Later she loaded at Manila for New York; sailed Mar. 18, 1853, and arrived home July 16th, in a run of 120 days. Captain Whipple now took command, and leaving New York, Oct. 5, 1853, arrived at San Francisco, Feb. 6, 1854, 123 days out. Was 33 days to the line; 18 days rounding Cape Horn; 22 days from 50° South, Pacific, to the equator and when within two days' sail of destination, was detained a week in a dense fog. After crossing to Hong Kong, she took her departure therefrom May 8th, about the poorest season for a quick run, and did not clear the Straits of Sunda until the 33rd day out. From Java Head, however, she was only 29 days to the Cape and 54 days to the equator, both of which runs were the fastest made by homeward bound Indiamen about that time. Reached New York, Aug. 25, 1854, in 109 days from Whampoa, and 76 days from Java Head.

After making quite a lengthy round voyage between New York and China, the *Eureka* again loaded at her home port for San Francisco, this time under command of Captain Canfield. She arrived out,

Aug. 26, 1856, after a passage of 120 days; was 26 days to the line; 55 days to 50° South; 10 days rounding the Cape; 31 days in the South Pacific and 24 days from the equator to destination. Then crossed to Shanghai in 54 days and remained for a time on the coast. In 1858, Captain Lane was in command. In 1859, following her sale at New York, she went out to China. On June 24, 1861, she arrived at San Francisco, 46 days from Hong Kong, under Capt. Benjamin F. Cutler, who subsequently was for many years prominent in the China trade in connection with his command, the *Mary Whitridge*. She sailed from San Francisco, Aug. 10, 1861, for Melbourne and ran down in 61 days.

The *Eureka* arrived at New York, Apr. 10, 1863, from Macao, Oct. 30, 1862, 89 days from Anjer and 39 days from St. Helena. In December 1863, as the British ship *Eureka*, Captain Hale, she was at Boston, loading for Melbourne. Captain Hale continued in command until she was condemned in 1866.

EUTERPE

MEDIUM clipper ship, built in 1854, by Horace Merriam, at Rockland, Maine; launched Dec. 7th. 234 x 43: 8 x 24: 6; 1985 tons, old measurement; 1509 tons, new measurement. Original owners, Foster & Nickerson of New York. She proved to be a fast vessel and was a good carrier, having on her first trip to California 3400 tons general merchandise, weight and measurement.

On her maiden voyage she sailed from New York, Jan. 31, 1855, under command of Capt. George W. Brown; was 24 days to the line and 66 days thence to Calcutta, arriving May 1st, in a passage of 90 days. Sailed from Calcutta (Saugor Roads) on Aug. 12th; was off the Cape in 39 days, equal to the record then and not known to have ever been beaten; was 46 days from the Cape to London, the whole run occupying 85 days, which was the best up to that time as well as for many years thereafter. She was the first ship to enter the new

Victoria Docks, being too large and deep for any of the other London docks.

Crossing to New York, the *Euterpe* loaded for San Francisco and sailed May 30, 1856, under command of Captain Arey; was 34 days to the line; passed the Horn, 62 days out; crossed the equator, in Pacific, in the fine time of 83 days from New York, but thereafter had light and head winds for the remaining 32 days; passage, 115 days according to dates, but Captain Arey claimed 112 days. There arrived at San Francisco, within a few hours after her, the *Robin Hood*, in 125 days; the *John Gilpin*, in 139 days; the *Thatcher Magoun*, in 121 days; and the *Nor'wester*, in 132 days, all first-class clippers, so the *Euterpe's* passage must be considered exceptionally fast for that season. From San Francisco she went to Callao, in 47 days, and from there reached New York via Hampton Roads, June 30, 1857, in 80 days. She again went out to San Francisco, arriving Jan. 15, 1859, in 135 days from New York. Captain Arey reported 39 days to the line; fell to leeward of St. Roque and lost three days beating; was 19 days off the Horn, in bad weather, having hatch-house and quarter-boat stove, sails split, etc.; was 23 days in the South Pacific and 24 days from equator to port, being within 300 miles of the Golden Gate for 10 days. Had head gales most of the passage, with more than half of the crew sick the entire trip. From San Francisco she went to Valparaiso and thence home.

The *Euterpe* arrived at San Francisco, June 25, 1860, in 118 days from New York. Entered the harbor with pilot aboard and grounded in the fog just outside of Fort Point; got off with four feet of water in the hold after lightering 140 tons of cargo; total expense (partial and general average), $24,000. Repaired and sailed for Callao, Aug. 1st, making the run to that port in 40 days, and was 78 days thence to Hampton Roads, an excellent round voyage. She made her last appearance at San Francisco on Nov. 2, 1861, in 132 days from New York, returning there direct in 94 days, according to Captain Arey's report; was 43 days to the Horn; 69 days to the line and had 11 days of strong northerly gales after passing the Bermudas.

From June 1862 until April 1863, the *Euterpe* was under charter to the United States Government and was used by the army as a hospital ship. She did not use her canvas but was towed between New York, Fortress Monroe and other points by navy steamers. In June 1863 she left Philadelphia for Panama with a cargo of coal and thereafter was engaged in general trade, principally in the Atlantic. She was at Shields, Feb. 1, 1865, from Hamburg, Captain Arey still in command. In the fall of 1867 she received considerable repairs at New York and was reported sold to A. Jacquemot. Captain Pennell was made commander but was succeeded by Capt. George W. Leach, who remained in command until her loss. She left Callao Apr. 28, 1871, for Falmouth, and June 2nd sprung aleak. Two days later she was abandoned and Captain Leach with 16 of the crew reached the coast of Brazil, in the long boat, June 14th. The mate and eight of the crew were lost.

EXPOUNDER

CALLED a medium clipper, but was built more for carrying capacity than for speed. Launched at Charlestown, Mass., in April 1856; Joshua Magoun was her builder. Dimensions for measurement purposes; 171 x 37 x 23; 1176 tons. Came out some months after the *Defender* was built by Donald McKay, which was so named after Daniel Webster, who was popularly known as "The Defender of the Constitution and Expounder of the same," hence the origin of *Expounder's* name. She was owned by Paul Sears and late in the 60's was registered in the name of J. Henry Sears & Co., of Boston, which firm had been established in 1863, after Captain Sears had retired from the sea, he having turned over the command of his ship *Franklin Haven,* to Captain Bartlett at San Francisco, in the summer of 1861.

The maiden passage of the *Expounder* was to England. She there loaded coal at Cardiff for San Francisco; arrived out Jan. 19, 1857, in 140 days' passage, Captain Foster in command. From San Francisco she went to Callao, in 61 days; arrived at Baltimore, Nov. 24,

1857, in 94 days from Callao. On Mar. 13, 1860, she was again at San Francisco, in 140 days from Boston, Captain Knowles; returned East, via Callao. These two runs are the only ones she made to San Francisco, prior to the summer of 1867. The *Expounder* stranded on North Breaker, Stone Inlet, South Carolina, Mar. 26, 1863, inward bound, indicating that she was then serving as a Navy transport. She arrived at Liverpool, Dec. 30, 1873, captain's name and port of departure not stated.

Capt. C. H. Allyn of Hyannis, commanded the *Expounder* some 8 or 10 years. Capt. R. Irvine was master in 1871.

For a time, Capt. George Crocker of Brewster, Mass., was in command. He had previously been in the ship *Wm. A. Cooper.* Captain Crocker died while in command of the ship *Electra,* in 1883, while on a passage from Batavia to Manila.

The *Expounder* was sold in October 1881 and converted into a barge of 651 tons. In the 1888 register she is listed as a two-masted schooner, owned by the Philadelphia and Reading Railway Co., of Philadelphia. Her depth was given as 15:7 and her tonnage, 651 net. Her name disappears from the registers in 1906.

FAIR WIND

MEDIUM clipper ship, built by E. & H. O. Briggs, at South Boston, Mass.; launched Oct. 12, 1855. 195 x 36: 10 x 24; 1299 tons. She was called a sister ship of the *Mameluke,* both being fairly good sailers and large carriers, their actual capacity being about 1700 weight or 2400 measurement tons. They were quite deep for their breadth, having two laid decks and beams for a third. The figurehead of the *Fair Wind* was an image of Aurora. Henry Hallet & Co., of Boston, were her owners.

On her first voyage the *Fair Wind* left Boston, Nov. 25, 1855, Captain Allen in command; was 32 days to the line; 65 days to the Horn and 12 days off it in heavy weather; crossed the equator, 112 days out and arrived at San Francisco, Apr. 11, 1856, in 138 days.

Sailed, May 2nd, for Calcutta; put into Batavia, July 12th, and arrived at Calcutta, Aug. 7th. Loaded for Boston and sailed from Sand Heads, Oct. 15th; was 54 days to the Cape; 75 days to the line and 33 days thence to Boston, arriving Jan. 31, 1857, in 108 days' passage. Captain Allen died at Calcutta and Captain Strout brought the vessel to Boston.

She left Boston, Apr. 1st, for San Francisco; put into Rio, May 27th, 56 days out, to obtain medical aid for the captain; left Rio, June 10th, and on the 12th and 15th had two severe gales, during which she had boats stove and deck gear damaged. Was 19 days from Rio to 50° South; 19 days thence to 50° in the Pacific, during 11 of which, off the Horn, had royals set continually in light winds; crossed the equator, 61 days from Rio, after which had light winds and calms and was within 700 miles of San Francisco for 12 days. The passage was made in 146 sailing days from Boston and 90 days from Rio. Her freight list on this voyage was $24,458, while that of the clipper *Flying Dutchman*, of about the same registered tonnage but of a much sharper model and hence smaller carrier, making the voyage at the same time, was only $18,275.

From San Francisco the *Fair Wind* went to Melbourne, thence to Peru for guano and sailed from Callao, May 20, 1858, for France. After crossing to New York, she went out to Valparaiso in 102 days; thence to the Chincha Islands and left Callao, Dec. 29, 1859, for Hampton Roads, under Captain Hatch. On Dec. 7, 1860, she arrived at San Francisco, 133 days from New York, with Capt. Elkanah Crowell, formerly master of the *Boston Light*, in command. Sailed Jan. 12, 1861, for Baker's Island and anchored off Honolulu on the 21st, in a passage of 8 days and 18 hours, which has never been beaten to this date. Her daily runs were:—209 miles (19 hours' run)—243 —261—213—224—254—215—260—225 (23 hours' run). Total distance made, 2104 miles; the shortest distance ever made on this run by a sailing vessel and only some 20 miles greater than the shortest possible direct steamship route. Continuing the voyage she loaded guano at Baker's Island, for Hampton Roads for orders, and when near destination, went ashore on Hog Island. She was finally pulled off by the tug *S. R. Spalding*, with three feet of water in the hold and a broken rudder. Men were sent to her to relieve the crew, who were exhausted by pumping, and also carpenters to make repairs, after which she was towed to New York, arriving Aug. 17th, 105 days from Baker's Island. After repairing damages she loaded coal for account of the Pacific Mail Steamship Company, for Acapulco, where she was reported in port discharging, Feb. 18, 1862; had cleared from New York, Oct. 14, 1861. Continuing this voyage she loaded at the Chincha Islands; sailed from Callao, Aug. 19th, for Cork; was ordered to Aberdeen, arriving there Jan. 5, 1863. Sailed Feb. 19th; went to Sunderland to load coal for Hong Kong; left Shields, Mar. 8th, and arrived at destination, June 29, 1863, in 113 days' passage. Went thereafter to Manila, crossing thence to San Francisco, where she arrived Jan. 16, 1864, 75 days out. Captain Crowell reported being 17 days in the China Sea and 36 days from the coast of Japan to destination, in head winds with much fog and rain. From San Francisco returned to New York direct in 114 days. She again loaded coal for the steamship company and reached San Francisco, Feb. 1, 1865, Capt. Seth Taylor in command, 137 days from New York. She remained in port until Mar. 2nd when she left with her inward cargo for San Juan del Sur, arriving about Apr. 8th.

Shortly after returning East, in 1866, the *Fair Wind* was sold for British account, continuing under her original name. In 1869 she was thoroughly overhauled. From 1870 to 1875 she is listed as owned by Moore & Rawle of Plymouth, England.

FANNY McHENRY

BUILT by A. & G. T. Sampson, at East Boston, in 1854. 194 x 39 x 23; 1237 tons. G. McHenry & Co., Philadelphia, Pa., owners. Sold to Thomas Richardson & Co., of Philadelphia, and renamed *Philadelphia*. Resold and went under British flag about December 1862, as *Sanspareil*, of Liverpool.

FEARLESS

EXTREME clipper ship, designed by Samuel H. Pook and built by A. & G. T. Sampson, at East Boston. Launched July 28, 1853. 191 x 36: 5 x 22; 1183 68/95 tons, old measurement; 909 tons, new measurement. She was a very sharp ship with beautiful yacht-like lines, very square yards, with single topsails and carried nothing above royals. She was owned by William F. Weld & Co., of Boston, whose fleet, which included many clippers, was the largest belonging to any firm in America. They were painted dark green or what painters called tea color, and their house flag, a leaping black horse, was always conspicuous among the burgees flying from lofty ships in Far Eastern ports, particularly in the East Indies.

The *Fearless* was a fast sailer and has a good record. On her second passage to San Francisco, Capt. Nehemiah Manson reported crossing the Pacific equator on Nov. 3, 1854; made the Farallon Islands on the 18th, some hours over 15 days, and entered port the following day. His total passage had been 124 days, but head winds and gales had been encountered all the way from the Platte to the latitude of Valparaiso. Her average of six trips from San Francisco to Manila is 49 days; fastest two, 36 and 39 days; slowest, 59 days. There were three runs from San Francisco to Hong Kong in 47, 56 and 48 days respectively; one to Singapore, via Batavia, in 79 days and one to New York, direct, in 97 days. Leaving Manila in March 1854, she arrived at Boston in 86 days, which is but two days longer than the record, having circumnavigated the globe in 9 months and 12 days including all detentions. The following year, leaving Manila in February, her time to Boston was also reported as 86 days, but on this run she was 77 days from Anjer as against 74 the previous trip. In 1856 she was 95 days, Manila to Boston, and in 1863, was 100 days on the same course. In 1860 she was 107 days from Boston to Hong Kong. Homeward bound she left Manila, Sept. 26th, and arrived at New York, Jan. 15, 1861, in a passage of 111 days. In 1865 she left Manila, July 22nd; was 26 days to Anjer, thence 30 days to the Cape, where was detained four days by heavy gales; was thence 25 days to the line and arrived at Boston, Nov. 8th, in 83 days from Anjer and 109 from Manila.

Aside from the outward passages mentioned, the *Fearless* made 11 other runs from Eastern ports, prior to 1868, all of which were to San Francisco; seven from Boston, and four from New York. Eliminating her last run, which was 163 days, in 1868-1869, her average for the 10 is 125 days; fastest, 114 days; slowest, 139 days. On her passage out, in 1856, Captain Manson had 57 days to the Horn, off which for 14 days he encountered the worst weather he had ever experienced but made the whole run in 127 days. While off Cape Horn, on her passage from Boston in 1867, second mate Haskell was shot dead in the cabin by third mate Guptill, who was taken to San Francisco in double irons. She arrived at San Francisco, Jan. 11, 1869, Captain Ballard in command, 163 days from New York, with a cargo of railroad iron. The *Rattler*, from the same port with the same cargo, arrived the same day in 130 days. The *Fearless* was 43 days to the line and 35 days off the Horn in strong westerly gales.

Between 1853 and 1858, the *Fearless* was commanded by Capt. Nehemiah Manson; then followed Captains Devens, Holt and George W. Homan, the latter having been in the ship *Edith Rose*. Captain Drew of Gardiner, Me., took the *Fearless*, late in 1864, and left her in 1868 to take the *Franklin*, belonging to the same owners. Captain Drew was very proud of his ship, painted several fine pictures of her and praised her performances in newspaper articles. Subsequently Captains Ballard, Cromwell, Rich, Andrew Smith and James F. Tilton, all had her between 1870 and 1875. On Apr. 22, 1874, while bound from New York to Shanghai, she had her bulwarks and part of her house washed away.

On July 28, 1875, the *Fearless* was sold by William F. Weld & Co., to George Leary, for $18,000. In October 1878 she was sold at Hamburg, for Norwegian account, for $6500, her name being changed to *Johanne*. She hailed from Mandal, was bark rigged and engaged in the timber trade with Nova Scotia. In June 1885 she was surveyed at Halifax, but had no class.

FLEETWING

MEDIUM clipper ship, built in 1854, by Hayden & Cudworth, at Medford, Mass., for Crowell, Brooks & Co., of Boston. 167 x 34 x 21: 8; 896 tons, American, old measurement; 829, by new system; 786 tons, British measurement. Her figurehead was an eagle. She was a handsome ship of rakish appearance and was recognized as a fast sailer although having no record passages to her credit. Capt. Laban Howes was in command until 1861; then Captain Kelly, until 1865, after which Captain Bray had her for two round voyages, Captain Thatcher for three and Capt. Uriel Doane for one. In 1873, Captain Guest took command, the ownership of the *Fleetwing* then being vested in Howes & Crowell of Boston. Her last American owner was Vernon H. Brown of New York.

From her maiden passage in 1854 until 1873, inclusive, all of the outward runs of the *Fleetwing* were to San Francisco, via Cape Horn, with the exception of one from Liverpool to Calcutta in 1861. In 1864 her run to San Francisco was from Rio, with the cargo of the condemned ship *Undaunted*, her passage being 85 days. Those from New York or Boston numbered 14, their average being 134 days. On seven of these she took her departure during the unfavorable season and averaged 38 days from port to the line, with 47 days as the longest, over that section. There also fell to her lot adverse winds in the South Atlantic, long spells of heavy weather off the Horn, and light and variable winds in the North Pacific, so that her average for these seven passages is 147 days, the longest being 158 days. On the other seven runs she left port during the fair to good season and her average for these is 120 days, there being two of 113 days; one each of 114, 121 and 122 days and two of 128 days. On two occasions she was 19 days from the Pacific equator crossing to destination and in another instance she ran up from 50° South, Pacific, to port in 41 days. On her passage in 1868, 128 days, Captain Bray reported that for 93 days the course had been full and by the wind, with the yards against the back-stays; was within 350 miles of the Golden Gate for 10 days.

Of her return passages from San Francisco, one was to New York in 103 days; two to Boston in 112 and 119 days and one to Cork in 120 days. From the Pacific guano islands to Hampton Roads she made one passage of 111 days and to Cork and Hamburg, one each, of 120 and 90 days. Two were from Calcutta to Boston in 98 and 97 days. In 1855 she was 44 days from San Francisco to Hong Kong and 108 days from Whampoa to New York. This was her only call at a port in China. She made three homeward passages from Manila but details are lacking. In 1870 and in 1871 she was six months, three days and six months, one day, from San Francisco to Liverpool via Mazatlan and Altata, long delays being experienced in loading her cargoes of dye woods. In 1864, bound to Baker's Island from San Francisco, she put into Honolulu, 10 days out, to receive gear and supplies for the Island.

In 1873-1874, the *Fleetwing* went out from New York to Melbourne, arriving Feb. 25, 1874; thence to Newcastle, where she loaded coal for Hong Kong; thence to Manila and New York. She again went out to Australia and was sold to go under the British flag, without change of name, but her rig was altered to that of a bark. She was employed, thereafter, in the lumber trade between British Columbia and ports in the Pacific. Finally, sailed from Victoria, B. C., Oct. 30, 1884, for Melbourne; and off Cape Flattery had a heavy gale lasting 14 days and sprung a leak; all hands being exhausted from pumping she was forced to put back. After part of her cargo was discharged she was repaired and sailed again Dec. 18th. She reached Melbourne, Mar. 27, 1885, where she was found to be in such poor condition that she was condemned.

"Empress of the Seas," 2197 tons, built at East Boston, in 1853

From a drawing by Charles E. Bateman

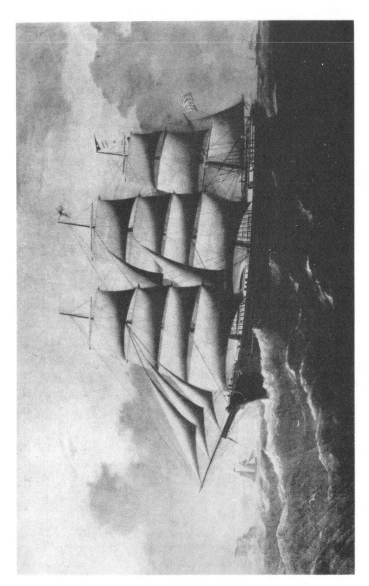

"EXPOUNDER," 1176 TONS, BUILT AT CHARLESTOWN, MASS., IN 1856

From a painting by an English artist showing the ship off Fastnet Light

"FEARLESS," 1183 TONS, BUILT AT EAST BOSTON, IN 1853

"FLYING CLOUD," 1782 TONS, BUILT AT EAST BOSTON, IN 1851

From an oil painting in the Macpherson Collection

FLEETWOOD

MEDIUM clipper ship, built in 1852, by George Raynes, at Portsmouth, N. H., 663 tons, old measurement. She was owned by Sewell, Johnson & Co., of Boston, and during her whole sea life was commanded by Capt. Frank Dale. Aside from her maiden voyage to San Francisco and a round between Boston and London, she was operated between her home port and Calcutta.

Completing her first passage she arrived at San Francisco, Apr. 13, 1853, in 130 days from Boston, a run considerably slower than was made by other ships of her size and class, about that time. From San Francisco she crossed to Shanghai, arriving June 29th. Sailed, Nov. 3rd, and put back next day for medical advice for Captain Dale. Sailed again, Nov. 14th, and made the passage to Boston in 124 days; 81 days from Java Head. Cleared from Boston, May 3, 1854, for London and arrived back at Boston, Sept. 13th, 39 days from the Downs and 32 days from the Lizard. Sailed from Boston, Oct. 25, 1854; was 34 days to the line and 82 days thence to Calcutta, a total of 116 days. Left Calcutta, Apr. 16, 1855, and arrived at Boston, Aug. 27th, 133 days out. Sailed from Boston, Oct. 16, 1855; was 112 days to Calcutta and on return arrived at her home port, Sept. 1, 1856.

In completion of her last India voyage, the *Fleetwood* sailed from Calcutta, July 22, 1858, and arrived at Boston, Dec. 10th, from Newport, where she had put in. On Feb. 12, 1859, she left Boston for Honolulu and Tahiti. Off Cape Horn she encountered very heavy weather and was driven backward. At 5 o'clock in the morning of May 3rd, while running under single-reefed courses and a close-reefed topsail, she collided with an iceberg and rapidly filled. She was well provided with boats, as besides her own three, she had two large mission boats. The mate and four seamen embarked in one boat while Captain Dale, his wife and son, the passenger and the remainder of the crew went in another. The latter boat and its 17 occupants were never heard of. The mate's boat was picked up by the

British bark *Imogene,* on May 8th, and its five men were landed at Pernambuco. The *Fleetwood* was insured for $30,000; her freight money for $10,000, and cargo, $71,266.

FLORA TEMPLE

MEDIUM clipper ship, built in 1853 by J. Abraham, at Baltimore, Md. Owned by Abraham & Ashcroft of the same port. She was a handsome ship with good lines and registered 1915 tons, old measurement.

Under command of Captain Meyers she arrived at San Francisco, Feb. 19, 1856, in 160 days from New York, with adverse weather conditions throughout. She was 36 days to the line and had 40 days of violent gales off Cape Horn; light trades, variable winds and calms prevailed in the run up the Pacific. From San Francisco she was 51 days to Callao and took guano from the Chincha Islands to Hampton Roads.

On Sept. 14, 1857, she arrived at San Francisco in 129 days from New York. Captain Cole, who was in command, reported being 34 days to the line; thence 30 days to 50° South; was two days getting through the Straits of Le Maire and then experienced a succession of strong southwest winds; crossed the equator 94 days out; in the North Pacific had a number of sails split in a severe gale. When 117 days out was 500 miles from San Francisco and was off port for six days. She then crossed to Hong Kong in 46 days.

The *Flora Temple* made no further passages to California but was employed in trade with China. On Oct. 9, 1859, she left Macao for Havana, with coolies. Six days later she struck an unknown rock in latitude 10° North, longitude 113° East and foundered. The coolies had laid a plan to take the ship a short time before the disaster but it was not caused thereby. The loss of life was very heavy, 18 out of the 49 whites aboard and 850 coolies being drowned.

FLORENCE

MEDIUM clipper ship, built by Samuel Hall, at East Boston, to the order of J. M. and R. B. Forbes of Boston, and their old and esteemed friend and employee, Capt. Philip Dumaresq; launched Feb. 23, 1856. Captain Dumaresq had practically retired from the sea when his wife and daughter unexpectedly died and to take his mind off the tragedy, he superintended the construction of the *Florence,* took her command and remained in her until the spring of 1859. He was a very capable shipmaster, having commanded such clipper ships as the *Surprise, Bald Eagle* and *Romance of the Seas,* besides many small opium clippers in the China seas. In June 1861, during a trip from Boston to New York on the steamer *Empire State,* he fell overboard and was drowned. Born in 1804, he first went to sea at the age of 16, for his health, and at 22 had a command.

The *Florence* was 171: 7, over all; 36: 6, extreme beam, outside; with 19: 4, as her depth of hold; 1045 tons, old measurement; 896 tons, new measurement; she could load 1650 measurement tons. While not a regular clipper, she made excellent passages through the skillful seamanship and "drive" of Captain Dumaresq and his worthy successor Capt. E. D. Wadsworth. Capt. J. T. Watkins, formerly of the opium clipper brig *Antelope* and the ships *Akbar* and *Paul Jones,* fast sailers in their day, was a passenger in the *Florence* from San Francisco to Hong Kong, in 1862, and called her the fastest ship he had ever sailed in.

On her maiden passage the *Florence* left Boston, Apr. 5, 1856; passed Java Head, 76 days out, 22 days from the Cape, and arrived at Hong Kong in 91 days from Boston; best day's run, 296 miles. Completing the voyage she reached New York, Mar. 23, 1857, 100 days from Shanghai. On her second voyage she left New York, Apr. 29, 1857, and arrived at Hong Kong, Aug. 1st, in 93 days, 8 hours' passage; 17 days from Anjer. Logged 12,474 miles to Java Head, with 298 miles as her best day's run in the Indian Ocean, the log reading, "took in and set royals occasionally." The following day she made 260 miles and "passed two barks under reefed courses standing the same way, we having topgallant studding-sails and royals set." She sailed from Shanghai, Dec. 4, 1857; passed Java Head in 20 days; on the 49th day out took in royals for the first time; passed the Cape, 57 days out; the equator on the 77th day, and arrived at New York, Mar. 18, 1858, 104 days from pilot to pilot; "topsail halyards started only once, and then only to single reef."

On her third voyage the *Florence* arrived at Penang, July 12, 1858, in 81 days, 10 hours from New York; logged 14,757 miles, an average of 179; topsail halyards started only once, to take in a single reef for a few hours; best day, 310 miles, near the Cape; on the 17th day from New York, she made 259 miles and "passed a ship under topsails bound in the same direction, we having royals set." The *Florence* was at Shanghai, Sept. 17, 1858, and later went to Japan, being the first American merchant ship to appear at Nagasaki. Returning to Shanghai, she took her departure therefrom, Dec. 26, 1858, for London; arrived at the Mother Bank, 92 days out. Her Japanese cargo, principally vegetable wax, was the first cargo to arrive in Great Britain from that country. Had passed Java Head, 16 days out and the Cape, on her 44th day, this being one day better than the time made by *Surprise* on her 83 days' run from Shanghai to New York in 1857. The *Florence* crossed the line 68 days out, best day thus far, 280 miles. When 17 days out she exchanged signals with the British ship *John Masterman*, Shanghai for London, 30 days out; on her 43rd day passed a ship, taken to be the *Akbar*, which had left Shanghai 12 days before her; had previously passed a bark under topsails and topgallants, the *Florence* being under royal studding-sails, and the next day passed a ship under double reefs, the *Florence* being under topgallants and flying jib. Nine days prior to her arrival, the *Florence* took single reefs in her topsails for the first time from China.

At London, Captain Wadsworth took command of the *Florence* and sailing May 24, 1859, had a passage of 101½ days to Hong

Kong. No information is available about her doings during 1860, but she arrived at New York, May 3, 1861, in 102 days from Foo Chow. She then went out to San Francisco in 141 days; thence to Hong Kong in 52 days and arrived at New York, Oct. 6, 1862, 125 days from Whampoa. She then crossed to England and was sold to Jones, Palmer & Co., of Liverpool, being renamed *Hypatia*. In 1887 she was the Norwegian bark *Hypatia*, of Skien, owned by L. W. Flood and others and had been engaged in the North Atlantic timber trade. The following year she was stranded and became a total loss but her crew were all saved.

FLYAWAY

EXTREME clipper ship, built in 1853, by William H. Webb, at New York, for Schiff Brothers & Co., of that city. 190 x 38: 3 x 21: 6; 1274 tons, American measurement; 912 tons, British measurement. She was very strongly built, her frame being iron strapped, and was of a beautiful model. She had neither figure nor billet head, the stem elongating to the bowsprit, there being a gigantic pair of spread wings, indicating flight over the waves. She was launched in May and sailed from New York, Aug. 20th, under command of Captain Sewall, for Melbourne where she arrived Nov. 11th, 83 days' passage, 80 days from land to land. Made 5000 miles in 17 days, an average of 295; best day's run, 346 miles. From Melbourne she was 55 days to Whampoa and left that port Feb. 25, 1854; arrived at New York, June 8th, 103 days' passage, 75 days from Anjer and 44 from the Cape.

On her second voyage she sailed from New York, Nov. 13, 1854, and was 109 days to San Francisco; crossed the equator in the Pacific, 91 days out and was 18 days thence to destination; lost her jibboom when near the California coast. Then crossed to Hong Kong in 43 days, beating both the *Bald Eagle* and *Phantom* which made the run about the same time. Went to Shanghai and Manila. Left the latter port, July 18, 1855, and was 106 days to New York. On July 29th, when going six knots, she struck on a coral reef; after jettison of about 100 tons of cargo, she got off three hours later and continued the voyage. She again left New York, Dec. 22, 1855, and was 108 days to San Francisco. Was 44 days to 50° South, Atlantic, and crossed the Pacific equator on the 82nd day; on the 98th day at sea she was 500 miles distant from the Golden Gate but then encountered a belt of very light winds. From San Francisco she went to Hong Kong in 47 days and thence to Foo Chow. Left that port, Jan. 27, 1857, and is reported to have made the run to New York in 94 days. On her next voyage, which was her last passage to San Francisco, she left New York, Aug. 7, 1857, and was 128 days on the run. Was off the Cape, 21 days in very heavy weather and had light winds in the Pacific. Her best day's run on the trip was 298 miles. She returned to New York direct, in 98 days.

Shortly after her arrival at New York she was sold for $50,000, and Captain Trundy succeeded to the command. She left New York, Aug. 21, 1858, and was 95 days to Sydney. Thence went to Manila where, in March 1859, she was sold to sail under Spanish colors and renamed *Concepcion;* hailing port Cadiz. For some years she was owned by Galway, Casada & Teller and later by J. Fide de Castro of Cadiz. In 1875 she is listed as the British bark *Bothalwood,* of Newcastle-on-Tyne, T. R. Miller owner and Captain Gifford master.

FLYING ARROW

MEDIUM clipper ship, built by Isaac Dunham, at Frankfort, Me.; launched in December 1852. 170: 8 x 37: 10 x 23: 4; 1092 tons, old measurement. Dead rise, 17 inches; swell of sides, 6 inches; sheer, 26 inches. She was built for account of James Arey & Co., under the superintendence of Captain Arey and was intended to be called the *Flying Yankee.* On proceeding to Boston, however, she was at once purchased by Manning, Stanwood & Co., and Thomas Gray, of that port, and became the *Flying Arrow.* She had no figurehead, a billet substituting, and her stern was square. She had rounded lines with long, clipper-like ends, her model being adapted for capacity as well as speed. Her mainmast was 84 feet long and topmast 45 feet. The yards on the fore and main masts were alike, being, from the lower yards upward, 72, 61, 48, 36 and 26 feet long. Her entire career, as an American ship, was one continuous series of disasters, so that she had no opportunity of demonstrating her ability in any direction.

Under command of Capt. Charles T. Treadwell, she left Boston, Jan. 20, 1853, for San Francisco. When four days out she was struck by a squall and totally dismasted, with all her boats overboard or crushed. For 22 days she drifted, her crew exhausted from pumping and their ship in imminent danger of foundering from a bad leak. Eventually she was picked up by the steamship *Great Western* and towed into St. Thomas, arriving Feb. 16th. All the cargo was discharged and the hull found to be in good condition. There being no large spars to be had, masts had to be built. Yellow fever broke out and nearly all on board were stricken; the fatalities among passengers and crew were very large. A new crew not being obtainable, the ship was forced to return to New York where she arrived Aug. 4th. Her passengers had a printing press on board and while at St. Thomas they published, for distribution to port officials and visitors, the initial issue of the "Ocean Spray," containing a full account of the disastrous voyage. A passenger, H. L. Weston, who edited the little paper, remained by the ship until her arrival in California, when he located in Petaluma and for many years published the "Argus."

The *Great Western* received $10,000 as salvage, and refitting and other expenses at St. Thomas were $5000. After arrival at New York, Captain Treadwell was presented by the underwriters with $500, "for his judicious and painsworthy management of his ship under very perplexing and adverse circumstances." He was worn out and sick and turned over the ship to Captain Clark. The voyage was resumed Aug. 10, 1853, and off Cape Horn the maintopgallant mast was carried away and the topmast sprung, in very heavy gales. Arrived at San Francisco, Dec. 31st, in 143 days. In completion of the voyage she arrived at New York, Sept. 19, 1854, in 85 days from Callao, via Hampton Roads.

Captain Treadwell resumed command and on her second voyage the *Arrow* reached San Francisco, Apr. 13, 1855, in 136 days from New York. When seven days out she was badly damaged by a gale; had to cut away all three topgallant masts and while lying to had the steering apparatus broken. The cargo shifted badly, requiring one week's hard labor to get the ship upright, and at one time there was three feet of water in the hold. Captain Treadwell got up stump masts and on the fore and mizzen, set royals to replace the topgallants. Considering her condition she had a good run of only 43 days from 50° South, Pacific, to the Golden Gate. From San Francisco she went to Melbourne.

The *Flying Arrow* left Melbourne, in ballast, for Batavia, on Nov. 9, 1855, and the following day was totally dismasted. After dragging close in to the breakers of the reef off New Years Island, Bass Straits, the crew, with the exception of four volunteers who stood by the ship, reached shore safely. Signals of distress, which had previously been set, finally brought assistance from Melbourne and all hands were rescued, the ship being towed into that port by the small steamer *Marion*. The latter was awarded £1200 salvage, while the man-of-war brig *Fantome*, whose crew had assisted in heaving up the anchors, received £200.

The following account of this disaster is taken from the log of the ship:

Thursday, November 8, 1855. At 4 A.M. weighed anchor from Shoreland Bluff and proceeded to sea; 8 A.M. pilot left; wind light from N.E. First officer, Mr. Winn, sick, second officer, Moore, acting first, and Cannin, third, acting second. Ends showery with light squalls of wind from N.E. to N. At 2:30 P.M. Cape Otway Light House bore N., 6 miles distant. Calm till 4 P.M. when took breeze from W. Furled royals and topgallants and reefed mainsail. At 8 P.M. tacked to N.; at 12, to S.W., Otway light bearing N.N.E., 10 miles; wind fresh from W. to N.W. Took in upper topsails and jib and reefed spanker. Ship under our lee bow supposed to be *Dashing Wave;* steam schooner coming up astern. Ends fresh gales and freshening. Latitude, 39: 50 south.

Saturday, Nov. 10, sea time, fresh gales and squally with rain. At 1 P.M. schooner on the weather quarter. At 10 P.M. sharp vivid lightning; sea one sheet of blaze with animalculae; wind hauling to N.N.E. with heavy rain. Took in mainsail and foresail at midnight when the gale burst with terrific force; blew away foretopmast staysail, which was new; spanker flew into ribbons, together with the mainsail; the topsail which was well secured was instantly blown to pieces. Sea making fast. Attempted to take in close-reefed fore and mizzen topsails; succeeded in fastening them to the yards but such was the force of the gale that it was at imminent peril that the crew reached the deck. At 2 A.M. wind hauled to N.W. and blew with unabated fury. The ship was completely submerged with water. Stood by with axes fore and aft to cut away topgallant and royal backstays, when the topgallant masts fell over the lee. Ship righted and gave a plunge when a tremendous gust struck her and the 3 lower masts broke off and came down with a terrific crash, the fore and main breaking off even with the deck, and the mizzen, even with the eyes of the rigging, the bowsprit breaking about 5 feet outboard. The mainmast fell fore and aft on deck on the port side, smashing in its fall, 2 boats and the upper cabin and cutting the lee rigging to pieces. All hands busy at work clearing the wreckage from alongside to keep it from staving a hole through the ship; there was great danger in getting it free. Day ends with wind blowing violently but with more uniformity. No observation.

Sunday, Nov. 11. Commences with fresh gales from N.W. with rain squalls. Bent a foretopmast staysail aft to keep ship's head to the sea. Bent an 8 inch hawser to a small anchor with a spar lashed to it and threw it out forward for a drag. Drew the boxes from the head pump and put the gutta-percha hose overboard to windward and kept them filled with oil to break the force of the sea which was running large. Mr. Moore, in clearing the wreck, smashed his hand

and was laid up. At 4 A.M. got up a new spanker, bent and reefed it; got up a jury foremast. At 10 A.M. a brig under our lee; set our colors, union down, but she did not notice us. Day ends blowing fresh with heavy sea. Latitude, 40:03, S. Monday, Nov. 12. Gale still continues, inclining to S.W. At work on jury foremast. At 4 P.M. judged ourselves to be 15 miles from King's Island, drifting 2½ miles per hour. At 9 P.M. wind at S.W. which brought the ship in the hollow of the sea, rolling sails under and making it difficult to work. Mainmast got adrift on deck and was secured with great difficulty. At 10 P.M. set steering sail on jury foremast, hauled in the drag and wore ship to W.N.W., trusting this would keep us from the land until daylight. At daylight, 5 A.M., land in sight about 8 miles off, breakers plainly visible from deck; no hope of safety but in our anchors. Got up stream anchor and bent on 2 8-inch hawsers; sounded in 40 fathoms, white sand and broken coral; ship, by lead, drifting about N.E. Let go the stream anchor which produced no effect in bringing ship to wind. Cleared away the 2 bower anchors and at 12 M. let both go; sounded in 32 fathoms, same bottom. Day ends blowing heavy, large sea; ship riding hard on chain but dragging steadily.

Tuesday-Thursday, Nov. 11-13. Ship continues to drive towards the breakers; at 2 P.M. putting bowsprit under. Parted small bower chain and stream cable leaving but the best bower to ride by. Situation now truly desperate; night approaching and with but little hope of beholding dawn; made ready the three boats with some small provisions; took all light spars and water casks and built a raft; put some clothing, provisions, etc., on it and at 8 A.M. launched it successfully, securing it astern by 2 hawsers; the main-land about 3 miles off. Sounded in 25 fathoms, ship dragging slowly. At 10 A.M. the second officer, with a boat's crew volunteered to attempt a landing; started off and in about 2 hours returned in their whale boat, reporting a large sea breaking on the reef about ½ mile from the main and thought that by passing this barrier, a landing could be made, though with great danger. Mustered all hands for a consultation and it was the opinion of all that we had better try to land. The carpenter and 3 men volunteered to remain in the ship with one boat. Lowered the boats without damage; lowered the Captain's family over the stern in a bowline and at 3 P.M. Nov. 14th, 3 boats left the ship to seek shelter on a desolate island; left the raft towing astern. At 5 P.M. reached the outer breakers; used oil freely from each boat; put them through the breakers and landed in safety, though wet as drowned rats. Found an old tent by the water, under which took shelter for the night. Ship driving about twice her length. Wednesday, gale abating and sea going down. Sent second officer and 3 men to the north end of the island for assistance. Visited the ship and procured provisions and bedding. A sail in sight; hoisted colors but she took no notice. Thursday, 15th. Pleasant weather and ship riding easily at her anchor. Remained on board nearly all day and brought away some provisions. Raft broke adrift and was lost with all the baggage. At 4 P.M. second officer returned accompanied by Mr. Forrester who has a cattle station at the north end of the island. There are only 5 persons on the island and to communicate with Melbourne we would be obliged to send over a whale boat. A crew immediately volunteered and the next day was set for their departure.

Friday, Nov. 16. Calm and sea smooth, preparing boat with sail and provisions to leave in the afternoon and remained during the night on New Year's island. At 3 P.M. a steamer in sight; manned a boat and Captain Treadwell boarded her. Found her manned with a first lieutenant of a man-of-war, a crew of seamen, Captain Ferguson of Melbourne, and others. The Government had sent them out on their errand of mercy, to render assistance if required. Part of our crew being on shore, it was not considered advisable to take them off but to start with the ship immediately before nightfall; the man-of-war brig, then in sight, would take off all hands in the morning. Put second officer in charge with some of the crew and went on shore to build fires as signals to the brig. The steamer proceeded with the ship to Melbourne and arrived in safety. The man-of-war brig *Fan-*

tome, passed us 8 miles from land and went to Melbourne. The steamer returned and after remaining a week on the island we were taken off and reached Melbourne in safety, though somewhat bruised in person.

The *Flying Arrow* was sold, Jan. 16, 1856, for $15,000 and was refitted and rerigged. On Mar. 20, 1856, she sailed for Calcutta. She was renamed *Wings of the Wind* and appeared registered as owned by G. Duncan & Co., of London.

FLYING CHILDERS

MEDIUM clipper ship, launched Nov. 11, 1852, from the yard of Samuel Hall, at East Boston, for J. M. Forbes and Cunningham Brothers of Boston. Keel, 175; deck, 183: 9; over all, 195 x 36: 4 x 22: 6; 1125 tons. Dead rise, 18 inches; sheer, 30 inches. Her bow rose boldly, was without head boards or rail and was ornamented with a carved racehorse. Capt. Robert B. Forbes stated that she was rigged after his plan, with double topsails, the topmasts fidded abaft, excepting on the mizzen. He speaks of her as a fine sailer and a fair carrier.

She left Boston, Dec. 18, 1852, under command of Capt. Jeremiah D. White, formerly of the ship *Epaminondas;* was 23 days to the line; 51 days to 50° South; 12 days thence to 50° in the Pacific; 91 days to the equator and was near San Francisco Heads, Apr. 7, 1853, 110 days out; anchored the 10th, 113 days from Boston. Sailed from San Francisco, Apr. 30th; arrived off Honolulu, May 15th, and, as a correspondent there wrote, "after lying to for a few hours, she squared away and under the strong trade winds, was off like a rocket on her westward passage." She arrived at Shanghai, 32 days later; went thence to Manila and was eight days from there to Hong Kong. Sailed from Whampoa, Nov. 10th; passed Anjer, Dec. 1st and arrived at Deal, Feb. 20, 1854, in 102 days; 82 days from Anjer. She then made a voyage to Russia under Capt. John M. Cunningham and returning, reached Boston, June 30th; from Cronstadt, May 14th;

Elsinore, the 25th; the Downs, June 3rd. She then crossed from Boston to London and left the latter port, Oct. 24, 1854, for Hong Kong, arriving out after a passage of 117 days. Loaded at Shanghai; sailed July 18th; passed Anjer, Aug. 8th and arrived at New York, Nov. 2, 1855, 107 days' passage; 86 days from Anjer. During 1856 she was trading between Boston and England. The following year she was 87 days from Hampton Roads to Melbourne, arriving Apr. 2, 1857; went thence to Manila where she loaded for New York and was 128 days on the run. In 1858 she was reported sold at New York for $53,000.

Leaving Boston, Jan. 30, 1859, Captain Horton in command, she was 24 days to the line; 52 days to the Horn and arrived at San Francisco, May 28th, a run of 117 days; went to Hong Kong in 44 days; then to Foo Chow, from whence she was 112 days to New York. Sailed from New York, Sept. 12, 1860; was 37 days to the line; passed Staten Island, 63 days out; was off the Horn in heavy gales and lost the upper part of her cutwater and figurehead; filled decks, washing away everything movable. Crossed the equator in the Pacific, 95½ days out and was 19 days thence to San Francisco. In latitude 30° North, Atlantic, was several days in company with the *Aurora* and off Rio was close to the *Webfoot* a number of days. Off the Horn she spoke the *Ringleader*, the latter arriving at San Francisco two days ahead of the *Childers*, which, in turn, dropped anchor 12 days before the *Aurora* and 18 days ahead of the *Webfoot*.

The *Childers* left San Francisco, Feb. 3, 1861, and was 120 days to Liverpool, her cargo being 1355 short tons of wheat. Arrived at New York, Sept. 8, 1861, three days from Boston. Left Boston, Oct. 27th, under command of Capt. William Lester, and was 131 days to San Francisco; thence 54 days to Hong Kong; loaded at Manila for London and arrived out Dec. 18, 1862, in 112 days. In January 1863 she was sold at London for £5050 sterling, to Mackay, Baines & Co., of Liverpool and renamed the *Golden South*. At the time of the sale she was owned by S. G. Reed of Boston. In 1865 she is listed as owned by Baines & Co., and commanded by Captain Faithful.

Later she became a coal hulk at Port Jackson and after many years of service, sparks from a burning ship set her on fire and she was entirely destroyed.

FLYING CLOUD

EXTREME clipper ship, built by Donald McKay, at East Boston, in 1851, for account of Enoch Train of Boston, and purchased by Grinnell, Minturn & Co., of New York, for $90,000. Keel, 208 feet; deck, 225; from knightheads to taffrail, 235 feet x 40: 8 x 21: 6; 1782 48/95 tons, American old measurement; 1139 tons, British. Dead rise, 30 inches; swell of sides, 6 inches; sheer, 3 feet. An angel holding a trumpet to mouth was the figurehead. Her entrance lines were slightly concave and although not as long as those of later clippers, were very sharp, her width on the level of the 'tween deck, 18 feet aft of the apron, being only 11 feet. A topgallant forecastle and a house on deck furnished accommodations for her crew and she had three cabins for officers and passengers. She was sparred as follows:—length of foremast, 82 feet; topmast, 46; topgallant, 25; royal, 17; and skysail-mast, 13. On the main:—88, 51, 28, 19 and 14½. On the mizzen:—78, 40, 22, 14 and 10. Yards; on the foremast:—70, 55, 44½, 32 and 22. On the main:—82, 64, 50, 37 and 24. On the mizzen:—cross-jack, 56; topsail, 45; topgallant, 33; royal, 25; skysail, 20. The foremast was 35 inches in diameter, the main, 36 and the mizzen, 26. Diameter of fore-yard, 20 inches; main-yard, 22; and cross-jack, 16 inches. The bowsprit was 28 inches in diameter, 20 feet outboard. The jibboom was divided at 16 feet and again at 29 feet, with a five foot end. The spanker boom was 55 feet long; gaff, 40 feet; and main spencer gaff, 24 feet. The masts all raked alike, 1¼ inches to the foot.

The *Flying Cloud* was launched Apr. 15, 1851 and arrived at New York on the 28th in tow of the tug *Ajax*. The command had been given to Capt. Josiah Perkins Cressy, a most competent navigator and a great "driver" who had made a name for fast passages in the China trade in the *Oneida*. The *Flying Cloud* sailed from New York,

June 2, 1851 and when three days out, lost the main and mizzen topgallant masts. She crossed the line 21 days out; was in 50° South on the 47th day and had the remarkable run of seven days thence to 50° South, Pacific; from that point was 17 days to the equator, then 71 days out; arrived at San Francisco, Aug. 31st, 89 days and 21 hours, from New York, anchor to anchor, the second fastest passage ever made over that course; her fourth voyage, in 13 hours less time, being the record. To San Francisco, her time of 40 days from Cape Horn and 36 days from 50° South, was very fast. Her best day's run on the passage was 374 nautical miles on which occasion she made over 18 knots during squalls; for four consecutive days she averaged 314, and in 26 consecutive days covered 5912 nautical miles, an average of 227 daily. She left San Francisco, Oct. 20th; passed Honolulu, Nov. 6th, and arrived at Hong Kong, Dec. 5th, in 45 days' passage. Left Whampoa, Jan. 6, 1852, and in spite of having a sprung mainmast, made the passage to New York in 94 days. Her masts and spars on the fore and main were then replaced, the yards on the foremast being made of the same dimensions as those on the main, which slightly increased her sail area. She was also refitted with new rigging.

The *Flying Cloud* left New York on her second voyage, May 14, 1852, and arrived at San Francisco, Sept. 6th, 115 days out. Captain Cressy reported 29 days to the line and 95 days to the Pacific equator crossing; a succession of light winds and heavy gales prevailed all the passage. On June 7th a number of sails were split and on the 16th the head of the foremast was sprung. On July 1st, in the South Atlantic, she had a little brush with the *N. B. Palmer* which proved that they were about equal in sailing ability. On July 8th, the *Cloud* was struck by a heavy sea which knocked down all the berths on the starboard side. The best day's run on this passage was 314 miles and the poorest, 35 miles. From San Francisco she went to Hong Kong, in 40 days, having passed Honolulu in 8 days and 8½ hours from the Golden Gate. Sailed from Whampoa, Dec. 1st; from Macao Roads, Dec. 2nd; cleared the Straits of Sunda on the 14th; had a series of gales for 14 days off the Cape of Good Hope and thereafter much light weather with many calm spells. Arrived at New York, Mar. 8, 1853, in 96 days' passage; best day's run, 382 nautical miles on Dec. 21st.

On her third voyage, the *Cloud* left New York, Apr. 28, 1853; crossed the line May 15th, 17 days or 408 hours out, having logged 3672 miles, an average of nine knots hourly; never had skysails in for more than three hours at a time; was 45 days to 50° South, and nine days rounding the Horn. On June 24th, in the South Pacific, chief officer Gibbs and a seaman were washed off the topgallant forecastle and lost. On the 27th she lost her jibboom and a number of sails and had a boat stove; was 27 days from 50° South, to the equator and 16 days from latitude 20° North, to San Francisco where she arrived Aug. 12th, in 105 days from New York. She anchored 45 minutes after the *Hornet* which had left New York two days ahead, but each had passed the other at some point on the voyage. The *Cloud* sailed from San Francisco, Sept. 5th, in ballast, for New York and during a heavy squall, when 12 days out, the rudder head was badly twisted and temporary steering apparatus had to be used the rest of the passage. Passed the Falkland Islands 51 days out and was 41 days thence to destination, a total of 92 days.

The fourth voyage of the *Flying Cloud* from New York to San Francisco, via Cape Horn, 89 days and 8 hours, anchor to anchor, is the record to this date, as is also her time from New York to Hong Kong, via San Francisco, 137 days gross and 127 sailing days. She left New York, Jan. 21, 1854, getting under way at 12, noon, civil time, in tow of the tug *Achilles*, off the foot of Maiden Lane; at 3:30 discharged tug and pilot and made sail and at 6 P.M. passed the lightship; crossed the line, 17 days out; passed through the Straits of Le Maire, 47 days out, and the next day passed Cape Horn; was 12 days between the 50's and 20 days from 50° South to the equator, which was crossed Apr. 5th, 74 days from New York; thence she had 15 days to San Francisco, arriving Apr. 20th. Total distance logged, 15,091 nautical miles; best day, 360 miles, when three days out; best day in the South Atlantic, 240 miles; best day rounding the Horn, 206 miles; in the South Pacific, 282 miles and in the North Pacific, 283 miles; poorest days, 26 miles in the North Pacific; 56, 63, 64 and 64 miles in the South Atlantic, and 45, 47 and 37 miles while rounding the Horn. She passed Rio, 28 days out; when 22 days out, Pernambuco bore southwest, 75 miles distant.

It has frequently been published that the medium clipper ship *Andrew Jackson* has equalled or beaten both of the 89-day passages made by the *Flying Cloud* but statements to this effect are false, full proof being available that the *Jackson's* run was 89 days and 20 hours, pilot to pilot, and 90 days and 12 hours, anchor to anchor.

In continuation of her fourth voyage, the *Cloud* was 37 days from San Francisco to Hong Kong. Sailed from Whampoa, July 20, 1854, and when a few days out, ran on a coral reef, but got off, leaking 11 inches an hour. The pumps were kept going continually until her arrival at New York, Nov. 24th, 115 days from Whampoa. For his success in thus saving his cargo, worth $1,000,000, Captain Cressey received a silver service and flattering commendation from underwriters and owners.

On her fifth voyage, the *Flying Cloud* arrived at San Francisco, June 6, 1855, 108 days from New York. She was 20 days to the line; 47 days to the Horn, off which had the unusual experience of encountering light winds and calms; crossed the equator, 80 days out, and was becalmed for 12 days between 10° and 14° North latitude. Sailed from San Francisco, June 22nd; passed Honolulu, 11 days out, and arrived at Hong Kong, Aug. 1st; total passage, 39 days. Sailed from Whampoa, Sept. 5th and Macao, Sept. 7th, and arrived at New York, Dec. 14th, in 97 days, being 72 days from Anjer.

On her sixth and last Cape Horn voyage, the *Flying Cloud* left New York, Mar. 13, 1856, under command of Captain Reynard, Captain Cressy staying ashore for a much needed vacation. The ship had been pronounced strong and fit, but on getting fairly at sea the bowsprit was found to be badly sprung and the vessel unworthy in several points. However, the run to the line was made in 19 days and Rio was passed when 31 days out. In the South Atlantic, from latitude 37° to 46°, very heavy gales with bad seas were encountered and the ship was so badly damaged in hull, spars and rigging, that on Apr. 29th, Captain Reynard set a course for Rio, where he arrived May 10th. After repairing, she sailed June 23rd and was 24 days to the Horn, off which had seven days of very bad weather and had to rig an addition to the rudder in order to properly steer the ship. Off the California coast had seven days of light winds and calms and arrived at San Francisco, Sept. 14th, in 82 days from Rio. As she had passed Rio when 31 days out, her actual passage, in sailing days from New York, would be 113. On this passage she made the fastest day's run in her career,—402 nautical miles,—28 miles better than her previous record. She was laid up at San Francisco until Jan. 4, 1857, when Captain Cressy, who had been sent out to resume the command, left in her for New York and made the passage home in 91 days.

For two years and eight months, the *Flying Cloud* was idle at New York and finally, having changed owners, she sailed Dec. 8, 1859, and made the fast passage of 17 days to Deal, Captain Winsor being in command. Loading at London for Hong Kong, she left Deal, Feb. 14, 1860, and arrived out May 21st, in 97 days' passage. Sailed from Foo Chow, Aug. 6th, and arrived at London, Dec. 7th, in 123 days. Left Deal, Feb. 28, 1861, and arrived at Melbourne, May 24th, 85 days out. Left Melbourne, June 28th, and was 67 days to Hong Kong. She was then offered for sale, freight or charter and was finally engaged to carry troops to London for the flat sum of £6000. She sailed from Hong Kong, Dec. 29, 1861; passed Anjer, Jan. 7, 1862; put into St. Helena, Feb. 26th, remaining in port until Mar. 9th and arrived at Gravesend, Apr. 20th.

Some time after her arrival in England, the *Flying Cloud* was sold to go under British colors without change of name and then went into trade between the mother country and Australia and New Zealand. Her spars had been cut down at Rio, in 1856, and again at

New York, in 1858, so that she could not carry sail as she did in her prime. In the early sixties she is said to have had a race out to Moreton Bay with the *Sunda* (formerly the American clipper ship *Gauntlet*), in which the latter beat by 18 miles in a four days' run, both ships often going 16 knots. In 1870, under command of Captain Owen, she left Liverpool, June 4th, and arrived at Hervey's Bay, Aug. 30th, in 87 days' passage. About this time her owners were reported as being Mackay & Son.

The later years of the *Flying Cloud* were spent in the timber trade between St. Johns, principally, and London. In 1874, shortly after leaving St. Johns, she went ashore on Beacon Island bar, on returning to port to escape a heavy gale. Her cargo was lightered and she broke her back, after which she was condemned and sold. She was finally burned for her copper and metal fastenings, in June 1875. At the time, her hailing port was given as South Shields and her owner as H. S. Edwards. The name of the captain is not stated but he is said to have been known locally as "Wild Goose."

FLYING DRAGON

CLIPPER ship, launched in June 1853, by Trufant & Drummond, at Bath, Me.; owned during her lifetime by Reed, Wade & Co., of Boston and Samuel G. Reed & Co., their successors. 187 x 38 x 22; 1127 tons, old measurement. Her figurehead was a typical Chinese dragon, with open mouth, from which a dart-like tongue protruded.

Under command of Capt. Judah P. Baker, formerly in the *Shooting Star*, she left Boston, July 21, 1853, and arrived at San Francisco, Dec. 16th, in 148 days' passage. Was 35 days off Cape Horn, having bowsprit sprung and jibboom carried away in heavy weather; crossed the equator in the Pacific, Nov. 20th, and on Dec. 7th, was in 35° North, 128° West. On Nov. 24th, Captain Baker died. She left San Francisco, Jan. 6, 1854, under Captain Horton; was 50 days to Callao and arrived at Norfolk, Va., July

12th, in 91 days from Callao. Capt. James A. Little took command and leaving New York, Oct. 30, 1854, went to Calcutta, arriving at Sand Heads, 101 days out. Sailed from Calcutta (Saugor), Mar. 20, 1855; was 52 days to the Cape of Good Hope, 80 days to the equator and arrived at Boston, June 28th, in a run of 100 days. On her third voyage, she left New York, July 31, 1855, and arrived at San Francisco, Nov. 23rd, in 114 days. Was 33 days to the line; 12 days between the 50's, and 22 days from the equator to port. From San Francisco she went to Calcutta in 80 days, being 65 days to Singapore. Sailed from Saugor, Apr. 24, 1856; was 71 days to the Cape, 97 days to the line and arrived at Boston, Aug. 27th, in a passage of 125 days. Sailed from New York, Nov. 27, 1856, and arrived at San Francisco, Mar. 5, 1857, Captain Little reporting his passage as some hours over 97 days. In 39° North, 60° West, three days out, had a violent gale, with very high sea, which lasted three days, during which the bulwarks were stove in and considerable damage done on deck. Crossed the line, 21 days out; was 47 days to the Horn; 17 days from 50° to 50° and had a remarkably fast run up the Pacific, crossing the line, 81 days out, and carrying the northeast trades to 22° North. Sailed from San Francisco, Apr. 18th and was 92 days to Calcutta, including detention at Singapore. Sailed from Saugor, Sept. 16th and passed the Cape of Good Hope, 49½ days out, bound to Boston. On her fifth voyage, she arrived at San Francisco, July 30, 1858, in 126 days from New York. Captain Little reported having northerly gales soon after leaving port; crossed the line, 30 days out; had calms and light winds to 26° South; thence a succession of southwest gales to 50° South; passed Cape Horn, June 2nd, 39 days from the line and 69 days out; was 14 days between the 50's in light winds; crossed the equator, July 4th, 101 days out and had light winds to port. Sailed from San Francisco, Aug. 17th and was 19 days to Jarvis Island; leaving there Oct. 7th and arriving at Boston, Jan. 17, 1859, via Hampton Roads.

Capt. Horace H. Watson, Jr., now took command and on arrival at San Francisco, Sept. 6, 1859, reported his passage as 119 days.

Sailed Oct. 3rd for Baker's Island, via Honolulu, and was 11 days, 16 hours, to Honolulu. Left Baker's Island, Feb. 7th, guano laden, for Hampton Roads and on Feb. 20, 1860, in 27° South, 176° West, was found to be leaking 60 inches an hour. Of her 1225 tons of cargo, some 400 tons were jettisoned and she reached Tongata-boo, Mar. 4th. Her crew had previously tried to force Captain Wat-son to abandon the ship and take to the boats but he resisted with arms and forced the men to continue at the pumps. The native Governor of Tongataboo sent a relief force to continue pumping; and some 600 tons additional cargo were discharged and after some of the leaks had been stopped, the ship proceeded to Sydney, where she was docked and repaired. She arrived at Hampton Roads, Nov. 1, 1860, after the very fast passage of 75 days from Sydney, and reached port before the papers in connection with the bottomry bonds had ar-rived, per steamer mail.

She again loaded at New York for San Francisco and arrived out June 24, 1861, in 116 days' passage. Sailed Aug. 11th and arrived at Melbourne, Oct. 4th,—a rapid run of 53 days, the fastest made about that time. At Newcastle, N. S. W., on Dec. 2, 1861, the *Dragon* started discharging her ballast, 500 tons, and on the 5th, at 2 P.M., took her departure for San Francisco with 1000 tons of coal laden in the interim. On entering San Francisco harbor, during the night of Jan. 29, 1862, being then 55½ days out, she struck on Arch Rock and foundered. When inside Fort Point, the weather being thick with heavy rain, she was struck by a terrific and unusual squall and let go her anchors, but the windlass proved defective and be-fore sufficient chain could be put out she struck the reef off the Rock and the strong flood tide kept her hard on. A tug was sent to assist and also soldiers from Alcatraz to pump, but all efforts proved unavail-ing and the next morning she fell over on the starboard side and soon disappeared. Nothing was saved. The pilot who was in charge at the time was fully exonerated, after an investigation. In many lists of fast passages from Australia to San Francisco, this run of the *Dragon* has been stated as only 45 days, but a thorough investigation estab-lishes as correct the dates and time heretofore quoted.

FLYING DUTCHMAN

EXTREME clipper ship, built in 1852 by W. H. Webb, at New York; launched Sept. 9th. 190 (200 over all) x 38: 6 x 21: 6; 1257 tons. Her model is said to have been faultless. She was one of the sharpest vessels ever built at New York and had 36 inches dead rise; was very strongly built, being diagonally braced with iron straps. Capt. Ashbel Hubbard was in command during her career which was of but five years' duration.

She left New York, Oct. 15, 1852, and arrived at San Francisco, Jan. 27, 1853, some hours under 104 days. Made fair time in the Atlantic but was 30 days rounding the Horn, in very heavy weather. Her time from 50° South, in the Pacific, to destination, 35 days, odd hours, was remarkably fast,—19 days to the equator crossing and 16 days therefrom. Sailed from San Francisco, Feb. 11th; crossed the line, in 119° West, on the 23rd, 12 days out; was in 40° South when 24 days out and arrived at New York, May 8th, in 85 days' passage. The clipper ship *Comet* left San Francisco the day after the *Dutchman* got away, but caught up with her in the South Pacific, Mar. 13th. They parted company but were together again in the North Atlantic, Apr. 30th. A passenger on the *Comet* wrote:—"It was an exciting race; the ships were frequently within pistol shot of each other. Sometimes one was ahead and sometimes the other, but the wind increasing, the *Comet* luffed up and shot ahead. The next morning the *Dutchman* was scarcely visible astern of us. She had crossed the line three days before the *Comet*. On May 3rd, while going at a rapid rate with a strong breeze, our mainsail split and had to come down and in consequence our rival came up and passed us in the night and was not seen thereafter. The *Comet* arrived at New York on the morning of May 7th, in 83 days and 18 hours from San Francisco, the *Dutchman* getting in the following day, in 85 days."

On her second passage, the *Dutchman* arrived at San Francisco, Oct. 7, 1853, in 106 days from New York. Had received her 'Frisco pilot on Oct. 5th and anchored on the bar on the 6th. Was 50 days to

50° South; eight days getting around the Horn, and crossed the equator, 78 days out. Prospects were very favorable for a passage of under 100 days, but were spoiled by light winds and calms in the North Pacific, 28 days being occupied between the line and destination. However, her passage of 106 days still stands as the record for any vessel making the Pacific equatorial crossing during the month of September. From San Francisco she crossed to Hong Kong in 44 days. From Hong Kong she was 102 days to London, a feature of the passage being her run of 30 days from Anjer to the Cape.

The third voyage of the *Dutchman* commenced at New York, Sept. 15, 1854. Maury quotes her as having an exceptionally long run, 40½ days to the line and 42 days to St. Roque; thereafter, however, she was but 39 days to Melbourne, a remarkable performance. Proceeding from Australia to China, she loaded at Shanghai; sailed Oct. 8, 1855; passed Anjer, the 31st, and reported arrival at London, Jan. 9, 1856, in a passage of 93 days. The fourth voyage was from New York to San Francisco, during 1856, and was made in 125 days, with generally light winds throughout. Proceeded to Valparaiso, going down in 45 days, and loaded at Copiapo, with copper ore for Baltimore.

On what was destined to be the final voyage of the *Dutchman*, she sailed from New York, May 30, 1857, and reached San Francisco in 102 days. On her 51st day out she was up with Cape Horn and was on the line in the Pacific on her 74th day. She then had a fine run to within 1000 miles of the California coast, but light and adverse winds required 18 days to cover that distance, her second possible two-figure passage being thus prevented. At San Francisco she loaded a cargo of produce, principally wheat and hides, to a total valuation of $150,000, for New York, and took her departure Nov. 1, 1857. She was making good time, for, when 42 days out, east of Cape Horn, she was spoken by the *Starlight*. However, she piled up on Brigantine Beach, New Jersey, prior to Feb. 13, 1858, and proved a total loss. Valued at the time at $50,000. On her last passage out to

San Francisco, her freight list was only $18,275, whereas on the run from New York to Australia she had received 60 cents per cubic foot.

FLYING EAGLE

CLIPPER ship, built by William Hitchcock, at Newcastle, Me.; launched in December 1852. Deck, 183: 9; over all, 195 x 36: 4 x 23 feet; 1094 tons, old measurement; 1004 tons, new measurement; could carry about 1370 dead weight tons. Dead rise, 15 inches; figurehead, an eagle on the wing. Her model was sharp, with long entrance and clearance lines. Owned by Frederick Nickerson & Co., of Boston, at which port she made her first appearance, Jan. 7, 1853, in tow of the *R. B. Forbes*, from Maine.

The *Flying Eagle* sailed from Boston, on her maiden passage, Feb. 22, 1853, for San Francisco and thereafter made 11 other trips to the same port, from New York or Boston; 12 in all, 6 from each. Her last run over the course was in 1869-1870. On her passages in 1853 and 1860-1861, she received such damage as to be obliged to put into ports for repairs. In 1854, 1857 and 1859, she lost important spars but was able to make repairs at sea. On four of these occasions she had taken her departure during the best season for making a fast passage, which advantage was thereby lost. In four other instances she also left Eastern ports in the favorable season but in only one of them did she have an opportunity to show what she could do. On the other three, light winds, particularly in the Pacific, effectually prevented her from making a good run. The single exception was in 1869-1870, when she left New York, Nov. 10th; was 23 days to the line; passed Cape Horn, 58 days out; crossed the equator on the 91st day, and reached destination 21 days later, Mar. 2nd. This passage of 112 days is her fastest western Cape Horn run.

On her maiden voyage she lost maintopmast and yard and all three topgallant masts, when five days out from Boston; put into Rio, 47 days out; refitted and sailed 25 days later. From Rio to the Horn, was 17 days, and to the equator, 63 days; thence 34 days to San

Francisco, arriving Aug. 10, 1853, in 144 sailing days from Boston and 97 days from Rio. On her second voyage she had a dead beat from Sandy Hook to the line, 35 days; was off the Horn 10 days, in heavy gales, having foretopgallant mast and main yard carried away; crossed the equator, 95 days out, and was 37 days thence to the Golden Gate where she arrived, Dec. 22, 1854, in 132 days' passage. On her third passage she left New York, Sept. 21, 1855, and was 37 days to the line. On the 65th day she passed through the Straits of Le Maire in one hour, in strong northwest breezes; was battling heavy gales for 15 days off the Cape, during which she lost and split sails; crossed the line 101 days out, on Jan. 1, 1856, and on Jan. 17th was within 100 miles of the entrance to San Francisco harbor, which was remarkably fast time. However, to do this remaining short distance required three days, she being under close-reefed topsails the last two days. Arrived Jan. 20th, in 120 days from New York. On her fourth passage she left Boston, Dec. 5, 1856, and was 30 days to the line. Off the Platte, in a heavy gale, carried away the bowsprit cap and the jibboom; was 15 days from 50° to 50° in light winds and calms; crossed the equator, 95 days out and was 23 days thence to port, making 118 days for the passage. In 1858, her time from New York was 132 days and arrival, June 22nd. Had 26 days to the line; thence, 32 days to the Cape, off which was 21 days in northerly gales and had very light winds in the Pacific. On her sixth passage she left New York, Feb. 28, 1859, and crossed the line, 30 days out. In a pampero off the Platte, had the mainmast sprung and was obliged to send down the topgallantmast; off the Cape lost the head of the bowsprit; crossed the equator, 125 days out and was thence 28 days to port, being off the Heads four days in fog; passage 153 days.

Sailed from New York, Nov. 8, 1860, and was 29 days to the line. When 48 days out, in 39° South, had a heavy pampero, breaking the bobstays, springing the bowsprit badly and staving bulwarks, boats and casks. Bore up for Montevideo, for a new bowsprit, arriving five days later and was in port 23 days. Passed Cape Horn, in 15 days from Montevideo, but was 18 days from 50° to 50°; was 36 days from passing the Cape to the equator crossing and 33 days thence to the Golden Gate, the last 20 of which were spent in covering the final 900 miles. Was becalmed off the Heads four days; the royals having been furled for only a few hours during the last 54 days. Arrived, Apr. 18, 1861, in 137 sailing days from New York and 84 days from Montevideo. Left Boston, Feb. 6, 1862, was 26 days to the line and 24 days off the Cape, in heavy gales; crossed the equator, 119 days out, and had the exceptionally long run of 40 days to port, making her passage in 159 days. In 1863-1864 she had 35 days to the line; passed Cape Horn, 72 days out, coming around in fine weather; was 107 days to the equator and 28 days thence; total, 135 days from Boston. Again left that port, sailing Sept. 24, 1864; had 34 days to the line, 18 days from 50° to 50°; passed the Cape, 69 days out; 41 days thereafter crossed the equator, 110 days out; made the South Farallon in 19 days from the equator, but was three days getting into port; passage, 132 days. Sailed from Boston, Dec. 14, 1866; was 29 days to the line; 33 days thence to 50° South; 19 days to 50°, Pacific; 29 days thence to the equator, 110 days out; thence, 31 days; total, 141 days, arriving May 4, 1867. Left New York, Nov. 10, 1869, and was 112 days to San Francisco, her fastest outward run.

Between the fall of 1865 and the summer of 1866, the *Flying Eagle* is said to have made a round between Boston, Australia and the Orient. In the latter part of 1867 she went out from New York to Australia, thence to San Francisco, arriving there June 18, 1868, in 67 days from Newcastle, N. S. W. Then went to Nanaimo, B. C., returning to the Golden Gate with coal. Late in 1870 she left an Atlantic port for Australia; thence to San Francisco from Newcastle, arriving Sept. 16, 1871, in 64 days' passage. Made the run over the Great Circle, being 35 days to the equator and 29 days thence; was three days between Point Reyes and the Heads, in a thick fog. From San Francisco she returned to Newcastle, in 51 days; then back to the Golden Gate, in 61 days, returning to Newcastle, in 52 days; arrival out being May 24, 1872. Sailed thence July 1st and was 57 days to

Hong Kong; went to Manila and passed Anjer, Jan. 15, 1873, bound for New York.

Eastward bound from San Francisco, the passages of the *Flying Eagle* were as follows. In 1853, 44 days to Callao; 85 days thence to New York. In 1855, 55 days to Callao, 71 days thence to Hampton Roads and five days thence to Philadelphia. In 1856, 70 days to Calcutta and 110 days thence to Boston; for 35 days not a sheet was touched and her wheel was lashed. In 1857 she was 48 days from San Francisco to Callao and thence 84 days to Hampton Roads, in very adverse weather; sprang a leak and had to jettison some cargo; had decks swept, main hatch stove and lost a suit of sails. In 1858 she got under way at San Francisco, at 1 P.M., July 9th; discharged pilot at 4 P.M., and came to, off Honolulu, July 19th, in a passage of 9 days and 22 hours; carried mail which had left New York, June 21st, per steamer, via Panama; said to be about the quickest time in transit, if not the record. Loaded at Honolulu, principally with guano received per brig *Josephine*, from Jarvis Island, and was 96 days to New York. In 1859 she was 14 days from San Francisco to Honolulu; thence 39 days to Singapore; thence to Akyab; arrived at Falmouth, June 14, 1860, and at New York, Sept. 13th, in 36 days from Sunderland. In 1861 she was 130 days from San Francisco to Liverpool and thence 46 days to New York, in very rough weather. In 1862 she passed Honolulu in 13 days from San Francisco and was thence 36 days to Hong Kong. Returned to San Francisco in 52 days, having had very heavy easterly gales in the China Sea and stormy weather off the California coast. Then went to Boston, in 111 days, arriving out July 9, 1863. In 1864 she was 97 days from San Francisco to Boston and the following year went over the same course in 113 days. In 1867 she went from San Francisco to New York in 106 days. In 1868-1869 her time from San Francisco to Cork was 102 days, one of the fastest passages that season, and the following year she was 116 days to Liverpool.

In the summer of 1873 she went to Melbourne from New York and thence to Newcastle, N. S. W., where she loaded coal for Hong

Kong, arriving out Mar. 16, 1874. Sailed hence, Apr. 21st, for Iloilo, to load for New York. Thereafter, she is said to have continued in the triangular run to Australia, the far East and home but no details of the few passages are available. She left San Francisco for the last time on Apr. 1, 1872.

The *Flying Eagle* arrived at Mauritius, July 22, 1879, in distress and was condemned and sold prior to Sept. 22nd.

Prior to 1874, her captains were as follows, in regular order;— Capt. W. Parker, one voyage; Captain Bates, five voyages; Captain Walden, five voyages; Capt. John Hayes, two voyages; Capt. E. Lewis, three voyages; Capt. W. Crowell assumed command in the summer of 1873 and was in her on her last voyage.

FLYING FISH

EXTREME clipper ship, launched in September, 1851, from the yard of Donald McKay, at East Boston. 207 x 39: 6 x 22; 1505 tons, old measurement; dead rise, 25 inches; a flying fish in green and gold, was the figurehead. In general appearance she resembled the *Flying Cloud*, but her ends were a trifle sharper and some authorities considered her the faster ship. Her spread of canvas was 8250 yards and, as will appear, she was not quite as lofty as the *Cloud*, but some of her upper yards were more square. Her fore lower-mast was 82 feet long; the topmast 46; topgallant, 24; royal, 16; skysail-mast, 12. On the main they were: 88, 49, 27, 18 and 14; and on the mizzen: 78, 38½, 21, 14 and 10. The corresponding yards were: 70, 55, 41, 32 and 22; 80, 64, 49, 39 and 31; 59, 44, 34, 26 and 21. The masts all raked 1¼ inches to the foot. She was owned by Sampson & Tappan of Boston and, except for one outward passage, was commanded, during her career as an American ship, by Capt. Edward Nickels, an old packet master and navigator of high rank.

As the *Flying Fish*, on all of her outward as well as homeward passages, left port during seasons unfavorable for fast runs, her record is phenomenal. The average of her seven Cape Horn runs to San Francisco, is 105 4/7 days, departures from Eastern ports all having been taken in September, October or early in November. Her average time to the line is 26 3/7 days, and in each of the seven instances, her run is the fastest quoted in Lieutenant Maury's tables for that particular month. Her average time from port to the pitch of the Cape is 54 5/7 days, 49 days being the shortest and 60 days the longest. The average of her time to the Pacific equator crossing is 85 6/7 days; shortest, 74; longest, 92 days. From equator to San Francisco, the average is 19 5/7 days, shortest, 16, longest, 23 days. From equator in Atlantic to a similar crossing in Pacific, average 59 3/7 days, shortest, 52½, longest, 64 days. From the pitch of the Cape to anchorage at San Francisco, average 49 5/7 days, shortest, 41, longest, 61 days. She had a run from 50° South, Pacific, to the equator, in 19 days, and from 170° East, Pacific, to San Francisco, in 12 days. In 1853 she passed through the Straits of Le Maire, in company with the *Onward* and *Skylark*, and reached San Francisco 4 days and 14 days respectively, in the lead. Her outward passages in 1855 and also in 1856, were much shorter than those of any other ship reaching port within a month before or after her. It was the boast of Captain Nickels that his ship had never been "crawled up to" or passed.

On her maiden voyage, the *Flying Fish* left Boston, in tow to the tug *Mayflower*, at 11:30 A.M., Nov. 6, 1851, and at sunset was 28 miles E. by S. of the outer station. At 2 P.M., Feb. 14, 1852, she received her San Francisco pilot and four hours later anchored off the bar, 100 days and 6 hours out and entered the harbor the following morning. This run is often incorrectly quoted as having been 98 days and 18 hours. Her best day's run was 336 miles; poorest, 49; best speed, 15 knots. She made 1194 miles the first four days out and when 14 days out, was in 9° 50' North, having averaged 213 miles daily. At noon, Nov. 20th, 19 days out, she was in 24' South, average thus far, 196 miles. Was in 50° South, 45 days out; passed Cape Horn four days later; was in 50° South, Pacific, on the 54th day; crossed the equator 23 days later and on the 88th day was just 1000 miles from the Golden Gate; then had light winds and calms to port. The New York clipper ship *Sword Fish*, which had left her home port Nov. 11th, had crossed 50° South, Pacific, on her 52nd day; the equator on her 71st day and had reached San Francisco, Feb. 10th, thus beating the *Fish* by 10 days. From San Francisco, the *Flying Fish* went to Manila in 51 days; left that port, May 17, 1852, and was 123 days to New York; 93 days from Anjer.

On her second voyage she sailed from New York, Oct. 31, 1852, and arrived at San Francisco, Jan. 31, 1853, in a passage of 92 days and 4 hours, anchor to anchor. She had to beat around Cape St. Roque, yet was up with 50° South, when 48 days out and passed the Cape on her 51st day; was seven days between the two 50's; crossed the equator 74 days out, 52½ days from the Atlantic crossing. Her run up the Pacific was very good; 19 days from 50° South, to the line, thence 18 days to port, a total of 37 days; from the pitch of the Cape to her anchor, she was 41 days. The medium clipper *John Gilpin*, leaving New York two days before her, arrived at San Francisco one day after her. Continuing her voyage, the *Fish* was 40 days from San Francisco to Manila. Left there, May 6, 1853, and was 107 days to Boston, 79 days from Anjer. Sailed from Boston, Sept. 20, 1853, and was 113 days to San Francisco, with very light winds throughout; best day only 260 miles; for 27 days averaged under 100 miles and for 22 other days the average was under 200 miles; was 600 miles from the Golden Gate when 101 days out. Went to Manila in 42 days. Sailed thence, Apr. 2, 1854, and arrived at New York, July 20th, in 109 days' passage, 80 days from Anjer. The clippers *Wild Pigeon* and *Sweepstakes* had reached port a few hours previously, 76 days from Anjer, and all had fallen in with each other on more than one occasion on the passage.

On her fourth voyage, the *Flying Fish* arrived at San Francisco, Jan. 10, 1855, in 109 days from Boston. Captain Adams, who had taken her out, reported light winds most of the passage; crossed the equator in Pacific, 92 days out and 14 days later was near the Farallons, in a thick fog which prevented her passing through the Golden Gate until three days later. Her skysails were set for 95 days of the passage. In the vicinity of Cape Horn, 57 days out, the rudderhead was twisted off and steering tackles were rigged to complete the voyage. From San Francisco she went to Manila in 57 days; thence to Batavia and Padang; left the latter port, May 20th, and was 86 days to Boston. Captain Nickels had resumed command at San Francisco. Sailed from Boston, Sept. 13, 1855, and reached San Francisco, Dec. 27th, in 105 days; crossed the line in 25 days and 2 hours from Boston Light; was in 50° South, on the 50th day; thence 19 days to 50°, Pacific; crossed the equator 89 days out; thence 16 days to port. Again went to Manila and Padang; left that port, May 19, 1856; had a succession of W. and S. W. gales from the Isle of France to off Algoa Bay; then very strong westerlies for several days. On June 25th, the rudder post broke, necessitating short sail being carried until the arrival at Boston, Aug. 22nd. Left Boston, Oct. 4, 1856, and had a light weather passage of 106 days to San Francisco; was 28 days to the line and 60 days thence to the equator in the Pacific. Sailed from San Francisco, Feb. 5, 1857. After crossing the bar it was discovered that her rudder was gone. She got some 90 miles offshore, when, a temporary one being rigged, she beat back in the face of strong northerly winds and was towed into port on the 10th. Sailed again, Feb. 22nd, and arrived at Manila about Apr. 6th; left there Apr. 29th; passed Anjer, May 25th; then had a fine run of 24 days to off Algoa Bay; light westerly winds and a strong easterly current delayed her passing the Cape until July 7th; touched at St. Helena, July 17th; arrived at Boston, Aug. 24th, 117 days from Manila, 91 from Anjer and 38 from St. Helena.

The seventh and last Cape Horn passage of the *Flying Fish* ended at San Francisco, Jan. 20, 1858, on her arrival in 114 days from Boston. She was 33 days to the line and 58 days thence to a similar crossing in the Pacific. She then crossed to Hong Kong and, returning to San Francisco, reached port, June 22nd, 46 days out. Had continuous head winds and much rain the first 30 days but from 170° East, to port, had fine breezes from S. W. to W. and covered that portion of the run in the record time of 12 days. She then returned to Hong Kong.

The *Flying Fish* loaded tea at Foo Chow for New York. On proceeding to sea, Nov. 23, 1858, and being nearly at the mouth of the river Min, the wind headed her and she was compelled to tack. Captain Nickels had always found her to work like a pilot boat and never to balk in stays; so, confident in her working qualities, he brought her to the wind and successfully made two tacks; on the third she failed to come around. There not being sufficient room for her to wear, the only recourse was to anchor and the working anchor was let go but fouled and hung under the bow. The best bower was then dropped but after 20 fathoms had run out, the chain fouled in the hawse-hole and the anchor failed to bring her up. She drifted on a sand bank and in the considerable swell that was running, her whole fore-body started to work; knees were broken, breast hooks displaced and she commenced taking in water. After two days she was got off and, the cargo being discharged, the displaced parts sprang back into position and only a slight leak was apparent. A thorough survey, however, developed the fact that she was very badly damaged and she was condemned and sold, a mercantile firm of Manila being her purchaser. She was then taken to Whampoa and rebuilt. For a number of years she was engaged in trade between Manila and Spain, being known as the *El Bueno Suceso,* and finally foundered in the China Sea.

FLYING MIST

MEDIUM clipper ship, launched Sept. 13, 1856, from the yard of James O. Curtis, at Medford, for Theodore and George B. Chase of Boston. Length over all, 200 feet x 39 x 24; 1183 tons, old measurement. She was a large carrier, having loaded 2200 tons of general cargo for San Francisco and she had 1922 tons of guano aboard on leaving Baker's Island in 1860. She is everywhere described as a fine looking ship, with slightly concave lines, a bold rak-

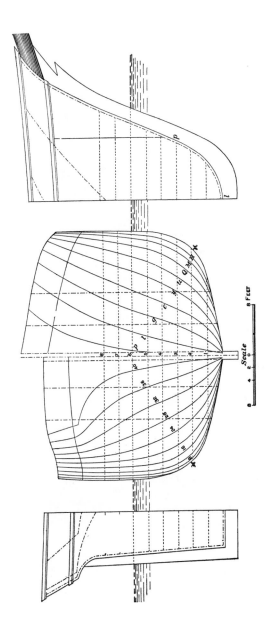

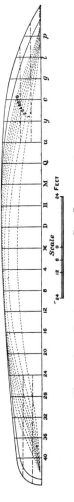

"FLYING CLOUD," 1782 TONS, BUILT AT EAST BOSTON, IN 1851

Lines from Hall's *Ship-Building Industry of the United States*, 1884

"Flying Fish," 1505 tons, built at East Boston, in 1851

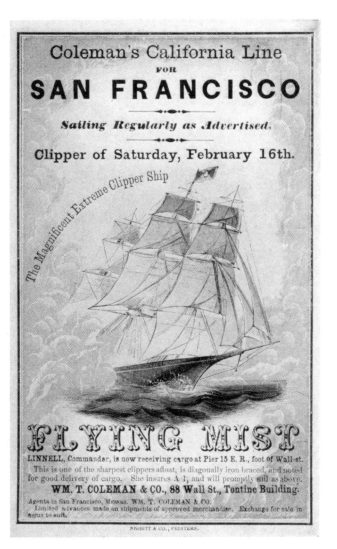

SHIPPING CARD ADVERTISING THE "FLYING MIST," 1183 TONS,
BUILT AT MEDFORD, MASS., IN 1856
From the Peabody Museum, Salem, Collection

"Galatea," 1041 tons, built at Charlestown, Mass., in 1854

ing stem and a neat, round stern. Her figurehead was a full-length female in flowing garments, a fine specimen of carving. Her lower masts were made sticks and she had double topsails and carried a main skysail. In all the ports she visited she was the subject of favorable comment.

She left Boston, Nov. 17, 1856, and arrived at San Francisco, Mar. 12, 1857, in 115 days; had 31 days to the line, 58 to Cape Horn; during 11 days of light winds and calms in the South Pacific she made only 374 miles and was off the California coast for three days. From San Francisco she was 43 days to Valparaiso; proceeded to Caldera and loaded for Philadelphia; sailed Aug. 23, 1857, and anchored off New Point, Chesapeake Bay, Oct. 13th, 51 days out, reporting only 37 days from Cape Horn,—very fast runs. Cleared from Philadelphia, Dec. 10, 1857, for Singapore and Hong Kong, arriving at the latter port on May 25, 1858; loaded at Manila for New York where she arrived Dec. 15, 1858.

In 1859 she was 123 days from New York to San Francisco; thence 42 days to Hong Kong, returning to San Francisco in 48 days. She then went to Baker's Island, sailing thence, guano laden, Aug. 14, 1860, and arrived at New York, Dec. 14th, via Hampton Roads. She again went out to San Francisco, arriving June 24, 1861, under command of Captain Foster, in 119 days' passage; sailed July 22nd, under Captain Stickney, for Queenstown, via Mazatlan; arrived out Jan. 30, 1862, leaving there Feb. 3rd, and reached London on the 8th. Here Capt. E. H. Linnell, who had been in the ship except for the last round voyage, again assumed command and proceeded to Glasgow to load merchandise and sheep for New Zealand, arriving at Glasgow, Apr. 7th, from Gravesend, Mar. 27th. Left the Clyde in May and arrived at Bluff Harbor, N. Z., Aug. 26, 1862, where she was properly anchored by the pilot but during the night was blown ashore and became a total loss. The crew, the 18 shepherds aboard and 820 out of the 1760 sheep aboard, were saved but the general cargo was lost.

FLYING SCUD

EXTREME clipper ship, launched from the yard of Metcalf & Norris, Nov. 2, 1853, at Damariscotta, Maine. Length of deck, 221 feet; beam, 41; depth of hold, 23; 1713 tons, old measurement. She was of sharp model, very strongly built and in every way a fine ship. After arrival at New York, from the builder's yards, she was purchased by parties in that city for $100,000, and soon became noted as a fast sailer.

On her maiden voyage, which was a round between New York and England, the *Flying Scud* did not realize the expectations of her owners or builders as to speed, due to experiencing much heavy weather outward and homeward. Captain Patten was in command and leaving New York, Mar. 23, 1854, she was 29 days to Liverpool. After return to New York she was chartered for the lump sum of $30,000, for a voyage to Melbourne and sailed, Sept. 28, 1854, under command of Capt. Warren Bearse of Hyannis. When two days out, in the Gulf Stream, she was struck by lightning twice, the first time forward, when several men were knocked down. In the second instance, she was hit between the main and mizzen masts when most of the men on deck were knocked down. The ship was not materially damaged but the needles of the compasses revolved with great rapidity, which was thought due to the iron cargo in the after hold having become magnetized. The ship had to be laid to and thereafter, until Dec. 7th, the compasses had to be used on a board extending 10 feet out from the port side. She crossed the line on Oct. 26th and on Nov. 5th was in 27° 41' South, 29° 30' West. The following day she ran 449 nautical miles. Then for a week had variable weather, calms and strong gales; often logged 15 and 16 knots. Ran her easting down in about 44° South and between Nov. 24th and Dec. 10th, made 106° 54' of longitude, the actual distance covered, as figured by Lieutenant Maury, being 4620 nautical miles, an average of 288 miles for the 16 consecutive days. She arrived at Melbourne in 80 days from New York. Then went to Calcutta in 45 days.

Sailed from Calcutta, Apr. 30, 1855, and was 110 days to Liverpool. Arrived at New York, in March 1856, from Marseilles, when Capt. Rodney Baxter of Hyannis, assumed command, Captain Bearse retiring to take the *John Wade*.

The *Flying Scud* sailed from New York, Apr. 14, 1856, and arrived at Bombay, July 4th, in a passage of 81 days. While this run is seven days longer than the record set by the *Sweepstakes* in 1857, it has otherwise been beaten but seldom and then only by a few days. The *Flying Scud* continued in trade between England and Indian ports and on Sept. 26, 1859, reached Liverpool in 92 days from Bombay. She then went out to China, returning to New York, where she arrived, May 15, 1861; from Whampoa, Feb. 5th; Java Head, Feb. 22nd; Cape of Good Hope, Mar. 29th; and the equator, Apr. 21st. Captain Harding, who was then in command, reported that after leaving Whampoa he had fine weather, with mostly light winds, until May 4th, during which period had furled skysails only once, in a squall. On May 4th, at 8 P.M., being then in 25° North, 66° 40′ West, the ship was struck by a whirlwind which carried away all three topgallant masts with the furled sails; the fore and main topmastheads and the head of the mizzen mast were sprung and the courses, topsails and jibs and the fore and main topmast staysails were blown away. After the squall passed, the spanker was the only sail left above deck.

At New York, in November 1861, a one-eighth interest in the ship was sold for $3500. She loaded for San Francisco and with Captain Harding still in command, sailed from New York, Feb. 28, 1862. The first 2½ days out had hard gales; in 66 hours ran 1053 miles; crossed the line 23 days out; thereafter had light winds nearly all the way, not having to reef topsails until just south of the equator in the Pacific. Arrived at San Francisco, June 27th, after a passage of 118 days. Leaving that port, July 28th, she was 44 days to Valparaiso. Arrived at Liverpool, Mar. 14, 1863, from Cobija.

The *Flying Scud* was sold at London, in April 1863, and became the British ship *Cestrian*, of Liverpool, J. Thompson owner. From

1865 to 1871 she is listed as owned in Liverpool, by G. H. Pickering, and commanded by Captain Fothergill and later by Captain Mc-Garrey.

FRIGATE BIRD

CLIPPER ship, built by J. A. Robb, at Baltimore, Md.; launched Jan. 12, 1853. 155 x 33 x 19; 567 tons, old measurement. Owned by C. H. Cummings & Co., of Philadelphia.

Her maiden voyage was from Philadelphia to San Francisco, arriving out Sept. 29, 1853, in 150 days' passage, Captain Cope in command. From San Francisco she went to Manila in 51 days; sailed thence Dec. 4, 1853, and was 121 days to Philadelphia. She was then operated in the China trade for a few years but returned to the California run in 1857.

On Jan. 6, 1858, she arrived at San Francisco in 165 days from Philadelphia, when Captain Cope reported being 45 days in getting around Cape Horn in the face of very severe weather. She then made a round voyage to Hong Kong, being 58 days on the outward passage and 46 days on return. On arrival at San Francisco she found the Frazer River gold excitement at its height and a great demand for tonnage to take miners and supplies to British Columbia. On returning to San Francisco in September 1858, she made the run down from Victoria in the fine time of five days. She then made another round voyage to Hong Kong, and after returning to the Golden Gate, went to Manila and from there to New York. Captain Cope was still in command.

In 1861, the *Frigate Bird,* under command of Captain Johns, crossed from Philadelphia to Liverpool and was sold after arrival, continuing under her original name. Under Captain Thompson she left Southampton, June 27, 1861, for Kurrachee and returning from that port, arrived at London in April 1862. In January 1863 she arrived at Victoria, B. C., with 48 passengers and 570 tons of cargo from London. After returning to England she loaded coal at Shields for San Francisco and arrived out Aug. 17, 1864, in 154 days' passage, Captain Watts in command. Then proceeded to Puget Sound, where she went ashore in Appletree Cove and filled with water. She was towed off, not materially damaged, and loaded a cargo of lumber for Valparaiso.

Registers of 1869 list her as the bark *Frigate Bird*, of Bergen, Norway.

GALATEA

MEDIUM clipper ship, launched Mar. 16, 1854, from the yard of Joseph Magoun, at Charlestown, Mass. 182 x 36: 6 x 23; 1041 tons, old measurement; 939 tons, new measurement. Owned by W. F. Weld & Co., of Boston.

The *Galatea*, under Capt. Harry Barber, sailed from Boston, June 4, 1854, and was 115 days to San Francisco, this being the fastest of her 13 passages from eastern ports to the Golden Gate; her last arrival out was in February 1871, in 120 days. Her longest run was in 1859, 144 days, and the average for the 13 is 130 days. Her shortest time to the line was 25 days; to Cape Horn, 51 days; from 50° to 50°, 8 days and 20 hours; from 50° South, Pacific, to the equator, 19 days; from Sandy Hook to the Pacific equator, 88 days on one occasion, 92 days in two instances and 93 days on her last westward run; best time from the equator, Pacific, to the Golden Gate, 22 days, when she sailed by log 2700 miles; these items applying to various voyages. In 1857 she was within 396 miles of the Golden Gate when 109 days out from Sandy Hook, but light and baffling winds prevented her getting into port until 10 days later. Her two fastest trans-Pacific passages were 40 days to Hong Kong and 43 days to Manila, from San Francisco. She made but one trip from the Golden Gate to Great Britain, 121 days to Queenstown, in 1861-1862. She arrived at New York, Jan. 13, 1860, in 84 days from Callao, via Hampton Roads, five days. In 1865 she was 123 days from Altata to New York. Her other homeward bound passages were from ports of the Far East and among them are noted:—Shanghai to New York, in 1855, 102 days; Whampoa to Liverpool, in 1856, 104 days; Calcutta to New York, in 1859, 101 days; Manila to New York, 1862-1863, 115 days; 1872-1873, 121 days over the same course.

In 1873 the *Galatea* went from New York to Melbourne and thence to Bombay; sailed from that port, June 23, 1874, for Havre; put into Mauritius to repair minor damage and left there July 21st. At Boston, on Dec. 24, 1875, she was sold by Weld & Co., the reported consideration being $18,000. The purchasers were Prendergast Brothers & Co. It was stated, at the time, that she was to load machinery at Philadelphia for the Brazilian Government. In July 1882 she was sold to go under the Norwegian flag to be operated in trans-Atlantic trade; her further career, however, appears to have been short as she is not listed in registers of 1887. In 1858, Captain Barber was succeeded by Captain Lunt; thereafter, in turn, came Captains Wendell, B. L. Cook, Elkanah Crowell, Gardner and Tisdale.

GAME COCK

EXTREME clipper ship, built by Samuel Hall, at East Boston, for Daniel C. Bacon, one of Boston's most successful merchants and ex-sea captains; launched Dec. 21, 1850. Length of keel, 182 feet; of deck, 190: 6; over all, 200 x 39: 10 x 22; 1392 tons, old measurement; 1119 tons, new measurement. She had very sharp ends and everything in her model was sacrificed for speed; her dead rise of 40 inches was greater than that of any other merchant ship with the exception of the *Nightingale*, which was built about the same time. Her swell of sides was six inches and sheer, 36 inches. The figurehead was a game cock, with outstretched neck and head as though ready for any contest. She was heavily sparred and in comparison with the much larger clipper *Flying Cloud*, she was nearly as lofty, within four feet at the main truck; and while her lower yards were a trifle shorter, the upper yards were squarer, the main skysail yard, by four feet. Her mainmast was 88 feet long; topmast, 49 feet; topgallant, 27; royal, 18; skysail mast, 14 feet. The main yard was 80 feet long; topsail yard, 64 feet; topgallant, 49; royal, 39; skysail yard, 31 feet. She spread 8000 yards of canvas in a single suit of sails.

While in speed the *Game Cock* never fully realized the expectations of her owners, yet, during her career of thirty years of hard service she bore throughout the reputation of being one of the fastest ships afloat and her captains all agreed in saying that she was a phenomenally fast ship going to windward. Under command of Capt. Clement T. Jayne, she left New York, June 10, 1859, and crossed the line on the 29th, a very fast run for any season but particularly so for the month of June. She was off Java Head on the 76th day; best day, by observation, 337 miles; during three days in the southeast trades, made 288, 290 and 292 miles, when, as Captain Jayne wrote, a candle on the capstan burned down to the socket, showing that she was going about as fast as the wind, which was on the quarter. She was at Batavia, 78 days from New York. On the return passage, from Colombo to New York, she fell in, off Mauritius, with the British clipper *Forward Ho*, from Foo Chow with tea, and although the *Game Cock* was deeply laden, they kept company for 13 days, and only parted on changing courses after clearing the Cape. *Game Cock's* best day, this passage, was 342 miles by observation and for seven consecutive days she averaged 306.

On the next outward passage, leaving New York, Dec. 8, 1861, she crossed the line in 17 days. On the 15th day out she spoke a British ship, bound north. Captain Jayne showed a blackboard on which was written, "15 days from New York," to which the John Bull response came, "It is a lie"; which reply might seem reasonable to any one. Captain Jayne stated that the most he ever got "honestly" out of the ship, during the four years of his command, was 15 knots. On his first voyage in her, the pilot was discharged off Sandy Hook at 2 P.M., June 10th. On the 11th there was no opportunity for an observation but on the 12th, at noon, observation gave 596 knots for the 46 hours, a rate of 13 knots, while he had thought she "was going along easy at about 9 or 10." The best day on her maiden passage, Captain Hollis in command, was 325 miles. Homeward bound on this voyage, she was 16 days from San Francisco to Honolulu; was off that port 12 hours and was thence some hours under 20 days to Hong Kong, which stands as the record run to this date. In spite of her slow time from the Golden Gate to off Honolulu, her total of under 36 days through to Hong Kong, is within three days of record. On her passage from New York to San Francisco, in 1854, in 114 days, she was only 16 days from the Pacific equator crossing to inside the Farallon Islands, being then detained two days by fog. In 1868, in the North Atlantic, she was in company for five days with the celebrated clipper *N. B. Palmer,* commanded by the driver, Capt. Charles Porter Low, both being bound in the same direction. In the early 70's she was 75 days from New York to Melbourne, Captain Sherburn in command.

She first left Boston, Jan. 23, 1851, and was 48 hours to New York; sailed thence Apr. 3rd; on the 24th sprung her mainmast and was forced to put into Rio, 38 days out; was there 57 days; thence 91 days to San Francisco; thence to Honolulu and Hong Kong, as stated; then made a round trip to Bombay; left Whampoa, May 20, 1852, about the poorest season, and was 123 days to New York. Her second outward passage was 115 days from New York to San Francisco; was within 500 miles of destination for nine days; then went to Callao in 51 days and was 76 days thence to New York. Captain Osgood succeeded Captain Hollis, and made the run from New York to the Heads, San Francisco, in 112 days; was thence 42 days to Shanghai and 111 days home, being 70 days from Anjer. On the fourth passage, Captain Osgood reported much light weather; 33 days to Cape St. Roque and 38 days thence to 50° South; crossed the equator in the Pacific, 121 days out; went to Shanghai in 51 days and arrived at New York, Mar. 26, 1868, 87 days thence, 76 days from Anjer. The following voyage was 97 days from New York to Bombay, thence to Calcutta and 94 days from there to Boston.

Between the summer of 1857 and the spring of 1859, she went

out to China, traded for a time between Hong Kong and Bangkok and returned to New York, but details of this voyage are lacking. On the following one, with Capt. Clement P. Jayne in command, she was 78 days from New York to Batavia; passed Fernando Norhona, 21 days out; from St. Paul and Amsterdam Islands, had adverse winds for a week or ten days. Left Batavia about Oct. 10th, heavily laden, and beating up the China Sea against a strong monsoon, was 48 days to Woosung. Went to Nagasaki, Japan, and at Hong Kong, in March 1860, was chartered by the British Government for six months at 22 shillings per ton register, per month, to transport horses, cattle, etc., from Japan, for use in the Peiho campaign. In January 1861, she was six days from Woosung to Singapore; thence to Padang and Ceylon; arrived at New York, Aug. 27th, in 87 days from Colombo, 35 days from St. Helena. Six days prior to arrival, a suspicious looking vessel, brigantine rigged, supposed to be a Confederate privateer, was seen steering directly for the ship, but after altering the course three times and being steadily followed, she finally got clear of her pursuer during the night.

On her following outward run, the *Game Cock* made the fast time of 17 days to the line, previously referred to. She was 58 days thence to Java Head and went up the China Sea in a very unfavorable season, February and March; her time from New York to Hong Kong was 112 days. She left Hong Kong early in May and was 17 days to Woosung; sailed from Shanghai, Nov. 24, 1862, and arrived at New York in 111 days, only a fair run for the season, but reported heavy westerly gales off the Cape. Sailed from New York, May 2, 1863, under command of Captain Williams; went out to Melbourne; thence to Otago; thence to Newcastle, N. S. W., where she loaded 1000 tons of coal and was 60 days to San Francisco, losing all three topmasts in a hurricane on the passage. She then proceeded to Shanghai and thence to Manila, where she loaded for New York. Sailed, Dec. 30, 1864, and was 103 days on the passage, 48 days from the Cape and 27 from the line. Capt. Benjamin Sherburn succeeded Captain Williams and has to his credit the fine runs of 92 days from New York to Hong Kong, in 1869, and 75 days from New York to Melbourne, previously referred to. Mar. 2, 1872, the *Game Cock*, still under Captain Sherburn, arrived at New York and reported that off Hatteras, in a violent gale, the vessel split and lost sails, had her bulwarks stove and received other damage.

Captain Stoddard was the next commander of the *Game Cock* and she was continued in trade between New York, Australia and China. In April 1875 she was at San Francisco, in 49 days from Hong Kong, going thence to Manila, in ballast. While at Shanghai, in June 1862, she was offered for sale but no transfer was made. Several years later she was sold to Robert L. Taylor and others, of New York, who were at that time owners of the celebrated clipper *Young America*. The *Game Cock* was finally condemned at the Cape of Good Hope, in February 1880.

GANGES

BUILT by Hugh R. McKay, at East Boston, in 1854. 192 x 39 x 23; 1254 tons. W. S. Bullard of Boston, owner. Sold to go under British flag, in May 1863.

GAUNTLET

CLIPPER ship, launched Sept. 5, 1853, from the yard of Thomas J. Southard, at Richmond, Maine. 230 x 42 x 23; 1854 tons, old measurement. On account of her great size, apprehension had been felt that she might foul a ledge of rocks after clearing the ways but no mishap occurred. A concourse of people from near and distant points had gathered to witness the scene, the *Gauntlet* being the largest vessel to be built in Maine up to that time. She was described as being the sharpest ship built north of Portsmouth and equal to anything afloat in beauty of model and strength of material. Her owners, Stephenson & Thurston of New York, gave the command to Capt. Samuel G. Borland.

The first voyage of the *Gauntlet* was from Bath to Mobile; thence to Liverpool, where she arrived Feb. 25, 1854, in 39 days from Mobile; reached New York, June 8th, in 28 days from Liverpool. Sailed from New York, July 14th; was 28 days to the line; thence 35 days to 50° South, in very bad weather, and was 18 days rounding the Horn. Arrived at Callao, Oct. 16th, in 94 days from New York. The return passage was 66 days from Callao to Hampton Roads. Sailed from Norfolk, Mar. 9, 1855, and was 27 days to Liverpool. Went to Marseilles and was under charter to the French Government as a transport to the Crimea. Left Malta, Sept. 20, 1856, for Havre; arrived at New York, Jan. 13, 1857, 30 days from Havre; lost two suits of sails in very heavy gales. From New York she went out to the west coast of South America and was reported at Valparaiso, Aug. 3, 1857. Later she loaded guano at the Chincha Islands; sailed from Callao, Oct. 21st, and arrived at New York, Jan. 3, 1858, from Hampton Roads.

Sailed from New York, Feb. 27, 1858; when 30 days out had the mizzenmast sprung; was 35 days to the line and 72 days to Cape Horn; in the South Pacific had foremast sprung; in the North Pacific had a succession of very light winds and calms and was off the Golden Gate several days in strong head winds. Arrived at San Francisco, Aug. 9th, in 162 days from New York. Sailed Oct. 12th and arrived at Hong Kong, Dec. 8th, via Johnson's Island. Arrived at San Francisco, May 29, 1859, in 46 days from Hong Kong, Captain Borland reporting very light winds and calms for 20 days in the China Sea. Sailed from San Francisco, Aug. 1, 1859, and arrived at New York, Nov. 5th, in 95 days' passage.

Sailed from New York, Jan. 13, 1860, and was 27 days to London. Loaded coal at Cardiff for Shanghai and sailed Apr. 6th and arrived at Woosung, July 24th, in 109 days' passage. Later she went to Hong Kong where she was reported sold, becoming the British ship *Sunda*, of Hong Kong, Smith, Archer & Co. being her registered owners. Under command of Captain Paul she went to Manila and Bangkok. Sailed from that port, Nov. 2, 1861; passed

Anjer, the 20th; the Cape of Good Hope, Dec. 25th and arrived at New York, Feb. 8, 1862, in 98 days from Bangkok. Sailed from New York, Apr. 16, 1862, for Hong Kong and was reported at Anjer, July 5th, 80 days out. After completing her outward passage she went from Hong Kong to London where she was sold for £8000. She was then put in trade between England and Australia, Captain Paul being succeeded by the famous "Bully" Bragg, a notorious character, who had been mate under "Bully" Forbes in the *Lightning*. Among sailors, the *Sunda* had the name of being a "hard" ship, but she made some very fast passages. On Sept. 25, 1863, she arrived at Brisbane, in 76 days from London, the record run up to that time. On one passage out to Moreton Bay she is said to have raced the *Flying Cloud* for four consecutive days, at the end of which she was 18 miles in the lead, both ships having frequently logged 16 knots during the period.

The *Sunda*, on a voyage from Norfolk for Liverpool, was reported burned at sea some time in 1878. Uninformed authorities have erroneously credited certain fast passages she made in 1863-1864 to a ship built in 1865 at Miramichi, under the name *Royal Arch*, but later named *Sunda*.

GAZELLE

EXTREME clipper ship, launched from the yard of William H. Webb, at New York, Jan. 21, 1851. On the same day, Mr. Webb also put afloat the Pacific Mail steamship *Golden Gate* and the Havre packet ship *Isaac Bell*. The *Gazelle* was 182 x 38 x 21; 1244 tons, old measurement. She had great dead rise and was very sharp, some authorities claiming that she was the sharpest ship ever built by Mr. Webb and that her model was never equalled. Although very strongly built, every other consideration was secondary to speed in draughting her plans. Robert L. Taylor, of Taylor & Merrill, her owners, was very emphatic in his condemnation of the inartistic figurehead originally attached, so it was removed and a billet substituted.

A published table of the time expected to be made by a number of clippers on their maiden runs out to San Francisco, in 1851, gave the *Flying Cloud* and *N. B. Palmer*, 95 days each, with *Gazelle* and *Ino* coming next, in 100 days. The *Gazelle*, however, due to light winds and the sickness of Captain Henderson throughout the entire passage, did not come up to expectations, being 135 days on the passage, against *Flying Cloud's* 89 21/24 days, *Palmer's* 106 days and *Ino's* 134 days. As a matter of fact the *Gazelle* never did realize the expectations of her builder or owners, as to speed, although her trans-Pacific and homeward bound runs were all fast. Her career was short and on her outward passages she always played in bad luck.

Following her maiden trip, she made three runs from New York to San Francisco: in 1852, 136 days; 1853, 119 days; and in 1854, 114 days. Her time from San Francisco to Hong Kong was 44 days, 39 days and 43 days and on her fourth run she was 35 days out when she was dismasted in a typhoon, 1500 miles east of destination. Her first passage from Hong Kong to New York was reported by Captain Dollard, who had succeeded Captain Henderson at San Francisco, as 98 days; her second was 99 days and her third and last, 91 days. In all instances she had left during the strength of the favorable monsoon.

On arrival at San Francisco, Oct. 1, 1852, Captain Dollard reported that when 53 days out, off Cape Horn, he had been in collision with a Spanish ship, losing jibboom, all headgear, cutwater and part of the stem, starting the catheads, ripping off copper and developing a leak of ten inches per hour. The accident occurred at 4 A.M., it blowing a gale with a bad sea on. A jury bowsprit was rigged but it was soon carried away and but little headsail could thereafter be carried, causing difficulty in steering. Fortunately light winds prevailed during the rest of the passage and on arrival at San Francisco extensive repairs were made. On this passage she was overhauled just north of the line in the Atlantic by the *N. B. Palmer* which had left New York six days after her. The two ships met again in the North Pacific, the *Palmer* having been obliged to put into Valparaiso to land mutineers and secure stores.

On her third outward passage, the *Gazelle* left New York, June 9, 1853, Captain Dollard reporting on arrival out, all light winds; the maintopgallant sail was furled for only three hours between the Platte and the Golden Gate; was off Cape Horn in calms three days. On her fourth run out she was 51 days to 50° South, thence 20 days to 50° in the Pacific; 20 days thence to the equator and was close to the California coast for 12 days in light winds and calms and off the Heads two days in the fog. Reached port, Sept. 27, 1854, in 114 days from New York.

The *Gazelle* sailed from San Francisco, Oct. 14, 1854, for Hong Kong. On Nov. 19th, in about 21° North, 141° East, and only 35 days out, she was struck by a typhoon and thrown on her beam ends. The mainmast broke off close to the deck as soon as it hit the water, taking the mizzenmast also. Slowly righting, a heavy sea struck her, rolling her over until the foremast was in the water, when it also went, taking the bowsprit with it. She righted with ten feet of water in the hold; 16 of the Chinese passengers in the 'tween decks, out of 189 aboard, were drowned. Mrs. Dollard and children who were in the cabin had a narrow escape. The Chinese were sent to the pumps and in 61 hours the ship was cleared of water and the crew had cut away the mass of wrecked spars and rigging and improvised a small jury rig. The only provisions on hand were 15 barrels of bread and two of beef, with 1500 gallons of water for the 210 persons left and there were no navigating instruments. The ship was finally towed into Hong Kong, Dec. 4th, a complete wreck. She was condemned and sold for $13,500 and then repaired and renamed *Cora*. In 1857-1858 she was under the Peruvian flag, hailing from Callao, and was reported as engaged in carrying coolies to the guano deposits. In 1861-1862 she is registered as ship *Harry Puddemsey*, owned by E. Bates & Co., hailing port, Liverpool.

GEM OF THE OCEAN

MEDIUM clipper ship, built in 1852, by Hayden & Cudworth, at Medford, Mass., for William Lincoln of Boston. 152 x 31 x 20: 6; 702 tons, old measurement; 629 tons, new measurement. She was a fine, dainty-looking craft with rounded lines but fairly sharp ends. Dead rise, 14 inches. A billet substituted for a figurehead.

The *Gem* made but one Cape Horn passage to San Francisco, such being her maiden run, arriving out Feb. 2, 1853, in 120 days from Boston. Capt. Freeman Crosby reported crossing the equator in the Pacific, 89 days out, being near the coast on the 110th day and off the Heads for five days. From San Francisco she went to Manila in 46 days and thence to Boston in 110 days, 85 days from Anjer; season unfavorable. Sailed from Boston for Fort Philip, Australia, Oct. 4, 1853, still under command of Captain Crosby. During 1854-1855 she was in the Australian and Calcutta trade and made passages from the latter port to Boston in 108 and 105 days. Between 1861 and 1863 she was running on the Indian coast, between Bombay, Madras and Calcutta, Captain Williams in command. Left Bombay, June 27, 1863, put into St. Thomas, Nov. 6th, and arrived at New York, Nov. 18th.

The *Gem* arrived at New York, Apr. 13, 1866, from Whampoa, Jan. 5th, in 98 days, 43 days from the Cape. Captain Pritchard was in command, he then taking her out to Hong Kong and thence to San Francisco, arriving there May 26, 1867. She then went to Alaska for a cargo of ice and from that date remained on the Pacific coast, having been purchased by McPherson & Wetherbee for $18,000, in gold. The firm had their headquarters at San Francisco and used her to transport lumber, principally to South American ports. In November 1867 she struck a sunken rock near Bellingham Bay but was floated and repaired, her rig being then changed to that of a bark. Cost of repairs $15,000. On Aug. 1, 1879, while bound from Seattle for San Francisco, she went ashore on Vancouver Island and became a total loss.

GEORGE PEABODY

BUILT by J. O. Curtis, at Medford, in 1853. 195 x 39 x 27; 1397 tons. Wm. F. Weld & Co., Boston, owners. Condemned at Valparaiso in May 1881.

GODDESS

FULL model, but a fine merchant ship. 1126 tons, old measurement, but carried 2100 weight and measurement tons cargo for California. 182: 10 x 36: 5 x 23: 9. Built at Medford, Mass., by Hayden & Cudworth, in 1855, for Baxter Brothers of Boston. Sold to N. C. Nash & Co., February 1861. Sold at London, England, in September 1864, for £6800. In 1868-1869 and later, was the Norwegian ship *Nordens-Dronning* of Stavanger.

Arrived at San Francisco, July 8, 1856, Capt. Zenas Crowell in command, in 133 days from Boston; was 28 days to the line; thence 27 to 50° South; 18 days rounding the Horn, in strong gales; 32 days from 50° Pacific to the equator, crossing June 2nd, 99 days out; thence 34 days. From 50° South, to port, had nearly all light winds and calms. Sailed from San Francisco July 27th; arrived at Calcutta, Nov. 22nd. Sailed from Calcutta (Sand Heads), Jan. 21, 1857, and was 51½ days to the Cape. The *Syren* and *Panther*, leaving at about the same time, had 47 and 45 days' passage, respectively. The *Goddess* arrived at Boston, May 3rd, in 101 days from Calcutta.

Arrived at San Francisco, Nov. 16, 1857, in 129 days from Boston. Captain Crowell reported 31 days to the line; 63 days to 50° South; 22 days rounding the Cape, in heavy gales, losing sails, etc.; 23 days from 50° South, Pacific, to the equator, crossing 108 days out. Best day on passage 225 miles; best day on the run out the previous year, 283. She had left Boston July 9th, within a few hours of the *Panther's* taking her departure, also for San Francisco. Both had light winds in the North Atlantic, but the *Panther* having a superior model and being a faster sailer, crossed the line 36 hours ahead. Off

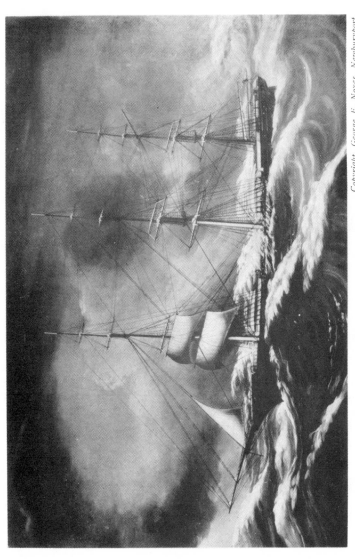

"GEM OF THE OCEAN," 702 TONS, BUILT AT MEDFORD, MASS., IN 1852

"Golden Eagle," 1121 tons, built at Medford, Mass., in 1852

From a Chinese painting showing the ship off Hong Kong

"Golden Fleece," 1535 tons, built at East Boston, in 1855

the Platte, the *Panther* encountered a very heavy gale and had to go east of the Falkland Islands, while the *Goddess* escaped the pampero and had a good passage to and through the Straits of Le Maire, thus gaining say, 15 days. From the Horn, each had about the same run to the line, the *Goddess* being 108 days out against the *Panther's* 119 days. The *Goddess* was then 22 days to destination while the *Panther* was 24, showing that the race is not always to the swift. The *Goddess* sailed from San Francisco, Dec. 7, 1857, for Mazatlan.

Arrived at San Francisco, Apr. 20, 1861, Captain Lathrop in command, in 157 days from Boston. Sailed June 2nd and arrived at Liverpool, Oct. 17th. Arrived at New York, Jan. 21, 1862, in 25 days from Liverpool. Arrived at San Francisco, Aug. 23, 1862, Captain Crowell* in command, in 127 days from New York. Sailed Sept. 14th and arrived at Callao, Nov. 16th. Sailed from Callao, Jan. 28, 1863; on Mar. 21st, 52 days out, was spoken in 34° 30' South, 30° 07' West; thence was 60 days to Antwerp, arriving May 20th, which would be 112 days from Callao. Sailed from Antwerp, July 8, 1863, and arrived at Cardiff, July 17th.

The *Nordens-Dronning* arrived at San Francisco, Sept. 7, 1870, in 201 days from Newcastle-on-Tyne. Had been in collision in the Channel and been forced to put into Cowes to repair damage. Sailed from San Francisco Oct. 3rd and arrived at Greenock, Feb. 8, 1871, via Queenstown. The *Nordens-Dronning* is listed as late as 1887, still hailing from Stavanger; tonnage, 1086, new measurement. She was at Pensacola in June 1886.

GOLDEN CITY

EXTREME clipper ship, launched Aug. 4, 1852, from the yard of Jacob A. Westervelt, New York, for account of Chambers & Heiser of that city. 154: 10 x 33: 10 x 20: 10; 810 tons, old measurement. She was rakish and was called a perfect little gem. Was one of the few clippers to be equipped with Cunningham's rolling top-

---

* Probably some other Crowell than the Zenas Crowell who was her first captain.

sails. Capt. Samuel F. Dewing, formerly in the bark *Isabelita Hyne*, well known as a fast vessel, was appointed to the command.

The *Golden City* sailed from New York, Sept. 8, 1852, and arrived at San Francisco after a passage of 118 days; was off the Farallons when 112 days out but was detained five days in a dense fog. From San Francisco she went to Manila in 47 days. Left there May 7, 1853, and was 111 days to New York, being 78 days from Anjer. The day after leaving Manila she was in collision with a Spanish brig, having jibboom and cutwater carried away. After arrival at New York, Capt. Richard Canfield took command and was 109 days to San Francisco, arriving Feb. 8, 1854. Sailed thence Feb. 28th and arrived at Woosung, Apr. 5th, a fast run of 35 days. Loaded at Shanghai; left Woosung, May 1st; passed Anjer, June 3rd, and arrived at New York, Aug. 19th, in 110 days' passage. Total time on the voyage around the world, 9 months and 28 days, including detention in ports.

On her third voyage she reached San Francisco, Apr. 10, 1855, in 132 days from New York; was 20 days off the Horn in heavy gales, losing main yard and fore topsail yard and off the California coast was becalmed five days. Sailed from San Francisco, Apr. 27th and was 39½ days to Shanghai. Reached New York, Nov. 2nd, after a rather long run from Shanghai, reported as 137 days. The command was then given to Capt. Latham B. Avery, an experienced navigator, who, while a lieutenant in the United States Navy, under Commodore Jones, had hoisted at Monterey, on Oct. 20, 1842, the first American flag that had been floated over California. On arrival at San Francisco, May 1, 1856, Captain Avery reported the passage of the *Golden City* as being 113 days from New York; was 24 days to the line; 19 days rounding Cape Horn and 84 days to the Pacific equator crossing. The ship then made a round voyage to Hong Kong and on reaching San Francisco, on return, Nov. 19th, after a good run of 42 days, Captain Lee was in command. She sailed again, Dec. 22nd, and was 55 days to Hong Kong. In September 1857 she was at Amoy loading for New York, where she arrived Feb. 3, 1858.

On Nov. 16, 1858, the *Golden City* arrived at San Francisco after a long passage of 144 days from New York. Captain Leary, then in command, reported having much light weather; 43 days to the line; 79 days to the Cape and 15 days getting 'round. From San Francisco she was 51 days to Shanghai, thence to Foo Chow and 140 days from that port to London. Crossed to Boston and arrived at Tahiti, May 30, 1860, after a passage of 105 days. Then went to Manila and Boston and arrived at New York, Mar. 25, 1861, four days from Boston, in ballast, Captain Moore in command. She was then reported as being owned by Henry A. Pierce of Boston. In May 1861 she crossed to England and sailed from Cardiff, July 10th, for the Cape of Good Hope; left Simon's Bay, Nov. 3rd and arrived at Bassein, Jan. 13, 1862. Left that port, Mar. 1st; hove to off St. Helena, May 15th, arriving at Cowes, July 7th, and at Antwerp, the 10th. On Nov. 18th she reached Table Bay from Sunderland; proceeded next day and arrived at Hong Kong, Jan. 31, 1863. Then went to Bassein and Falmouth.

After arrival in England, late in 1863, she was reported as having been sold to go under British colors, continuing her original name. In registers of 1870, her owners are given as Houlder Brothers of London. In January 1873 she was at Hong Kong, as the British bark *Tokatea*, owned in Sydney. She then crossed to San Francisco, in 72 days of very heavy weather, but discharged her cargo in perfect condition. Thereafter she was engaged principally in the lumber trade out of British Columbia, trans-Pacific and with the antipodes, and in March 1877, was at San Francisco, 65 days from Hong Kong. On Nov. 18, 1878, she left Victoria, B. C., for Australia. Returning from Sydney, with coal for Honolulu, she was lost, Dec. 1, 1879, on Wollstock Island, South Pacific. The crew, comprising three whites and 15 Chinese, reached Tahiti in the ship's boats. The wreck was sold for $150.

GOLDEN EAGLE

EXTREME clipper ship, launched from the yards of Hayden & Cudworth, at Medford, Mass., Nov. 9, 1852. 192 x 36 x 22; 1121 tons; dead rise, 20 inches; a gilded eagle on the wing was her figurehead. She had the old style single topsails and carried three skysails; spread 7000 yards of canvas in a suit of sails. She is described as a handsome ship and was built to the order of William Lincoln & Co., of Boston, under the superintendence of Capt. Samuel A. Fabens, who was her commander until 1858 and who was subsequently master of the celebrated *Challenge*. At the time of the destruction of the *Golden Eagle* she was owned by E. M. Robinson of New Bedford and John A. McGaw of New York and hailed from New Bedford.

She sailed from Boston, Dec. 3, 1853, for San Francisco and when 36 days out, in 38° South, 48° West, and four days ahead of the time made by the *Flying Cloud* on her first 89-day passage to San Francisco, she shipped a tremendous sea forward, which instantly crushed in the gratings over the head, breaking off and splitting all the knees, breast hooks, etc., and opening the topgallant forecastle. The main rail was torn off and the outer planking above the main deck stripped off as far as the catheads. The ship was immediately brought before the wind and as daylight showed that the damage was impossible of repair at sea, a course was set for Rio. Repairs took about a month and the passage from Rio to destination, occupied 78 days, the run up the Pacific from 50° South being made in 40 days. Having passed the latitude of Rio when 32 days out from Boston, the whole run would be equivalent to 110 sailing days. From San Francisco she went to Callao in 43 days; thence to the Chincha Islands, where she loaded 1120 tons of guano; left Callao, Sept. 26th; arrived at Hampton Roads, Dec. 8th, in 73 days' passage; was considerably damaged in sails and spars and rigging on the voyage.

On her second voyage she was 124 days from New York to San Francisco; was 17 days off the Horn, yet was on the line on the 91st day out; thence to port, however, she had 33 days of light winds and calms. From San Francisco was 40 days to Callao; left there Oct. 22nd; put into St. Thomas, Dec. 25th, 64 days out; sailed the 27th and arrived at New York, Jan. 8, 1855. The log of the third outward passage shows;—Left New York, 1: 30 P.M., May 10, 1855; crossed the line June 1st, sailing 4063 miles; July 3rd, 54 days out, was in 50° 30" South, 63° 12" West, total distance 7723 miles; July 6th, noon, passed through the Straits of Le Maire; 7th, noon, made land about Cape Horn, Cape S. W. by W.; at 11: 30 P.M., Cape bore N. W. by W. July 16th, after five days of heavy weather, crossed 50° South, in the Pacific, 67 days out; total distance, 8800 miles. Aug. 4th, crossed equator, 86 days out; then had 20 days of light winds and calms and at 2 A.M., Aug. 24th, lay to for daylight, when received a pilot and at 9 A.M. anchored in San Francisco harbor, in 106 days' passage. Total distance sailed, 15,437 miles; best day, 280 miles. The run up the Pacific, 39 days, was very good. From San Francisco she crossed to Hong Kong in 43 days; loaded Chinese coolies at Swatow for Havana and was about 80 days from Anjer to destination.

On arrival at San Francisco, Dec. 1, 1856, Captain Fabens reported having covered the different sections of the passage as follows:— 36, 24, 12, 26 and 30 days; total from New York, 118 days. Sailed from San Francisco, Dec. 25th, at noon; discharged pilot 1: 30 P.M.; crossed the line in 101° West, Jan. 13, 1857; during the four days between Feb. 3rd and Feb. 7th, noon to noon, made 221, 281, 270 and 266 miles; on the best day the course was N. E. by N., wind E. by S. Feb. 9th, midnight, lying along the land with calms and light airs and anchored at 2 A.M., in Callao Roads, 44 days from San Francisco, sailing 6742 miles. Left Callao, guano laden, June 14th, and arrived at Havre, Sept. 3, 1857, 81 days out. Crossed to New York, in ballast, in 28 days. The fifth voyage was made under Captain Harding and started auspiciously with 21 days to the line and 49 days to 51° South; thereafter heavy gales were met with for 22 days, during which decks were swept and bulwarks, hatch house, water casks, etc., were stove. Crossed the equator 103 days out and arrived at San Francisco, June 11, 1858, in 135 days from New York. Sailed again July 15th and arrived at Honolulu, the 27th, 12 days out. Having made good connection with the Panama steamer at San Francisco, she landed mails at Honolulu which had left New York 36 days previously, which is said to be record time to that date. From Honolulu she took a cargo of whale oil to New Bedford, arriving out Mar. 5, 1859, after a passage of 100 days, beating the *Elizabeth F. Willetts*, *Skylark*, *West Wind* and *Anglo Saxon*, all having left the Islands at about the same time.

On her sixth voyage, the *Golden Eagle* reached San Francisco, Dec. 24, 1859, Captain Luce, then in command, reporting a long and hard passage of 217 days from New York, less six days in port at Talcahuana. Adverse weather in the Atlantic prolonged her run to the Horn to 85 days and she then had 90 days of heavy gales and mountainous seas before getting into the Pacific. Lost fore and main yards; had bulwarks stove; the furled jibs were washed from the boom and in 58° South, 59° West, she was under bare poles for six successive days with decks constantly flooded and drifting six degrees to eastward. Fifteen of the crew were on the sick list and on arrival at Talcahuana, Nov. 12th, where she put in short of water, only ten seamen were fit for duty. Left that port, Nov. 18th, and in spite of the fact that she was becalmed five days in 30° North, her time to San Francisco was 36 days. Completing this voyage, she proceeded to Callao and left there, guano laden, June 8, 1860, for Hampton Roads. On arrival at New York, Captain Swift assumed command and had a fine run of 110 days to San Francisco; returned direct to New York in 103 days. On July 21st, just north of the equator, in Atlantic, 81 days out, was in company with the *Mary L. Sutton*, which had left the Pacific port eight days after her and both reached their common destination the same day, Aug. 12th. The *Golden Eagle* then made a voyage as a United States transport, returning to New York, Feb. 21, 1862, seven days from Port Royal, in ballast. Again loaded for San Francisco and made the run out in

117 days; proceeded to Howland's Island and loaded guano, sailing about Nov. 20, 1862, for Cork, for orders. All went well until the morning of Feb. 21, 1863, when 90 days out and in 29° North, 45° West and with three other sailing vessels in sight, the smoke of a steamer was perceived. Fearful that it might prove to be the *Alabama*, Captain Swift signaled his nearest consort, the bark *Olive Jane*, from Bordeaux for New York, and both sailed off in different directions to distract the attention of the steamer, which was then in full chase. The *Alabama*, for so she proved to be, sped after the bark as being the slower sailer and offering the promise of an easier capture, but the captain of the *Jane* kept doggedly on his way, evidently determined, if he could not escape himself, at all events to do his best to increase the chances of the *Golden Eagle*. Finally a round shot through the rigging of the bark brought her to and then the *Alabama* under sail and a full head of steam, started in the direction of the ship, which was making the best of her way off and was some 15 miles distant. However, the steamer was going at the rate of three to one of the chase and by the end of a couple of hours she also was brought to, with the Stars and Stripes flying and her maintopsail to the mast. Both the *Olive Jane* and the *Golden Eagle* were set afire and burned. In the case of the latter the claim filed and allowed, was $56,000 for vessel, $30,000 for freight and $27,522 for cargo.

GOLDEN FLEECE (1)

MEDIUM clipper ship, launched July 2, 1852, from the yard of Paul Curtis, at Boston, and built for Weld & Baker of that city. She capsized while being rigged but was righted without having sustained any material damage. 173 x 35 x 21; 968 tons, old measurement. Captain Freeman was in command during her career, which was very short, and under conditions which allowed no opportunity of showing what she could do in the way of speed.

On her maiden voyage she sailed from Boston, Aug. 16, 1852, and arrived at San Francisco, Jan. 4, 1853, in a passage of 140 days, in practically all unfavorable weather. The clippers *Golden City*, *John Wade* and *Malay*, taking their departure from eastern ports a month later than the *Golden Fleece*, experienced much more favorable winds, each of the three making the passage in 116 days. From San Francisco the *Fleece* returned to Boston via Manila.

On her second voyage she arrived at San Francisco, Apr. 10, 1854, after a passage of 128 days from New York. Was 14 days off Cape Horn, in strong gales, during which she lost an entire suit of sails. Had light winds in the Pacific, being 18 days covering the final 1300 miles. The clipper *Polynesia*, which had left New York 24 days after her, passed through the Golden Gate in company, her time being 104 days.

The *Golden Fleece* cleared from San Francisco for Manila, on Apr. 21, 1854, and while proceeding to sea the next day, she missed stays and being caught in an eddy, drifted broadside on the rocks just outside of Fort Point, Golden Gate. The tugs *Hercules* and *Resolute* could not pull her off and she soon bilged. The following day being Sunday, she was visited by thousands of sightseers. Her mizzen mast and fore and main topmasts went over the side when she stranded, but the hull did not break up until Oct. 23rd, although the surf had been very heavy at times. The hull was sold for $2600 and sails and rigging for $580. The pilot in charge said that her loss was due to "Letting go the lee main braces before the order was given."

In 1855, her former owners had a second *Golden Fleece*, of 1535 tons, built by Mr. Curtis, and this ship had a long and successful career.

GOLDEN FLEECE (2)

MEDIUM clipper ship, launched Nov. 20, 1855, from the yard of Paul Curtis, at East Boston, and is said to have been his finest production. Length for tonnage, 210; over all, 222 x 37: 9 x 25; 1535 tons, old measurement; 1475 tons, new measurement. Dead rise, 14 inches; swell of sides, 12 inches; sheer, 4 feet. Her figurehead was a knight in armor. In size and model she was practically a duplicate of the *Reporter*, a product of the Curtis yard, in 1853, and as to sailing qualifications, both ships stand very high in the class of medium models. The capacity of the *Fleece*, in dead weight cargo, was 2000 short tons. She was employed in the California trade during her whole career and was a prime favorite, owing to the excellent condition in which her cargoes were delivered and to her uniformly good passages. In 1876, a survey showed her timbers to be perfectly sound. Her original owners were Weld & Baker of Boston. About 1872 she was purchased by Thayer & Lincoln of the same port.

All but one of the passages from eastern ports, made by the *Golden Fleece*, were to San Francisco. In 1871 she left Boston for Bombay, but almost immediately met with disaster, as will appear, and the voyage was temporarily abandoned. In 1856, 1858 and 1865, her departures were taken from Boston, her passages out being 113, 112 and 126 days respectively, an average of 117 days. Between 1857 and 1876, she made 12 passages from New York, those under 120 days, being 118 days, in 1859; 111 days in 1870, her fastest westward; and 116 days in 1874. In 1873 she was forced to put back from the Straits of Le Maire, to Rio, and was 108 days from the latter port to San Francisco. Her average of the 11 direct runs from New York is 125 days, with 143, 130 and 130 as the three longest. Her average of the 14 direct runs from Boston and New York is 123 1/3 days, in spite of the fact that she took her departure during the best season for short passages, on only four of them. Her average time from port to the line for these four runs is 22½ days; average of the other ten, 32 days. Fastest time to the line, 21 days, made on two occasions; fastest from port to 50° South, 51 days; to 50° South, Pacific, 65 days; from 50° to 50°, 12 days; to the Pacific equator crossing, 87 days; thence to San Francisco, 20 days. On her passage of 121 days in 1875, she crossed the equator Nov. 17th, 101 days out, and 12½ days later, she was 200 miles from the Golden Gate, a run which is very close to record over that particular section. However, six days of calms and light airs, with a heavy westerly swell, followed by a day of strong northerly winds and a high sea, delayed her arrival into port until Dec. 7th, 20 days from the equator. On arriving at San Francisco, Feb. 12, 1870, 111 days from New York, Captain Adams reported having crossed the equator 90 days out; then having a fine run to 32°, but four days of calms ensuing, effectually prevented the accomplishment of his anticipated 105 day passage. She reached San Francisco, Oct. 29, 1860, in company with the fast clipper *Golden State*, both being 128 days from New York; their positions and runs in the Atlantic had been widely divergent but from the Horn to port both encountered practically the same conditions of wind and weather and made the same time.

The passages of the *Golden Fleece* from San Francisco, were as follows:—to New York, 102, 95 and 113 days; to Boston, 98 days; to Liverpool, 119, 125 and 106 days; to Cork, 122, 112 and 111 days; to Callao, 46 and 46 days; to Honolulu, 13, 24 and 14 days; to Hong Kong, 44 days, this being in 1868, she arriving out three days ahead of the fast clipper *White Swallow* which had passed through the Golden Gate two days before her. In 1865-1866, she was 43 days from Honolulu to Manila, thence going to Cebu and being 133 days from there to New York. In January 1867 she was 30 days from Honolulu to Hong Kong, on which occasion a Chinese merchant paid $600 for a stateroom for himself and family. Completing this voyage, she returned to San Francisco via Yokohama, reaching her destination, July 1, 1867, 27 days from the Japanese port,—a good passage. In 1870 her time from Honolulu to Hong Kong was 34 days. In 1857-1858 she was 94 days from Callao to Queenstown, reaching Boston, June 28, 1858, in 33 days from London. In 1863, following her arrival at Liverpool from San Francisco, she crossed to New York in 29 days with a cargo of salt.

For a vessel engaged in trade, particularly in the Cape Horn run, for as great a length of time as was the *Golden Fleece*, she was exceptionally fortunate in escaping damage from the elements, the most serious instance being on her outward passage in 1873. Leaving New

York, Mar. 3rd, all went well until she reached 37° South. From there to Staten Island she had very heavy weather, spars and rigging being damaged and all her sails were split or entirely blown away. She was forced to put about and run for Rio, arriving June 4th, and remaining in port until July 5th. Serious damage was done to her cargo on her second voyage when, on entering San Francisco harbor, June 21, 1857, a pilot in charge, she struck heavily on Four Fathom Bank, otherwise known as the Potato Patch, off Point Bonita. In spite of hard work at the pumps, she had 14 feet of water in her hold by the time she was run up on the mud flats in the bay. In 1871 she was the victim of a very unique mishap. On July 1st she sailed from Boston, under command of Captain Bray, with 1902 tons of ice for Bombay. At 3 A.M. of the third day, the sawdust and shavings used in packing the ice were found to be on fire, in the lower hold near the fore hatch. All efforts to extinguish the fire were futile, so Captain Bray shaped a course for the nearest port, Halifax, which was reached during the night of the fifth day. She was immediately berthed at Tobin's wharf, the hatch uncaulked and opened and streams of water forced below, but without effectual result. The ship was then scuttled, 20 feet of water being allowed to enter. When the fire was extinguished, supposedly, a steam fire engine pumped her dry but later the fire again broke out and water had again to be applied. The fire is supposed to have originated from stevedores smoking while stowing the cargo. She arrived back at Boston, July 24th, and was overhauled and repaired but it was not until Oct. 26th that her readiness to receive cargo was announced.

On Nov. 19, 1877, the *Golden Fleece*, under command of Captain Horton, bound from New York to San Francisco, grounded on the English Bank, at the mouth of the Rio de la Plata, and put into Montevideo. A survey showed her to be badly damaged and she was condemned and subsequently sold. Her cargo was forwarded to destination by the ship *Granite State*.

The first master of the *Golden Fleece* was Capt. Alfred M. Lunt, formerly of the ship *Humboldt*. Capt. John L. Manson succeeded, being in charge from 1858 until 1865; he was later in the *Valparaiso* and *Young America*. Then followed Captains Hubbard, Nelson, Willcomb, Robert C. Adams, Bray, Horton, formerly in the *Ocean Express*, and Humphrey.

GOLDEN GATE

EXTREME clipper ship, launched July 12, 1851, from the yard of Jacob A. Westervelt, New York, for Chambers & Heiser of the same city. 186: 8 x 40: 4 x 21: 6; 1349 tons, old measurement. She had long and sharp ends and was in every way a handsome ship. During her short career she did some very good work. A sister ship, the *Golden State*, built in the same yard, for the same owners, a year later, had a sea life of 34 years and ranked as one of the fastest of the clipper fleet.

On her maiden voyage, the *Golden Gate* sailed from New York, Oct. 13, 1851, under command of Captain Truman, arriving at San Francisco, Feb. 5, 1852, in a passage of 115 days. She encountered light weather in all sections of the run and her best day's work was only 296 miles. It took eight days to cover the final 300 miles. From San Francisco she went to Hong Kong, in 55 days, and on her run thence to Manila, she had an interesting race with the clipper bark *Arco Iris*, from the northerly end of Luzon to Manila. In head winds, accompanied by squalls of rain, thunder and lightning, the two vessels were in sight of each other daily, for nine days, often passing close aboard on opposite tacks. Both arrived at the entrance to Manila Bay on the evening of May 25th. The bark ran in and anchored at sunrise, while the *Golden Gate* stood offshore and did not come to her moorings until late in the afternoon when she found that her smaller competitor had secured the only profitable charter offering. From Manila, the *Golden Gate* returned to New York, via Batavia, in 103 days.

On her second voyage she left New York, Dec. 6, 1852, under command of Captain Barstow, and arrived at San Francisco, Mar.

20, 1853, in a passage of 104 days. She was 20 days to the line; 22½ days thence to 50° South; 11 days rounding the Horn; 26 days in the South Pacific; crossed the equator, 80 days out, and had 24 days thence to destination. Captain Barstow reported being off the pitch of the Cape, 47 days out, and in the latitude of Valparaiso, 13 days later, having then every prospect of making a rattling good passage, but here the fine breezes and weather, theretofore encountered, forsook her. From San Francisco she went to Hong Kong, in 42 days, thence proceeding to Shanghai. Left that port, Sept. 26th, and arrived at New York, Jan. 10, 1854, in a passage of 106 days, 78 days from Anjer.

On her third voyage she sailed from New York, Apr. 2, 1854, with Captain Dewing in command, and crossed the line on the 20th, some hours under 18 days from Sandy Hook. She then had a top-gallant-mast carried away and in consequence fell to leeward of Cape St. Roque. However, she was in 24° South, when 32 days out and on the 50th day was at the entrance to the Straits of Le Maire, but was three days getting through, in the face of heavy gales. Made the Cape Horn passage in 16 days; crossed the equator 91 days out, and was 29 days thence to San Francisco; arrived Aug. 1st, in 120 days from New York. She then crossed to Shanghai, in 43 days, and loaded for London. On Dec. 4th, when 9½ days out from Shanghai, she put into Batavia, with loss of jibboom, through having been run into by the bark *Homer*. On arrival at London, early in March 1855, it was stated that she had made the run to Deal in the unprecedented time of 86 sailing days from Shanghai. She was then chartered to load troops and stores for the Crimea, on French account, for $7500 per month and a bonus of one franc per ton, if she reached Constantinople in 15 days from Marseilles.

The *Golden Gate*, Captain Dewing, sailed from New York, Apr. 11, 1856, for Bombay. On May 9th she put into Pernambuco, partially dismasted. On May 26th, when nearly ready for sea, a fire broke out and the wind blowing a gale, she was soon burned to the water's edge. Boats from the British ship *John Lynn*, took off her crew. She was valued at $60,000 and was fully insured; her freight money was insured for $25,000. The hull and such gear as was not burned was sold at auction for $700. The second officer was suspected of having set the fire.

GOLDEN HORN

BUILT by Clark & Wood, at Wiscasset, Me., in 1854. 186 x 37 x 23; 1193 tons. H. Clark, Wiscasset, owner. Sold to go under British flag, 1863. In 1886, was the Norwegian bark *Golden Horn*, of Christiania.

GOLDEN LIGHT

MEDIUM clipper ship, built by E. & H. O. Briggs, at South Boston, in 1852; launched Jan. 8, 1853. The *Golden Light* was built to the order of James Huckins & Sons and her construction was superintended by Captain Huckins. 167½ feet, keel; 182, deck; 193, over all; 36 feet, beam; 22½, depth of hold; 1140 60/95 tons. She had a dead rise of 27 inches; swell of sides, 6 inches; and sheer, 2½ feet. Her wedge-like bow was slightly concave below, merging into convex above, and her cutwater, as it rose, sprang outward and terminated in a torch staff grasped by a golden hand, from which blazed a golden light. Her stern was elliptical and beautifully ornamented with carved work.

Under command of Capt. Charles E. Winsor, she sailed from Boston, Feb. 12, 1853, for San Francisco. About midnight on Feb. 22nd, in 22° 23′ North, 47° 45′ West, she was struck by lightning and set afire. Every exertion was made to save the ship but at 6 P.M., on the 23rd, her people were forced to abandon her, she then being entirely in flames. At 10 P.M., the foremast burned off and fell; a half hour later the mizzenmast followed; and by midnight she was almost entirely consumed. The people, 35 in all, were in five boats, amply provisioned and watered, and were advised by Captain Winsor to steer southwest and keep together, the three boats which had compasses to lead. On the morning of the 24th, one boat was missing and the fourth night after leaving the ship, another boat was missing. The other three were picked up five days after the abandonment, by the British ship *Shand*, Captain Christie, from Calcutta, and the occupants were landed in Boston, Mar. 20th. One of the missing boats, having seven occupants, reached Antigua, Mar. 5th, while the fifth boat with eight men was never heard from. The *Golden Light*, with her cargo, was insured for $288,000.

GOLDEN RACER

MEDIUM clipper ship, built in 1852, at Thomaston, Maine, by J. C. C. Morton. 160 x 34 x 19; 837 52/95 tons, old measurement. Her model is described as that of a clipper, with the clear deck and large, well appointed cabins of a packet ship. She was launched under the name of *Hyperion*, but this was changed to *Golden Racer*, probably on account of her immediately engaging in trade with California. Originally owned in Boston, she was sold by auction, at New York, in October 1855, for $45,000.

The *Golden Racer* was lost on her third voyage, before its completion, but her short career is very creditable. On her first passage, that from Thomaston to Boston, where she was to load for San Francisco, she logged 120 miles in eight consecutive hours. Sailed from Boston, Jan. 29, 1853; was 35 days to the line; thence 21 days to 50° South; 19 days rounding the Horn; 22 days to the equator, which was crossed on the 96th day out; then had very light winds and was 34 days to destination, being 100 miles from the Golden Gate four days before her arrival, June 9th; passage 130 days. Off the Horn, the maintopmast was sprung and some other damage to spars received. From San Francisco she was 53 days to Callao; loaded guano at the Chincha Islands; left Callao, Oct. 11th, and was 80 days to Hampton Roads.

On her second voyage she arrived at San Francisco, Aug. 9, 1854, in 135 days from Baltimore. Off the Horn, lost the mainyard; had very light winds all the way up the Pacific, being becalmed for 16 days in 19° South and having the very long run of 37 days from the equator crossing to destination. Then went to Calcutta, where she loaded for Boston and arrived, Apr. 11, 1855, 90 days from the Sand Heads, a very good passage.

On her third voyage she left New York, Nov. 16, 1855; was 27 days to the line; passed around Cape Horn, in fine weather, 57 days out; had a heavy gale in 50° South, Pacific, during which bulwarks were stove, sails split, etc.; crossed the equator 95 days out and was close to the California coast for five days; arrived at San Francisco, Mar. 13, 1856, 117 days from New York. Arrived at Shanghai, May 16th, 43 days from San Francisco. Was subsequently stranded in the River Min and became a total loss. Was fully insured; had no cargo aboard.

Capt. Benjamin M. Melcher had the *Golden Racer* on her first voyage; Captain Nagle, on the second, and Capt. George Henry Wilson, on the third. The latter had been in the ship *Tonquin*, which, on entering San Francisco, in November 1849, from New York, was stranded and lost on Whaleman's Spit (afterwards known as Tonquin Shoal), just inside the Golden Gate. In 1850, he took the ship *Samoset* of Boston. This ship was lost at Fort Point, Golden Gate, on entering San Francisco harbor, Dec. 1, 1852, from New York.

GOLDEN ROCKET

FULL modelled ship, built at Brewer, Me., and launched in the fall of 1858. Owned by Moses Giddings and E. S. Dole of Bangor. 608 tons. Was advertised to leave Bangor on initial voyage, Nov. 11th, for Boston, a large number of passengers having engaged passage. She was put on the berth for San Francisco, at Boston, and reached the former port, May 18, 1859, after a passage of 158 days. Captain Pendleton had been in command, outward, but on leaving the Pacific port she was cleared under Captain Collins, destination being given as Malden Island, where she was to load a cargo of

"Golden State," 1363 tons, built at New York, in 1852
From a photograph showing her in dock at Quebec in 1884

"GOLDEN WEST," 1441 TONS, BUILT AT EAST BOSTON, IN 1852
From an oil painting showing the ship leaving Boston harbor

"GREAT REPUBLIC," 4555 TONS, BUILT AT EAST BOSTON, IN 1853

From an oil painting in the possession of Nichols L. McKay, showing the ship lying at her dock in New York, after the fire

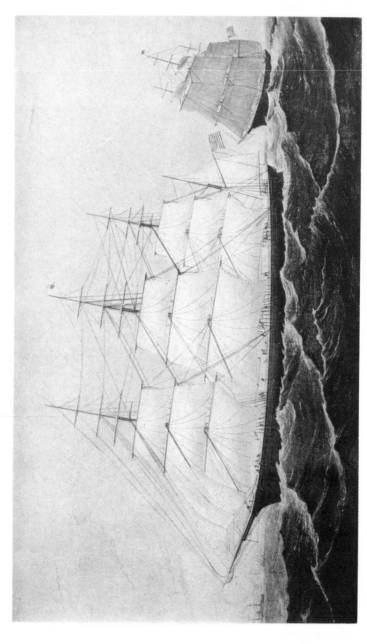

"GREAT REPUBLIC," 3356 TONS (AS REBUILT), BUILT AT EAST BOSTON, IN 1853

The largest clipper ship ever built. From an oil painting in the possession of Nichols L. McKay

guano. On Sept. 24th, however, she was reported as arriving at Valparaiso.

Her career was short. On July 13, 1861, while on a voyage in ballast, from Havana to Cienfuegos, under Captain Bailey, she was captured and burned by the Confederate privateer *Sumter*, Captain Semmes. The privateer's crew was jubilant over the capture of the *Rocket*, which was their first prize, while Captain Bailey was very indignant over the treatment accorded him, which included his being robbed of $200, private means. Captain Semmes' sentiments regarding his action towards his first prize were expressed in the "Index," of May 1, 1862, as follows:

"It was about 10 o-clock at night when the first glare of light burst from her cabin hatch. Few, few on board can forget the spectacle. A ship set on fire at sea! It would seem that man was almost warring with his Maker. Her helpless condition—the red flames licking the rigging as they climbed aloft, the sparks and the pieces of burning rope taken off by the wind and flying miles to leeward; the ghastly glare thrown upon the dark sea as far as the eye could reach and then the deathlike stillness of the scene—all these combined to place the *Golden Rocket* on the tablet of our memories forever."

The capture occurred off the Isle of Pines. The *Rocket* was beating to windward, steering a course that would almost bring her into contact with the *Sumter*. The latter displayed British colors until the vessels were about a mile apart, when they were replaced by the Stars and Bars and a shot across the bows of the victim soon made her astonished captain heave to. The crew were taken aboard the *Sumter*.

GOLDEN RULE

BUILT by Hitchcock & Co., at Damariscotta, Me., in 1854. 185 x 37 x 23; 1185 tons. F. Nickerson & Co., Boston, owners. Reported in 1900 register.

GOLDEN STATE

EXTREME clipper ship, built in 1852, by Jacob A. Wester-velt, at New York. 188 x 39: 8 x 21: 6; 1363 tons, old measurement; 944 tons, new measurement. Owned, at first, by Chambers & Heiser of New York; later, by A. A. Low & Brother of same city. She was launched, Jan. 10, 1853, with part of her cargo aboard. She had very fine lines, her ends being long and sharp and was a beautiful vessel, alow and aloft. She was a favorite vessel with shippers and also a profitable one to her owners.

On her maiden voyage she left New York, Feb. 8, 1853, under command of Capt. L. F. Doty, and on the third day out came up with the ship *Northern Crown,* bound for San Francisco. Eight hours later, the *Crown* was out of sight astern. The next day she fell in with the medium clipper *Ariel,* from New York for China, and in nine hours she was out of sight, to leeward. On the night of Feb. 18th, when ten days out, she carried away all three topmasts with everything attached. The day previous she had made 327 miles under royals and every thing looked propitious for a short passage but as it was she had to put into Rio, practically dismasted. After repairing she sailed from Rio, Apr. 6th, and arrived at San Francisco, July 12th, 97 days from Rio and 133 net sailing days from New York. Captain Doty reported 26 days off the Horn and light winds from the equator to port. Sailing from San Francisco, Aug. 2nd, she was 54 days to Shanghai and arrived at Deal, Feb. 9, 1854, 94 days from Woosung and 82 from Anjer. From London she crossed to New York in ballast.

Her second voyage was made under Captain Barstow, leaving New York, May 25, 1854, and arriving at San Francisco, Sept. 28th, a passage of 125 days. She had fallen to leeward of St. Roque and lost a week in beating around; was within 700 miles of the Golden Gate in 14 days from the line, but had light winds and calms the rest of the way. She had made Staten Island, 61 days out, and two days later, off the Horn, in heavy gales, saw the clipper *Golden West,* under single-reefed topsails, also bound west. Both ships crossed the line in the Pacific the same day, the *State* three degrees to the eastward of her competitor, thereby gaining better trades and leading into San Francisco by four days. The *State* sailed from San Francisco, Oct. 14, 1854, in company with the clipper *Galatea* and both had the same passage to Shanghai, 42 days. The *State* left Shanghai for New York, Jan. 1, 1855; cleared Java Head the 14th; was on the equator, 67½ days out, and 21 days later anchored in New York harbor, in a passage of 88½ days.

The third voyage was a round between New York and China, she going out to Hong Kong in 90 days and returning in 105 days from Foo Chow. The fourth voyage was over the same route, 114 days on the outward passage and 95 days on the return. Captain Hepburn then took command and leaving New York, Mar. 19, 1857, was 93 days to Hong Kong and also 93 days from Foo Chow to New York. On the homeward run she was 31½ days from Java Head to the Cape, which, for that time, was beaten only by the *Challenge*. The *State* was 74 days from Anjer to port.

On her next voyage the *State* had an experience which was becoming rather common, that of mutiny on board. On the outward passage to Hong Kong, when off Penang, the crew refused duty on the plea that the food was insufficient and the officers and boatswain were fearfully beaten with handspikes. The mutineers escaped in boats to Penang where they were taken into custody. The first mate died of his wounds. After arrival at Hong Kong, the *State* made a round voyage to Bangkok, followed by one to Australia. On this latter outward passage, she reached Sydney in a leaky condition, the passengers and crew having been compelled to pump day and night to keep her afloat. She left Hong Kong, Dec. 2, 1859, and made a short stop at Batavia; passed the Cape of Good Hope, Jan. 21, 1860, and arrived at New York, Mar. 2nd, in a passage of 91 days gross but claimed as only 84 days actual sailing time. Near Mauritius she spoke the clipper *Electric Spark* which had left Hong Kong nine days after her but had not put into any intermediate port. The *Spark* reached New York three days after the *State*, her time from Hong Kong being also 84 days.

Capt. C. Ranlett now took command and had a light weather passage of 128 days from New York to San Francisco, thence 94 days to Cork. Her cargo was 1195 short tons of wheat, which was considerably under her original register tonnage. After crossing from Liverpool to New York, in 20 days, in ballast, she again loaded for San Francisco and went out in 120 days, in light winds. Then went to Yokohama and China. Arrived at New York, Dec. 15, 1862, 127 days from Amoy and 78 from Anjer. She again changed masters and under command of Capt. Rowland T. Delano, went from New York to San Francisco, arriving July 6, 1863, 121 days out. Went to Callao and loaded guano at the Chincha Islands for Hamburg. When 71 days out was in 25° North, 37° West, a good run thus far. Eight days later, in a heavy gale, the decks were swept and the mate and two men were lost overboard. Arrived off the Start, Apr. 4, 1864, 100 days out from Callao.

The *Golden State* made no subsequent passages around Cape Horn to the westward and but one to the eastward, that of her return from San Francisco to New York, in 107 days, in 1873. Her operations were confined to trade between New York, China and Japan, she always being a favorite and having the longest career of any vessel ever so engaged. In May 1867, it was stated that her cargo of tea, recently imported, was the largest ever received at New York and that it had been sold prior to arrival for $1,000,000. Leaving New York in June 1867, she went out to Hong Kong, Amoy, Hong Kong again and arrived back at New York in under eight months on the round, including all detentions. In 1869 she had large repairs made at New York, being practically rebuilt. On Nov. 22, 1872, she reached San Francisco in 34 days from Shanghai, a very fast run.

In 1873-1874, Captain Berry was in command, Captain Delano having remained ashore to take a much needed vacation at his home in Fairhaven, Mass. Captain Berry, however, is said to have later again taken the ship, being reported as in command when the *Golden*

State took her last departure from New York as an American ship on Jan. 13, 1883. She was then bark rigged and was bound for Anjer. In the North Atlantic she sprung a bad leak in very stormy weather and in March put into Rio in distress. Her cargo was discharged and she was sold to D. & J. Maguire of Quebec, who renamed her *Anne C. Maguire* and put her under the Argentine flag. She was operated in the Atlantic trade until December 1886, when she went ashore on Cape Elizabeth, near Portland, Maine, and broke up.

GOLDEN WEST

EXTREME clipper ship, launched Nov. 16, 1852, from the yard of Paul Curtis, East Boston, to the order of Glidden & Williams of Boston. Dimensions: deck, 196 feet long; over all, 210 x 39 x 23: 4; 1441 tons, old measurement. She had a long, sharp entrance, her lines being at first almost straight, becoming convex to meet the swell of the sides. Figurehead, a gilded eagle.

On her maiden voyage she left Boston, Dec. 12, 1852, under command of Capt. Samuel R. Curwen, and was 124 days to San Francisco. When 21 days out she was 53 miles north of the line but was unable to get into south latitude until seven days later, having been forced in the meantime to cover 1200 miles, mostly to the north and east. The passage of the Horn occupied 14 days, in light winds and calms, and when 101 days out, she crossed the equator in the Pacific. From San Francisco she went to the Chincha Islands for guano and arrived at Hampton Roads, Jan. 20, 1854, in 69 days from Callao. On her second voyage she left Philadelphia, May 10, 1854, and was 145 days to San Francisco. Had the long run of 39 days to the line and was off the Horn 20 days, in heavy gales. The *Golden State*, which arrived out four days ahead of her, had met her off the Horn and both ships had the same run thence to the equator. From San Francisco the *Golden West* was 55 days to Manila, thence to New York, where she arrived, May 17, 1855, in 99 days. On the passage she struck on a reef in Gaspar Straits but got off after 200 tons of hemp had been jettisoned.

Her third voyage was made under Captain Putnam, 175 days from New York to San Francisco. Off Cape Horn lost jibboom, foretopmast, had steering apparatus broken, sails split and was otherwise damaged. Put into Valparaiso, when 111 days out, and was in port 26 days. From Valparaiso she was 39 days to San Francisco, a very fast run. She then crossed to Hong Kong, via Honolulu, in 56 days gross. Captain Folger assumed command and sailing from Hong Kong, Apr. 17, 1856, she made the passage to San Francisco in 47 days. On May 13th she left the coast of Japan and on June 2nd, made the Farallon Islands, a run of slightly over 20 days during which time she logged 4876 miles. This is the record from Japan to San Francisco to this date. She then returned to Hong Kong, under Captain Putnam, in 62 days. After taking a rice cargo from Bangkok to Shanghai she left the latter port, May 17, 1857, and was 103 days to New York, being 79 days from Anjer.

At New York, Captain Curwen again took command and she sailed Feb. 25, 1858, arriving at Sydney, Aug. 8th. Had lost her rudderhead and put into Simon's Bay for repairs. From Sydney she went to Hong Kong in the fast time of 40 days, thence crossing to San Francisco in 60 days. Left San Francisco, Sept. 8, 1859, under Captain Pinkham, and arrived at New York in 126 days. Captain McKenzie then took her and crossed to London, thence 100 days to Melbourne. Thereafter, until late in 1862, she was trading in the Far East with Captain Lunt in command. Captain Crandall then took her to New York, reaching port, Apr. 18, 1863, in 101 days from Shanghai. She then crossed to Liverpool and later was sold at auction for $25,000. For some time previously she had been owned in New York by J. A. & T. A. Patterson.

In 1864 the *Golden West* was listed as hailing from Liverpool, J. G. Ross being her owner, and Captain Jewett master. In 1866 she was transporting coolies from China to Peru.

GOOD HOPE

BUILT by J. O. Curtis, at Medford, in 1855. 187 x 38 x 23; 1295 tons. R. L. Taylor, New York, owner. Sold to George F. Burritt of New York. Resold to E. E. Morgan's Sons, New York. Condemned at Bahia, June 1873. Repaired and continued as Swedish ship *Solide;* at one time named *Frederick Hasselman;* lost near Quebec, in 1881.

GOVERNOR MORTON

MEDIUM clipper ship, built by James M. Hood, at Somerset, Mass., for Handy & Everett of New York. Launched, fully rigged, Nov. 22, 1851. 192 x 39 x 26; 1429 tons, old measurement; 1303 tons, new measurement; capacity about 1740 dead weight. She was a sharp, deep ship, with three laid decks, having been built to run between New York and Liverpool, in the Handy & Everett Line. The great demand then prevailing for tonnage to California, however, caused her diversion in that direction and the third round voyage she made was her only experience as a trans-Atlantic liner. Of her 25 years of active service, no less than 20 years were passed in the California trade, in which she was always a popular ship, particularly from the early sixties down. During the years 1856-1861, she was engaged in general business.

On two, out of her total of 13 passages from New York to San Francisco, the *Morton* was forced to put into ports in distress, and on two others, her runs, due to continuous adverse conditions, were no criterion of her ability as a sailer. Of the other nine passages, the shortest was 104 days, in 1855; longest, 133 days, in 1873; average, 121 2/3 days. From San Francisco she made following passages:— to New York, four, in 103, 115, 107 and 105 days, an average of 107½ days; to Great Britain, four, in 130, 136, 117 and 117 days, an average of 125 days; to Callao, two: the first in 68 days, the second in 55 days; to Calcutta, two, the first being 82 days, she going thence to London; to Honolulu, one, 13 days, thence to Phoenix Island to load guano for Europe.

In trade, other than to California, some of her voyages were;—in 1854, Liverpool to New York in October, 23 days' passage, with 400 passengers; in 1856-1857, London to Melbourne, 91 days; 1857-1858, London to Sydney, 107 days; 1859-1860, New York to China, thence to Havana with coolies. Mar. 3, 1861, the *Morton*, Captain Dunbar, left London for New York; from the Downs, the 13th. Three days out she collided with an unknown vessel and sustained some damage, arriving at her port of destination, Apr. 18th. She then resumed her place in the California fleet, under Captain Smith.

The *Morton* was undoubtedly a fast sailer but an analysis of the memoranda of her several passages shows that she was unfortunate both as to meeting with mishaps and encountering unfavorable conditions of wind and weather. On her maiden passage it was predicted by authorities that she would make the run out to San Francisco inside of 100 days, but she met with light winds throughout and was 33 days from the Pacific equator crossing into port; the whole passage from New York being made in 125 days. On the return to New York she had much heavy weather and had her bowsprit sprung, yet she made the passage in 103 days. On her second passage she lost two topmasts and jibboom in a squall in the South Pacific; was 15 days getting rerigged and 50 days thence to San Francisco, in light winds; total time, 124 days. Her third passage, 104 days to San Francisco, was her fastest westward run. She crossed the line in 20 days and 11 hours from Sandy Hook, sailing 3664 miles; was 45 days to the Horn, having been only 19 days from St. Roque to 50° South; was 16 days rounding the Horn and 46 days from 50° South, Pacific, to destination. In 1862, on her run of 115 days from San Francisco to New York, she was 26 days to the line; 26 days thence to 50° South; 14 days rounding the Horn, in heavy weather; had a hurricane of 36 hours during which she was lying to, a portion of the time with lee rail and end of fore-yard under water; ship laboring, with cargo shifted; was 92 days to the equator and 33 days thence to port, being within 200 miles for five days. In 1864 she passed Rio when 27 days out from New York.

While loading at New York, in the spring of 1867, in competition with the *Prima Donna*, the *Morton*, as well as her rival, received much attention and one newspaper has the following:—"Both being of nearly equal sailing capacity and having charts marked out as accurately, only an accident can give one an advantage." How accurate this writer's judgment was, is evident by the fact that three hours after Captain Horton entered the Golden Gate in the *Morton*, Captain Herriman also brought in his charge, the *Prima Donna*. Both had crossed the line, had passed through the Straits of Le Maire and been on the equator in the Pacific, on the same day. Their passages were 123 days. In 1870, the passage of the *Morton* was 119 days from New York. She was but 42 days from 50° South, Pacific, to San Francisco, while the following year she was 72 days covering the same ground, having had but eight days of trades during that time. On her next run out, 133 days, Captain Howland reported being 62 days to the Horn and 71 days thence, all in very light winds. In 1874 she was 22 days from New York to the line and 20 days from the Pacific crossing to San Francisco, having mostly light winds and calms the intervening 76 days. The *Morton's* trip in 1875 was her last as well as her slowest westward run, being 175 days. She had either light winds, calms or gales and did not take in a single sail for the 51 days between 45° South, Pacific, and San Francisco.

In addition to the mishaps already recounted the *Morton* was ashore in 1859, on a reef, while bound from Havana to New York, but got off the next day. Much more serious was her experience in 1862, when she was forced to put back from near the Falkland Islands, on account of a bad leak. She went into Montevideo where the cargo was discharged and repairs occupied over three months. After leaving there she was damaged off the Horn, having all head rails carried away and only saving the head by lashing chains about it; lost two men overboard at different times. After arrival at San

Francisco, 279 days from New York and 104 from Montevideo, she was repaired at a cost of $27,500. In 1861, on the passage from London to New York, while in the British Channel, she carried away the crossjack yard and lost and split sails and shortly after was run into by some vessel and received considerable damage. In 1868, outward bound to San Francisco, she experienced bad weather off the Horn and was damaged to such extent that she put back to Rio for repairs which occupied 28 days and cost $7000. In 1863 she was rebuilt at New Bedford, at a cost of $30,000.

On July 2, 1877, while loaded with cotton and staves for Grimsby, England, and anchored at the South West Pass, Mississippi River, she was struck by lightning, took fire, was scuttled in 20 feet of water and burned to the water's edge. About 800 bales of cotton were saved and the vessel was sold as she lay for $2500. She was raised and towed to New Orleans and there libelled, vessel and cargo, for salvage, by the boats and tugs that had assisted. The vessel and cargo were valued at $250,000.

The first captain of the *Morton* was John A. Burgess of Somerset, under whose supervision the ship was built. He had previously been in the *Narragansett* and subsequent to his leaving the *Morton*, after making a number of voyages in her, he was in the celebrated clipper ship *David Crockett*. In June 1872, while on a passage from San Francisco for Liverpool, 61 days out, he was lost overboard in a severe squall. He had intended to give up the sea at the termination of the voyage. Other masters of the *Morton* were Captain Dunbar, Captain Smith, Capt. L. W. Horton and Capt. J. E. Howland, who had her from the summer of 1868 until the fall of 1876. Captain Davis was in command when she was burned. According to the Register of 1875 she was then owned by Burling and Davis, hailing port, New York.

GRACE DARLING

MEDIUM clipper ship, built in 1854, by E. & H. O. Briggs, at South Boston. 185: 5 x 37 x 23: 6; tonnage 1197, until 1865, when, by new measurement, it became 1042. She was not as sharp as most of the medium clippers and was said to be about the same model as the *Alarm* and *Fair Wind*. Neither was she very fast but she was always a favorite with shippers and was singularly free from the accidents so common with clipper ships of her day. Her dead rise was 15 inches and a female attired in white garments was her figurehead. Her original owner was Charles B. Fessenden of Boston. In 1858 she was bought by Baker & Morrell for $37,000 and during the latter part of her sea life she was owned by Adams, Blinn & Co., who had large mills at Seabeck, on Puget Sound, and who used her in the lumber trade.

On her maiden voyage she left Boston, June 17, 1854, under Capt. S. H. Doane, and arrived at San Francisco, Nov. 7th, in a passage of 143 days. Reported being 78 days to the Horn and ten days off, in heavy gales during which she lost flying jibboom and fore and main topsail yards. Crossed the equator, Oct. 8th, in 113° West, 113 days out, and had a fine run to within 700 miles of the Golden Gate, which latter distance occupied 16 days. The whole voyage was not up to expectations but homeward bound she did better, being 56 days from San Francisco to Singapore and 74 days to Calcutta. From Sand Heads she was 50 days to the Cape, 81 days to the line and 104 into Boston.

On her second voyage she left Boston, July 25, 1855, and arrived at San Francisco, Dec. 1st, in a passage of 129 days; thence to Manila, via Honolulu, and back to Boston. On her third voyage to San Francisco, Capt. Allen H. Bearse had her and arrived out, Oct. 14, 1858, in 124 days from Boston. Captain Baxter replaced Captain Bearse and took her out to Shanghai and then returned East. Her next arrival at San Francisco was on Apr. 8, 1861, Captain Bearse again in command, in 129 days from Boston. Loaded 27,264 one hundred pound sacks of wheat and sailed, May 1st, for London. Arrived out, Aug. 16th, after a passage of 107 days. The *Mary L. Sutton*, which left San Francisco eight days after the *Darling*, caught up with and spoke her off the Horn and was 95 days to New York. The next voyage of the *Darling* was from Sunderland to Bombay, with coal, arriving out Feb. 17, 1862, and sailing thence, June 5, 1862, for Liverpool. She arrived at San Francisco, May 9, 1863, in 132 days from Liverpool and loaded again with wheat and was 114 days to Queenstown. Crossing to Boston she loaded for San Francisco, Captain Hotchkiss taking her out, and arrived, Oct. 24, 1864, in 144 days. Returned to Boston in 106 days.

Captain Gibbs now took command and arrived at San Francisco in 130 days. Had a good run as far as the equator in the Pacific, which he crossed Jan. 2, 1866, and 19 days thereafter was within 300 miles of the Golden Gate, requiring 12 days to make that distance and being in sight of the Farallon Islands for the last five days of the passage. Had it not been for this unfortunate ending the run would have been a good one and her best westward passage. She loaded a cargo of quicksilver, copper ore and hides and returned East. She made two more passages to San Francisco in 134 and 135 days respectively and in 1868 was sold, as has been stated, to Adams, Blinn & Co.

Her new owners put Captain Smith in command and chartered the *Darling* to load guano at Baker's Island for Cork. On this voyage she arrived at Honolulu, in 10 days 20 hours from San Francisco, a very fast run. For the next seven years she was chiefly used in the lumber and coal business in the Pacific; in 1870 under Captain Spear and later under command of Captain Blinn. She arrived at San Francisco, Apr. 22, 1875, in 55 days, from Lyttleton and this is believed to be her last off-shore voyage. Her remaining days were spent in carrying coal from Departure Bay, B. C., to San Francisco. In the summer of 1877 she was commanded by Captain Gilmore. She left San Francisco on her last voyage, under Captain Harrington, on Oct. 28, 1877, and arrived at Victoria, B. C., Nov. 6th. Sailed from Nanaimo, Jan. 3, 1878, and was sighted by the *Melancthon* on the 18th, when she was hove to in a heavy gale. Nothing thereafter has been heard of her and she is supposed to have foundered. Eighteen lives were lost with her. Valued at $25,000 and insured for $21,000.

GRANITE STATE

BUILT by Badger & Co., at Portsmouth, N. H., in 1854. 174 x 34 x 24; 1108 tons. H. D. Walker & Co., Portsmouth, owners. Wrecked in 1868.

GREAT REPUBLIC

THE extreme clipper ship *Great Republic* was built in 1853, by Donald McKay, at his yard in East Boston. She was designed and built by Mr. McKay at his own risk and from the hour her keel was laid the newspapers of this country and England kept their readers informed of her progress and made frequent predictions of her success or failure. There were really two *Great Republics*; the first, the vessel as originally built by McKay; the second, the same vessel as reconstructed in New York after her partial destruction by fire. The original *Great Republic* was the largest merchant sailing ship ever constructed in the United States and was designed to carry 6000 tons, dead weight. Published descriptions give her dimensions as 335 feet, by 53 feet, by 38 feet; registered tonnage, 4555. She had four decks, the height of each of her between decks being eight feet. All her accommodations were on the upper between deck. The after cabin was wainscoted with mahogany, had recess sofas on each side and the furniture was mahogany with velvet coverings. Mirrors, paintings and stained glass were freely used in decoration. The state-rooms for passengers were luxurious and there was a fine library for the use of the crew. Her figurehead was an eagle's head and across her stern was an eagle with extended wings, holding a shield in his talons on which was inscribed her name and hailing port. Her ends were very long and sharp and her lines slightly concave, forward and aft. She had four masts, the after or spanker mast being fore and aft rigged. Her square-rigged masts, counting from the foremast, were 130, 131 and 122 feet long and the corresponding yards 110, 120 and 90 feet long. The mainmast was 44 inches in diameter, the main yard 28 inches in diameter and other spars in proportion. The spanker mast was 110 feet in length, the topmast 40 feet and she carried a gaff topsail and gaff topgallant sail. The spanker boom was 40 feet long and the gaff 34 feet. Her bowsprit was 30 feet outboard, jib-boom, 18 feet outside the cap and flying jibboom, 14 feet. She spread 15,653 yards of duck; had four anchors, the best bower weighing 8500 pounds. She was provided with a 15 horse power engine to hoist sails and handle the cargo. There were employed in her construction 1,500,000 feet of hard pine, 3500 tons of white oak, over 326 tons of iron and 56 tons of copper exclusive of sheathing. She carried a crew of 100 men and 30 boys and was commanded by Lauchlan McKay, a brother of the builder.

The launch of the *Great Republic* took place, Oct. 4, 1853, at noon, in the presence of the largest number of people ever attending a similar event in this country. Special trains were run and all the morning people poured in from all parts of Massachusetts and many from other states. It was estimated that 30,000 persons crossed the East Boston ferry, while Chelsea bridge, the Navy Yard and every point of advantage were crowded with spectators. As noon drew near Capt. Alden Gifford stood ready with a bottle of Cochituate water to christen the new ship and at 12 M. the giant vessel slid into the water amid a babel of cheers, the peal of bells and the notes of the East Boston band.

It was decided to send the *Great Republic* to New York to load for Liverpool and for a few days before her departure she was thrown open for the inspection of the public at a trifling charge and the receipts, which amounted to $1000, were given to the Seamen's Aid Society. She was towed to New York, loaded with a cargo of provisions valued at $300,000, her sails bent, her crew engaged and their advance wages paid and a few more days would have seen her at sea, when, Dec. 26, 1853, a great fire broke out in New York. The fire started about midnight in the Novelty Baking Company, 242 Front Street, and a strong wind carried the blazing cinders to the wharf where the *Great Republic* lay, setting the vessel on fire. Every effort was made to save her; her masts were cut away and she was scuttled, but the water was too shallow and all her upper works, except the shell of the bow as far aft as the fore chains and the bowsprit, were burned to the water's edge. Mr. McKay came on to see her and decided to give her up to the underwriters. The insurance on the vessel amounted to $180,000 and on the cargo to $275,000. Thus ended the career of the original *Great Republic*, without her having had a chance to show what she could do. That she would have proved a profitable ship is very doubtful, for the cost of running her was estimated at $10,000 a month and her great draft would have obliged her to lighter her cargo at most ports; still, it must always be a matter of regret to all lovers of marine architecture, that the largest sailing merchant vessel in the world, built by the greatest shipbuilder of his time, had no chance to show her speed. Mr. McKay always believed she would have beaten anything afloat, and her career, even under her reduced sail plan, fully confirmed the correctness of his opinion.

THE SECOND GREAT REPUBLIC.

The wreck of the *Great Republic* was raised by building a temporary stern and drawing canvas around the ship so that four steam pumps were able to clear her of water. One third of the cargo was found spoiled by fire and the rest damaged by water. She was bought by A. A. Low & Brother and rebuilt at Greenpoint, Long Island, by Sneeden & Whitlock, under the superintendence of Capt. N. B. Palmer. The upper deck, which had been burned, was not replaced, leaving her with three complete decks, and all her spars were considerably reduced. Instead of swinging a 110-foot foreyard and a 120-foot mainyard, these spars were now 90 feet and 100 feet, respectively. The foremast, originally 130 feet long, and the mainmast, 131 feet, were each 17 feet shorter and all other spars in proportion. She was fitted with Howe's rig and the Harris system of lightning conductors. Her depth of hold was reduced to 29 1/6 feet and her registered tonnage to 3356. The *Great Republic* loaded at New York and sailed for Liverpool, Feb. 24, 1855. She was commanded by Captain Limeburner and carried a crew of 50 men, less than half the number the original *Republic* would have required. Owing to her great draft, 25 feet, she was unable to enter the dock at Liverpool and had to go to the "Long Reach," to discharge her cargo. Her captain wrote from Liverpool to her owners: "We made the run from land to land in 12 days. Passage a rough one. Reached Liverpool in 19 days. The ship behaved nobly." Soon after her arrival she was chartered by the French Government for transport service in the Mediterranean at the rate of 17 shillings per ton per month. In January 1856 she was loading stores at Marseilles, in company with the American ships *Monarch of the Sea, Ocean Herald, Queen of Clippers* and *Titan*. After several voyages in the French service she crossed over to New York and loaded 5000 tons of mixed cargo for California; discharged her pilot Dec. 7, 1856, outside the light ship, at 3 P.M.; the fifth day out made 413 knots; made 360 knots in 19 hours, an average of 19 knots and at the rate of 456 miles in 24 hours; crossed the line in 15 days and 18 hours from Sandy Hook,—the fastest time on record; passed Cape St. Roque, 19 days and 14 hours out; passed the longitude of Cape Horn in 45 days and 7 hours from Sandy Hook, coming around with skysails set; was 52 days from Sandy Hook to 50° South, Pacific; crossed the equator in the Pacific on Feb. 17th, in 118° West, 21 days from 50° South and 73 days out, and was 19 days to San Francisco. Passage 92 days. She was within 500 miles of the Heads for five days in calms and fogs.

From San Francisco the *Great Republic* went to Callao, in 54 days; loaded guano at the Chincha Islands and sailed for London. Off the Falkland Islands she shipped a tremendous sea which stove in the deck between her fore and main masts and broke four of her deck beams. She was carrying 4500 tons of guano and the water in the

"GREAT REPUBLIC," 3356 TONS (AS REBUILT), BUILT AT EAST BOSTON, IN 1853

From a wood engraving in *Gleason's Pictorial*, 1853

"GREAT REPUBLIC," 3356 TONS (AS REBUILT), BUILT AT EAST BOSTON, IN 1853

From a rare photograph made in San Francisco, in 1860

"GREAT REPUBLIC," 3356 TONS (AS REBUILT), BUILT AT EAST BOSTON, IN 1853
From the painting by François Roux, 1882, in the Musée de Marine du Louvre

"HARVEY BIRCH," 1488 TONS, BUILT AT MYSTIC, CONN., IN 1854

From a painting by D. McFarlane, at the Peabody Museum, Salem, showing the burning of the
ship in 1861, by the Confederate cruiser "Nashville"

hold, mixed with guano, reached the ship's provisions. Threatened with famine she put into the Falkland Islands, Sept. 8, 1857, and despatched the schooner *Nancy* to Montevideo, for provisions and material for repairs. She finally arrived at London on Jan. 11, 1858. At London she was obliged to lighter part of her cargo before she could enter the Victoria dock; her draft being 25 feet and 6 inches while the dock admitted only 24 feet.

The *Republic's* following three voyages were: New York to San Francisco, 1858-1859, 120 days; return to New York in ballast in 100 days. In 1859-1860, same voyage, 110 days out; 98 days home, in ballast. In 1860-1861, New York to San Francisco, 104 days; thence to Liverpool with grain, 96 days; Liverpool to New York in ballast, 32 days. Her outward trip to San Francisco, in 1858, was prolonged by unfavorable winds in the North Atlantic, she having the long run of 41 days to the line. On her return passage she left San Francisco in company with the *Talisman* and was beaten by the latter four days to New York. On the following voyage she left New York, Nov. 23, 1859; was 51 days to Cape Horn; crossed the equator in 110 and was thence 19 days to San Francisco. The extreme clipper ship *Ocean Telegraph* arriving there the same day beat the *Republic* one day. The latter, however, reported a series of calms and light winds from the Platte, for days together not making over four knots an hour. On the succeeding voyage she sailed from New York, Oct. 24, 1860; crossed the line Nov. 17th; passed the Horn, Dec. 18th; had a heavy gale from the 20th to the 23rd; was 11 days from 50° South to 50° South; crossed the equator, Jan. 16, 1861, and for the last few days of the passage had light winds.

In 1861, the *Republic*, at New York from Liverpool, was seized by the surveyor of the port on account of the majority ownership of the vessel being in the South,—five-sixteenths being held by Virginia parties and the same amount by citizens of South Carolina. These shares were sold,—A. A. Low & Brother, co-owners, taking them over. She was then chartered to the United States Government for transport purposes and made a voyage to Port Royal and return.

In February 1862, she was fitted up for the Butler expedition and went to Ship Island. Soon after her arrival at the Island, during a southeast gale, she swung foul of another transport, the *Idaho*, and both vessels went ashore. The *Republic* was hauled off without injury but two weeks later was again ashore at the mouth of the Mississippi. Sometime in June she returned to New York and prepared to resume her California trade.

Two additional round voyages to San Francisco complete the record of the *Great Republic* while under the American flag. In 1862-1863 she was 102 days from New York to San Francisco; thence 43 days to Callao; loaded a cargo of guano at the Chincha Islands and sailed from Callao for London, Aug. 24, 1863. Sailed from London, Apr. 7, 1864, and arrived at New York, May 4th. In 1864-1865 she was 114 days from New York to San Francisco, returning in 120 days. On the first voyage of this new series the *Republic* left New York, Nov. 24, 1862; was 23 days to the line; 50 days to 50° South; thence 12 days to 50° South, Pacific, and crossed the equator, Feb. 16, 1863, in 117° West. On Mar. 1st, being 96 days out, she was 577 miles west of destination and had it not been for unfavorable weather during the last week of the passage she should have made the run in under 100 days. On her last voyage to San Francisco she sailed from New York on Oct. 24, 1864; was 27 days to the line; thence 30 days to the Cape and nine days off it in strong westerly gales; had 29 days from the Horn to the equator and thence 19 days to San Francisco. On this voyage she was under command of Capt. Josiah Paul, as successor to Capt. Joseph Limeburner, who had had the ship from the commencement of her career. The crew on this passage were insubordinate and inefficient.

On her return to New York, in 1865, she was laid up for a year and in 1866 was sold to parties in Yarmouth, N. S. Her managing owner was Capt. J. Smith Hatfield.

In 1868 she ran from St. John to Liverpool, in 14 days. In 1869 she was purchased by the Merchants Trading Company of Liverpool, for £3500 sterling and renamed *Denmark*. Jan. 18, 1872, she sailed from Rio, in ballast, for St. John, N. B., to load lumber for Great Britain, and on Mar. 2nd, in 32° North, a strong northwest gale set in and continued until the next day. The ship began to leak alarmingly, the water gaining steadily on two double-action pumps. On Mar. 5th, the storm lulled but the carpenter reported 12 feet of water in the hold and the captain ordered out the boats. The vessel was abandoned and all hands reached Bermuda in safety.

GREY FEATHER

BUILT by C. S. Husten, at Eastport, Me., in 1850. 135 x 30 x 19; 610 tons. L. H. Sampson & Co., New York, owners. Sold in 1862. Renamed *Ida;* of Bremen.

GREY HOUND

BUILT at Baltimore, Md., in 1848. D. Stewart, Baltimore, owner. 538 tons. Sold to go under Chilian flag, in 1856.

GUIDING STAR

BUILT by J. Currier, at Newburyport, in 1853. 165 x 33 x 23; 900 tons. Charles Hill & Co., Newburyport, owners. Sold to S. G. Reed & Co., March 1867. Condemned at Hong Kong, 1870.

HAIDEE

BUILT at Providence, R. I., in 1854. 395 tons. Sold in 1857 to E. Sanchez Doiz of New York. While operating as a slaver, was scuttled and sunk off Montauk, in September 1858.

HARRIET HOXIE

BUILT by Irons & Grinnell, at Mystic, Conn., in 1851. 678 tons. Post, Smith & Co., Mystic, owners. Sold to Callaux, Wattell & Co., of Antwerp, in 1859.

HARRY BLUFF

BUILT by Jotham Stetson, at Chelsea, Mass., in 1855. 184 x 37 x 24; 1244 tons. Charles R. Green, New York, owner. Lost on Nantucket, South Shoal, Feb. 26, 1869, while on voyage from Cadiz to Boston. Four lives lost.

HARRY OF THE WEST

BUILT by Robert E. Jackson, at East Boston, in 1855. 182 x 36 x 23; 1050 tons. Calvin Adams, New York, owner. Burned in November 1865, near South West Pass, mouth of Mississippi, while bound to Liverpool from New Orleans.

HARVEY BIRCH

BUILT by Irons & Grinnell at Mystic, Conn., in 1854. 196 x 40 x 28; 1482 tons. J. H. Brower & Co., New York, owner. Captured and burned by the *Nashville*, Nov. 19, 1862, while bound to New York from Havre.

HERALD OF THE MORNING

MEDIUM clipper ship, designed by Samuel H. Pook, built by Hayden & Cudworth, at Medford, Mass., and launched in December 1853. She was 203 feet long between perpendiculars, x 38 x 23: 6; 1294 tons, old measurement; 1108 tons, new measurement. Her lines were sharp, approaching those of an actual clipper, yet she could carry in dead weight close to 1600 tons. She was well sparred and crossed three skysail yards. An Aurora was the figurehead. She was described as a perfect gem in hull and rigging, not at all unlike one of those long, light-heeled privateers that Marryatt and Cooper were wont to introduce into their novels. With clear and roomy decks and two fancy brass cannon mounted on her poop deck, her saucy and fighting appearance was further enhanced. During her career of twenty years as an American ship, she made eighteen passages to the westward, around Cape Horn, and when in ports of the Pacific, she was always the recipient of favorable comment. She made no outward passages around the Cape of Good Hope and only two of her homeward runs were by that route. Her record as a fast sailing ship is well established.

On her maiden voyage she left Boston, Jan. 21, 1854, and in spite of meeting with an undue proportion of head winds, without an opportunity of making even one day's good run, she made the passage to San Francisco in the fast time of 106 days. When 100 days out she was within 180 miles of the Golden Gate and a feature of the voyage was her run of eight days between the two 50's of South latitude. From San Francisco she was 45 days to Callao; sailed thence Sept. 4th, and put into St. Thomas, 66 days out; reached New York, Nov. 21st, in 78 days after leaving Callao. Sailed from New York, Feb. 5, 1855, and arrived at San Francisco, May 16th, in 100 days and 6 hours, anchor to anchor; 99 days and 12 hours, pilot to pilot. Was 18 days to the line; 44 days to 50° South; eight days rounding the Horn; crossed the equator, 79 days out; best day's run, 340 miles. When just south of the line in the Atlantic, was in company with the fast clipper ship *Winged Racer*, and off the Horn signalled the *Adelaide;* led both into San Francisco, by 5 and 17 days, respectively, and beat their passages by 14 and 18 days. From San Francisco she was 50 days to Callao; thence 56 days to Port Louis, Mauritius; thence 74 days to Deal; arrived at Boston, May 6, 1856, in 32 days from London. She then went out to Callao in 86 days from Boston; returning, reached New York, May 4, 1857, in 79 days from Callao. Capt. Otis Baker, Jr., in command thus far.

On her fourth voyage, the *Herald* arrived at San Francisco, Nov. 15, 1857, in 132 days from New York, her captain, Lothrop, reporting having experienced head winds and variables and being 27 days rounding the Horn; best day's run, 255 miles, only. From San Francisco she went to Guaymas and Mazatlan, and arrived at London, July 6, 1858, and thence crossed to Boston in 36 days. On

Mar. 18, 1859, she was again at San Francisco from Boston in 116 days; was 800 miles from the Golden Gate when 104 days out. A feature of this passage was her run from 50° to 50° in seven days, in fine weather. From San Francisco she was 38 days to Callao and arrived at Hampton Roads, Nov. 7th. Captain Mitchell took command and sailing from Boston, Feb. 7, 1860, had the fine run of 18 days to the line; passed Cape Horn, 52 days out and crossed the equator on the 84th day; arrived at San Francisco, May 25th, in 108 days from Boston. Went to Callao in 41 days; thence was 80 days to Hampton Roads. Sailed from New York, Mar. 23, 1861; crossed the line in 25 days; had very heavy weather in the South Atlantic, and off the Horn had the bowsprit sprung, bulwarks stove, and the forward house started, causing the between deck cargo to be considerably damaged by salt water. Passed Cape Horn, 69 days out and was 46 days running up the South Pacific to the line; arrived at San Francisco, Aug. 16th, in 146 days from New York. Loaded grain for London and was 102 days to Deal. Then went from London to Callao in 96 days; thence to Queenstown in 79 days and arrived at Boston, Apr. 7, 1863, in 36 days from London.

On her ninth voyage, being her seventh to San Francisco, she arrived out Sept. 20, 1863, in 127 days from Boston. Captain Williams, who was now in command, reported having had moderate weather throughout; passed Cape Horn on the 80th day; thence 47 days to destination. Completing this voyage, she returned East via Baker's Island. On Feb. 17, 1865, she was again at San Francisco after an uneventful passage of 124 days from Boston. Then made the fast run of 36 days from the Golden Gate to Callao, and returned East with guano. Took her departure from Boston, June 3, 1866, under command of Capt. Cyrus Sears of West Yarmouth, and was 134 days to San Francisco. Encountered over 50 immense icebergs off the Horn; was 32 days from the Pacific equator crossing to port; during one stretch of 44 successive days of the passage, the skysails were clewed down only once. From San Francisco went to Liverpool in 106 days. Passed through the Golden Gate, Oct. 15, 1867, in 124 days from

New York, to which port she then returned direct in 123 days. Capt. Alexander Winsor took command and on Sept. 1, 1868, anchored his ship at San Francisco, after the good run of 118 days from New York. Was 20 days rounding the Horn in practically one continuous gale from the West; snow squalls were frequent and at times the ship was so badly iced up as to be perfectly unmanageable. Good trades were found in the Pacific and the run from 50° South to the equator was made in the exceptionally fast time of 16 days. This voyage was completed by her passage of 114 days to Boston, direct. She then returned to San Francisco, arriving Aug. 20, 1869, in 128 days from Boston and then went to Liverpool in 121 days.

On Nov. 9, 1870, the *Herald* reached San Francisco, in 147 days from New York, the slowest run in her history. For 48 days she was unable to steer her course and during 44 consecutive days, the skysails were taken in only once. From San Francisco she was 50 days to Singapore, thence proceeding to Rangoon and Akyab, Falmouth and Marseilles. Arrived at San Francisco, Sept. 3, 1872, 139 days from Marseilles, 124 days from Gibraltar; crossed the line in 17 days from the latter port, but thereafter had nothing but light winds. At San Francisco, the command was taken by Capt. Daniel McLaughlin, formerly of the ship *Swallow* also owned by the Magoun firm, and the *Herald* went to Liverpool in 119 days. On her last direct run from an eastern port to San Francisco, she arrived out Oct. 8, 1873, in 141 days from New York. Made the Cape Horn passage in 13 days, in moderate weather, aside from which she had nothing but light and variable winds; the skysails were set for the first 46 days out and also all the way up the South Pacific; was 34 days from the equator to port, being becalmed for seven days in 27° North. From San Francisco she went to Liverpool, in 99 days, the second fastest passage that season. Crossed to New York and loaded coal for the Pacific Mail Steamship Company's depot at Acapulco. After discharging all but 350 tons, she proceeded to San Francisco, arriving Nov. 26, 1874. Sailed Jan. 13, 1875 for Cork via Tahiti; arrived at Papeete, Feb. 2nd, a very fast run of 20 days;

logged 4200 miles. Arrived at Queenstown, June 21, 1875, in 102 days from Tahiti; proceeded thence to Hamburg, where she was sold for $25,000 to James B. Tibbets and Isaac Benham. For some four years she continued under the American flag, operating in the Atlantic. She then went under the Norwegian flag, her hailing port becoming Arendal and her rig being changed to that of a bark. In 1890 she appears under the British flag, W. J. Smith of London, owner.

In 1859, while off Cape Horn, from Callao for Hampton Roads, the *Herald of the Morning* was struck by an immense sperm whale, which appeared to have been badly injured by the impact; the ship lost part of the stem, which caused such a bad leak that the pumps had to be kept going until arrival at destination. On her voyage from Shields to Boston, in December 1865, with coals and chemicals, she encountered very bad weather; five men were lost overboard at different times, and the ship had to be run into the Gulf Stream to thaw out the ice. When making the port of Boston, during the night of Feb. 14, 1866, then 61 days out from Shields, she struck the spit close inside the light and the next morning was found to have nine feet of water in the hold. Tugs and pumps were furnished and after a portion of her cargo had been lightered, she was towed off. In December 1871, shortly after leaving Marseilles, with a cargo of steel rails for San Francisco, she met with very heavy gales, sprung a leak and was badly strained. She was forced to return to Marseilles, where repairs occupied four months.

HESPERUS

BUILT by J. T. Foster, at Medford, in 1856. 1019 tons. Thomas B. Wales & Co., Boston, owners. While at anchor at Woosung, just arrived from Liverpool with coal, was destroyed by fire, Jan. 8, 1861.

HIGHFLYER

MEDIUM clipper ship, launched from the yard of Currier & Townsend, Newburyport, Mass., on Jan. 13, 1853, for the owners of the Red Cross Packet Line plying between New York and Liverpool, of which D. G. Ogden of New York, was agent and one of the owners. 180 x 38 x 25; 1195 tons, old measurement. She was described as a vessel "that her owners need not be afraid of comparing with any New York built ship."

On account of the demand for tonnage to California, at the time the *Highflyer* was built, she was put into that trade and on her maiden voyage she arrived at San Francisco, Sept. 2, 1853, in 148 days after leaving New York. Capt. Gordon B. Waterman, who was in command and who had a considerable interest in the ship, reported that she had sprung a leak in the North Atlantic and the pumps becoming choked, he had been obliged to put into Rio. The passage thence to San Francisco was 82 days, and the actual sailing time from New York, 138 days, many days of light and baffling winds being experienced. From San Francisco she was 54 days to Hong Kong and returned to New York in 90 days from Whampoa. She then made two round voyages between New York and Liverpool, the first being 24 days outward, 31 days returning, while her second homeward passage was 21 days. She then loaded at New York for San Francisco arriving out, Oct. 8, 1855, in 144 days, with light winds generally prevailing. She was within 500 miles of the Golden Gate for 14 days.

She left San Francisco, Oct. 25, 1855, under Captain Waterman, for Hong Kong and was never heard from. The prevailing opinion was that she had been surprised and captured by Chinese pirates off Formosa, the crew murdered and the ship burned. A war vessel sent in search of her found the wreck of a vessel which had been stranded and burned, but identification was impossible, although a spyglass believed to have been the property of Captain Waterman was found. The Red Cross Line had a short time before lost two of their packet ships, the *St. George* and the *St. Patrick*, and following the loss of the *Highflyer*, three others of the fleet, the *Driver*, the *Racer* and the *Andrew Foster* met their fate, leaving the *Dreadnought* as the only surviving member.

HIPPOGRIFFE

MEDIUM clipper ship, built at East Dennis, Mass., by the Shiverick Brothers, for Capt. Christopher Hall and Prince S. Crowell; launched Apr. 5, 1852. She was the second ship to be built at East Dennis, the *Revenue* being the first. She was provided with jury masts, yards and sails and proceeded to Boston under her own canvas to receive permanent spars and rigging. She was fitted with Forbes' double topsails and her topmasts fidded abaft the lower mastheads. She was a small ship of but 678 tons, old measurement.

The maiden voyage of the *Hippogriffe* was from Boston to San Francisco, arriving out Oct. 20, 1852, in 155 days' passage, Capt. Anthony Howes in command. She returned East via Callao and then went to Calcutta from Boston, in 110 days; from Calcutta, was 112 days to Philadelphia. Her next voyage was from London to Calcutta in 107 days, returning to Boston in 108 days. Crossed to England and loaded a cargo of coal at Cardiff for San Francisco; arrived out Nov. 24, 1856, in 142 days' passage, Capt. David S. Sears in command. Returned east via Callao. Her next voyage was a round to China. In the China Sea she struck an uncharted rock but worked clear and proceeded, arriving at Hong Kong, May 22, 1858. On being placed in dry dock, a piece of rock was found imbedded in her bottom, so large, that had it fallen out she must inevitably have foundered. The obstruction she struck was later charted under the name of Hippogriffe Rock. On July 6, 1860, while on a passage to Callao, she was forced to put into Montevideo, damaged in heavy weather. Her cargo had shifted and some 40 tons were jettisoned.

The *Hippogriffe* sailed from Cardiff, Nov. 27, 1862, for Hong Kong, under command of Capt. J. H. Addy, son-in-law of Prince S.

Crowell and formerly master of the ship *Christopher Hall*. From China she went to Calcutta where, in December 1863, she was sold for 70,000 rupees and went under the British flag.

HOOGLY

MEDIUM clipper ship, built in 1851, by Samuel Hall, at East Boston. Keel, 185; deck, 190; over all, 200 feet; 1264 tons. Dead rise, 15 inches; sheer, 3½ feet. A female figure in flowing white garments ornamented her forward. She was described as being a beautiful ship in model designed both for speed and carrying capacity. Her owners were D. C. Bacon & Sons of Boston.

The *Hoogly* arrived at San Francisco, May 28, 1852, her commander, Captain Chadwick, reporting his passage as being 127 sailing days from Boston. When three days out she had carried away her fore and main topmasts and later had put into Rio to refit. She sailed from San Francisco, July 1, 1852, for Shanghai and the Alta, California, newspaper describes her departure as follows:

"One of the most beautiful harbor sights that has occurred here for some time came off yesterday. The magnificent clipper *Hoogly*, which had been lying at the end of Broadway wharf, loosed her sails about noon, cast off her lines, swept away majestically from the end of the wharf and put directly to sea. This is an occurrence which has only happened in San Francisco two or three times before and was very creditable to all concerned. She carries a crew of 25 men; they were all on board at the appointed hour; the jib, foretopsail and maintopmast staysail were loosed; the bow line cast off. The mizzen topsail was then loosed and the stern line cast off. The ship leaned over and shot swiftly away without accident. A large number of spectators were on Broadway, Pacific, Commercial and Market Street wharves, viewing the scene."

The *Hoogly* touched at Honolulu, 12 days out. On Aug. 20th, while bound up the river to Shanghai, she stranded and became a total loss. She was reported to be insured for $74,000.

HORNET

EXTREME clipper ship, built by Westervelt & Mackay, at New York, and launched June 20, 1851. 207 x 40 x 22; 1426 tons. She was very sharp, had a flush deck and was one of the finest modeled and best constructed vessels afloat. Chamberlain & Phelps of New York were her owners.

Her maiden passage was 155 days from New York to San Francisco and being made in the face of extreme difficulties, was no criterion of what her sail abilities were. She made nine passages, subsequently, from eastern ports to San Francisco, averaging 121 5/9 days; shortest, 106, 111 and 113 days; longest, 131 and 135 days. On the fastest run she was 19 days from New York to the line and 18 days from the equator to the bar off San Francisco. On two other occasions she had the excellent runs of 19 days and 18 days from the equator in the Pacific to anchorage in San Francisco Bay. In 1854 she was ten days between the two 50's and in 1855 had 17 days from off Cape St. Roque to 50° South. On her passage of 124 days in 1863 she made the excellent run of 56 days from 50° South in the Atlantic and 41 days from 50° South in the Pacific, to San Francisco. On some of her homeward passages she also did most excellent work. San Francisco to Panama in 33 days, anchor to anchor, in 1852; in 1853, San Francisco to Callao in 34 days, having made Pt. St. Elena, Gulf of Guayaquil, when 21 days and 22 hours out. This is the record passage to Callao by the eastern route and within two days of record by the western course. In 1857 she was only 47 days from Calcutta to the Cape of Good Hope; in 1859, 88 days from San Francisco to New York and the following year, 96 days over the same course. In 1861 her passage from New York to Bristol, England, was 14 days and 20 hours and in 1865, 58 days from Tomé, Chile, to New York.

On her first run she left New York, Aug. 21, 1851, deeply laden, drawing 20 feet and 6 inches. On deck she had two boilers with stacks, totaling 49 tons weight, for the steamer *Senator*, and these had to be thrown overboard during a severe gale in which the ship was laboring hard. Except for one good day of 318 miles, she had no chance; gales, light winds and calms prevailing throughout. In addition to this, Captain Lawrence was sick and on arrival out the mate and steward were under arrest. She was 73 days to the Horn, off which she was 17 days; thence 36 days to the equator and 26 days from there to port. Sailed from San Francisco, Mar. 1st, with 300 passengers for Panama and made the run in 33 days; thence about 90 days to Hong Kong and 117 days from Whampoa to New York.

On her second voyage, the *Hornet* left New York, Apr. 26, 1853, and two days later the *Flying Cloud* sailed, both for San Francisco. The *Hornet* had a very poor start, as on Apr. 29th the *Cloud* had caught up with and passed her, being about 12 miles in the lead; this lead was slowly increased in the Atlantic and in rounding the Horn an additional five days was gained, the *Cloud* being seven days ahead at the crossing of 50° South, in the Pacific. The *Hornet* gained two days thence to the line, crossing in 113° West, after which Captain Knapp made practically a direct course to destination, thereby recovering not only all her handicap but actually arriving off San Francisco Bar one day ahead of the *Cloud*. Cressy, in the *Cloud*, crossed the line three degrees to the eastward of the *Hornet*, but then stood much further to the westward, going out to longitude 140° 43′, and as far north as latitude 38° 30′, thereby covering a much greater distance. Both ships arrived in San Francisco harbor, Aug. 12th, the *Hornet*, 45 minutes ahead; she had been off port one whole day in the fog. The *Hornet's* passage, 106 days; best day, 281 miles; *Flying Cloud's* passage, 104 days, best day, 316 miles. Off the Horn, the *Hornet* saw the clippers, *Eclipse* and *John Land* and led them into San Francisco, 5 days and 14 days, respectively. Continuing this voyage the *Hornet* was 34 days to Callao and from there went to Philadelphia, arriving Apr. 9, 1854.

The third voyage was made under Captain Benson and was 126 days from Philadelphia to San Francisco, with 1½ days calms off the Horn and five days calms north of the line in the Pacific. Had skysails set for 91 days on the passage. Returned to New York via

Mazatlan, Mexico. Captain Benson again took the *Hornet* out to San Francisco, being 113 days from New York, but was close to the California coast on the 107th day, then having six days of calms. Went to Calcutta in 69 days and was thence 102 days to New York; crossed to London and thence to Calcutta; passed the Lizard, Jan. 12, 1857, and was 97 days thence to destination. Sailed from Calcutta, June 28, 1857, and on the 47th day was off the Cape of Good Hope.

On her fifth passage to San Francisco, the *Hornet* arrived out, May 28, 1859, Captain Mitchell in command, in 128 days from Boston. The *Flying Childers* reached port the same day, in 117 days from the same port. The *Hornet* returned to New York, direct, in 87 days. The following year she reached San Francisco, Sept. 4th, in 135 days from New York. Had light winds and calms nearly all the passage except 12 days of severe gales off the Platte and 15 days of heavy weather off the Horn. Returned to New York, direct, in 96 days; passed the Horn, 47 days out. From New York she crossed to Bristol, England, in 14 days and 20 hours and returned in 27 days, in ballast. On the outward passage had a hurricane of 20 hours in which she had bulwarks stove, decks cleared and cabin filled. On the return had much fog and generally light and baffling winds. She then loaded for San Francisco and was 131 days on the passage; then went to Valparaiso in the fine time of 42 days; thence to Iquique and Pisagus and arrived at Philadelphia, July 23, 1862; reached New York, Aug. 4th, two days from Philadelphia, with nitrate of soda, part of her inward cargo. Again loaded for San Francisco and arrived out Feb. 17, 1863, in 124 days. Was 30 days to the line; 38 days thence to 50° South, in gales and calms; in a pampero, had bulwarks stove, lost sails and had jibs washed from the booms; was 15 days between the 50's, 21 days to the equator and 20 days to port. From San Francisco took a wheat cargo to Liverpool, in 120 days; loaded coal for New York and was 32 days crossing over, the final 20 days being nearly a calm. Arrived at New York, Oct. 3, 1863.

In December 1863, the *Hornet*, Captain Harding, and the *Star of the Union*, Captain Reed, were loading at New York for San Francisco. The two captains bet $500 each that their respective ships would arrive out in 120 days or less. Both lost as the *Star* reached port Apr. 1st, in 121 days, while the *Hornet* was at the Heads, but not at anchor, on her 120th day. The *Hornet* had been 23 days to the line; 53 days to 50° South; 18 days rounding the Horn; 103 days to the equator and 18 days thence to port. She returned to New York, direct, in 101 days. Went back to San Francisco, in 111 days; thence to Valparaiso; thence to Tomé where a cargo of wool was loaded and the passage to New York was made in 58 days.

At New York, Capt. Josiah A. Mitchell again took command of the *Hornet* and after loading a full cargo, including 45 barrels and 2000 cases of oil and 6195 boxes of candles, she sailed Jan. 11, 1866, for San Francisco. Light winds were experienced from the start, the line being crossed 30 days out; on May 2nd they were on the equator, in the Pacific, 111 days out. The following morning, at 7 o'clock the mate went below to draw some varnish, when his lantern caused an explosion, the flames from which shot up through the open hatch and ignited the crossjack, which was hanging clewed up. The fire spread and in a short time the whole ship was in flames and all hands were obliged to leave the ship in haste. Captain Mitchell took two passengers, the third mate and eleven men in the long boat; the first mate and eight of the crew were in one quarter boat and the second officer and six men in the other quarter boat. At 8 o'clock the masts went over the side and at 5 A.M., May 4th, the ship went down. The position was latitude 2° North, longitude 112° 30′ West, being 1250 miles south of Cape St. Lucas and about 2500 miles southeast of the Island of Hawaii. The three boats kept together for 19 days before separating, at which time they divided what few remaining stores were left and then parted on different courses. The captain's boat reached Lapahoehoe, Island of Hawaii, on June 15th, two natives swimming out through the surf and assisting in the rescue. All the 15 were in a pitiable condition after being in the boat 43 days, being practically starving; latterly had been reduced to eating scrapped boot leather and an occasional flying fish which blundered into the boat. The consul at Hilo promptly relieved Captain Mitchell of the care of his men.

Nothing was ever heard of the fate of the two quarter boats, containing the first and second mates and fourteen members of the crew. The *Hornet* and cargo were insured for $400,000.

HOTSPUR

MEDIUM clipper ship, launched early in 1857, by Roosevelt & Joyce, New York, for account of Frank Hathaway and parties in New Bedford; later owned by Wisner, McCready & Co., of New York. 154: 9 x 35 x 20; 862 tons. Her whole career was spent in trade between New York and China. She has to her credit a number of fast passages and while most of her runs, both out and home, were made during the favorable season at each end, yet in instances she reached port in advance of accredited "flyers" doing the same course at the same time and which she had met on the way.

On her maiden run the *Hotspur* left New York, Apr. 4, 1857, under command of Captain Potter, and arrived at Hong Kong, July 3rd, in 90 days; returning left Hong Kong, about the end of August, passed Anjer, Sept. 30th, and arrived at New York, Dec. 18th, in 79 days from Anjer and about 107 days from China. Left New York on her second voyage, Jan. 28, 1858; arrived at Hong Kong, May 6th, in 98 days' passage. On her third homeward run she passed Anjer, Oct. 19, 1859; the Cape, Nov. 28th; St. Helena, Dec. 6th and arrived at New York, Jan. 12, 1860, in 85 days from Anjer and 45 days from the Cape. Captain Potter reported five days of northerly gales between the Bermudas and Hatteras.

Capt. W. O. Johnson now took command and returning on his first voyage, left Hong Kong, Oct. 31, 1860, and arrived at New York, Feb. 2, 1861, reporting his time as 95 days. In the Straits of Sunda, Nov. 23rd, met the *Sea Serpent* which had left Hong Kong the day after him, but the *Hotspur* later passed her larger and faster competitor and led her into New York by nine days. On Apr. 25, 1861, the *Hotspur* took her departure from New York; reported at Anjer, July 10th, 76 days out; was 18 days going up the China Sea and arrived at Hong Kong, July 28th, in company with the clipper bark *Maury* which had left New York two days after her. The *Maury* reported passing Anjer, 76 days out, but thereafter gained two days on the *Hotspur*. From Hong Kong, the *Hotspur* went up the coast to Shanghai; left Woosung, Nov. 5, 1861; sailed from Hong Kong, Jan. 25, 1862; put into Batavia, Feb. 3rd, leaving on the 11th and arrived at New York, May 13th, in 100 sailing days from Hong Kong and 91 days from Batavia; was within two days' sail of Sandy Hook for six days. Captain Johnson reported that on Apr. 22nd, in 6° North, Atlantic, he was in company with the *Surprise*, which had left Batavia two days before him. He led the latter into New York three days.

On the following voyage, which was never to be completed, the *Hotspur*, under command of Captain Bennett, sailed from New York, June 17, 1862; had a long run to the line and to the Straits of Sunda, not passing Anjer until Sept. 25th, 100 days out; arrived at Hong Kong, Oct. 24th, in a total passage 129 days. Thereafter she went up the coast and loaded a cargo valued at $1,000,000, at Foo Chow, for New York. On Feb. 17, 1863, she ran on the Paracels Reef and proved a total loss. The captain and 18 others took the long boat; the two mates had each seven others in their respective boats and an attempt was made to keep together but they were soon separated. The occupants of the long boat were picked up by a Chinese junk and taken to Bangkok; the second mate's boat reached Cape Patterman, but the occupants were kept prisoners by the natives for seven days; they then escaped, boarded an English vessel and were landed at Saigon. The third boat also reached shore in safety, but a passenger, Mrs. Abbe, died on the way.

HOUQUA

THE *Houqua* is classed as a clipper ship although she was built to be sold to the Chinese Government for use as a vessel of war, she having eight gun ports on each side. However, on her first arrival in China she was found to be too small to answer the original purpose and during her whole career she was operated as a merchantman by A. A. Low & Brother of New York, for whose account she had been built by Brown & Bell, at New York, in 1844. She was named after the most prominent Hong merchant of Canton, a close friend of her owners, who was to have negotiated her sale. She was called a very handsome ship, in all respects, although small. Her tonnage was 581, old measurement.

Excepting her voyages, No. 7, in 1850, and No. 10, in 1853, when she went from New York to San Francisco, the whole life of the *Houqua* was spent in the China trade, including some visits made in later years to Japan. The two passages to San Francisco were made in 131 and 144 days respectively, on the latter she being a month rounding the Horn in very heavy weather. In completion of these particular voyages she reached New York, Feb. 24, 1851, in 95 days from Shanghai and 77 from Java Head; and on Apr. 26, 1854, from Foo Chow, also in 95 days and 77 from Java Head.

Between July 1, 1844, when she left New York on her first voyage, until Jan. 8, 1850, the *Houqua* made six rounds between her home port and China, on the fifth being nine months on the China coast, trading between Hong Kong and Shanghai. Her passages outward and homeward were made in excellent time but this particular period was conspicuous for the high percentage of fast passages made by vessels employed in the trade and the *Samuel Russell*, *Sea Witch* and *Rainbow* shared honors in this respect with *Houqua*. In 1848, the *Sea Witch* made the run from Whampoa to New York in 77 days and odd hours, the fastest on record to this date, while the 78 days and 6 hours' passage from Macao to New York, land to land, made by the *Natchez*, in 1845, was phenomenal. The latter ship was an old

New York-New Orleans packet, 130 x 30 x 15 feet, and her best day on this run was only 276 miles but she had exceptionally favorable winds throughout and it is said that she did not have to tack once. On her first outward passage, the *Houqua* was 72 days from New York to Anjer and 12 days thence to Hong Kong. She sailed from Whampoa, Dec. 9, 1844; was 15 days to Anjer; 70 days to the Atlantic equator crossing and received her pilot off Barnegat on the 87th day out but did not get into New York harbor until three days later; logged 14,272 miles on the passage. On her second homeward run she left Whampoa, Dec. 9, 1845; was 16 days to Anjer and 75 days thence to New York. Left the latter port in May 1846 and was 72 days and 14 hours to Java Head; thence 14 days and 3 hours to Hong Kong, a total of 86 days and 17 hours. The fourth voyage was made in the fine time of under seven months, on the round, but details are not at hand. On the fifth outward voyage she was totally dismasted in the Indian Ocean, arriving at Hong Kong, Mar. 14, 1848, in 131 days from New York, being under jury rig the final 55 days. Sailed from Hong Kong, Nov. 29, 1848; was eight days to Anjer; passed the Cape 42 days out and was on the equator on the 62nd day; between latitude 34° North and New York she was detained ten days by calms and heavy gales, so that Captain Low's anticipated passage of 85 days was prolonged to 98 days. On the following passage she was 90 days from New York to Hong Kong, returning in 109 days from Macao and 42 days from the Cape. In 1851 she left Shanghai, Aug. 19th, and was 129 days to New York. Her run home, in 1852, was in 111 days from Shanghai. These last three runs were made during the unfavorable season. In 1854 she was 128 days from New York to Hong Kong, returning to New York in 100 days from Shanghai.

In 1857, the *Houqua* was rerigged as a bark and left New York, May 28th; was 96 days to Anjer and 127 days to Hong Kong. On July 19, 1862, she arrived at New York, from Kanagawa (Yokohama), via Whampoa, Mar. 18th; Anjer, Apr. 5th; the Cape, May 16th, and the equator crossing, June 18th. She arrived at Hong

Kong, Jan. 23, 1863, from New York; sailed from Foo Chow, Apr. 25th and arrived at New York, Aug. 23rd in 120 days' passage, 50 days from the Cape and 25 from the line. She sailed from Yokohama, Aug. 15, 1864, for New York and was never thereafter heard of. It is supposed that she foundered in a typhoon.

The first commander of the *Houqua* was Nathaniel B. Palmer, who was succeeded by his brothers Alexander and Theodore D., in turn. On voyages No. 5 and No. 6, she was commanded by Capt. Charles Porter Low, who had joined her as third officer on her maiden passage. Captain McKenzie then had her for three voyages, being followed by Capt. Richard W. Dixie, who was succeeded by Captain Cartwright. Captain Dixie was in command when she sailed from Foo Chow in January 1854, she being the first ship to leave that port for America. His second and third mates, Millett and Symonds, had the honor of raising the first American flag at the port of Foo Chow, it being floated over the consulate at the request of Mr. Hunt of Salem, the consul.

The fifth voyage of the *Houqua*, it being Captain Low's first, as master, was momentous. Leaving New York, Nov. 4, 1847, the equator was crossed on the 23rd day out and all went well until Jan. 15th, when, in a hurricane, she lost all three topgallant masts and the jibboom. The ship being hove on beam ends and in danger of foundering, the main and mizzen masts were cut away, going close to the deck; the ship was half full of water. After extraordinary exertions she was got under control, pumped dry and on Feb. 7th, put into Cajeli, Island of Bouro, under jury rig as a brig. After arrival at Hong Kong, her cargo of cotton goods in bales was found to be scorched and so hot that it was a miracle that she had not been destroyed through spontaneous combustion. On Feb. 3, 1853, while in New York harbor, ready to sail for San Francisco, she was run down by the ferryboat *Tonawanda*, in the fog, losing part of her cutwater and had to go upriver for repairs. Subsequently, off the Horn, on this passage, she had very heavy weather, lying to, off and on, for many days. On May 5th, in a violent squall, a meteor, apparently about the size of a man's head, broke at the masthead, throwing out most brilliant sparks. Coming down the mast, it passed to leeward and two men standing near were sensibly affected and much frightened. In February 1863, after leaving Hong Kong for Shanghai, she was forced to return to port, having sprung a bad leak, and repairs took over a month.

HURRICANE

EXTREME clipper ship, built by Isaac C. Smith, at Hoboken, N. J.; launched Oct. 25, 1851. Length of keel, 206 feet; deck, 215 feet; over all, 230 feet x 40 x 22; 1608 tons, old measurement. Her stern terminated in a gilded eagle's head with a ribbon flying from its mouth on which the name was inscribed in gilt letters. She had Cunningham's rolling topsails and across the lower part of the foretopsail her name appeared in large black letters. She had 40 inches dead rise and her long and extremely sharp entrance and clearance lines were so intensified that she could hardly carry her registered tonnage in heavy cargo. Some authorities claimed that she was the sharpest sailing ship ever constructed by any builder, being in fact too sharp and with the collapse of the extremely high freight rates of the early 50's she was not a profitable carrier. Her owners were C. W. & H. Thomas of New York and during her career as an American ship she was commanded by Capt. Samuel Very, except on her last voyage. As will appear she proved to be a very fast sailer, having many voyages and parts of passages quite close to record. On her maiden voyage, according to published accounts, she covered in one day 400 nautical miles, at times logging 18 knots per hour.

Her first departure from New York was on Dec. 17, 1851, and 16 days later, when in latitude 18° North, she had her fore and main topmasts and mizzen topgallant mast carried away in a white squall, necessitating Captain Very's putting into Rio to refit. In spite of this disaster she crossed the line when 27 days out; reached Rio, Jan. 28th, 26 days after the mishap and 42 days from New York. Left Rio, Feb. 9th and 24 days thereafter was in 50° South, Pacific;

thence had the fine run of 18 days to the equator; thence 24 days to San Francisco. Her gross time from New York was 120 days; net sailing days, 108. From Rio she was 66 days, which time has only once been beaten and only twice equalled. From San Francisco she crossed to China, returning to the Golden Gate, Oct. 20th, in 43 days from Whampoa. Captain Very reported having heavy weather throughout for 21 days. She then went to Hong Kong in 44 days and loaded at Whampoa for New York. Sailed Feb. 12, 1853, the season getting late. However, she cleared Java Head, 21 days out; was off the Cape on the 54th day; crossed the equator, 72½ days out and arrived at New York, May 18th, in a passage of 94½ days.

On her second voyage the *Hurricane* left New York, Aug. 9, 1853, and was 123 days to San Francisco. Her run of 25 days from Sandy Hook to the line is said to have never been bettered and seldom equalled for August departures. She was in 50° South, when 51 days out; thence 19 days to the same latitude in the Pacific; from there, 30 days to the equator and 23 days thence to destination. In the vicinity of Cape Horn she lost from 10 to 40 miles daily for 14 days and in 18 days gained only 373 miles on her course; lost jib-boom and foretopgallant mast. In the South Pacific much calm weather was experienced and for five successive days she was becalmed off the island of Masafuero. For 19 days of the whole passage she averaged under 50 miles daily and for 42 days, under 100 miles. Her best day was 263 miles in the North Pacific. She left San Francisco, Dec. 31st, for New York, in ballast; crossed the equator 19 days out; was in latitude 37° South, 33½ days out and arrived at New York, May 26, 1854, in 96 days from the Golden Gate.

On her third voyage she sailed from New York, May 26, 1854, and in spite of encountering much light and calm weather she was within 1040 miles of San Francisco when 85 days out and had good prospects of completing the passage in 90 days. This was within 153 miles of the position of the *Flying Cloud's* corresponding day on her first 89 day run. The *Hurricane* was, however, here headed off by light northerly winds and calms, often having barely steerage way and being forced to cover during the final 15 days, 1777 miles. From Sandy Hook to the line she logged 4090 miles in 22 days and 16 hours; crossed the equator, in the Pacific, 76 days, 16 hours out and was thence 23 days to San Francisco. Her time of crossing the tropics in the Atlantic was 15 days and 17 hours, logging 3087 miles; in the Pacific, 15 days and 22 hours, logging 3154 miles; average in each instance, over eight knots an hour. Total distance sailed from New York to San Francisco 17,384 miles by log; average over seven knots. Total distance made in a straight line, from noon to noon each day, 16,357. Best day's run, 288 miles. Sailed from San Francisco, Sept. 21st; passed Honolulu, nine days out and arrived at Hong Kong, Nov. 1st, in a 40 days' passage. Later, continuing on to Calcutta, she was seven days from Hong Kong to Singapore. Sailed from Calcutta (Saugor), Feb. 3, 1855, she was 48 days to the Cape of Good Hope and arrived at London, 100 days out.

The fourth voyage of *Hurricane* was a round from London to Calcutta and return. On the outward voyage her time from passing the Needles, Aug. 12, 1855, to the mouth of the Hooghly, was 82¼ days, a record at that time and not beaten or equalled for many years thereafter. Returning she left Calcutta, Jan. 10, 1856, and arrived at Gravesend, May 13th, in 124 days' passage. Again sailed from London and arrived at Hong Kong, Oct. 5, 1856, 103 days out. Sailed from Hong Kong, Jan. 20, 1857, and arrived at San Francisco, Mar. 13th, in a 51 days' passage. Had either heavy gales with high seas or light head winds practically all the passage. Sailed from San Francisco, June 16, 1857; was 55 days to the Horn and arrived at New York, Sept. 28th, in a 104 days' passage.

During the remainder of 1857 and all of 1858, the *Hurricane*, with many other fine ships, was laid up, due to low freights and the general financial depression throughout the United States. Extreme clippers of small carrying capacity in proportion to register, could not properly operate. Towards the end of 1858, the *Hurricane* was again put on the berth at New York for San Francisco, Captain Sherman in command. She sailed Jan. 8, 1859; was 22 days to the line;

60 days to 50° South and 20 days rounding the Cape, in heavy westerly gales. Contrary winds in the South Pacific forced her to cross the equator in 105° West. She made land, 125 days out, in 28° North, off lower California, and thereafter had 17 days, practically all of calms, to the Golden Gate; total passage 142 days; arrival May 30, 1859. Sailed from San Francisco, Sept. 3rd, and was reported as arriving at Singapore, Nov. 7th.

While in port at San Francisco, in March 1857, the *Hurricane* was offered for sale but there were no offers made. Early in 1860, she was reported as having been sold at Singapore, for $30,000. She went under British colors, becoming *Shaw-Allum* of Singapore. In October 1863 she was in port at Mauritius and appears in registers as late as 1876.

HUSSAR

BUILT by G. W. Jackman, at Newburyport, in 1852. 151 x 32 x 23; 721 tons. Bush & Wildes, Boston, owners. Sold to G. Hussey, of New Bedford, in July 1854. Sold at Singapore, in November 1864.

INDIAMAN

BUILT by Hugh R. McKay, at East Boston, in 1854. 1165 tons. Sampson & Tappan, Boston, owners. Sold to go under the British flag in 1862. Name changed to *Indian Merchant*. Last report, 1883.

INO

EXTREME clipper ship, launched by Perrine, Patterson and Stack, at Williamsburg, N. Y., on Jan. 4, 1851. Deck, 160: 6 x 34: 11 x 17: 5. Draft, 17: 6, forward; 18: 9, aft. Tonnage, 895, old measurement; 673, new measurement. Original owners: Sifkin & Ironside of New York. She was heavily sparred, spreading 9491 yards of canvas and in every port she visited she was conspicuous for her handsome model and rakish rig. As will appear she proved to be a fast sailer, justifying the anticipations of both builder and owners. The first three outward passages of the *Ino* were from New York to San Francisco. Thereafter, until 1861, she was employed as an East Indiaman. On her maiden voyage she left New York, Mar. 12, 1851, and passed through the Golden Gate 134 days later. Capt. R. E. Little, in command, reported 27 days to the line; 66 days to 50° South, Pacific; thereafter light winds and was 34 days from the equator to port. Completed the voyage by going to Singapore in 57 days and thence 89 days to New York; 77 days from Java Head. Capt. Kimball R. Smith took command and had a fine run of 111 sailing days to San Francisco; 76 days from Rio, where she had put in and been detained seven days. Went to Manila in 60 days; thence to Singapore and was 90 days from there to New York. The third voyage was made under Captain Plummer in 121 days from New York to San Francisco; 49 days thence to Manila and 108 days from there to New York, arriving Apr. 4, 1854.

Leaving New York harbor, Dec. 11, 1857, Captain Plummer still in command, she passed Anjer in the fast time of 71 days, but the season being unfavorable, she was 20 days from there to Singapore. Later she proceeded to Hong Kong and thence to Shanghai. Sailed from Woosung, Nov. 21, 1858; was at Anjer, Dec. 9th, but did not get clear of Java Head until the 14th; then had the excellent run of 26 days to the Cape; thence 23 days to the line and 18 days later received her pilot off Sandy Hook, Feb. 19, 1859. If allowance is made for detention in the Straits of Sunda, five days, her passage would be 88 days from Woosung to anchorage; 85 days to pilot and 67 days from Java Head to pilot. Shortly after arrival at New York she was sold to Goddard & Thompson of Boston.

On Aug. 30, 1861, the *Ino* was purchased by John M. Forbes and others, for the United States Government, for $40,000. She was equipped with eight 32 pounders and a complement of 144 men and was rated as a ship-of-war, 4th class. Some months later her armament was increased by one 20 pounder Parrott rifle. Under Acting

Volunteer Lieutenant Josiah P. Cressy, of *Flying Cloud* fame, she started on her first cruise, Sept. 23, 1861, returning to Boston, Jan. 10, 1862. In reporting to Secretary of the Navy Welles, Lieut. Cressy wrote;—

"The ship fully justifies all expectations in regard to the service required; she carries her batteries well, in no way affecting her strength or fastenings. Cruised in the vicinity of the equator a long time; latterly she has been very tender on account of the consumption of stores and water."

On her second cruise she left Boston, Jan. 29, 1862, in search of the *Sumter* and arrived off Algeciras, Spain, Feb. 25th. Her run to Cadiz was reported as 12 days, being the fastest on record; had heavy weather, sustaining some damage and losing a boat; repaired at Palermo. Commander Craven, of the *Tuscarora*, having taken exception to the way in which Lieut. Cressy was obeying instructions, filed charges against him and in May the *Ino* was ordered to return from Cadiz to Boston. Thereafter the *Ino* had different commanders, among whom were: Acting Masters Edward F. Devens and James M. Williams, also Acting Vol.-Lieut. Charles A. French. On different occasions she was sent out to cruise in search of the *Alabama* and *Florida*, when she would be disguised by having the guns screened and the hull repainted a different color, so as to appear as a merchantman. Other cruises were made to the Newfoundland Banks to protect the fishermen; to the Western Islands and vicinity for the benefit of the whalers and to the equator and Cape St. Roque to cover merchantmen. On May 29, 1863, she left New York as convoy to the ship *Aquila*, which had the knocked-down ironclad *Comanche* on board for San Francisco and left her when well south of the line. At other periods she was attached, as a cruiser, to the various blockading squadrons, at times having one or two armed schooners as tenders. In June 1865 she was sent north from Key West and her four years of strenuous service as a vessel of war were ended. All of her commanders spoke well of her. On arrival at New York, in 1863, Captain Williams reported having sailed 18,000 miles on his cruise of five months ten days, during which time he had communicated with 132 vessels; the greatest distance sailed in 24 hours was 310 miles; least, 13 miles; maximum speed, 14 knots.

In 1867 the *Ino* was sold by the Government, to Samuel G. Reed & Co., of Boston and renamed *Shooting Star*. She loaded 900 tons of coal at Alexandria, Va., and under command of Captain Peck sailed for San Francisco, June 10, 1867, leaving Hampton Roads, July 4th. She was in sight of the Capes of Virginia for five days before she could get an offing, after which she had a gale lasting seven days; crossed the line 18 days from Hampton Roads; was 41 days from the line to 50° South, Pacific; thence had an excellent run of 19 days to the equator and was thereafter 23 days to port, in light winds and fine weather. Total passage from Hampton Roads, 102 days or 97 from the Capes of Virginia. Shortly after arrival at San Francisco she was purchased by Rosenfeld & Birmingham and was used principally to carry coal to that port from the mines at Nanaimo, B. C. Her voyages were made with the regularity of clockwork, eight round trips annually. She was kept in fine condition and her general appearance was always noteworthy. She generally carried between 950 and 1000 tons, being loaded like a sand barge. Latterly she was bark rigged. In 1876 she left the Pacific, taking a cargo of ore from the west coast of Mexico to Hamburg. In June 1877 she was at Philadelphia, to load oil for Bremen. Later she was sold foreign and in May 1886 was at Barcelona as the Russian bark *Ellen*, of Wasa, owned by her captain, Dahlstrom, and others.

INTREPID

THE medium clipper ship *Intrepid* was built in New York, in 1856, by William H. Webb, for Bucklin & Crane. She was commanded, during her whole career, by Capt. E. C. Gardner, who had a financial interest in her and who had previously been master of the *Celestial* and the *Comet*, owned by the same firm and productions of the same shipyards. The *Intrepid* was a handsome ship and a fast sailer. Captain Gardner was very proud of her and claimed she had never met her equal in sailing qualities, a bit of probable exaggeration, though pardonable.

She measured 1173 tons and was built for the China and California trade. She completed two round voyages and was lost when homeward bound on the third. On her maiden voyage she left New York, July 1, 1856, and arrived at San Francisco, Nov. 26th, Captain Gardner reporting his passage as 146 days. The run was prolonged by contrary winds and heavy weather in the Atlantic and off the Horn and she was not in the Pacific until the 94th day out. From San Francisco she crossed to Shanghai, making a fair run, and after going to India for a cargo of rice, left Shanghai in November 1857, for New York. Shortly after sailing she fell in with the wreck of the ship *Waverly*, from Shanghai for Swatow, from which she took off 96 Chinese passengers and landed them at Hong Kong, Nov. 24th; continued her voyage the 26th, cleared the Straits of Sunda, Dec. 16th, and was thence 38 days to the Cape of Good Hope. Her actual sailing time from Shanghai to New York was 110 days.

On her second voyage she reached San Francisco on Mar. 5, 1859, Captain Gardner reporting 132 days from New York. She returned to her home port in ballast, sailing Mar. 25th, and arriving out June 20th, a fast passage of 87 days.

Her third and last voyage, which was never completed, was to have been a round trip between New York and China. She went out to Shanghai in a fair run and left that port in ballast for Hong Kong about the first of March 1860. On going to sea she was side by side with the fast mail steamer *Yang Tsze* also bound for Hong Kong and arrived two hours ahead of her rival. At Hong Kong she loaded teas, silk and a general Oriental cargo, including a large consignment of firecrackers, all to the value of $660,000. She weighed anchor off Macao, Mar. 17, 1860, and it was hoped she might make New York before July 4th, on account of the firecrackers aboard. She was doing well, for the lateness of the season, being on the equator 14 days out, but aiming to make the Western or Macclesfield passage of the

Straits of Gaspar, she got ashore on Belvedere Reef, Mar. 31, 1860, Banca Island being in sight, 18 miles southwest. There were 26 in the crew, all of whom had been nearly a year with the vessel; the second mate and several of the seamen had been with Captain Gardner for years and Ah Ling, his steward, had been with him since boyhood, so that he found willing workers in his endeavor to save the ship. Immediately after she stranded, efforts were made to kedge the vessel off the reef and considerable of the cargo was jettisoned, but to no purpose. The masts were cut away to prevent the Malay pirates from discovering her position but the next morning many proas filled with men came down on the ship and a fierce battle ensued. As was customary in the China trade the ship was armed, carrying two nine-pound cannon besides boarding pikes and small arms. At one time the pirates gained the deck but the defenders rallied and drove the Malays back, using boiling water with good effect. Many of the Malays were killed aboard the ship or in the proas and one of the crew of the *Intrepid* lost his life. At length a vessel was sighted coming towards them and the *Intrepid* was set on fire and all hands took to the boats. Another attack made by the pirates on the boats was repulsed and the officers and crew of the *Intrepid* were picked up by the French clipper *Gallilei* who landed them at Anjer. On receipt of information concerning the position of the wreck of the *Intrepid*, a small vessel, the *Shandon*, was sent from Singapore to salvage any of the cargo remaining, but on arriving at the scene of the disaster they found the wreck completely surrounded by a fleet of Malay proas, while their piratical owners were plundering the ship of everything movable. Two Dutch gun-boats finally drove the pirates away and the *Shandon* was able to salvage cargo to the amount of $2000 and land it at Singapore.

INVINCIBLE

EXTREME clipper ship, launched Aug. 6, 1851, from the yard of William H. Webb, New York. Keel, 225; deck, 238; over all, 245; extreme breadth of beam, which was several feet forward of the center, 42: 10; depth of hold, 25: 6; 1769 tons, old measurement; 1325 tons, new measurement. She was very strongly built, iron braced throughout and cost $120,000. Her entrance and clearance lines were long and sharp and slightly concave. The bow rose nobly and with a liberty cap as a billet head, backed by the American coat of arms, neither head nor trail boards, had a beautiful yet very strong appearance. The handsome, round stern bore a carved eagle in relief, surrounded by scroll work. The bulwarks, including monkeyrail, were only 4½ feet high and she had a beautiful sheer. The masts raked 1¼, 1 1/3 and 1½ inches to the foot, the lower masts being "made" sticks; bowsprit, 38 inches in diameter, 30 feet outboard; jibboom, 17 inches in diameter, 33 feet long; flying jibboom, 14 feet with a 3 foot end. Spanker boom, 13 inches by 56 feet; gaff, 9 inches by 35 feet. Her spars and rigging were snug and handy but very strong and well adapted for heavy weather and she appears to have consistently escaped the damage aloft that was experienced by many other of the early clippers.

The *Invincible* was designed for the Liverpool passenger business, the main deck being practically free from obstructions, while the two 'tween decks were each 7½ feet high in the clear. In model for speed, she surpassed the few other clippers built especially for transAtlantic packets and her record is very good. Her first owner was James W. Phillips of New York. In 1860 she was purchased by Spofford & Tileson of New York, for $60,000, becoming a regular packet in their line to Liverpool, until February 1863, when Henry Hastings of Boston, became her owner. Captain Norton, who had been selected for her first commander, died on the day she was launched and Capt. H. W. Johnson was appointed in his stead. On account of the great demand for tonnage to California at the time, the ship was diverted to that trade, and her first two outward passages were to San Francisco. Then, for about five years, she was operated between England and Australia as a White Star packet. Between 1860 and 1863 she plied between New York and Liverpool and her remaining years were spent in trade with California. Her passages were always good and she was considered one of the fastest sailing vessels afloat. Her best day's run on her maiden trip, New York to San Francisco, 400 miles, was never exceeded or equalled on that route except by the *Flying Cloud* and *Great Republic*, both of which, in a single instance, over-run her record by a few miles. She was a favorite ship in every trade in which she was engaged.

The *Invincible* made five passages from New York and one from Boston to San Francisco, her time being, 113 (sailing days); 111; 134; 109; 119 and 119 days respectively. On her first run she was forced to put into Rio, when 37 days out, short of water due to a leaky tank and was 76 days from Rio to San Francisco. On her second run out, she was 48 days to 50° South and 23 days rounding the Horn, losing her main-yard, a number of sails, etc. In 1863, her longest passage, 134 days, she was 35 days off the Horn and 34 days from the equator to the Golden Gate. Her last three runs were faster than any made by other clippers at about the same time, she beating the *Dreadnought*, 25 days in 1864 and eight days in 1865. In 1866 she was 22 days from 50° South, Pacific, to the equator, and 19 days thence to San Francisco, her passage of 119 days not being equalled about that time. It is noted that on five of her westward Cape Horn runs she left eastern ports during midsummer, the poorest season for fast passages.

From San Francisco, homeward, the *Invincible* made passages to New York in 90, 107 and 96 days; to Boston in 108 days, and to Philadelphia in 114 days. On her first voyage she crossed from San Francisco to Hong Kong, arriving out July 11, 1852. She experienced a typhoon, July 6th and 7th, and Captain Johnson wrote home:

"Just as I got the royal yards down, it came buzzing enough to blow one's hair off; relieving tackles were hooked on and led down to the main deck to keep the men on their feet; the sea was tremendous but it was beautiful to see her behave; not a shiver or shake, no water on board, and lying to without a rag of sail. While many others would be dismasted, our good ship did not do $5 damage and on the 8th came out in fine weather, like a new pin."

Completing this voyage she was 112 days from Whampoa to London, having left the China coast during the unfavorable monsoon. Sailed from London, Feb. 14, 1853; passed the Scilly Islands on the 16th and was six days and three hours to the eastern edge of the Banks, latitude 48°, called the best run on record; best day, 306 miles; best speed, 15½ knots; received pilot off Fire Island, Mar. 5th, and anchored in New York harbor on the 7th.

While engaged as a White Star packet, between England and Australia, she made two runs out to Melbourne in 76 days and 79 days respectively, on one of which occasions her time equalled that made by the *James Baines* that season. She completed her 1854 voyage by going from Melbourne to Bombay; whence she was 92 days to Liverpool. After her last voyage to Australia she went on to China and arrived at New York in October 1859, 126 days from Whampoa and 78 days from Anjer.

Between Sept. 21, 1860, and Jan. 19, 1863, she completed eight round voyages between New York and Liverpool. Her fastest was the first, 19 days out and 16 days home, Captain Hepburn in command. In February 1862 she was 19 days on the homeward run and the following voyage was 22 days out and 35 days return. Most of the voyages occupied about 2½ months on the round, including detention at Liverpool. In the spring of 1863, Captain Hepburn was succeeded by Captain Kellum, who made one voyage. Capt. William Lester, formerly in the *Pampero* and *Flying Childers*, then took her and continued in her until her end.

The last passage of the *Invincible* was from San Francisco to Philadelphia, arriving out May 16, 1867. She later proceeded to New York and loaded for San Francisco. On Sept. 11th, while lying opposite the Pierpont Storehouse, near Montague Street, Brooklyn, the watchman was awakened at 12: 30 A.M. by smoke and found the vessel on fire. Before the fire department could reach her, the flames had made such headway that it was determined to tow her into the stream and scuttle her; the smoke, however, prevented this latter being done and she lay all night in the stream with two fire boats playing on her. The next morning Mr. Hastings, her owner, ordered her to be towed to the foot of Dover Street, but finding no hope of saving her, she was beached on Governor's Island and proved a total loss. Insurance reported to be $100,000.

JACOB BELL

EXTREME clipper ship, launched Nov. 12, 1852, from the yard of Jacob Bell, New York, who died while she was in frame and she was completed by his son, Abraham C. Bell, his successor. Dimensions: keel, 195; deck, 200: 11; over all, 215; beam, 38: 5; depth, 22; 1381 43/95 tons, old measurement. She is described as being of faultless model and exquisite symmetry, everywhere attracting admiration as being a perfect specimen of naval architecture and the foremost production of that famous yard. The spacious deck was broken only by a highly polished frame on which were stowed the launch and lifeboats. A notable feature was the helmsman's platform, which was of brass in the shape of a heart.

The maiden voyage of the *Bell* was from New York to San Francisco, the arrival out being on Apr. 10, 1853, in 122 days' passage. Captain Kilham reported a succession of light winds most of the way. From San Francisco she returned to Philadelphia, in ballast, in 87 days. Loaded for San Francisco and arrived out, Jan. 14, 1854, in 122 days' passage. Had light winds throughout, excepting 13 days of heavy gales off the Horn; carried three skysails from latitude 25° South, Pacific, to 28° North. From San Francisco she crossed to Shanghai, in 39 days. Left Woosung, May 1st, and was 109 days to New York. Then went to Singapore, in 90 days; thence to Shanghai and passed Anjer, Nov. 5, 1855, bound for New York.

Under command of Capt. F. W. Behm, sailed from New York, Mar. 15, 1856, for Bombay; crossed the line, 18 days and 1 hour out, logging 3703 miles, an average of 8.55 knots per hour; was 78 days from New York to Bombay. Homeward bound she is said to have been 113 days from Manila. With the exception of a passage from New York to San Francisco in 1860, she was henceforth kept in the China trade, by her new owners, A. A. Low & Brother of New York, who had purchased her early in 1856. Leaving Manila, Aug. 6, 1857, she was 119 days going home, 69 days from Anjer, 40 from the Cape and 22 from the line.

Under Capt. Charles P. Low, formerly of the *N. B. Palmer*, who had been ashore on sick leave, she left New York in January 1859; was 83 days to Anjer and 114 to Hong Kong; thence went to Foo Chow, in 10 days. When about ready to sail for New York she got ashore in the river Min; got off, but after getting to sea, Aug. 24th, she developed a leak and put into Hong Kong the 31st; repaired and sailed Oct. 13th; was 27 days to Anjer; thence 33 days to the Cape; thence 23 days to the equator and received her pilot 102 days from Hong Kong, one of the fastest passages from China made about this time. She then loaded for San Francisco, arriving out, July 15, 1860, in 116 days' passage. Captain Frisbie reported 22 days to the line, 66 to the Horn, off which had 12 days of heavy gales, thence 24 days to the line in the Pacific; in 46° South, Pacific, had a tornado lasting 24 hours which carried away some head gear; in 50° South, Pacific, was in company with the *Witchcraft*, which had left New York with her and led her into San Francisco 14 days, the latter reporting unfavorable weather all the way up the Pacific. She crossed from San Francisco to Hong Kong, in 51 days; returned in 45 days; went from San Francisco to London, in 110 days; thence in ballast to New York, in 46 days.

The *Bell* sailed from New York, Nov. 12, 1861; was 84 days to Anjer and 115 to Hong Kong, arriving Mar. 7, 1862. In a typhoon, July 27th, she was driven ashore in a paddy field near Whampoa and had to discharge to get off. Later, went up the coast to Foo

Chow and sailed, Nov. 5, 1862, for New York, with a cargo, principally on English account, valued at $1,500,000, and consisting of choice tea, cassia, camphor and fans. Passed Anjer, Nov. 30th. On Feb. 12, 1863, when 99 days out and in latitude 24° North, longitude 65° 58′ West, about 100 miles from the Sombrero Reef, she was captured by the *Florida* and burned the following day. Captain Frisbie gave the details as follows.

About noon discovered a steamer in pursuit under full head of steam and all sail set. After a chase of over four hours she fired a shot which struck about twice a ship's length astern and we hove to; the steamer, carrying the Federal flag, sailed around the *Bell* three times, presented her broadside, ran up the rebel flag and sent a boat aboard. Our officers, crew and passengers, including Mrs. Frisbie and child and another lady, were allowed half an hour to collect a few necessities, the prize crew appropriating what remained. All our people were then taken aboard the *Florida*, which set off in pursuit of a schooner, after leaving instructions as to the *Bell's* course during the night. The next morning the *Florida's* crew were so busily engaged in transferring plunder as to neglect the management of the ship and the *Bell*, with sails set, bore down on the *Florida*, the rigging of which had to be manned to shove the *Bell* off. She was then set afire and burned to the water's edge. Four days later all the *Bell* people were transferred to the Danish brig *Morning Star*, which landed them at St. Thomas, Feb. 19, 1863.

The cargo of the *Bell* was reported as well covered by insurance in England and New York. The value of the ship and her freight money was stated as being $50,000 and $22,783 respectively and that portion of her cargo belonging to American citizens, $308,290.

JAMES BAINES

THE *James Baines* was the third of a quartette of extreme clipper ships built by Donald McKay, at East Boston, Mass., to the order of James Baines & Co., of Liverpool, for operation in their "Black Ball Line" of Australian passenger packets. Her predecessors were the *Lightning* and *Champion of the Seas*, and she was followed by the *Donald McKay*, each in its turn being somewhat larger than its predecessor, and each as it was built, being respectively the largest merchant ship flying the British flag. The *Baines* was launched July 25, 1854, and was 266 feet long, over all, by 44: 9, by 29 feet; tonnage, 2515, American measurement and 2275, British measurement. Dead rise, 18 inches. Her bow was long and sharp with slightly concave lines. Her figurehead was a bust of Mr. Baines. It was the product of an English carver and was called an excellent likeness. Her stern was round and was regarded as the neatest and most handsome of any ever put on a McKay clipper. It was ornamented with the arms of England and America, between which was a bas-relief of the globe, done in gilt. In general appearance of hull and rig she was more pleasing to the eye than the *Lightning* or any of her predecessors. She was a three decker and her accommodations for all classes of passengers were unsurpassed. Her lower masts were shorter than those of the *Lightning* but this was offset by the greater length of those above and by the greater squareness of her yards. Counting from the foremast, her lower masts were in length, 63¾, 71 and 61 feet; topmasts, 47, 50 and 42 feet; topgallants, 29, 29 and 26 feet; royals, 19, 19 and 15 feet. The corresponding yards were; 90, 100 and 74½ feet; 69, 75 and 51 feet; 49, 54 and 42 feet; 36, 49 and 30 feet. She crossed a skysailyard on the mainmast only, its length being 39 feet, and its mast, with pole, 19 feet long. In very light winds she set moonsails and spread in a single suit of sails, 13,000 running yards of canvas, 18 inches wide.

Under command of Capt. Charles McDonnell, who had been in the *Marco Polo*, first as mate and later as master, the *Baines* sailed from Boston, Sept. 12, 1854, and made the run from Boston Light to Rock Light, Liverpool, in 12 days and 6 hours, a record run. She was in ballast and uncoppered and this was her captain's first experience in a clipper. At times she logged 20 knots, yet her best day's run was only 337 miles. She sailed from Liverpool, Dec. 9, 1854, with 1400 tons of cargo and 700 passengers and made the run to Melbourne in 65 days and 5½ hours, her time from Rock Light to Hobson's Bay being 63 days and 18 hours. In 23½ consecutive hours, running her easting down, she covered 423 miles; another day's run, noon to noon, was 407 miles. Sailed from Melbourne, Mar. 12, 1855, and made the run to Liverpool in 69½ days, with 420 miles as her best day. Left Liverpool, Aug. 5, 1855, and arrived at Melbourne, 79 days out. Returning to Liverpool, she was 85 days, with light and variable winds.

She sailed from Liverpool, Apr. 7, 1856; did not clear Cape St. Roque until 29 days out and was 48 days and 6 hours thence to Cape Otway. Ran 2276 miles in seven days. On May 28th she made 2 degrees, 15 minutes of latitude and 8 degrees, 7 minutes of longitude, calculated as 404 miles, the log showing—"Brisk gales with occasional heavy squalls and rain and wind increasing." On June 15th, the entry is: "Commenced fresh breezes with rain and sleet; at 8 A.M., more moderate. At noon sighted a ship ahead under double reefed topsails, we having main skysail set and going 17 knots. At 1 P.M. alongside the ship, the *Libertas*. At 2 P.M. she was out of sight astern." The entry of June 18th is: "Wind freshening; at 8 P.M. took in all starboard stu'nsails; mainskysail set; ship taking out 21 knots. Fine clear night; fresh gale until nearly noon with snow squalls." Four days later, in a squall which fortunately lasted only three minutes, the ship broached to; blew away all head sails, the foretop and topgallant sails, two sails on the mainmast and all the staysails, besides carrying away the main and the maintopgallant yards. Such a terrific gust of wind had never before been experienced by Captain McDonnell and the barometer had given no warning.

The *Baines* sailed from Melbourne, Aug. 7, 1856, and had but two good day's runs, 356 and 340 miles, to the Horn which was passed 36 days out. A further series of light or baffling winds was encountered in the South Atlantic and the line was not crossed until the 65th day out. On the 84th day out, in latitude 29° North, she fell in with the *Lightning*, which had left Melbourne 21 days after her but had gained 12 days on the run to the Horn and an additional nine days in the South Atlantic. The two ships were in company, off and on, for five days, in light and variable winds, neither having any advantage. Both arrived in the Mersey, Nov. 20th.

In January 1857, the *Baines* left Liverpool for Melbourne and was beaten five days on the run to Melbourne by the *Lightning*, which sailed Feb. 5th. On the homeward run, however, the *Baines* squared accounts by beating her rival six days. Both ships, as also the *Champion of the Seas*, were then chartered by the Government to take troops and stores to India. The *Baines* left Portsmouth, Aug. 8, 1857, having on board the 97th regiment, 1000 men, and arrived off the mouth of the Hooghly River in 103 days. On Apr. 16, 1858, she arrived at Liverpool from Calcutta, in the fast time of 77 days from the Sand Heads. The cargo in the between decks was duly discharged and on the 21st the lower hold hatches were taken off in the presence of surveyors, everything then appearing to be in first class condition. The next morning, however, smoke was observed issuing from the main hatch and efforts made to get at and quench the fire proved futile. The ship was scuttled but there not being sufficient depth of water in the dock to smother the flames, the ship was burned to the water's edge, the masts falling over the side. The cargo remaining in the ship at the time consisted of 2200 bales of jute, 6213 bags of linseed, 6682 bags of rice and 40 bales of hides. The wreck was sold at auction for £1080, sterling, and was later converted into a landing stage. The value of the ship and the cargo destroyed was estimated at $170,000.

In the Sept. 2, 1854, issue of the "Boston Semi-Weekly Atlas," appeared the following account of the *James Baines*, viz.:

This magnificent ship, like the *Lightning* and the *Champion of the Seas,* is designed for James Baines & Co.'s line of Liverpool and Australian packets, and is larger, and said to be more beautiful than either of them. She is 266 feet between perpendiculars on deck, has 44¾ feet extreme breadth of beam, 29 feet depth of hold, with three decks, a poop, two houses and a topgallant forecastle, and registers 2525 80-95ths tons. She has a long, rakish, sharp bow, with slightly concave lines below, but convex above, and it is ornamented with a bust of her namesake, which was carved in Liverpool, and which is said by those who know the original, to be an excellent likeness. It is blended with the cutwater, is relieved with gilded carved work, and forms a neat and appropriate ornament to the bow. She is planked flush to the covering-board, has a bold and buoyant sheer, graduated her whole length, and it rises gracefully at the ends, particularly forward; and every moulding is fair and harmonizes finely with the planking and her general outline. Her stern is rounded, and although she has a full poop deck, her after body surpasses, in neatness, that of any vessel her talented builder has yet produced. Our most eminent mechanics consider her stern perfect. It is rounded below the line of the planksheer, is fashioned above in an easy curve, and only shows a few inches of rise above the outline of the monkey rail; and as this rise is painted white, and the rest of the hull black, when viewed broadside on, her sheer appears a continuous line along her entire length. The stern is ornamented with carved representations of "the great globe itself," between the arms of Britain and the United States, surrounded with fancy scroll work, has carved and gilded drops between the cabin windows, and her name above all— the whole tastefully gilded and painted.

Her bulwarks are built solid, and are surmounted by a monkey rail, which is panelled inside, and their whole height above the deck is about six feet, varying, of course, towards the ends. She has a full topgallant forecastle, which extends to the foremast, and is fitted for the accommodation of her crew, and abaft the foremast, a large house, which contains spacious galleys, several state-rooms, store-rooms, an ice room, and shelters a staircase, which leads to the decks below. She has a full poop deck, between 7 and 8 feet high, under which is the ladies' cabin, and before it a large house, which contains the dining saloon and other apartments. The outline of the poop and the house is protected by rails on turned stanchions, and the enclosure forms a spacious and beautiful promenade deck. She also has a small house aft, which shelters the helmsman in a recess, protects the entrance to the captain's cabin, is also a smoking room for the passengers, and answers a variety of other purposes.

The ladies' cabin is aft, and is 30 feet long by 13 wide and 6½ high. It is pure white, with gilded carved work on the panels, and has papier maché cornices, and ventilators between the beams. Aft is a beautiful sofa, fitted to correspond with the curve of the stern, and over it is a neat bookcase, containing among other works, a full and uniform edition of the British Poets. The forward partition is ornamented with a large plate-glass mirror, which gives a reflected view of the cabin abaft it. The Captain's cabin and sleeping room are on the starboard side, and communicate with the wheel house on deck, so that it will not be necessary for him to enter the ladies' cabin. Besides these the cabin contains 11 spacious state-rooms, a bath-room and other useful apartments.

The dining saloon is 35 feet long by 15 wide, is wainscotted with mahogany, has enamelled white panels and pilasters, ornamented with flowers and gilding, and its cornices, which are of papier maché, are edged with gilded flower work and other ornaments. The ceiling is plain white, except the corners of the beams, which are also edged with papier maché mouldings. Two of the after panels, on each side, are mirrors, and a large square mirror ornaments the forward partition also. The alternate panels along the sides, are stained glass windows; and the casings around the mizzenmast and rudder-trunk, are beautifully variegated with national emblems and other ornaments. Permanent settees are fitted along both sides of the saloon, and on each side there are walnut tables extending fore and aft. The furniture of the saloon, as well as the after cabin and state-rooms, is of the most costly kind, finished in the highest style of art. It was made by Messrs. Jas. H. Beal & Brother, who have furnished nearly all the splendid ships which have been built by Mr. McKay.

The entrance from the deck to the saloon is 2½ feet wide, and extends across the house with a door on each side; and opposite to the midship door of the saloon is the pantry, which is spacious and fitted up in superior style. In front of the saloon-house are the state-rooms of the first and second officers, and the windows of these rooms are of stained glass, and have the ship's name in them.

We will return to the saloon. A staircase in its after part leads to the main deck, where are the gentlemen's sleeping apartments. These consist of 24 staterooms, with two berths in each room, and extend along the sides, leaving a spacious cabin outside. This cabin is painted pure white, relieved with gilded carved work, and receives light and air through two large ventilators amidships, the forward one of which passes through the deck below, and both extend to the skylights on the poop, and have glass in their sides. Every stateroom, too, along the sides has a square port in it, and the rooms adjoining have ventilated blinds, which admit light as well as air.

The deck before the gentlemen's sleeping cabin has three large cargo ports opposite the hatchways, one on each side, and square ports suitable for staterooms along the sides. This deck, when she arrives at Liverpool, will be fitted up for the accommodation of second class passengers, and the deck below for others. These decks are ventilated amidships with trunk-skylights, which pass through the house forward as well as the cabin and the saloon aft. Along the sides of the houses there are also ventilators and skylights, like those on board the *Champion of the Seas*. The height between each of her decks is 7½ feet, and over the main and after hatchways are large ventilated skylights, with double companions, which lead to the decks below. On the poop deck there are two oblong square skylights, the after one extending from the wheelhouse to the mizzenmast, and the forward one is over the pantry. The ascent from the quarter deck to the poop consists of two staircases, one on each side, built into the front of the poop.

Before the mainmast there are three gallows frames, upon which her spare boats are stowed, bottom up, and over the sides she carries quarter-boats, suspended to iron davits, which can be swung inboard when required. She has copper-chambered pumps, six capstans, a crab-winch on the forecastle, a patent windlass, Crane's self-acting chain stoppers, a patent steering apparatus, and a large variety of other modern improvements.

Notwithstanding the vast space occupied by her forecastle, houses and poop, she still has spacious deck-room for working ship and looks splendidly. Her bulwarks and houses are painted white, and her waterways blue, and in this style she is also painted below.

Of her materials and the style of her construction, it is not necessary to say much, for she is nearly the same, in these particulars, as the *Champion of the Seas,* a full and accurate description of which was published in the Atlas of May 20. Like her, the frame is of white oak, the ceiling, planking, deck-frames and keelsons, of hard pine, and she is diagonally braced with iron, and square-fastened, and all her keelsons and waterways are scarphed and keyed. Her ceiling is also scarphed and keyed, and bolted edgeways every three feet. The style in which her hull is finished, both inside and outside, has not been surpassed, if equalled, by any ship which Mr. McKay has built; and this is saying much when we call to mind the number of beautiful vessels he has "turned out of hand."

She is very heavily sparred, and will spread about 13,000 yards of canvas in a single suit of sails. Her mast-heads and yards are black; the lower masts, from the truss bands to the fife-rails, are bright and varnished, their hoops white, and the tops and down to the truss bands, are also white. She has iron caps, and is rigged in nearly the same style as the *Champion of the Seas,* so we learn from Messrs. Francis Low & Co., who rigged them both. Messrs. Porter, Mayhew & Co. made her sails. The length of her lower masts, in the following table, are above the deck. Owing to the vast spread of her yards, the lower masts look short; but they will certainly stand better and receive more support from the rigging, than if they were longer. The following are the dimensions of her masts and yards:

MASTS.

	Diameter. Inches.	Length. Feet.	Mast-heads. Feet.
Fore	40	63¾	17
Top	20	47	10
Topgallant	15	29	0
Royal	13	17	pole.. 9
Main	42	71	17
Top	21	50	10
Topgallant	16	29	0
Royal	14	17	0
Skysail	10	11	pole.. 9
Mizzen	36	61	14
Top	16	42	8½
Topgallant	12	26	0
Royal	10	15	pole.. 8

YARDS.

Fore	24½	90	yard arms.. 5
Top	19	69	5½
Topgallant	13¼	49	4
Royal	9	36	3
Main	26	100	5
Top	21	75	5½
Topgallant	14	54	4
Royal	11	40	3
Skysail	8	30	1½
Crossjack	21	74	4½
Mizzentop	16	57½	5
Topgallant	10	42	3½
Royal	8	30	2

The bowsprit is 20 feet long outboard; jibboom divided at 15 and 14 feet outside of the cap for the two jibs, with six feet end; spanker boom 58, gaff 44, main spanker gaff 24 feet 9 inches, and the other spars in proportion. She is more heavily rigged and spreads more canvas than the *Great Republic* will when she is refitted. Capt. N. B. Palmer, who now owns this ship, is having the fourth deck taken off her, and intends that her mainmast shall be only 66 feet above deck, and the mainyard 90 feet square, and that she shall be rigged in this proportion fore and aft. Capt. L. McKay, however, who is both a scientific shipbuilder and a sailor, contends that these alterations will spoil the *Great Republic's* sailing qualities, and he is also of the opinion that the *James Baines* is fully able to bear her canvas nobly, and that she is rigged in just proportion to her hull.

She is commanded by Capt. Chas. McDonnell, formerly of the famous ship *Marco Polo*, in which he made one of the shortest voyages on record, between Liverpool and Australia, and who, for his uniform kindness to his passengers, received from them a valuable service of plate. The fact that he is entrusted with the command of such a magnificent ship shows the high estimation in which he is held by those who know him best. We wish him and his beautiful ship the best of luck. In a few days she will sail for Liverpool, and there take her place in the "Black-Ball Line" of Liverpool and Australian clippers. For the same Line there is now on the stocks at East Boston, a clipper of larger stowage capacity than the *Great Republic*, and which will be named the *Donald McKay*, as a compliment to her builder.

JOHN BERTRAM

EXTREME clipper ship, launched from the yards of Ewell & Jackson, East Boston, Dec. 9, 1850, 61 days after her keel had been laid. She was built under the supervision of Captain Glidden and was the pioneer vessel in the "Glidden & Williams Line" of San Francisco-Boston packets. Flint Peabody & Co., of San Francisco, were joint owners. She was named after the well-known sea captain and merchant of Salem, John Bertram. Keel, 173 feet; deck, 180; over all, 190; by 37; by 20; 1080 tons, old measurement; 778 tons, new measurement. She was very sharp, being designed specially for speed and her run was as clean as that of a pilot boat. For a figurehead there was a representation of an eagle on the wing and on her stern was a medallion bust after her namesake. Dead rise, 40 inches; sheer, 26 inches; swell or rounding of sides, 6 inches. Length of lower masts, 76½, 81 and 67 feet; rake, 1¼, 1½ and 1¾ inches to the foot.

Under command of Capt. Frederick Lendholm, she left Boston, Jan. 11, 1851, and when off the Platte had the mainmast and bowsprit sprung, on account of which she put into Valparaiso, when 77 days out, for repairs. Was there 17 days and was thence 49 days to San Francisco; total days out from Boston, 143; sailing days, 126. She sailed from San Francisco, July 5th; arrived at Rio, Sept. 2nd, in 58½ days, very fast time; was in port at Rio, nine days; was below Boston, Oct. 18th, 37 days from Rio and 96 sailing days from San Francisco, but was blown out by a gale. Anchored on the 21st, in 108 days, gross, from San Francisco. On her second voyage, she left Boston, Dec. 12, 1851, saw Staten Island, 54 days out and from there made the remarkably fast run of 51 days to San Francisco. Was 12 days between the 50's; 20 days in the South Pacific and 19 days from the equator to port. Passage 105 days. From San Francisco she went to Shanghai in 41 days. Left Shanghai, Aug. 12th, and put into Singapore in distress, Sept. 26th. In a typhoon lasting 14 hours had carried away trestle- and cross-trees; had all the close-reefed topsails and storm sails blown from the bolt ropes and lost two men overboard; eleven of the crew were on the sick list at the time. On resuming her voyage, she cleared the Straits of Sunda, Oct. 18th, and was off the Cape, 31 days later, the fastest run made about that time and half a day better than that of the *Sword Fish* and the *Sea Serpent*. On her third voyage, she sailed from Boston, July 1, 1853, and arrived at San Francisco, Oct. 24th, in 115 days' passage. Captain Lendholm reported having much light winds and calms; best day,

260 miles; poorest, 14 miles, with a number of days between 20 and 50 miles. Had, however, an excellent run up the South Pacific, being 18 days from 50° South to the equator. Sailed from San Francisco, Nov. 2nd; touched at Honolulu; left there the 26th; arrived at Manila in 32 days. From Manila she went to Canton and was 91 days thence to New York.

The following excellent description of the working of a vessel at sea is taken from the account of this voyage of the *John Bertram*.

"Leaving the Sandwich Islands we flew away over to the China Sea, at the entrance to which we were saluted with a fierce typhoon, and on the 28th December we made the light on the island of Corregidor, at the entrance to Manila Bay. We had a splendid breeze, just abaft the beam, until we got within 12 or 15 miles, when, the wind suddenly shifting, headed us off on every tack. Anxious, however, to get in, we crowded on all sail and at it we went and by dint of taking advantage of every puff we managed, little by little, to shorten our distance. It is a beautiful sight to see a clipper ship of 1000 tons, with a spanking breeze, working up a narrow channel. Scarcely is she about on one tack than she must go in stays for another, and, as may be imagined, on board all is excitement and everyone kept actively employed. As our barometer indicated bad weather, we felt it important to get in that night and therefore every nerve was strained to get the most out of the vessel we could, and in order to make the most of a favorable slant, we would often shave the reef so closely that the slightest mistake in manoeuvering would have lost the ship. The crew never left their stations from daylight till dark. I was stationed at the wheel to 'con' it, to see that the helmsman did his duty, and watched with great pleasure the pilot-boat qualities of our ship.

"About dark, just when we were thinking that we would be obliged to stay outside all night, we got a favorable breeze and rapidly shot inside the island of Corregidor. Darkness came down upon us but the flashes of the revolving lantern made us sure enough of our position to venture in, so, squaring away, we went flying up the bay. Just before four bells were struck, the lookout forward sung out, 'Land close aboard,' when, luffing up in the wind, letting every-thing fly, we let go an anchor and brought up all standing, when, sure enough, within only a few lengths of us lay a long black object. What it was we could not imagine but as the lead gave us plenty of water, we did not trouble ourselves. Daylight, however, solved the prob-lem, it proving to be an immense battery made of timber and brush-wood, used by the natives as a fishery."

She sailed from New York, June 14, 1854; passed Anjer, Sept. 4th and was reported arriving at Manila, 96 days out. Arrived at Boston, Jan. 29, 1855, 90 days from Manila, a run which has seldom been beaten; she was 73 days from Anjer.

After arrival home she was sold for $45,000, to William F. Schmidt of Hamburg and was engaged in trade between that port and New York, for many years, as a regular passenger liner. In 1859 she was owned by R. M. Sloman of Hamburg and commanded by Captain Knudson. In 1860 she was reported as having made the very fast run of 18 days from New York to Hamburg. In April 1863, while bound from Hamburg, via Havre, for New York, with 336 passengers and a full freight, she had a heavy gale for 48 hours during which she lost four of the crew overboard, had eight dis-abled, and all her storm sails blown away. Arrived at New York, May 22nd, in a leaky condition. She was later sold to J. Rod & Son of Tonsburg, who put her in the timber trade between Quebec and London. She left Quebec, June 19, 1882, and arrived at London, July 12th. The old clipper *Nightingale*, which had left Quebec in company, reached London, July 8th. On Jan. 18, 1883, she arrived at New York and there loaded for Rotterdam, sailing Feb. 22, 1883. Captain Dahl, of the Norwegian bark *Oxo*, on arrival at London, Mar. 29th, reported that he fell in with the wreck of the ship *John Bertram*, Mar. 17th, and took on board her crew. Part were trans-ferred to another ship and ten were landed in London.

JOHN ELLIOT THAYER

BUILT by Paul Curtis, at East Boston, in 1854. 1918 tons. Enoch Train & Co., Boston, owners; afterwards Benjamin Bangs and John E. Thayer & Bro., of Boston. Burned Sept. 13, 1858, while loading guano at the island of Patos, Gulf of California.

JOHN GILPIN

MEDIUM clipper ship, designed and built by Samuel Hall, at Boston, in 1852. Keel, 175 feet; deck, 195; over all, 205; by 37; by 22; 1089 tons, old measurement. Dead rise, 20 inches; swell of sides, 6 inches; sheer, 2 feet. She had sharp ends, with slightly convex lines; her bow flared outward three feet from the line of the plank-sheer. A gilded billet took the place of a figure-head, while the handsome oval stern was ornamented with a representation of her famous namesake, galloping at full speed. The mainmast was 80 feet long; topmast, 45 feet; topgallant, 25½ feet; royal, 15½ feet, with a 5 foot pole. The fore and mizzen lower masts were a few feet shorter than the main but all above were alike. She was well sparred and very rakish. Owned by Pierce & Hunnewell of Boston.

On her maiden voyage, the *Gilpin* left New York, Oct. 29, 1852, under command of Capt. Justin Doane and arrived at San Francisco in 93 days and 20 hours, from port to pilot. Her best day's run was 315 miles. The clipper ship *Flying Fish* had entered port the day ahead of her in 92 days and 4 hours from New York. The *Gilpin* sailed from San Francisco, Feb. 24th; was 13 days to Honolulu and 37 days thence to Singapore; later proceeded to Calcutta and Penang. Sailed from the latter port, Aug. 7th; passed the Cape, 38 days out and crossed the line, 24 days later; arrived at Boston, Nov. 10th, in 95 days' passage, Captain Sheer in command. On her second voyage she left New York, Jan. 28, 1854, under command of Captain Ring; had generally light winds and passed Cape Horn in fine weather with royals set; crossed the equator, 91 days out and arrived

"HERALD OF THE MORNING," 1294 TONS, BUILT AT MEDFORD, MASS., IN 1853

"HIGHFLYER," 1195 TONS, BUILT AT NEWBURYPORT, IN 1853

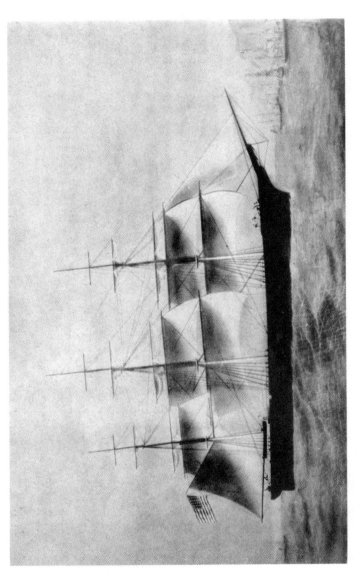

"HIPPOGRIFFE," 678 TONS, BUILT AT EAST DENNIS, MASS., IN 1852

From a painting by a Chinese artist, showing the ship off Hong Kong

BURNING OF THE "JACOB BELL," BY THE CONFEDERATE CRUISER "FLORIDA"

From a wood engraving in *Harper's Weekly*, Mar. 21, 1863

at San Francisco, May 23rd, in 114 days from New York. Sailed June 4th and was 80 days to Calcutta. Left the Sand Heads, Nov. 4th; passed the Cape, 37½ days out and crossed the line, 24 days later; arrived at Boston, Feb. 12, 1855, in a passage of 100 days. Off the Cape she was in company with the *John Bertram,* from Manila for Boston, the latter reaching port 13 days in advance of the *Gilpin.* Captain Ring reported, however, that he had been 20 days north of Bermuda and 13 days off the coast in continual gales and very cold weather.

The third voyage of the *Gilpin* was from Boston to Honolulu, she arriving out Aug. 27, 1855, in a passage of 133 days in light winds; for 41 consecutive days could not carry a studding sail nor steer a direct course; did not close reef a topsail on the run. After discharging cargo she proceeded to Manila, arriving Nov. 11th; loaded for New York and sailed Dec. 6th. Arrived out Mar. 26, 1856, in 111 days and 88 days from Anjer. Sailed from New York, May 5, 1856, and was 139 days to San Francisco. Was 68 days to 50° South and 23 days rounding the Horn, in terrific weather, with many icebergs in sight at times. In 30° South, Atlantic, spoke the *Santa Claus,* also bound for San Francisco, the latter reaching port one day ahead. Completing this voyage the *Gilpin* was 18 days from San Francisco to Honolulu where she loaded whale oil for New Bedford. Sailed Jan. 3, 1857, and made the passage in 117 days.

In June 1857, the *Gilpin* left Boston for Honolulu and arrived out Oct. 2nd, in 116 days' passage. Loaded 7500 barrels of whale oil and with 15 passengers in the cabin, took her departure, Nov. 30th, for New Bedford. All went well until Cape Horn was rounded. At 2:30 A.M., Jan. 29, 1858, a heavy shock was felt which was thought at first to have been caused by an extra heavy sea but it was later found that she had struck the submerged portion of an iceberg. The following day, her captain, John F. Ropes, decided to abandon ship, she then having 15 feet of water in the hold. In the hurry of securing necessaries from the cabin, the ship took fire, supposedly from the lamps, and when last seen the mizzenmast had gone overboard.

All hands were picked up by the British ship *Hertfordshire*, from Callao for Cork, which later put into Bahia. A portion of the *Gilpin's* crew arrived at New York, Apr. 14th, in the clipper ship *Sunny South*, which had sailed from Santos, Feb. 26th.

At New York, the carpenter and three of the seamen made sensational charges against Captain Ropes and sued to recover wages as for a completed voyage. They alleged that at the time of the disaster the ship was close hauled on the wind, the weather being tolerably good and that the pumps were not sounded until 10 A.M. the following day. The ship was kept on her course for a time, when she was squared away for the Falkland Islands, going at good speed before the wind, and could have made port. They claimed further that the captain unnecessarily abandoned the ship which was then only 150 miles from the Falklands and that they would have continued in her and kept her afloat but were peremptorily ordered out of her and into the *Hertfordshire*, after which Captain Ropes deliberately set the ship afire. Captain Ropes denied these charges in toto and they were not substantiated.

The most celebrated and famous ship-race that has ever been run, came off on the New York-San Francisco course in the autumn of 1852, when navigators were beginning fully to reap the benefits of Lieutenant Maury's researches with regard to the winds and currents, and other facts connected with the physical geography of the sea. It is reprinted from "The Physical Geography of the Sea." by M. F. Maury, New York, 1858.

Four splendid new clipper ships put to sea from New York, bound for California. They were ably commanded, and, as they passed the bar at Sandy Hook, one by one, and at various intervals of time, they presented really a most magnificent spectacle. The names of these noble ships and their masters were, the *Wild Pigeon*, Captain Putnam; the *John Gilpin*, Captain Doane—alas! now no more; the *Flying Fish*, Captain Nickels, and the *Trade Wind*, Captain Webber. Like steeds that know their riders, they were handled with the most exquisite skill and judgment, and in such hands they bounded out upon the "glad waters" most gracefully. Each, being put upon her mettle from the start, was driven, under the seaman's whip and spur, at full speed over a course that it would take them three long months to run.

The *Wild Pigeon* sailed October 12; the *John Gilpin*, October 29; the *Flying Fish*, November 1; and the *Trade Wind*, November 14. It was the season for the best passages. Each one was provided with the wind and current charts. Each one had evidently studied them attentively; and each one was resolved to make the most of them, and do his best. All ran against time; but the *John Gilpin* and the *Flying Fish* for the whole course, and the *Wild Pigeon* for part of it, ran neck and neck, the one against the other, and each against all. It was a sweepstake with these ships around Cape Horn and through both hemispheres.

The *Wild Pigeon* led the other two out of New York, the one by seventeen, the other by twenty days. But luck and chances of the winds seem to have been against her from the start. As soon as she had taken her departure, she fell into a streak of baffling winds, and then into a gale, which she fought against and contended with for a week, making but little progress the while; she then had a time of it in crossing the horse latitudes. After having been nineteen days out, she had logged no less than thirteen of them as days of calms and baffling winds; these had brought her no farther on her way than the parallel of 26° North, in the Atlantic. Thence she had a fine run to the equator, crossing it between 33° and 34° West, the thirty-second day out. She was unavoidably forced to cross it so far west; for only two days before, she crossed 5° North, in 30°—an excellent position.

In proof that the *Pigeon* had accomplished all that skill could do and the chances against her would permit, we have the testimony of the barque *Hazard*, Captain Pollard. This vessel, being bound to Rio at the same time, followed close after the *Pigeon*. The *Hazard* is an old hand with the charts; she had already made six voyages to Rio with them for her guide. This was the longest of the six, the mean of which was twenty-six and a half days. She crossed the line this time in 34° 30', also by compulsion, having crossed 5° North, in 31°. But, the fourth day after crossing the equator, she was clear of Cape St. Roque, while the *Pigeon* cleared it in three days.

So far, therefore, chances had turned up against the *Pigeon*, in spite of the skill displayed by Putnam as a navigator, for the *Gilpin* and the *Fish* came booming along, not under better management, indeed, but with a better run of luck and fairer courses before them. In this stretch they gained upon her—the *Gilpin* seven and the *Fish* ten days; so that now the abstract logs show the *Pigeon* to be but ten days ahead.

Evidently the *Fish* was most confident that she had the heels of her competitors; she felt her strength, and was proud of it; she was most anxious for a quick run, and eager withal for a trial. She dashed down southwardly from Sandy Hook, looking occasionally at the charts; but feeling strong in her sweep of wing, and trusting confidently in the judgment of her master, she kept, on the average, two hundred miles to leeward of the right track. Rejoicing in her many noble and fine qualities, she crowded on her canvas to its utmost stretch, trusting quite as much to her heels as to the charts, and performed the extraordinary feat of crossing, the sixteenth day out from New York, the parallel of 5° North.

The next day she was well south of 4° North, and in the doldrums, longitude 34° West. Now her heels became paralyzed, for Fortune seems to have deserted her a while—at least her master, as the winds failed him, feared so; they gave him his motive power; they were fickle, and he was helplessly baffled by them. The bugbear of a northwest current off Cape St. Roque began to loom up in his imagination, and to look alarming; then the dread of falling to leeward came upon him; chances and luck seemed to conspire against him, and the more possibility of finding his fine ship back-strapped filled the mind of Nickels with evil forebodings, and shook his faith in his guide. He doubted the charts and committed the mistake of the passage.

The "Sailing Directions" had cautioned the navigator, again and again, not to attempt to fan along to the eastward in the equatorial doldrums; for, by so doing, he would himself engage in a fruitless strife with baffling airs, sometimes re-enforced in their weakness by westerly currents. But the winds had failed, and so too, the smart captain of the *Flying Fish* evidently thought, had the "Sailing Directions." They advise the navigator, in all such cases, to dash right across this calm streak, stand boldly on, take advantage of slants in the wind, and, by this device, make easting enough to clear the land. So, forgetting that the charts are founded on the experience of great numbers who had gone before him, Nickels, being tempted, turned a deaf ear to the caution, and flung away three whole days, and more, of most precious time, dallying in the doldrums. He spent four days about the parallel of 3° North, and his ship left the doldrums, after this waste of time, nearly upon the same meridian, at which she entered them.

She was still in 34°, the current keeping her back just as fast as she could fan east. After so great a loss, her very clever master, doubting his own judgment, became sensible of his error. Leaving the spell-bound calms behind him, where he had undergone such trials, he wrote in his log as follows: "I now regret that, after making so fine a run to 5° North, I did not dash on, and work my way to windward to the northward of St. Roque, as I have experienced little or no westerly set since passing the equator, while three or four days have been lost in working to the eastward, between the latitude of 5° and 3° North, against a strong westerly set"; and he might have added, "with little or no wind."

In three days after this he was clear of St. Roque. Just five days before him, the *Hazard* had passed exactly in the same place, and gained two days on the *Fish* by cutting straight across the doldrums, as the "Sailing Directions" advised him to do.

The *Wild Pigeon,* crossing the equator also in 33°, had passed along there ten days before, as did also the *Trade Wind,* twelve days after. The latter also crossed the line to the west of 34°, and in four days after had cleared St. Roque.

But, notwithstanding this loss of three days by the *Fish*, who so regretted it, and who afterward so handsomely retrieved it, she found herself, on the 24th of November, alongside of the *Gilpin*, her competitor. They were then both on the parallel of 5° South, the *Gilpin* being thirty-seven miles to the eastward, and of course in a better position, for the *Fish* had yet to take advantage of slants, and stand off shore to clear the land. They had not seen each other.

The charts showed the *Gilpin* now to be in the best position, and the subsequent events proved the charts to be right, for thence to 53° South, the *Gilpin* gained on the *Pigeon* two days, and the *Pigeon* on the *Fish* one.

By dashing through the Straits of Le Maire, the *Fish* gained three days on the *Gilpin*; but here Fortune again deserted the *Pigeon*, or rather the winds turned against her; for as she appeared upon the parallel of Cape Horn, and was about to double round, a westerly gale struck her "in the teeth," and kept her at bay for ten days, making little or no way, except alternately fighting in a calm or buffeting with a gale, while her pursuers were coming up "hand over fist," with fine winds and flowing sheets.

They finally overtook her, bringing along with them propitious gales, when all three swept past the Cape, and crossed the parallel of 51° South, on the other side of the Horn, the *Fish* and the *Pigeon* one day each ahead of the *Gilpin*. The *Pigeon* was now, according to the charts, in the best position, the *Gilpin* next, and the *Fish* last; but all were doing well.

From this parallel to the southeast trades of the Pacific, the prevailing winds are from the northwest. The position of the *Fish*, therefore, did not seem as good as the others, because she did not have the searoom in case of an obstinate northwest gale.

But the winds favored her. On the 30th of December the three ships crossed the parallel of 35° South, the *Fish* recognizing the *Pigeon*. The *Pigeon* saw only a "clipper ship," for she could not conceive how the ship in sight could possibly be the *Flying Fish,* as that vessel was not to leave New York for some three weeks after she did; the *Gilpin* was only thirty or forty miles off at the same time. The race was now wing and wing, and had become exciting. With fair winds and an open sea, the competitors had now a clear stretch to the equator of two thousand five hundred miles before them. The *Flying Fish* led the way, the *Wild Pigeon* pressing her hard, and both dropping the *Gilpin* quite rapidly, who was edging off to the westward.

The two foremost reached the equator on the 13th of January, the *Fish* leading just twenty-five miles in latitude, and crossing in 112° 17′; the *Pigeon* forty miles farther to the east. At this time the *John Gilpin* had dropped two hundred and sixty miles astern, and had sagged off several degrees to the westward.

Here Putnam, of the *Pigeon,* again displayed his tact as a navigator, and again the fickle winds deceived him; the belt of northeast trades had yet to be passed; it was winter; and, by crossing where she did, she would have an opportunity of making a fair wind of them, without being much to the west of her port when she should lose them. Moreover, it was exactly one year since she had passed this way before; she then crossed in 109°, and had a capital run thence of seventeen days to San Francisco.

Why should she not cross here again? She saw that the fourth edition of "Sailing Directions," which she had on board, did not discountenance it, and her own experience approved it. Could she have imagined that, in consequence of this difference of forty miles in the crossing of the equator, and of the two hours' time behind her competitor, she would fall into a streak of wind which would enable the *Fish* to lead her into port one whole week? Certainly it was nothing but what sailors call "a streak of ill luck" that could have made such a difference.

But by this time *John Gilpin* had got his mettle up again. He crossed the line in 116°—exactly two days after the other two—and made the glorious run of fifteen days thence to the pilot ground of San Francisco. Thus end the abstract logs of this exciting race and these remarkable passages.

The *Flying Fish* beat: she made the passage in 92 days and 4 hours from port to anchor; the *Gilpin* in 93 days and 20 hours from port to pilot; the *Wild Pigeon* had 118. The *Trade Wind* followed, with 102 days, having taken fire, and burned for eight hours on the way.

The result of this race may be taken as an illustration as to how well navigators are now brought to understand the winds and the currents of the sea. Here are three ships sailing on different days, bound over a trackless waste of ocean for some fifteen thousand miles or more, and depending alone on the fickle winds of heaven, as they are called, to waft them along; yet, like travelers on the land, bound upon the same journey, they pass and repass, fall in with and recognize each other by the way; and what, perhaps, is still more remarkable, is the fact that these ships should each, throughout that great distance, and under the wonderful vicissitudes of climates, winds, and currents which they encountered, have been so skillfully navigated, that, in looking back at their management, now that what is past is before me, I do not find a single occasion, except the one already mentioned, on which they could have been better handled.

There is another circumstance which is worthy of notice in this connection, as illustrative of the accuracy of the knowledge which these investigations afford concerning the force, set, and direction both of winds and currents, and it is this:

I had computed the detour which these vessels would have to make, on account of adverse winds, between New York and their place of crossing the equator. The whole distance, including detour, to be sailed to reach this crossing at that season of the year, was, according to calculation, 4115 miles. The *Gilpin* and the *Hazard* only kept an account of the distance actually sailed; the former reaching the equator after sailing 4099 miles, the latter 4077; thus accomplishing that part of the voyage by sailing, the one within thirty-eight, and other within sixteen miles of the detour which calculation showed they would be compelled to make on account of headwinds. With his way blazed through the forest, the most experienced backwoodsman would have to make a detour greater than this on account of floods in the rivers. Am I far wrong, therefore, when I say that the present state of our knowledge with regard to the physical geography of the sea has enabled the navigator to blaze his way among the winds and currents of the sea, and so mark his path that others, using his signs as fingerboards, may follow in the same track?

JOHN LAND

A MEDIUM clipper ship, named after Capt. John Land, a veteran navigator, at one time master of the renowned *Rainbow* and *Challenge*. The *John Land* was built by E. & H. O. Briggs, at South Boston, and was launched Mar. 26, 1853. Her owners, Baker & Morrill of Boston, had been so pleased with the performances of their ship *Winged Arrow*, a product of the same yard in 1852, that they ordered the *Land* to be an exact duplicate. The dimensions were: deck, 176 feet; beam, 36 feet; and depth of hold, 22 feet; tonnage, 1054. The *Land* proved to be quite a fast sailer, having to her credit the average of 113 1/3 days for the three passages she made from Boston direct to San Francisco, the runs being 126, 105 and 108 days respectively. On her other two westward voyages she was forced to put into ports in distress and her career was not very successful from the underwriters' point of view. Her first homeward passage was via Calcutta, her time being 88 days from Sand Heads to Boston, a very fine run. Her second homeward trip was 108 days from Manila to Boston, a fair passage, considering the season. On her third return she carried a cargo of whale oil, valued at $630,000, from Honolulu to New Bedford, in 101 days, which is better than average time. Her best work, outward bound, was in 1858 when she crossed the line in 18 days and 18 hours from Boston; was

47 days to 50° South; thence 15 days to 50° in the Pacific, 62 days out, and was on the equator on her 83rd day. Off the Horn, she spoke the *Ringleader*, bound the same way and led her three days into port although her rival had caught up with and passed her ten days before arrival. Her fast time of 105 days, in 1857, was due to a short run round the Horn and up the South Pacific and while the whole passage was three days shorter than the following one, it did not show up so signally as to speed.

On her second outward voyage she left Boston, July 1, 1854, and put into Valparaiso, leaky, Oct. 28th; made repairs and sailed Nov. 2nd. When in latitude 4° North, longitude 102° West, and leaking some 7000 strokes per hour, she was fallen in with by the whaling ship *D. M. Hall*, whose captain, Pratt, forced Percival, of the *Land*, to transfer to the *Hall*, $50,000 worth of cargo before he would render any assistance. Captain Pratt further wanted the *Land* to be abandoned to him, but Percival refused this and both ships proceeded to Nukahiva and thence to Tahiti, arriving in December 1854. Repairs were made to the *Land* and she proceeded on her voyage, reaching San Francisco, May 3, 1855, 310 days from Boston, 192 days from Valparaiso and 32 days from Tahiti. The awards for salvage were:—$26,684, to the owners of the *Hall*; $3000, to Captain Pratt; and $33,348, to his officers and crew.

On her fifth and last outward passage to San Francisco, the *Land* left Boston, Nov. 25, 1859. On Feb. 1, 1860, off the Horn, after 18 days of very heavy weather, she was found to be leaking 3500 strokes per hour. A course was set for Valparaiso where she arrived on Feb. 23, 1860, with four feet of water in the hold. A survey showed her to be badly strained and the cargo was discharged and a part sold. After being repaired she proceeded to San Francisco, arriving Aug. 21, 1860, in 51 days from Valparaiso and 270 days from Boston. She completed the voyage by going to Manila and thence home. On Mar. 26, 1861, she put into Holmes Hole, having on board the crews of the British ship *Columbus*, from Pensacola for Dublin, rescued Mar. 16th; and of the schooner *C. S. Lochman,* from Louisiana for Baltimore, rescued the following day.

She then went in trade between Europe and the East Indies, taking coal from Sunderland to Singapore, returning from Batavia to Amsterdam or Bremen. Her average passages to and from Anjer were about 78 days. On Feb. 28, 1864, she left Newport, England, for New York and on the second day out sprang a leak but it was kept under by the pumps for a time. On Mar. 25th, in 39° North, 65° West, then having eight feet of water in her, she was abandoned after pumping for 72 hours. All hands were taken off by the British bark *T. R. Patello* and landed at Portland. The captains of the *Land* were: Peleg Howes, first voyage; Percival, second; Warren H. Bearse, the following three voyages; and Hotchkiss, thereafter, until her end.

JOHN MILTON

MEDIUM clipper, built at Fairhaven, Mass., in 1855; owned by G. Hussey and others, of New Bedford. A fine ship of 1444 tons with but a short sea life.

She arrived at San Francisco, July 14, 1855, in 136 days from Boston, Captain McCleave in command. Had very heavy weather off the Horn and was 25 days from 50° South, Pacific, to the island of Masafuero; was 32 days from the equator crossing to port, in light winds and calms. She completed the voyage by taking guano from the Chincha Island to Hampton Roads.

On May 6, 1857, she reached San Francisco in 149 days from New York. Capt. Ephraim Harding, who was in command, reported being 40 days to the line; 80 days to Cape Horn, off which had fine weather except for one severe squall; had light and baffling winds and calms for the 35 days from the equator crossing to port. At San Francisco, 13 of the crew were put ashore for inciting mutiny and new men were shipped. Sailed from San Francisco, June 12th, and arrived at Callao, Aug. 10th, then proceeding to the Chincha Islands to load guano.

On Feb. 14, 1858, she arrived at Hampton Roads for orders and two days later left there for New York, light favorable winds prevailing. On the morning of 17th had strong winds and double-reefed the topsails. During the latter part of the day, a snow storm prevailed. The latter part of the 18th the weather became more moderate and the reefs were shaken out. The latitude was then 36° 56′ North and this was the last entry in the log book. The storm continued and on the 19th it was of terrific violence. That night another storm blew up, blowing on shore with great fury and the *Milton*, flying before the gale in a heavy snow storm, struck on a rock near Montauk, a quarter of a mile off shore, the morning of the 20th. The shock was terrific and the vessel melted under it like a lump of sugar. An eye witness said:

"I was one of the first on the spot. The shore looked like a wrecked shipyard. But for the breakers you could have walked for yards on broken masts, spars and timbers. There was the mainmast, four feet through, snapped off like a pipe stem. Every plank was made into kindling wood and every timber torn out of her. Only a part of the bow was left tossing and crunching on the rock where she struck, being held there by the attached anchors. The bodies of the crew, all frozen stiff, were on the beach, some covered with snow or thrusting up a hand or arm above the drift. One negro must have come ashore alive for he had dragged himself some distance up the sand but had soon frozen. The ship's log book came ashore, also some trinkets and furniture, but that was all."

The captain, three mates and the crew of 22, being all-hands aboard, were drowned or perished. The three mates and eighteen of the crew were buried in the old churchyard at Easthampton. The ship was valued at $80,000; cargo, $60,000 and freight money, $30,000.

JOHN STUART

THE *John Stuart* was the first medium clipper ship built in New York for the European trade and came out in 1851, from the yards of Perrine, Patterson & Stack. Her model was quite sharp, though not of the extreme type, and she was a lofty and heavily sparred ship. An ex-mate, in romantically describing how she steered like a pilot boat and carried sail, said that above the sky-sail she carried a main moonsail and above that, consecutively, a cloud-cleaner, a stargazer, a sky-scraper and an angel's foot-stool, the latter, however, being set only in dead calms, when the watch on deck were not allowed to cough or sneeze for fear of carrying it away. She had three full decks with a depth of hold of 28 feet and 2 inches, and on the occasion of her departure from New York for San Francisco, in the spring of 1854, she drew 24 feet and 6 inches, said to have been the greatest depth of any sailing vessel theretofore leaving port. Her length was 206 feet and her extreme breadth of beam 41 feet and 8 inches; tonnage, 1653, old measurement. Her original owners were B. A. Mumford, James Smith and others, of New York. She was sold in November 1859, at auction, in New York, for $36,750, to A. A. Lawrence of Boston. Vessels at the time were selling very low.

The *John Stuart* never showed up signally, as to speed. In the trade between New York and Liverpool, in which she was first employed, Capt. Watson Ferris was in command. Two westward trans-Atlantic passages are recorded, 38 and 31 days respectively. In 1853, Captain Ferris left New York for San Francisco and made the run in 134 days. In 1854, Captain Ellery was 136 days making the same voyage. In 1856, Captain Chamberlain had 132 days and in 1860, Captain Bernese had 125 days. The runs from Sandy Hook to the line were 35, 37, 35 and 23 days respectively, while from the equator crossing in the Pacific to the Golden Gate, they were 24, 34, 19 and 31 days, the memoranda showing light and adverse winds in northern latitudes except in one instance. On her 1854 passage she was but five days off Cape Horn, but on her other three runs she was from 20 to 30 days. The return voyages from San Francisco were made via South American West Coast ports, as follows: from Guayaquil, 90 days; from Callao, 87 days and again, 86 days to New York. Captain Hardie was then in command, having relieved Captain Chamberlain, at Hong Kong, after the ship had arrived 53 days from San Francisco. The return from China to California was made in 57 days.

On the return voyage from Callao, in 1857, the *Stuart* put into Rio, in July, in distress, having been struck by a heavy sea which did much damage to the upper works and sprung the bowsprit. Captain Sherman was reported very sick. After arrival at New York, on Jan. 16, 1861, 86 days from Callao, via Hampton Roads, three days, she loaded for Liverpool and on the passage collided with the British bark *Respigadera*, of and for Liverpool. The latter was much damaged in her upper works and the *Stuart* stood by her until it was found she was not leaking and then kept on her course, arriving Apr. 19, 1861. She then took on a cargo of coal, at Cardiff, and went to Callao and thence was 100 days to Antwerp, with guano, arriving July 8, 1862. She then took coal to Aden; went to Bombay and sailed thence, June 27, 1863, for Liverpool, Captain Bernese in command. While at Bombay she had been sold for 110,000 rupees and then resold at an advance of 18,000 rupees. She went under the British flag without change of name and the registers of 1868 and 1870 give her owner as B. F. Camoa; hailing port, Bombay.

On two occasions during her return, on her first Cape Horn voyage, she narrowly escaped disaster. While beating out to sea from San Francisco, on June 2, 1853, she missed stays in tacking outside Fort Point, Golden Gate, and nearly got ashore. The anchor was let go and 60 fathom of chain just brought her up, but very close to the rocks. The other instance was on Aug. 8th, when, near the Chincha Islands, she came in collision with the bark *Greenpoint*, sinking the latter immediately. The *Stuart* was considerably damaged but was able to get into Guayaquil, arriving Aug. 28th, and was drawn up on the beach and repaired.

JOHN WADE

MEDIUM clipper ship, built in 1851, by Hayden & Cudworth, at Medford, Mass., for Reed & Wade of Boston, and was the first sharp ship put out by her builders. She was 152 feet, over all; 145, on deck; by 32; by 16½ feet; 638 tons. Although not an extreme clipper, she had 17 inches dead rise, a sheer of two feet and is described as a beautiful little vessel, very rakish in appearance. She had single topsails and carried a main skysail. A bust of Captain Wade was her figurehead.

She was put on the run to California and China and between Sept. 5, 1851, when she left Boston on her maiden voyage, until her arrival at New York, June 16, 1854, had completed three round voyages, as follows: First, 131 days to San Francisco; thence 47 days to Hong Kong; thence 118 days to New York. Second, 117 days to San Francisco; 46 days trans-Pacific and 106 days to New York. Third, 120 days to the Golden Gate; 52 days across and 96 days home. She appears to have encountered much light weather on all these passages, according to her memoranda, one instance being recorded of ten consecutive days at an average of two knots an hour. On one occasion, off the Horn, she spoke the clipper *Golden City*, which had left New York four days ahead of her, but her rival reached port three days ahead.

After discontinuing her operations in the California trade, which was due to her purchase in the summer of 1854, by J. J. Dixwell of Boston, for the "Augustine Heard Line," she was kept entirely in the China business with New York and with London, besides doing some Asiatic coasting. In 1856, she made a long passage from Foo Chow to London, being badly beaten by the extreme clipper bark *Maury*, but this was in a measure retrieved by a good return run of 99 days to Hong Kong. In the fall of 1858, she left Shanghai for southern ports and in March 1859, shortly after leaving Bangkok for Hong Kong, she struck an uncharted rock in the Gulf of Siam and became a total loss. Her first commander was Captain Willis, one voyage; then Captain Little had her, being succeeded by Captain Harding. Captain King was in charge at the time of her loss, Mar. 28, 1859, all hands being saved.

JOSEPH PEABODY

MEDIUM clipper ship, built in 1856, by E. & H. O. Briggs, at South Boston, for Curtis & Peabody of Boston; launched June 7th. 186 x 38: 1 x 23: 6; 1178 tons, net; 1204 tons, gross. She was a fair sailer and good carrier.

On her first voyage she arrived at San Francisco, Dec. 6, 1856, in 145 days from Boston. Her commander, Captain Weston, reported being 40 days to the line; 75 days to the Horn, having had only seven days from Boston on which she could lay her course. Was 17 days off the Cape, in bad weather; crossed the equator, 121 days out, having had skysails set for 60 days. Left San Francisco, Jan. 2, 1857, and was 56 days to Shanghai; returned to the California port in 63 days from Hong Kong; went back there in 49 days and again returned to San Francisco, arriving Mar. 1, 1858, after a passage of 50 days. Newspapers reported that during her absence from Boston, 20 months, she had never started a topsail sheet at sea and never lost a mile in leeway.

Left San Francisco, Apr. 3, 1858, and in common with other ships sailing about that time had a slow run to Callao of 72 days. Was in port only five days when she proceeded to Elide Island, Lower California, and took her departure thence Aug. 6th. In 1859 she went out to Australia, thence to Callao, where she arrived Apr. 11, 1860, in 39 days from Melbourne. Mar. 9, 1861, she arrived at Bristol, Eng., from St. John, via Cardiff, and Apr. 9th, was at Swansea, loading patent fuel,—coal and coal tar mixed and made into square cakes for use in steamers. Sailed about Apr. 24th, for Shanghai, and arrived Aug. 27th, having had the long passage of 30 days up the China Sea. While in port she was coppered and caulked and Dec. 13th sailed for Hong Kong, arriving the 18th; freight list,

"James Baines," 2515 tons, built at East Boston, in 1854

From a lithograph, after the drawing by S. Walters, in the Macpherson Collection

"JOHN BERTRAM," 1080 TONS, BUILT AT EAST BOSTON, IN 1850
From the painting by Clement Drew, at the Peabody Museum, Salem

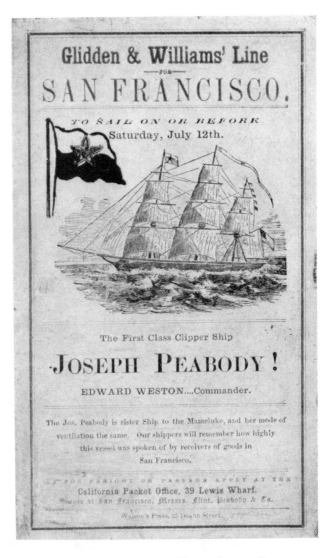

SHIPPING CARD ADVERTISING THE "JOSEPH PEABODY," 1204 TONS
BUILT AT SOUTH BOSTON, IN 1856
From the Peabody Museum, Salem, Collection

"LIGHTNING," 2083 TONS, BUILT AT EAST BOSTON, IN 1854

$5000. From Hong Kong she went to San Francisco, arriving Mar. 28, 1862, Captain Whitney in command, in a 60 days' passage, the ship in leaky condition and cargo damaged. At San Francisco she was chartered for the Chinchas and London, sailing May 9, 1862, and was 52 days to Callao. Captain Whitney reported light winds and calms on the passage and though the run was a slow one, it compared favorably with other ships sailing about the same time. On the passage the rudderhead had been twisted and the ship was detained some time at Callao for repairs. On July 23rd, Captain Whitney wrote that he was once more at the Chinchas and hoped to be loaded in 45 days, as he had paid $1000, extra, for dispatch. His hopes were not realized, however, and it was 73 days before he got clear of one of the most God forsaken places on the earth. Luckily he found many old friends there: Captain Lane in the *Ivanhoe*, Captain Emmerton in *Neptune's Favorite*, Captain Williams in the *Herald of the Morning*, Captain Bangs in the *Renown*, Captain Doane in the *Black Hawk*, Captain Crowell in the *Fair Wind*, and others. The *Fair Wind* was sister ship to Captain Whitney's former command, the *Mameluke*, and the captain states that, on his first visit to her, it seemed as if he was back in his old sea home. At the Chinchas there was nothing to do on the Islands and little on board ship, but the captains of the American vessels contrived to pass the time pleasantly. Almost every day two or three of them went a-fishing and then adjourned to one of the ships in port where turtle soup, turtle steak, the catch of the day and fruit were served for dinner; and after dinner they played cards, whist or euchre. There were some twenty ladies at the Islands, the wives and daughters of the captains in port, and dances, picnics and concerts were not infrequent. On one occasion, boats from the various vessels had a regatta and Captain Whitney's boat took the prize. Sept. 7th, the *Peabody* had 800 tons of guano aboard and 60 tons a day going in. After completing loading, she sailed for London and arrived at Margate Roads, Jan. 26, 1863, being badly beaten by the *Ivanhoe*, which sailed about the same time. Soon after arrival,—Mar. 14th,—she was sold for £7650, to go under the British flag, and from 1865 to 1869 was registered as the ship *Dagmar*, owned by T. Morrison; hailing port, Liverpool. In the register of 1874, she appears as a bark, owned by T. Emerson, still named the *Dagmar*, of Liverpool.

The following excellent account of the Chincha Islands and the guano shipments therefrom, reprinted from Littell's "Living Age," Volume XL, is inserted here in order to give an intimate description of a trade in which so many of the American clippers were engaged.

Chincha Islands,
Coast of Peru, Thursday, Nov. 10, 1853.

The ship *Albus*, in which I am a passenger, arrived here from Callao, Oct. 3. We found here a fleet of nearly 200 sail, all but three or four English and American. I shall send you a list of arrivals and departures for the last month with this. By it you will see how important these islands and all that relates to them are becoming, and how little is known respecting them at home.

The Chinchas are three small isles, neither of them more than a mile across, and about the same distance apart, lying in a line north and south, 14 miles from the main land, and about 90 miles, following the trend of the coast S.S.E. from Callao. They consist of porphyritic or volcanic rock, upheaved from the sea, and except a few narrow beaches, their sides are naked precipices, jagged and indented with caves, and surrounded here and there with rock masses. All of them are covered with nothing but guano, which lies upon the rock just as if it had been sifted upon it till it had formed rounded hills. The rocks are from fifty to two and three hundred feet high round the shores, and the guano is heaped upon them highest in the middle, where it may be 200 feet through. It has only been dug from the north and middle islands, and where they have been cut away they appear from the shipping like some very deep railroad cuttings through light ochre colored alluvial hills. Upon the islands are numerous shanties or frail huts of bamboo-like cane, peculiar to the country, for the Government officers and the Chinese laborers.

On the North Island is the principal station. Here is a Deputy Commandant (Serrate), subordinates, interpreter, doctors, hospital (so called), a few soldiers, women, negro drivers, and the like. The habitations are mere flat-roofed huts of matted cane, except one or two of the principal. The guano blows through and through everything. I spent a night here with a gentleman in the medical department. The room was an attic of matting, just enough for a shelter from the nights, which are cool. The floor was carpeted with guano; books, clothing, everything was yellow with it. But it is not so annoying or any more annoying than would be so much soil; it is strongly ammoniacal; it has a cleansing property in washing; nothing lives in it worse than fleas, to which I am almost insensible, and small lizards, which are glad to get out of one's way. The Peruvian soldiers are in reddish, snuff-colored uniform; they average four feet, are broad in the beam, narrow in the shoulders, which are round and stooping, and have noses like the Mexican idols. Their appearance here and at Callao is extremely impressive. Have you any recollection of the armies of supes we used to see at the Park long ago?

On the Middle Island there are fewer laborers and shanties— only one appropriated to the overseer, who is, as fortune will have it, a Hungarian, and signs himself Kossuth. He calls himself Kossuth's brother, but, I suspect, does not care much if intelligent persons doubt this. He told me, however, that he was one of those who came with Kossuth to New York in 1850; and finding Ujhazy had only got land, he pushed off South, went to New Orleans, was concerned in the Lopez affair, went to Mexico, thence to San Francisco, joined Flores and so reached Peru, where he entered the service and now has got this place, where, he says, he "means to make some money." He has a good salary, and it is hinted that among all these ships waiting out the lay days of their charter parties for their cargoes, there are those which find out that it is possible to secure his preference. The English say he rather favors the Americans; but this, and all things concerning him are very mysterious. He is, I should think the general opinion to be, a smart scamp, who likes to direct matters, can give if not take a joke, is cruel enough for his place, and does not require to be taught anything in particular. The South island is an untouched hill of guano, scattered with the skeletons of sea lions, and usually covered with birds.

The guano is dug from the hills and conveyed to depots, or mangueras, as the Peruvians call them, on the edge of the cliffs in barrows. On the North Island are two steam "paddies," which also cut it away and load cars, which are pushed to the same places of deposit on temporary rails. These places are large enclosures of cane, supported on the sloping face of the rock by chain cables, and reaching to the very verge of the cliff. At the lower ends of these are openings connecting with canvas pipes or "shutes," through which the guano is emptied into launches, or directly into vessels lying at the bases of the cliffs below. The shore is so bold that notwithstanding the swell, ships may be loaded at the shutes at both islands. Overseers are stationed at the top to see how much goes into launches; whose turn it shall be to get a load, etc. When a ship or launch is loading she is in a complete smother, as if ashes were poured into her from a hundred and fifty feet overhead. With their yards cock-billed, and rolling their royal masts almost against the face of the rock, all covered with guano, you would hardly recognize some of the finest clippers, that before they left New York or Boston were praised in the papers, visited by ladies, and, instead of guano, had their cabins perfumed by champagne. But the dust is easily washed off; the sea birds smooth their plumage when they commence their homeward flight.

The *Albus*, on board of which I am now writing, lies about midway between the North and Middle Islands. She is loading from launches. Around us are more than fifty other ships and barks, and there is a still larger number on the north side of the North Island. I returned this morning from a visit there, on board the *Bornado*, the flag-ship of the fleet, which was just hauling from her anchorage to the shute. Through the stern windows I see the hull of the *Plymouth Rock*, which carried me to Australia; and near by, within a square mile, lie the *Storm King, Witchcraft, Dacotah, Empress of the Seas, Governor Morton* (commanded by an old college friend), *New York, Danube,* and many others, whose names are as familiar as the piers and wharves where I have seen them lying. The sun is within a few degrees of being vertical at noon, yet the heat is not oppressive, and the nights are cool. We have nearly the same change of breeze and calm every day; the loading goes on very easily after ballasting, dunnageing, etc., and there is no lack of society. There are quite a number of ladies—the wives and daughters of captains in the fleet —and we make calls and visits and even have evening parties. Every night I can hear, out of my stateroom window, the sea lions blowing.

Mackerel are very abundant and whales come among us almost daily. It was a fine sight to see one the other afternoon make a complete breach scarcely two ships' length from us. I might even boast of going in a boat as a tender to a whale boat chasing them last week. We came very near, but did not succeed in striking one. The rocks are bristling with pelicans, and the divers and guano birds are "too numerous to be mentioned." I have seen six acres at least covered with them at one time—the blue by themselves, and the white by themselves, in compact bodies, like some great army. The rocks and caverns of the Islands are the most singular and romantic I ever beheld. No fairy scene, upon the act-drop of the theatre, could go beyond them in fanciful extravagance. The Ballista Isles, seven miles south, are entirely perforated. We rowed through sublime arches, worn by the long swell of the great Pacific, and into dark domes, filled with loud echoes and the voices of ten thousand birds. Such antres vast are the palaces of the sea lions. Over the bay, on the main land, is the town of Pisco, and beyond it the Andes, some of the loftiest peaks of which, if not the very loftiest, are said to belong to the range in this latitude. We see them sixty miles inland. In the afternoon they seem a long range of yellow summits—the sunlight gives the snow this look, I suppose—rising ten degrees or more above the horizon. And even these, I am told by a gentleman who has crossed them, are but the spurs of the great ridges which lie beyond. No view of them that I have ever seen conveyed anything like the effect of the reality. Indeed, these Islands would afford the best studies for a landscape artist, who could do them justice. I would most strongly recommend some of our young artists to follow me in this voyage.

The guano is dug by Chinese coolies or laborers, who are brought here by English ships from the free ports of their native coasts. The poor fellows are made to believe they are going to do well, by engaging to serve as laborers for five years at a "real" (York-shilling) a day, and a scanty allowance of rice. They fancy, it is said, they are coming to labor in the mines of California. However this may be, it is certain that they are shipped here in English vessels, and transferred or assigned (or whatever the word for such a transaction should be) to the Peruvian Government. I have known Englishmen who spoke of having been engaged in the traffic. The Government place them on these islands, avowedly under their original contract, to labor for five years; but who is to know how far this contract, if such it can be called, is adhered to? The truth is, the poor Chinamen are sold into absolute slavery—sold by Englishmen into slavery —the worst and most cruel perhaps in the world. Here are about eight hundred of the unfortunate creatures at work on these islands at a time;—as fast as death thins them out, the number is increased by new importations. The labor is severe—much more so than that of the negroes on our Southern plantations. They are kept at hard work, in the hot sun, throughout the day. On the middle island they are "stinted," each one, strong and weak alike, to dig from the hill and wheel to the mangueras five tons of guano, each, per diem! The guano is compact, like hard, claylike loam, and as dusty, when dug, as ashes. On the North Island, it has to be blasted for the steam paddies. It has to be wheeled from a hundred yards to a quarter of a mile—the nature of the labor may be conceived. The Chinese work almost naked, under a tropical sun, where it never rains. They are slender figures, and do not look strong. Negro drivers—the most ugly looking blacks I ever saw, are stationed among them, with heavy thongs, which I have seen them use. The poor coolies have no hope of reward—no days of rest. The smoke of their torment goes up on Sundays as well as on week-days. It blows away, in a yellow cloud, miles to leeward; and I never see it without thinking what a hell on earth these islands must be. That I do not exaggerate in this account any one who has been here will readily bear witness. The fact that some of the Chinese, almost every week, commit suicide to escape their fate, shows the true state of their case. Kossuth told me that more than sixty had killed themselves during the year, since he has been stationed here, chiefly by throwing themselves from the cliffs. They are buried, as they live, like so many dogs. I saw one who had been drowned—it was not known whether accidentally or not—lying on the guano, when I first went ashore. All the morning, his dead body lay in the sun; in the afternoon, they had covered it a few inches, and there it lies, along with many similar heaps, within a few yards of where they are digging. On the North Island, the Chinese carry heavy water-casks, slung on poles between two, up the steep hill; they can, in this way, as well as in barrows, take weights altogether disproportionate to their slender forms. They look unhappy, as well they may. We know that the Chinese are strongly attached to their native soil. Wretched and half-barbarous as they may be, dark as may be their souls, they still have human feelings, and I am not so constituted that I can witness the injustice of their treatment and their suffering without compassion—without indignation. It ought to be made known wherever English law prevails, that these poor creatures are deceived and sold into a servitude from which they almost daily seek escape through death—by Englishmen. It is not domestic slavery in which they are placed; they were not born slaves; they are not protected by any laws; there are no women with them; their condition is worse than that of any criminals, exiles, or prisoners, in civilized nations. It ought to be everywhere known. Americans, who have to bear the reproaches of the English for institutions entailed upon them, and which they could not avoid, have a right to reply that the worst slavery that exists among the civilized nations of the earth is maintained by the British subjects, who transport coolies to the Chincha Islands. It is not the fault of the English that the same system is not carried on in Australia. The coolies brought there, however, have not turned out a good speculation. But the taking and selling free men to such taskmasters as these Peruvians, who are little better than the Chinese, is an outrage to humanity, and a reproach to British rule. Let the next slaver the English cruisers capture, be some one of their own ships, with a cargo of coolies for this market.

Before this reaches you, you will have had the news of the outrage committed by the Peruvian Commandant here upon the American Captains. The memorial of the Captains to Mr. Clay, our Minister at Lima, with his reply, will, probably have been furnished in the Times. The memorial, which is a brief summary of the facts of the outrage, does not give anything like a full history of it, and conveys nothing of the deep feeling it created here, and which has not by any means subsided. The shipmasters were careful to present to the Minister only a simple detail of the circumstances of the outrage. Probably a greater or more unprovoked and brutal insult was never offered to the American flag; nor were ever American citizens so treated by an official of any foreign nation with whom their own was at peace. The statement of the memorial shows that some thirty American shipmasters (all here but two or three, who were unavoidably absent) waited on the Commandant, on board the hulk, to inquire respecting the detention of a boat's crew for an alleged infringement of the regulations, and to ascertain the views of the Commandant in similar cases. They were unarmed; they went in a peaceful, proper manner, with no other than a perfectly proper and justifiable intention, and no suspicion that they could be subjected to insult, and, least of all, to danger to life and limb. The Commandant was the agent of their charterers; he was also the Peruvian man of authority here. They wished to know what regulations he intended to enforce, in order that they might conform to them, or remonstrate, if they should deem them arbitrary, as they had a right to do, through the legal and proper channel. Nothing was further from their purpose than to oppose the measures of the Peruvian Government, or show themselves hostile to it, or offended with it. They certainly cannot be supposed to have gone on board an armed vessel unarmed, to insult or intimidate her commander. He was not on board. The officer of the deck, instead of sending for him, as would have been courteous, allowed them to send one of their own boats. When he came, he refused to hear them. He refused to grant a hearing to a committee from them, of one or more; but from some sudden freak of jealous obstinacy, or the mixture of cowardice and ferocity which seems to belong to the Spanish-American blood, ordered up a file of soldiers, and before the shipmasters were aware what was to happen, had them bayoneted off the deck and down the gangway! It was the merest accident, I have heard repeatedly from those who were present, that some of them were not killed. As it was, several were wounded—some of them severely. It was not through misunderstanding that this was done; for the Commandant could speak and understand English enough to understand, and did understand, the object of the Captains in their visit. No explanation can be given of his course, except that it was in keeping with other acts of his, though it could not have been supposed he would resort to actual violence, and only be hindered by the hesitation of his own soldiers from butchering unarmed American citizens upon his own deck. He is a Mexican, who came from his native country not long ago to Peru, and brought with him all his national prejudice against Americans. He had previously shown that he meant to make all the trouble and delay he could to our shipmasters. He fancied himself in a position to treat them with military contempt, and all that sort of insulting manner which inferior Peruvian officials, who live by cheating their Government, are so fond of affecting towards foreigners. The shipmasters had felt this in the way of business; some had endeavored to conciliate him, others had been made indignant by finding themselves so far at the mercy of such a petty tyrant—there was no doubt a good deal of feeling against the man, but nothing like a determination to resist his authority; and I am sure the thought of insulting or menacing him, or exposing themselves in any way to violence from him, could never have entered their minds. Such an intention would have been as far from their interests as from their duty; and to have placed themselves in such a position, with any such intention, would have been the height of madness.

I write within view of the locality where the outrage occurred; many of the shipmasters present are still here, and I have heard the views of almost all of them. I am convinced that they were most brutally treated; that they were exposed to imminent danger of their lives, and some of them severely wounded by stabs and bruises, without any reasonable provocation; and I think it due to the honor of our country, and necessary to the future safety of American citizens, that our Government should take the matter in hand, and compel such redress as shall teach these Peruvians the necessity of caution. I hope they will be made to pay for it roundly. . . .

The character of our shipmasters must also be considered, as well as their position. Here were thirty American men, each of whom was entrusted with the sole care of a large amount of property, and the sole government of a crew of men sailing under our flag. You are aware what sort of men must be selected by our merchants for such a command. In addition to the experience and skill necessary for the safe management of large and valuable ships, they must have the firmness and coolness, and knowledge of men to secure discipline on board; they must be familiar with the usages of trade all over the world, with the laws regulating their own in relation to freight, wages, crew, passengers, etc., under all the contingencies of long and hazardous voyages. There are no class of men in all the various business of the world to whom is committed so great a trust: —they are so many generals in the armies of Peace. Within their sphere of business, their powers are unlimited; on the decks of their vessels they are absolute. Here are several masters of vessels whose names will be recognized in the list enclosed, whose ships and freights are each worth more than the stock of a large wholesale store, or than a large manufactory. The safety of all this as well as its proper management, must often depend upon their lives and their discretion alone. Men are not selected for such commands whose passions or prejudices are deemed liable to mislead them; it is no part of their business to embroil themselves in difficulties with foreign authorities; they have too much at stake. They are used to look into the passions and prejudices, and bear with the suspicions of other men. I do not think that out of all our citizens, a set of men could be selected more cool-headed and fair-minded and capable of acting a manly part in any emergency, than our shipmasters; and I think their judgment and opinion in cases where themselves and their business is concerned, their views as to the propriety of what they do, and the treatment they receive, altogether likely to be correct. They are, if any can be, men of the world, used to deal with men of all countries, and knowing that it is for the despatch of business to deal fairly, and to conform to foreign customs. . . . I hope, for the honor of our country, and for the sake of the shipmasters here whose hospitality I have enjoyed, that something will be done in the matter. The Peruvians have already removed their officer; let them now make amends for injuries inflicted by him when acting under their authority. It will teach them to select in future fitter agents—if they can.

Affairs are by no means satisfactorily arranged here now. There is nothing like business order and despatch. Kossuth is as arbitrary as such a soldier of fortune might be expected to be; he is capricious, uncertain, and unreliable to the last degree, causing a good deal of unnecessary trouble. The Commandant Serrate is probably as thorough an old scoundrel in his way as Peru can produce—which is saying something. He and Kossuth do not merely compel some vessels to lay out their full time, while others are preferred for no known reason, but they give and withhold supplying guano capriciously, apparently for no other purpose than to irritate. The whole thing is badly managed, and it is shameful that so many of our finest ships should be subjected to needless inconveniences. Another trouble is with the crews when lying here. Most of them have to be shipped at Callao, and are natives (Peruvians or Chilenos, called "Cholas"). They are a poor diminutive race, half black, and said to be passionate and treacherous. Mixed with English and American crews they create constant trouble, increased by the disagreeable nature of the work in loading. The consequence is frequent trouble with men. No longer ago than yesterday a serious disturbance, in which knives and pistols were used, took place on board a ship near by. Some of the men will have to be—are already, I believe, sent on board the Peruvian guardship. They will get off, it is likely, without such punishment as is necessary to secure discipline—and so in many other cases. All the difficulties arising out of this state of things can only be appreciated by sea-going persons. It has continued long enough. There ought to be an American vessel of war sent here at once. Had there been one at the time, the outrage to our shipmasters could not have occurred. An English frigate visited here soon after, under Admiral Moresby, who immediately, at the request of our Captains, remonstrated strongly with the Commandant upon his conduct; and had it been inflicted upon Englishmen, serious retribution would have followed at once. It is humiliating that our merchantmen should be compelled to look for protection to the ships of England, and made to feel how true it is that English seamen are better protected than ours.

It ought to be mentioned in this connection that the Commandant, it has been ascertained, had applied to the captains of two French ships then here, the *Ville de Lima* and *Pomone,* anticipating a rupture with the Americans; they both promised him their aid; and when the American shipmasters were driven at point of bayonet and at peril of their lives, down the gangway of the hulk, the crew of the *Pomone* gave three cheers! This is of a piece with the doings of the French Government elsewhere in the Pacific. There is a French frigate here now, surveying all round the islands. Perhaps the next movement will be to take possession. Doubtless there is not a port in the world where there is so much American shipping that is left so unprotected as this. It is a subject of daily conversation and complaint among our shipmasters here, and any intelligent observer must confess, for the reasons above given, and many others which will readily occur to seafaring men, that their complaints are just. . . . In such a Government as this the subordinates require to be kept in check by the presence of an authority which they shall feel it to be dangerous to trifle with. They change so often that they care but little for the slow redress through diplomatic agents, of wrongs done to our citizens. They are fond of show and only to be reached through direct appeals to the senses; their regard for law and order would be much increased by the sight of an American frigate anchored off these islands, and the business of freighting our ships here would go on much more expeditiously and more in accordance with the usages of commercial nations.

G. W. P.

KATE HOOPER

MEDIUM clipper ship, built at Baltimore, in 1852, by Hunt & Wagner, for J. A. Hooper of that city. 205 x 39: 6 x 24; 1488 tons, old measurement. Capt. John J. Jackson was in command for about the first half of her career, being succeeded by Captain Johnson. She had the reputation of being a good carrier as well as a smart sailer. On one occasion she made the run from the Pacific equator crossing to the Heads, San Francisco, in 19 days. In 1856 she had only 37 days from San Francisco to Hong Kong, while on her final voyage she made the run from Anjer to Melbourne in 29 days. The fastest of her three passages from New York to San Francisco, was 130 days, on which occasion she was 30 days between the line in the Atlantic and the latitude of Rio, in light winds, and then had the misfortune to lose her jibboom, off Cape Horn. On the subsequent voyage, which was in 1856, she was close to the California coast, in 117 days from New York, and on this run she also suffered damage during 18 days of heavy weather off the Horn. In 1862 she was partially dismasted, shortly after leaving New York, and on one westward trans-Pacific run she reached Hong Kong partially crippled. The elements were not the only menacing forces she had to contend with. Late in 1857, her freight of 600 coolies, bound from China to Havana, mutinied and several times tried to take possession of the ship before Anjer was reached. After leaving Gaspar Straits they had control of the 'tween decks and had fired the ship in three places. The officers restored order after shooting four and hanging one of the Chinamen. Captain Jackson was sick at the time and on Nov. 23rd asked a Dutch man-of-war to tow his ship into Melbourne. On arriving at Havana, the crew mutinied and the vessel was detained 11 days. The ringleaders were sent to the United States to be tried.

The *Hooper*, under Captain Johnson, sailed from Hong Kong, Oct. 28, 1862; passed Anjer, Nov. 16th, and arrived at Melbourne, Dec. 15th. On the 29th, while lying in Hobson's Bay, she was discovered to be on fire. About 300 tons of cargo had been discharged into lighters, leaving 1500 tons still aboard. She was scuttled in 18 feet of water and burned to the water's edge. The fire was believed to have been set by a Chinese member of the crew. The vessel and cargo was sold for £2400, sterling, to Bright Bros. of Melbourne. She was raised, repaired and rigged as a bark and under the name *Salamander*, of 929 tons, as rebuilt, was registered as late as 1871, owned as above, and commanded by Captain Hudson. Her name does not appear in registers of 1874.

The following account, by Edgar Holden, of the coolie trade and a mutiny on board a New York vessel in the year 1857, is taken from "Harper's Monthly," June 1864.

The term "Coolie" belongs of right to a predatory tribe living near the Gulf of Cutch, in Africa; but as applied to the trade, it is merely a European title for the lowest class of laborers in most Eastern countries, and there seems to be no connection between the two names. The Coolie Trade that has excited the greatest interest and developed the worst atrocities is the Chinese.

The lowest class of Chinamen were collected under every variety of pretext, there being no Government superintendence or protection, and shipped to Peru and the adjacent Chincha Islands, or to Cuba. Upon arrival they were disposed of to the highest bidder, the price being sometimes as high as three hundred dollars, though I have rarely known them to cost more than eighty on board ship. The terms upon which this class of Coolies were induced to leave their country were simply these: Their transportation to be free; they were to be bound for seven years at a salary of eighteen dollars a year, and at the end of their term of service they were to be free: that time, however, was sure to find them each deeply in debt to his master, and his chance of escape rendered each day more and more distant.

So large were the profits of the business that a margin could be allowed for bribery of officials, and restrictions and prohibitions alike became almost dead letters. Vessels were known, in 1856 and 1857, to kidnap full cargoes within sight of Macao. Owners of vessels from American ports would enter into contracts with parties in the West Indies or South America to transport Coolies at from fifty to eighty dollars a head, freighting the ships often for some other than a Chinese port, but eventually arriving at Macao or Hong Kong, fitted and ready for the trade.

Such was the condition of the trade in 1857, when the ship *Norway*, of nearly 3000 tons, sailed from New York loaded with coal for the United States naval squadron in the China seas. It would be little to the purpose of the narrative to enter into a detailed account of the outward voyage, the waiting at Hong Kong, the transportation of laborers from China to the Australian mines, or describe the thousand incidents of a long stay in a Chinese port. Enough to say that nearly three-fourths of a year elapsed ere our human cargo was ready. During the latter part of this time extensive preparations were made to receive them.

Down the whole length of both lower decks were built tier on tier of berths, or rather shelves—for they were without sides or dividing partitions. Large quantities of beef, port, rice, etc., were stowed away. Hundreds of water-casks filled the holds, and on the upper or spar deck were erected galleys for cooking. Over every hatchway save one were set iron gratings to prevent too free access from below to the upper deck; that one, the main and nearly central one, was covered by the ordinary housing. As the covering of these hatches was afterward of vital importance to us, a word of description will be necessary. The gratings were made of bars of iron, arched in the centre, and having a circular opening of eight or nine inches diameter at the summit of the arch. The housing was merely the continuation of the ordinary one in which were the galleys, the door of it opening outward. In addition to these preparations on the spar deck a barricade was built, running athwart ship, from rail to rail, a short distance in front of the captain's cabin, twelve feet wide, ten feet high, and arranged so that a guard of armed men could, from their station on top, command the whole deck, while within it were accommodations for their sleeping. When all was ready we sailed for Macao, from the vicinity of which port the cargo was to be received.

Thousands had been collected from every quarter of the kingdom, under every pretext, and crowded into barracoons, amidst not less fearful horrors than characterize those of the slave districts of Africa. Many had been induced to leave their homes under the most cruel misrepresentations, and once at the barracoons, cowed by the lash or torture, were taught to reply as their masters commanded to the questions of Government officials who, at long intervals, came to inspect them. These barracoons are termed *Chu-tze-kwan*, "Pig-

Pens"—and from their usual filthy condition well deserve the name. Many Coolies died of diseases incident to such confinement, and suicides among them were not uncommon.

We lay off shore several miles, and it was therefore necessary to bring the Coolies to the ship in boats. These boats are termed *sampans*, and are capable of carrying from thirty to one hundred men besides the rowers. A woman usually sits in the stern to steer, and sometimes to scull the boat, while the rowers, unlike our own, stand on planks projected over the side.

The Coolies mounted the side one after another, most of them naked to the waist, wearing only the loose Coolie trowsers and broad-brimmed straw-hat. Slung at the belt were a pouch and purse, and a little case for the chop-sticks. A few were in good humor, but most were sullen or desponding. They were tallied over the gangway like so many bales of cotton, mustered in rows upon the deck, and their baggage and persons searched for opium or weapons. When all were on board a Government official came ostensibly to see that none were unwilling emigrants. A public announcement was made that any one who was on board against his will should step forward. Only one had the hardihood to do so, they knowing full well the improbability of getting nearer their homes than the dreaded barracoon. The man who came forward was immediately set ashore, and as the wind promised fair all hands of the crew were turned to getting ready for sea. The whole number of Coolies received was one thousand and thirty-seven, and each was stowed away as rapidly as the confusion and bustle incident to such a barbarous gathering would admit. The embarkation consumed the greater part of two days. Besides the Coolies there were several lady passengers and children returning by way of Cuba to their homes to the United States. They occupied a part of the cabin protected by the barricade.

It was evening ere the anchors were weighed, the sails loosed, and the ship under way, yet every one worked with energetic zeal, stimulated by the prospect of returning home, and none but those who have been long separated from home and friends can appreciate the exhilarant feeling that fills the breast of a sailor as the ship flies along on her homeward voyage. There were two interpreters on board, who had come from Havana, whose experience in the trade had been as varied as extensive. They were a sort of half Chinaman half Portuguese, and were in nowise friendly to the mass of Coolies on board. Warned by their representation of the treacherous nature of our barbarous freight, guards were stationed at all necessary points, a police force appointed, and indeed every precaution taken to subdue any disaffection that might arise. The necessity for such precaution may be appreciated if the comparatively small number of our crew (sixty, all told) be considered. The barbarians, moreover, were constantly quarreling, and within the very first twenty-four hours several were brought up and flogged after the old approved navy style. One or two suicides occurred, and one man was found strangled, whether by his own hand or by some of his companions was never ascertained.

A word or two regarding the way in which these Coolies passed their time and deported themselves generally may not be uninteresting. They were not usually unclean in their habits, but, on the contrary, were fond of dabbling in water like children, and some of them wore around their necks pieces of muslin to use as towels. Many had tooth-brushes, and little pieces of bone used for scrapping the tongue—a habit, strangely enough, which they religiously observed. They had but two meals daily, principally of rice and salt fish, with, at noon, or about eleven o'clock, a bowl of tea. Their rice was boiled at the galleys on deck in baskets, and the whole number of Coolies being divided into messes, the portion for each was served and carried below in other baskets. They then sat around on the deck, and, helping themselves each to a quantity in a small china bowl, fell to a rapid demolition of the contents with their chopsticks. Much of their time was spent in gambling, almost always with dominoes, and when not engaged at this they were either quarreling or playing on musical instruments, of which they had a great number. Their barbarous music would hardly strike the ear of an American virtuoso as melodious. It was a most ingeniously discordant variation, from the tum-tum-ti-tilly of a one-string violin to the hoarse uproar produced by enormous clarionets without keys, flutes six feet long, cymbals, gongs, drums, and marine trumpets. Occasionally, but more particularly toward the end of a voyage, they will attempt a rough sort of theatricals to while away the monotonous hours, yet in point of scenery or incident the most absurd.

But to proceed to our departure from Macao: The Coolies were allowed perfect freedom, in limited numbers, on the forward part of the upper deck, and their food carefully prepared and served. Had it not been for a providential mischance on the evening of the third day out the terrific incidents that followed would have come upon us totally unprepared. A not unusual quarrel had occurred on the lower deck, the shouting and altercation soon running to blows. The police, some of whom it may be remarked were Coolies, were quickly on the spot, and after great difficulty succeeded in quelling the riot; not, however, in time to prevent one man being cut down with a cleaver. This man, quite seriously wounded, together with four of the principal rioters, was brought up, and the latter chained by the wrist to the combings of the after-hatch. The former, immediately upon being alone with the surgeon and interpreter, asked for the captain, and in the heat of passion and revenge laid out the details of a plot the most coldblooded and inhuman.

The leaders were desperadoes who had voluntarily come to the barracoons, having studied the plot for weeks; and ere they had been on board an hour were at work, urging, with every plea of cupidity or revenge, the rising *en masse*, murdering every man who opposed, seizing the ship and cruising as they chose. The exact object of the seizure was not clear, but the plan was simply this: The temporary berths were to be torn down to furnish clubs and materials for building a fire under the foremost hatch. A large number was to be ready, when the flames should rise and the crew run forward to extinguish it, to rush up the main-hatchway, massacre every man as he came in their way, and thus gain possession. They had chosen their captain, navigator, and other officers, and it was concerning this choice that altercation had arisen. The opinions about the truth of this statement were various—the captain ridiculing the idea as absurd, but the two interpreters joining in their belief that it was true, and ominously shaking their heads at the captain's disbelief.

For two days the matter rested, nothing farther being heard concerning the mutiny. The ship was bowling along finely before a nine-knot breeze toward midnight of the third day, the moon shining beautifully, and all quiet save the rippling of the water under our bows, and the regular tread of the sentry at his post. We were expecting to make the land at Angier Point about daylight. Suddenly a bright gleam of flame shot up from the forecastle, and a yell like that of ten thousand demons burst on the still night. It needed no farther alarm to arouse every body from sleep. Every man was up and at his post as the fearful conviction of his imminent danger presented itself. The door of the main hatch, the only means of egress, was instantly locked; every blunderbuss, cutlass, and pistol passed out by the stewardess, who, with great presence of mind, had run to the arm chests; the ship put about, and the pumps manned in less time than it takes to describe it.

Knowing that a crowd was collected under and on the ladder, the top of the main housing was broken in in order to dislodge them; but, meanwhile, several of the foremost rioters were striving to force the door with cleavers stolen from the cooks, and had partially succeeded in prying it open against a dozen men who were endeavoring to fasten a spar across outside. In spite of the utmost exertion the door yielded far enough to allow an arm to be thrust through and a blow struck, wounding an officer. Quick as thought the muzzle of a pistol was against his breast, and with its explosion the Coolie reeled backward, carrying with him all on the ladder, and allowing the door to be effectually closed.

Then commenced a scene the most terrific and appalling. The foiled wretches, maddened at defeat in the very outset, rushed with furious yells from one hatch to another, swinging lighted firebrands or striving to wrench away the iron bars that covered them, or hurling bolts and clubs at every face that peered down from above. The red glare of the flames lit up the sky, reflecting grimly against the swelling sails, and in spite of a constant stream of water from the pumps appeared scarcely to diminish.

Tarpaulins were then thrown over the forward hatches and the stream of water directed upon them. The smoke thus confined filled the ship, and the Coolies, who had been burning the oil stolen from the ship's hold to increase the blaze, were obliged to crowd aft to get fresh air; but men, stationed at every loop-hole and crevice, shot down with remorseless vengeance every one of them who appeared within range, till ere long not one could be seen from any point on deck. After a few moments the tarpaulins were raised, the better to direct the water from the pumps, but a draft re-established, the flames burst forth again, and simultaneously a rush was made by the crowd to the main hatch. It was in vain; the door had been too securely fastened, and the guard were on the watch.

Gradually there fell an ominous lull in the uproar, and we feared that some means had been found to force an exit. Although I have stated that the rioters could withdraw out of sight of those on the upper deck, yet below there was a bulk-head, or partition, of very thick plank, shutting off their part of the deck and allowing a space between it and the cabin. Through cracks in this partition it was found that a tolerably good view of the whole scene of riot could be obtained, and through these the miscreants could be seen gliding hither and thither, their dark forms tinged with a dusky red glare from the smouldering flames, or grouped together in consultation. Suddenly, as if animated by one impulse, they would start, and with terrific yells rush from one end of the deck to the other, making one's blood almost curdle at the conviction that they had actually found a way of escape. Unsuccessful by this means in calling away the watchful marksmen, while fearful death-dealing weapons only found new victims as they passed in view, they abandoned the plan and again withdrew from sight, probably to the first or lowermost deck.

Meanwhile it must not be supposed that the spar deck was free from Coolies. More than a hundred had come up early in the evening, but unarmed, and, even if evil-inclined, unwilling to show any sympathy with the mutineers until they should at least gain some advantage, they kept themselves well forward and as much as possible out of sight.

The four men who had been previously chained around one of the hatches were from time to time noticed in communication with those below, apparently giving information of every movement and cheering them on. At the same moment it was found that two had succeeded in freeing themselves from their irons, and waited only an opportunity to join in the melée. The instant they were discovered they sprang to their feet only to fall stunned and bleeding beneath the clubbed muskets of the guard. One was afterward found to have been killed; the other, recovering in a few minutes, started again to run forward, but was riddled with shot from a blunderbuss fired from the barricade.

Another of the four, fearful of the fate of his companions or anxious to join those below, succeeded in wrenching his hands from the irons, and, being a small man, tried to squeeze himself through the circular opening in the summit of the arched grating. Too late he saw his error, for, stimulated by the fear of being shot before he could succeed, he had forced himself through and hung by his hands over the hold. Unable from the depth of the combing to swing himself clear so as to fall between decks, and seeing only the black hold, with a fall of thirty feet and certain death below, he was struggling to get back when a rifle-shot from the barricade pierced his brain and he fell into the abyss.

Amidst such horrors passed the night, the flames being at times completely extinguished, as the Coolies had abandoned the use of oil on account of the smoke, and burned only what they called "josh paper" to give great blaze and not really do much damage, for of course they had no intention of burning the ship. Their only hope, after finding their plan foiled, seemed to be to terrify us by the fear of the ship's burning into abandoning her in boats and leaving her in their hands; and had those above deck been willing to assist them, or the captain been a less brave man, the daylight would never have come again to any of us. But come it did, and with it a demand was made to the rioters to surrender the ringleaders of the mutiny. Instead of complying, one of them dipped a stylus in the blood upon the decks and wrote on a slip of paper to the following effect:

"Three hundred Coolies to be allowed on deck at one time. They shall navigate the ship, and take her to Siam, where a certain number may leave her, after which she shall be allowed to proceed on her course. No signals of any kind shall be made to attract attention of other vessels."

In addition to these demands was the threat that, unless instantly complied with, the ship should be burned.

The yards were backed, the boats made ready to rescue the ladies and crew, every Chinaman above decks was bound so that he could give no assistance to the mutineers, and when all was ready the captain returned answer to "Burn and be ———"; but every man of them should be smothered and burn in her. The result of this decisive stand was a consultation below, and another message, written in blood, to the effect that no more fires should be built until night at any rate.

A temporary quiet was then restored, the yards again squared, and the ship put on her original course. Arms were re-examined, extra guards stationed, and the strictest surveillance maintained. The ladies bravely devoted themselves to providing food, making cartridges, and indeed doing every thing in their power to render assistance.

Two serious difficulties were now presented, the chief of which was the want of fresh water, all the water-casks being stowed away upon or below the lower decks. The second, that, as the pumps on which the supply of salt-water for extinguishing the fires depended, passed directly up among the Coolies, they had succeeded in disabling them. The latter, however, was not of so much moment, since, after the captain's reply to their demands, they would scarcely dare to start their fires again. The decks, moreover, were now thoroughly saturated with water.

The demand for fresh water became every moment more urgent. One of the ladies suffering from effects of long illness, with a young infant demanding her constant care, was sinking under the accumulated horrors. At any moment the mutineers might succeed in gaining the upper deck, and by force of mere numbers overpower and massacre all on board. The torture of increasing thirst, however, soon overruled even our thoughts of peril, and some effort must be made to supply fresh water. To ask the fiends on the berth deck to pass it up was folly; they only laughed, and offered the black bloody water on the decks. To go for it would have been madness. Providentially there was a small engine on board used for loading and unloading ship, and the plan of condensing steam was suggested. An extemporaneous condenser was soon made, and ere long we had satisfaction of collecting water enough for every immediate want.

Effort was then made to cleanse the upper deck. The wounded were collected, and the few who had been killed were thrown overboard. Many were found hidden away in all sorts of positions, to which they had fled during the previous night, and one or two stiff and gory corpses were dragged from the concealment to which the poor wretches, mortally wounded, had crawled to die.

A demand was meanwhile made to the Coolies to pass up the dead bodies. Hours passed, and no disposition to comply being manifest, it was proposed toward night to send down one of the Coolies who was bound on deck. This proposal was humanely rejected, for to the Coolies on deck the mutineers attributed their defeat at the outset, and his instant death would be certain. A volunteer came forward from the crew, and, though it seemed madness, he was lowered down, his companions, armed to the teeth, standing ready to jump to his rescue or die with him. Whether the boldness of the act, or the fact that they themselves were anxious to be rid of the bloody corpses strewn around restrained them, it is impossible to say. Certain it is he was unmolested, and one or two even proffered assistance.

Night came as the task was completed, and soon began a repetition of the orgies of the last, though in a far less terrible degree. The Coolies tried unsuccessfully to force off the gratings and to break open the ports. They rushed with demoniac shrieks along the decks, burning their "josh paper" and waving torches or clubs about their heads. But it would be useless to attempt to picture either the fury of the mutineers or the feelings of the defenders. Every means of egress was tried and retried in vain. Only one or two were shot during the night, but we waited in torturing anxiety the events of each succeeding hour.

Ere daybreak, satisfied of the impossibility of succeeding in their purpose, quiet was restored, and the tired wretches slept. The following day, after long consultation, they sued for pardon.

From that time onward, and particularly after rounding the Cape of Good Hope, no signs of insubordination arose during the passage. The Coolies had the satisfaction of sleeping for four months about the decks as they could find space, no berths or accommodation of any kind being allowed them. Only a limited number were allowed on deck at any time, and the police force was increased at every point. It was a long time before it was deemed safe to allow any of the crew to go below for even the most necessary provisions and water, and then only at intervals and in small numbers.

Upon arriving at Havana the whole mortality of the voyage was found to be about one hundred and thirty, of which number seventy were killed, or died from wounds received in the mutiny of the first few days, and a large portion of the rest from an epidemic of dysentery which occurred while lying at Havana before commencing to disembark.

KATHAY

EXTREME clipper ship, built by Jacob A. Westervelt, New York, in 1853. 209 x 38: 4 x 21: 6; old measurement, 1438 tons; British measurement, after transfer, 1123 tons. Owned by Goodhue & Co., of New York. She was under construction, June 18, 1853, on which day the clipper ship *Sweepstakes* was launched, alongside. The latter careened, breaking stagings along the *Kathay*, which precipitated many spectators into the water, but fortunately without fatalities. The *Kathay* was to have been launched on Aug. 11th, but the prevailing high temperature having melted the tallow between the ways, the hull refused to move even after powerful levers and jack screws had been applied. The launching ways had to be relaid, tallow renewed and eighty hours of hard labor were required before the vessel took the water.

She was built for the California and China trade, but on account of low freight rates, then prevailing to the Pacific Coast, her maiden voyage was from New York to London; thence to Sydney, Canton, and home. She reached Sydney, Apr. 29, 1854, in 86 days from London and arrived at New York, Nov. 21st, in 104 days from Macao and 78 days from Anjer. The following voyage, in 1854, was out to San Francisco, thence to China and then home. In 1859 she made a similar round. These were her only two westward passages round the Horn and the time out to San Francisco was 121 days in each instance. In the first case she was up to 50° South, in the Pacific, when 62 days out, but thereafter had continuous light winds and did not furl a royal for the final 55 days. Was within 800 miles of the Golden Gate for ten days. On the 1859 run, she lost her maintopmast, off the Falklands, and the day prior to reaching destination made 187 miles, her best day's work on the passage. The homeward run from Shanghai, in the fall of 1855, was in 98 days; 73 from Anjer; arrival at New York being Jan. 12, 1856. She then went out to Sydney, in 84 days, and reached New York, Jan. 18, 1857, in 92 days from Shanghai. In the winter of 1859-1860, she was 93 days from Amoy to New York, being 74 days from Anjer. On Mar. 5, 1861, she arrived at New York in 89 days from Amoy and 77 days from Anjer, 39 from the Cape. On Jan. 20th, near the Cape, spoke the *Competitor* and lead her into New York, nine days.

Early in 1863, the *Kathay* crossed from Hong Kong to San Francisco, having very rough weather throughout the 48 days of the passage. She returned to China and shortly thereafter went under British colors and although actual ownership was reported to continue for a short time with American citizens, her port of registry became Liverpool. Under Captain Popham, she left Bombay, Oct. 7, 1866, for Howland's Island, to load guano for Europe; arrived Jan. 6, 1867, after a long passage of 90 days. Had 400 tons of guano aboard on Jan. 20th, with good prospect of completing her cargo of 1600 tons in 25 days, when a sudden shift of wind hove her broadside on the reef, where she instantly bilged. She soon slid off and within the space of one hour had sunk in deep water. Everything was lost, effects included. All hands remained on the island until Feb. 15th, when they proceeded to Honolulu, on the schooner *San Diego*. Captain Popham had always been very proud of his command, speaking in the highest terms of her seaworthiness and sailing qualities.

While under the American flag, the *Kathay* was commanded by Captain Stoddard, most of the time; the final year or so, Captain Rennel had charge. In 1866, the *Kathay* is registered as owned by D. Atwood, hailing port, Liverpool.

KINGFISHER

EXTREME clipper ship, built by Hayden & Cudworth, at Medford, Mass.; launched Aug. 18, 1853. 217 x 37 x 21; 1286 tons, old measurement; 999 tons, new measurement; carrying capacity, 1350 tons, dead weight. She is described as being as sharp as a steam boat and had 20 inches dead rise. A billet head, with carved trail boards, was her forward ornamentation. Her original owners were William Lincoln & Co., of Boston. In later years she belonged to Samuel G. Reed & Co., also of Boston.

The *Kingfisher* made four passages from Boston and two from New York, to San Francisco, her average for the six being 126½ days; fastest, 114 days; slowest, 135 days. The 114 day run was her maiden trip, leaving Boston, Oct. 3, 1853; was 37 days to the line; thence 57 days to the equator in the Pacific and was off the San Francisco Heads, five days in a dense fog. Reached port, in company with the *Bald Eagle*, 115 days from New York. In 1859, her passage being 130 days from Boston, she was 22 days to the line but had adverse weather in the South Atlantic and was off the Horn, 30 days. On arrival at San Francisco, Oct. 27, 1862, in 132 days from New York, Captain Freeman reported being off the Horn 24 days, during two of which he went through the most severe gale he had ever experienced. The bulwarks were started, hatch house stove in, sails split and other damage received. Forty miles south of the Cape, spoke the *Fleetwing*, from Boston for San Francisco, and led her into port four days, both ships having very light winds in the Pacific. On her slowest passage, reaching San Francisco, Sept. 22, 1869, in 135 days from Boston, she was 25 days to the line; 42 days thence to 50° South, in the face of continual head gales; was 12 days making the Cape Horn passage and 29 days to the equator, from 50° South.

The *Kingfisher* made three passages from Hong Kong to San Francisco, in 75, 49 and 50 days respectively. On the first occasion she left Hong Kong, Feb. 11, 1861, and was 18 days in the China Sea; had an entire suit of sails blown away; then had light northeast winds to the coast of Japan. Put into Yokohama, for water, when 39 days out and took six days to water from small boats. While beating out of the harbor, the pilot ran the ship ashore on a mud bank, on the Kanagawa side, and she had to lighter to get off, which took eight days. Finally, left Kanagawa (Yokohama), Apr. 6th, and arrived at San Francisco, Apr. 27, 1861, in a passage of 22 days, which is within 12 hours of the record and otherwise only once equalled.

Completing her first voyage, the *Kingfisher* was 50 days from San Francisco to Callao and 69 days thence to New York, via Hampton Roads. In prosecution of her second voyage, she left San Francisco, June 16, 1855, and arrived at Honolulu on the 26th, in 9 days, 20 hours from port to port, which was announced as being the fastest on record up to that date. From Honolulu, she was 35 days to Hong Kong and then went to London from Shanghai. In 1859, she was 50 days from San Francisco to Valparaiso, thence taking copper ore to Swansea. In 1861, she was 99 days from San Francisco to New York, Captain Freeman reporting 47 days to the Horn, off which had the mainmast sprung and was seven days from Cape Hatteras to destination. On first attempting to leave San Francisco, on this passage, in tow but with no pilot on board, she was put on a mud bank close inshore, and although she came off at high tide, she had received injuries which cost $24,000 to repair, her sailing being delayed some six weeks. In 1867, she was 123 days from San Francisco to Liverpool and the following year, took 1300 tons of guano from Baker's Island to England. In 1869, she was 130 days from San Francisco to Queenstown, with a cargo of wheat.

Of voyages other than those referred to, there are noted: a round between London and Hong Kong in 1856-1857, the return being 109 days from Foo Chow to the Lizard. From London she went to Melbourne, arriving July 10, 1857, in 78 days from the Lizard; thence went to the West Coast of South America and was 96 days from Callao to Liverpool. In 1860, after her arrival in China from England, she was chartered for use as a transport in the Peiho campaign against the Tai-Pings. In the winter of 1861-1862, she made a round voyage from Boston to Ship Island, at the mouth of the Mississippi, as a United States Army Transport, under command of Captain Tay. On the return to Boston, she went ashore about midnight, Feb. 1, 1862, on Peaked Hill bar, near Provincetown, during a thick snowstorm. She was hauled off by tugs on the 12th and taken to Boston, slightly damaged and making but little water. In 1863 and 1864 she was on the coast of Asia and made a round between Hong Kong and Melbourne. In 1867 and in 1870, she made passages from England to China.

The *Kingfisher* left New York, June 20, 1871, for San Francisco, Captain Knapp in command. In heavy weather she sprung a leak and was forced to put into Montevideo in distress. After survey, she was condemned and in November 1871 was sold, bringing $6150. The sound portion of her cargo was forwarded to destination, per bark *Moonbeam*. Her purchasers were the wealthy and influential family of Cibils, owners of theaters, dry docks, piers and a fleet of ships, and who had done much to improve the port. The *Kingfisher* was repaired, renamed *Jaime Cibils*, and under the Uruguayan flag, operated in trade on the Atlantic until 1890, when she was sold at auction to Calcagno Hermanos of Montevideo. They had her dismantled and broken up on Bellavista Beach, in the northern part of Montevideo Bay, according to information just received from Captain Botel, who was her last master.

The first captain of the *Kingfisher* was Tully Crosby, formerly in the *Antelope*, who retired from the sea in 1854. Capt. Zenas Crosby of Brewster succeeded, and died on board, while the ship was on the West Coast. In 1858, Capt. Kimball Harlow was in command, and was followed by Captain Cushman. In 1862, Capt. William Freeman took the ship, and in 1866, Captain Harding. In 1868, Captain Gibbons was in command and in the following year, Capt. William Caldrey. Captain Knapp took charge before she left New York, on what was to be her last voyage as an American ship.

KIT CARSON

BUILT by Shiverick Brothers, at East Dennis, Mass., in 1854. 173 x 36 x 22; 1016 tons. Prince S. Crowell, East Dennis, owner. Sunk off Rio during the Brazilian war.

LADY FRANKLIN

BUILT by Jarvis Pratt, at East Boston, in 1852. 475 tons. Owned by her captain, Nagle, and later by William Ropes. Abandoned in October 1856, while on a passage from New York to Trieste.

LANTAO

BUILT by Samuel Hall, at East Boston, in 1849. 593 tons. Owned by D. N. Spooner, Boston, and afterwards sold to Salem. Sailed from Caldera, Chile, Oct. 26, 1856, for Boston, missing, and never heard from.

LEVANTER

BUILT by Metcalf & Norris, at Newcastle, Me., in 1852. 182 x 33 x 22; 868 tons. Smith & Boynton and Naylor & Co., of New York, owners. In 1863 by E. Wheelwright, Boston, sold to T. Cotter of Cowes, to go under British flag, 1865.

LIGHTFOOT

EXTREME clipper ship, built by Jackson & Ewell, at East Boston, in 1853. Length, over all, 237 feet; by 42; by 23; 1995 83/95 tons, old measurement. She was of a beautiful model, light and graceful and cost $140,000. She was built for the California and China trade and was owned in New York. The command was given to Capt. Sumner Pierce of Barnstable, who, a few years later, when in command of the ship *Sunshine*, lost his life at Callao, through poison administered to the ship's officers by a member of the crew. It is to be regretted that her sea life was so short as to give her small chance to show the speed which her early performances indicated.

On her maiden voyage, the *Lightfoot* left Boston, Sept. 7, 1853, under command of Capt. Reuben Snow, and New York, Dec. 12, 1853, and arrived at San Francisco, Mar. 25, 1854, in a passage of 114 days. Her log shows that she was 24 days to the line, with generally light winds, her best day being 288 miles; from the line to 50° South, she was 22 days, 304 miles being her best day's work. Rounding the Horn occupied 22 days, in alternate calms and storms, and she was 25 days from 50° South, Pacific, to the equator, with 300 miles as her best day; had a dead beat from 40° to 33° South, after which had light, baffling winds. She crossed the equator, 93 days out, and during the following eight days, made 1636 miles; then, for 12 days, logged only 1049 miles and was within 500 miles of the Golden Gate for eight days. Captain Pierce reported having had to tack 75 times to get around Cape Horn. From San Francisco she went to Honolulu, in 12 days, and was 28 days thence to Hong Kong. Sailed from Whampoa, Aug. 5th, and was 40 days beating down the China Sea to Anjer. Cleared Java Head, Sept. 15th and was off the Cape, 26½ days later, one of the fastest runs reported for September departures. She arrived at London Dec. 5th, in 122 days from Whampoa and 81 days from Java Head.

From London she went to Calcutta and on June 29, 1855, was totally wrecked near Saugor, mouth of the Hooghly river.

LIGHTNING

THE *Lightning* was the first of four world-famed extreme clippers built at East Boston, Mass., by Donald McKay, to the order of James Baines & Co., of Liverpool, for operation in their "Black Ball Line" of Australian passenger packets. The others of the quartette were the *Champion of the Seas, James Baines* and

Donald McKay, each, in its turn, being somewhat larger than its predecessor and also, when coming out, being the largest merchant ship of its time to fly the British flag. The *Lightning* left the ways on Jan. 3, 1854, and was 243 feet long, over all; by 44; by 23 feet; tonnage, 2083. She had two laid decks and a poop deck which latter was subsequently extended forward to form a third deck in connection with the house amidships and the topgallant forecastle. She was very sharp, a chord drawn from the cutwater to the fore-chains at the water line, showing a concavity of 16 inches. However, after she had made two round voyages, this hollow was filled in with timber work, her captain or owners not understanding the principle on which she was built and thinking that the alteration would increase her speed. One side of this false bow was washed off on its first try-out and after her arrival at Melbourne, the other side was cleared off, experience demonstrating that her original model was practically perfect. Her dead rise was 20 inches; a carved female in flowing drapery was the figurehead. She crossed a skysail yard on the mainmast only, its length being 32 feet, and its mast with pole, 13 feet long. In very light winds she set moon sails on all three masts. Her cabins were elaborately furnished and handsomely decorated. The quarters of the steerage passengers were in the 'tween decks and those of the second cabin, in a large house amidships. On one of her outward passages she had 368 in the steerage and on another occasion she had 47 saloon, 73 second class and 253 steerage passengers. Her crew numbered 87.

The *Lightning* sailed from Boston, Feb. 18, 1854, under command of Capt. James Nicol Forbes, formerly in the *Marco Polo,* and made the run from Boston Light to the Rock Light, Liverpool, in 13 days and 20 hours. Left Liverpool, May 14th, and in a light weather passage was 77 days to Melbourne, the topgallant sails not once being furled. Left Melbourne, Aug. 20th; carried away the foretopmast eight days out, yet was up with Cape Horn in 19 days and odd hours, from Port Philip, a record run over that section. Received pilot off Point Lynas, 63 days and 16 hours from Port Philip;

arrived at Liverpool, Oct. 23rd, in 64 days and 3 hours' passage. She had in treasure, gold dust to the value of £1,000,000. Her round voyage was two days faster than that of the *Red Jacket*.

Captain Forbes then left her to take the *Schomberg*, in course of construction at Aberdeen, his place being taken by Anthony Enright who had been in the tea clipper *Chrysolite*. On Mar. 20, 1855, the *Lightning* reached Melbourne, in 73 days from Liverpool, 67 days from land to land; was 16 days between the tropics. Returned to Liverpool in 79 days, being 50 days from Cape Horn in light winds. The following passage to Melbourne was made in 81 days, this being the occasion on which the use of a false bow was tried. Captain Enright calculated that its partial breaking off impeded his ship's progress three knots an hour for the 40 days following. Left Melbourne, Dec. 28, 1855; passed the Horn, 23 days out and was thence 63 days to Liverpool, all but three days of which were of head or light winds or calms. Sailed from Liverpool, May 6, 1856, and was 68 days and 10 hours to Melbourne. Left Port Philip Heads, Aug. 28th; passed Cape Horn, 22 days out; crossed the line on the 44th day and was thence 40 days to pilot, off Point Lynas. Of her passage of 84 days, 51 were of calms, head or light winds. When in latitude 8° North, she was in company with the clipper ship *Tornado*, bound in the same direction, the wind being variable, accompanied with squalls of rain. After a lively brush in which at times one ship was ahead and then the other, the *Lightning* finally left her rival astern.

Leaving Liverpool, Feb. 5, 1857, the *Lightning* made the passage to Port Philip Heads, in 69 days and 6 hours. The distance from the equator to Cape Otway, 9449 miles, was covered in 35 days and 15 hours. Homeward bound, she cleared Port Philip Heads, May 11th; passed the Horn, 31 days out; crossed the line on the 56th day and arrived at Liverpool after a passage of 82 days, on 75 of which she was on the starboard tack. Shortly after her arrival she was chartered to carry troops and stores to Calcutta and the "London Times" referred to her as follows:—

"The *Lightning*, the most celebrated of the Black Ball Line has

been visited by hundreds during the short time she has been here. Our readers do not need to be reminded who or what vessel she is; her name is a household word. She has a regular clipper look, long, low and narrow like a yacht. She is rather heavy aloft, with yards almost sufficient to overpower her with canvas; in fact she is a perfect clipper and one in which the builder has thrown aside the minor points of symmetry to produce a fleet and useful vessel. Her appearance on the water is by no means comparable with that of the *James Baines* or *Champion of the Seas*, but in capacity for stowage and as a safe and rapid vessel, the *Lightning* is considered without a rival."

She left Portsmouth, Aug. 25, 1857, having on board the 7th Hussars, numbering 650 men and officers, under Lt. Col. Haggart, and arrived at the Sand Heads, 87 days out. The *James Baines* and *Champion of the Seas*, under similar charters, were 101 and 103 days respectively on the run, but leaving some three weeks before the *Lightning*, encountered lighter winds.

On returning home from Calcutta, the *Lightning* resumed her place in the Australian trade and was always a prime favorite. In December 1862, while outward bound and near the Port Philip Heads, the pilot being still on board, she experienced a sharp shock as though she had struck ground, but her headway was not stopped. It being deemed impossible that she could have grounded, she proceeded to sea. A later survey of the spot, however, showed two shoals near the fairway and it was one of these that she had struck. They were charted as the "Lightning Rocks," being so known until their removal in 1882.

On Oct. 30, 1869, the *Lightning*, then under command of Capt. Henry Jones, was at the wharf at Geelong, Melbourne Harbor, having completed her dockside loading, and was to finish, in the stream, the next day. At 1 o'clock on the morning of 31st, it was discovered that she was on fire. An attempt was made to scuttle her but it failed. She was then towed into the stream and was finally scuttled, sinking in 24 feet of water. A considerable portion of her cargo of wool, copper ore, tallow and leather was salved, but the ship had to be destroyed as it was a menace to navigation.

It was always a mooted question as to which was the faster ship, the *Lightning* or the *James Baines,* and there was great rivalry between their captains. As records speak for themselves, there appears to be no choice between these two and the *Great Republic* and several others of the California-China clippers. The *Lightning,* on her maiden passage, logged 436 miles in 24 hours. Her best day's work, on her first trip to Melbourne, was 348 miles. On returning, she covered 412 in one day and 3722 in 10 days. On her second outward run she made 325 miles in one day but went at times 17 knots under three single-reefed topsails, the foresail, trysail and foretopmast staysail. On this passage her best day was 390 miles and best speed, 18 knots. On her fourth homeward run she made, during the first week, 1908 miles and during the first 18 days, 5244 miles. On her fifth voyage, outward, she made 2188 miles for the week ending July 4th, with 382 miles on the best day. This week's run was, according to her captain, the best in her history to that date. On her sixth outward passage, she made, on Mar. 19, 430 miles which was followed, the next three days, by runs of 360, 308 and 348 miles, an average, for the four days, of 361½ miles. On the return passage of this voyage, she made 1723 miles in one week, the best day being 384.

In the Feb. 8, 1854, issue of the "Boston Atlas," appeared the following account of the *Lightning,* viz.:—

This splendid ship is 226 feet long at the load-displacement line and 243 over all, from the knight-heads to the taffrail, has 44 feet extreme breadth of beam, 23 feet depth of hold, including 7½ feet height between decks, and registers about 2000 tons. Her keel for 30 feet forward gradually rises from a straight line, and the gripe of her forefoot, instead of being angular, is arched where it blends with the stem. This gives increased strength compared with the angular forefoot, and in the event of her taking the ground forward, her gripe will not be the first to encounter resistance. In working ship, too, the arched form will facilitate her movements.

She has sharper ends than any clipper ever built in the United States, and her lines are decidedly concave. At the load displacement line, a cord from the extreme of the cutwater to the rounding of her side, would show a concavity of 16 inches, the curved line representing the segment of an ellipsis. The stem rakes boldly forward, and the bow flares as it rises, but preserves its angular form to the rail, and is there convex in its outline. She has a full female figure head, placed to correspond with her fore-rake, and this is her only ornament forward, for she has neither head nor trail boards, nor any other appendage for the sea to wash away. Her sides swell 10 inches, her rise of floor is 20 inches at 11 feet from the keel, and her sheer is 4½ feet, which is graduated her whole length, and rises gracefully towards the ends. The stern is semi-elliptical in form, and has the planksheer moulding for its base. The run is very long and clean, but is much fuller than the bow, and under the stern it is rounded, so that it has no hollow counter for the sea to strike against when the ship settles aft. Her after motions, therefore, will be easy in a heavy sea, and when she is going at her highest speed, the after vacuum in the water will be filled by the run, so as to enable her to sail upon the same lines forward and aft. It is well known that ships with hollow counters, when in a heavy sea, bring up aft with a tremendous splash, that makes everything crack fore and aft, and that when going swiftly through the water, they settle down almost to the taffrails. The *Lightning's* after body was designed with special reference to obviate these defects.

Her stern is ornamented with gilded carved work, but, this, at best, is only an excrescence, and adds nothing to the beauty of the hull. The ship will be coppered in Liverpool, at present her bottom is copper colored, and the rest of her hull outside is painted black, inside she is pearl color, relieved with white, and the water ways are lead color.

The whole height of her bulwarks is 7 feet, and she has a full topgallant forecastle, which extends to the fore rigging, and its deck is connected with the top of a house, which is continued aft, and is 48 feet long, and 19 wide at the after end. The top of this house is connected with the poop by two gangways, so that the men can pass forward and aft, without descending into the waist. She has a full poop deck 90 feet long, the outline of which is protected by a mahogany rail, on turned stanchions of the same wood.

There is a spacious house over the wheel, designed, in part, for a smoking room, and it also protects a staircase on the starboard side, which leads to the captain's stateroom and the after cabin. The after cabin is 34 feet long, 12 wide, and 7 high, and is wainscotted with mahogany, enamel, polished ash and other fancy woods, relieved with rosewood pillars, papier mache cornices, and flowered gilding. It has 4 staterooms, 2 sofa recesses, and other apartments, a splendid sofa aft, rich carpeting, a circular marble table in each recess, and a mahogany extension table amidships. All the staterooms are furnished differently, for the sake of variety, we suppose, and their furniture is of the choicest kind, arranged with consummate skill. Every stateroom has a square window in the side, and a perforated ventilator between the beams, so that, for light and air, all has been done that could be desired. There are 4 stern windows, and a large oblong square light in the after cabin, and similar skylights over the dining saloon, which is connected with the after cabin. The skylights are set in mahogany frames, and nearly all the windows are of stained glass. In the recesses and partitions of the after cabins, there are plate glass mirrors, which give reflected views of every part of the cabin. A more beautiful cabin or one more richly furnished we have never seen.

The dining saloon, which leads from it, is also wainscotted, is painted pure white, like enamel, and is tastefully relieved with gilded mouldings and flower work. It is 48 feet long, 13 feet wide aft, and 14 forward, and has a large mahogany table its whole length, with settees along its sides. It has spacious staterooms and other apartments on each side, its whole length, and these rooms are admirably designed for the accommodation of families. In richness of furniture, light, and ventilation, they are equal to those in the after cabin. At the foreward partition there is a costly sideboard of marble, and rising from it is a large mirror. Another mirror and sofa ornaments the after part, so that the saloon is reflected from both ends.

The chief officer's stateroom is on the starboard side, forward, and the pantry opposite, and between these are two doors, which lead to the quarter deck. The front of the poop deck projects about 5 feet, and shelters the entrance to the saloon.

The accommodations for her second class passengers are in the house before the main hatchway, which has an entrance amidships, aft. It is 36 feet long and has a passage amidships, 5 feet wide, which leads to 6 staterooms on each side, and these rooms are well lighted and ventilated, and tastefully furnished. The forward part of this house contains the galley, and before it, on each side, are staircases which lead to the between decks. Her crews' accommodations are under the topgallant forecastle, and are neatly fitted up.

The between decks are designed for the accommodation of passengers, and have 10 plate glass ports on each side, skylights and ventilators along the sides of the house above, so that they are well supplied with light and ventilation, and will be fitted up in superior style, when the ship arrives in Liverpool.

As the top of the house projects 3 feet on each side, a water proof awning will be spread from it to the rails, so as to shelter the waist, that the passengers may always have an opportunity of coming on deck without exposure to wet weather.

Her accommodations forward and aft are upon a liberal scale, and are most admirably designed for health, comfort and safety.

The ship herself is amply found in the best of ground tackle, has a good, substantial windlass, three capstans, a patent steering apparatus, and copper chambered pumps, and below she has an iron water tank of 5000 gallons capacity.

The leading details of her materials and fastening will show that she is well built. Her frame, all the knees in the hold, and her hooks and pointers, are of selected, seasoned white oak, and her scantling is of hard pine. The knees in the between deck are of hacmatack, the lower deck is of hard pine, and the upper deck of white pine, and her fastening varies from 1¼ to 1 inch iron and copper. Her ends have 4 tiers of uprights, which are bound to the keel and keelsons with massive oak knees, and they are almost filled with hooks and pointers.

Her keel is of white oak in two depths, sided 15, and moulded 30 inches, each depth 15 inches square. Its scarphs are 12 feet long, bolted with copper, and its parts were also bolted together before the frames were raised. The floor timbers are sided from 12 to 14 inches, and moulded, and the frames are chocked with oak above and below every joint, and bolted together fore and aft. She has 3 tiers of midship keelsons, each tier 15 inches square and double sister keelsons of the same size on each side, one over the other. The whole of these keelsons are bolted through the timbers and keel with 1¼ copper and iron, the bolts within a foot of one another. The sister keelsons are also bolted horizontally through the midship keelsons and each other. All the keelsons are scarphed and keyed, and fitted close as jointer work.

The whole of her ceiling is of hard pine, and that on the floor is 5 inches thick, and square fastened. Over the first futtocks there are two bilge keelsons, each 15 inches square, placed alongside of each other, and these, like the other keelsons, are scarphed and keyed. They are square fastened through the timbers, the bolts having been driven alternately from both sides and riveted, and they are also bolted together edgeways. The ceiling above the bilge keelsons up to the lower deck, is all 9 by 12 inches, all bolted together edgeways every three feet, and square fastened through the timbers. The lower deck beams are 14 by 16 inches amidships, tapered an inch or two toward the ends, and the knees connected with them are of white oak. The hanging knees are sided from 10 to 12 inches, have 5½ feet bodies, 4 feet arms, are moulded about 22 inches in the angles, and have 20 bolts and 4 spikes in each. Their lower ends rest upon a lapstrake or stringer of 6 inches thick by 12 inches wide, which is bolted through the ceiling and the timbers. This strake forward and aft is beamed and kneed in the angles of the ends, and forms a strong horizontal hook. The lodging knees are sided 8 inches, are scarphed together with every berth, and closely bolted. The stanchions are very stout, are clasped with iron, and are kneed to the beams above and to the keelsons below. There are 4 massive pointers of oak forward, ranging from 20 to 50 feet in length, and two of these are filled in the angles with hooks, and the others are fayed to the keelsons below and to the beams above. They are 12 inches square, and are bolted from both sides, through the cants and timbers. Her ends are as strongly secured as a Davis' Straits whaler. The run is secured in the same massive style as the bow.

Her between decks waterways are of hard pine 15 inches square with a strake of 9 by 12 inches inside of them, morticed over the beams and bolted through them, and another strake of 12 by 14 inches over them. These extend her whole length, are bolted vertically through the beams, and horizontally through the timbers. The ceiling above is 5 inches thick, and the clamp under the upper deck beams is 9 by 14 inches, and like the other ceiling, it is square fastened. The upper deck beams are 9 by 14 inches, and the knees connected with them are of hacmatack, about the same size as those below and are fastened in the same style. The stanchions under them are oak turned, and have bolts through their centers which are keyed on the upper deck beams and set up with nuts and screws to the beams below, thus binding both decks together. The planking of the lower deck is of hard pine, 3½ inches thick, and the upper deck is white pine of the same substance. In every berth between the hanging knees, she is diagonally cross braced with hard pine of 9 by 7 inches over the ceiling, and these braces are bolted through the ceiling and the timbers. Her hooks forward and aft between decks are beamed and kneed in the same style as those below. She has 32 beams under the upper deck and 30 under the lower deck, with a corresponding number of carlines. All the mast-partners and hatchways are strongly kneed in every angle.

The upper deck waterways are 12 by 14 inches, with a thick strake inside of them champered off towards the deck, and her bulwarks, like those of a ship of war, are built solid and outside. The bulwarks are 5 feet high, surmounted by a monkey rail of 2 feet which is panelled on the inside. Her garboards are 8 by 12 inches, the second strake 7 by 12, the third 6 by 12, champered off to 4½ inches thick, the substance of the planking on the bottom. The wales are 5½ by 8 inches and she is planked flush to the planksheer moulding. Outside as well as inside she is square fastened, and is butt and bilge bolted with copper.

The mouldings of the planksheer and rail are relieved with raised strakes above and below them, which are also moulded on the edges and outside she is polished smooth as marble, and every line and moulding is graduated in exact proportions fore and aft.

She is a fullrigged ship, and looks grandly aloft. Her lower masts and bowsprit are built of hard pine dowelled together and bolted, and are hooped over all with iron. The topmasts and jibbooms are also of hard pine. The following are the dimensions of her masts and yards:—

MASTS

	Diameter Inches	Length Feet	Mastheads Feet
Fore	37	86	15
Top	18½	46	10½
Topgallant	12½	23	..
Royal	10½	15	Pole.. 7
Main	38	90	16
Top	19½	50	11
Topgallant	14½	23	..
Royal	11½	15	..
Skysail	8½	13	Pole.. 8
Mizzen	30	79	13
Mizzen Top	15½	40	8
Topgallant	11½	18	..
Royal	8½	13	Pole.. 6

YARDS

	Diameter Inches	Length Feet		Mastheads Feet
Fore	23	87	Yard arms..	4
Top	18½	72		6
Topgallant	13	52		4
Royal	9½	40		1½
Main	24	95		4
Top	19	72		6
Topgallant	14	52		4
Royal	10	40		2½
Skysail	7	32		1
Crossjack	19	72		5
Mizzentopsail	15	52		4
Topgallant	10	40		1½
Royal	7	32		1

The bowsprit is 20 feet outboard, and has 34 inches diameter, divided at 19 and 14 feet for the inner and middle jibs, and the flying jibboom is 15 feet outside from wyth to the stay, with 6 feet end, spanker boom 50 feet long and spanker gaff 38 feet, with 6 feet end. The lower masts, commencing with the fore, are 65½, 72 and 60 feet high, above the deck. The whole height of the mainmast, from the deck to the skysail truck is 164 feet. All her caps are of wrought iron, the fore and main are 1 inch thick and 10 inches wide, and the others in like proportion. The heels of her topmasts and topgallant masts, in the wake of the lower and topmast rigging, are curved out to correspond with the eyes of the rigging, so that the topmasts and topgallant masts are wood-and-wood, or close together, in the doublings. This is very snug, and what is more, very strong, for it not only diminishes the lever weight upon the trestle-trees, but the heels and heads of the masts are bound together below the caps by iron bands, which set up with screws. Under the topmast trestle-trees, around each masthead, let into the wood, is a massive iron screw band to give additional support to the cross trees and all above them. Her standing rigging is of Russia hemp, four stranded and wormed. The fore and main rigging, fore and main topmast backstays, double topgallant backstays, lower and topmast stays are all 11½ inches, the mizzen rigging of 8½ inches, and the other in proportion. She has 6 shrouds to the fore and mainmasts on each side, 3 topmast backstays, double topgallant backstays, and 3 shrouds to the topmast rigging. The lower rigging, topmast backstays, etc., set up with lanyards and dead eyes, and most of the other rigging on its ends. She has chain bobstays and bowsprit shrouds, martingale stays and back ropes, iron futtock rigging, patent trusses and parrels, chain topsail sheets and ties, and all the other improvements of the day. Although her masts are of very heavy dimensions, they are so compactly fitted in the doublings, that they appear comparatively light, and her yards, too, though very square, are so neatly tapered toward the arms, that altogether, aloft, she appears the lightest sparred clipper of her size we have ever seen. Her mastheads are crowned with gilded balls, the doublings and lower masts are white, the yards black, and the booms bright, with black ends. The sails are of cotton canvas, with Manila roping, have crossed diagonal roped bands between the reefs, and are also roped from opposite clews to opposite earings. Her running rigging is mostly of Manila hemp, and her blocks are large and iron strapped. Aloft, as well as below, everything which skill, without regard to cost, could produce, has been abundantly supplied.

This magnificent ship is owned by Messrs. James Baines & Co. of Liverpool, is designed for their Line of Liverpool and Australia packets, and is commanded by Captain James N. Forbes, who superintended her outfits. Captain Forbes is well known as the former commander of the famous ship *Marco Polo*, in which he made two successive voyages from Liverpool to Australia in less than 12 months, including detention in ports. Her builder, Donald McKay, has a world wide reputation, his ships, for beauty, strength and speed, have no superiors on this side of the Atlantic, and as the *Lightning* is the first ship ever built in the United States for an English house, he has done his best to make her perfect in every detail.

She is the largest ship belonging to Liverpool, and we believe she will prove the finest ship of her size that has ever been produced, on either side of the Atlantic.

She now lies at Constitution Wharf, and is loading in Train & Co.'s packet line for Liverpool. We advise everybody to call and see her.

Mr. McKay has now on the stocks, for the owners of the *Lightning*, a clipper ship of 2500 tons, named the *Champion of the Seas*, which will be launched in April. She is 245 feet long, has 45 feet breadth of beam, 29 feet depth of hold, and three decks. Also, another clipper ship of 3000 tons named the *James Baines*, which is 310 feet long, has 46 feet extreme breadth of beam and 29 feet depth of hold, with three decks and will be launched in September. These ships have white oak frames, will be diagonally cross braced with iron and built in the best style.

LIVE YANKEE

EXTREME clipper ship, built in 1853, by Horace Merriam, at Rockland, Maine. 212 x 40 x 23: 6; 1637 tons, old measurement. She was sold by her builder to George W. Brown and others, of New York, but soon after, Foster & Nickerson of New York, appear as her owners. At the time of her loss, she belonged to Lawrence Giles & Co., of the same port. About the time that she was launched, there came off the ways, in the yard of George Taylor at Rockland, the larger clipper ship *Red Jacket* and it was always considered a mooted question as to which was the faster vessel. Their respective admirers frequently wagered considerable sums on their favorite. The *Live Yankee* was a very handsome ship in model, rig and in every respect and was undoubtedly a very fast sailer. On her first passage to San Francisco she logged at times as high as 18 knots and in one day made 327 miles, both of which performances are exceptionally good on that run.

Starting out from Rockland, the *Live Yankee* was four days to New York, in ballast, and then made a round voyage to Liverpool. On return to New York she loaded for San Francisco and sailed June 29, 1854. Was 34 days to the line and 17 days from Cape St. Roque to 50° South; passed Cape Horn, 65 days out; was 19 days between the 50's; from 50° South, Pacific, to the equator, 16 days; thence 24 days to port in light winds and calms, with no trades; passage from New York, 113 days. Her runs of 17 days down the South Atlantic and 16 days up the South Pacific, were very fast. Her time from 50° South, to 10° South, Pacific, was faster by two days than that made by the *Flying Cloud* on her first passage of 89 days and 20 hours from New York. From San Francisco, the *Yankee* was 48 days to Hong Kong; thence 10 days to Singapore and 17 days from there to Calcutta. Left the Sand Heads, Mar. 21, 1855; was 54 days to the Cape and 50 days thence to London. From London she returned to Calcutta, being only 58¾ days from the line in the Atlantic to the Sand Heads. Left Calcutta in February 1856; was off the Cape, 51 days out, and 42 days thence to London, the latter portion of the passage being exceptionally fast.

In December 1857 she was reported as arriving at Melbourne, 82 days from London, and sailed, Jan. 20, 1858, for Batavia, passing Cape Leeuwin on the 30th; arrived at Hong Kong, May 26th, from Batavia. Sailed from Macao, early in 1859, with 788 Chinese coolies for Havana and made the passage in 90 days. Lost by sickness only 12 members of her human freight, a much smaller percentage than usual on voyages of this kind. From Havana she went to New York in ballast; loaded for Hong Kong and arrived out in March 1860. She then made a second voyage as a coolie ship, taking 728 Chinese to Havana. Sailed thence, in February 1861, and was five days to New Orleans. Left there Mar. 27, 1861, for England. After loading at Liverpool for Kurrachee, India, she sailed

June 26, 1861, and was wrecked on the coast of Galicia. The chief officer and six of the crew were drowned.

She was commanded at times, by captains Thorndike, Gove, Brown and Boyle. The latter was master at the time of her loss.

LIVING AGE

BUILT by Jotham Stetson, Medford, in 1848. 727 tons, for Edward D. Peters & Co., Boston, and afterwards sold to William Appleton & Co., of New York. Wrecked on Pratas Shoal, Dec. 31, 1854, while on a voyage from Shanghai to New York, with tea and silks.

LOOKOUT

CLIPPER ship, built by Chase & Davis, at Warren, R. I., for E. Buckley & Sons, of New York, and launched Oct. 4, 1853. 198 x 38: 4 x 21: 9; 1291 tons, old measurement; 1068 tons, new measurement. She is said to have been designed for the Australian trade and made one round voyage between New York and England. Thereafter, until sold in 1871, she was operating almost entirely between New York and San Francisco and was a prime favorite on that run.

The first arrival of the *Lookout* at San Francisco was on May 5, 1854, and her last from New York, May 9, 1871. Her outward passages numbered 16. On the final one she was forced to put into Port Stanley, in distress. On her second passage she was 153 days, and on her fifteenth, 147 days, both of which long passages were due to exceptional detentions by bad weather off Cape Horn and subsequent light winds in the Pacific. The average of the other 13 runs is 121 days. Of her five fastest passages, the longest was 117 days; fastest, 108 days; slowest of the 13, 138 days. In 1858, her time being 112 days, she was 21½ days to the line; passed Rio on the 29th day; Montevideo on the 34th day and Cape Horn on the 47th day. In 1860 she crossed the equator in the Pacific on the 86th day from

New York, as against 113 and 119 days on her two very slow passages.

From San Francisco she made eight runs direct to New York and one to Boston. The four fastest were: 97, 90, 98 and 96 days; average of the nine 100 5/9 days; slowest, 112 days. In 1856 she put into Rio, when 71 days out from San Francisco, and was detained there several weeks.

In completion of her first voyage to the Pacific, she was 51 days from San Francisco to Callao; thence 91 days to New York. In 1863 she loaded at Chamala, west coast of Mexico and was 84 days thence to New York. In 1864 she was 98 days from Honolulu to New Bedford. In 1861 and 1869 respectively she was 121 and 123 days from San Francisco to Liverpool.

In 1855 she crossed from San Francisco to Hong Kong, in 53 days. Two days before reaching destination she fell in with the British clipper ship *Invincible*, which had just sunk the ship *A. Chesebrough* through collision. The *Invincible* was about to be abandoned, but by the united exertions of the crews of the three ships she was gotten into Hong Kong. The *Lookout's* share of the salvage money was about $25,000. After loading for San Francisco, the *Lookout's* pilot was discharged off Hong Kong, Feb. 4, 1856; the Bashee Islands were passed 4½ days later; the Loo Choo's were passed 7½ days out and Fatisio Island, off Japan, on the 12th day from Hong Kong. After crossing the 180th meridian, on the 21st day, she had fresh westerly gales and for several days made 250 to 290 miles under only the foresail and close-reefed maintopsail. She passed within the Heads, San Francisco, on the 38th day from Hong Kong.

The *Lookout* met with several serious mishaps. Leaving San Francisco in August 1866, for Boston, she returned to port a month later, leaking badly; repairs occupied two months, the total cost and damage being $48,000. In July 1870 she left New York, on what was to be her last run out to San Francisco. On Oct. 20th, off Cape Horn, had the foremast sprung, the mizzenmast split and was otherwise crippled besides becoming leaky. She arrived at Port Stanley, Oct.

25th, where temporary repairs were made by Captain Nugent and his crew and the voyage was resumed on Feb. 16, 1871. Arrived at San Francisco, 82 days thereafter, 292 days after having left New York. Insurance loss, in this instance, $18,000. After arrival at San Francisco she was sold to P. B. Cornwall and her subsequent operations were entirely in the Pacific Ocean, both off shore and coastwise, in the lumber and coal trade. On Jan. 20, 1872, while beating down the Straits of San de Fuca, bound to San Francisco, she narrowly missed destruction by striking one of the Race Rocks, in a thick fog, but got off with the loss of part of her stem and leaking badly; was taken to Port Townsend for repairs.

The *Lookout* left Shanghai, Sept. 7, 1878, for Puget Sound and got to sea on the 10th; on the 12th she was partially dismasted in a typhoon and then driven on the reef off the island of Kutsunoshima. Three of the crew who volunteered to launch a boat to attempt a landing were drowned. Fishermen ashore later assisted the rest of the crew to land. After being 16 days on the island, they embarked in two fishing boats and five days later they were picked up by a Japanese steamer and taken to Kagoshima, about 100 miles from the scene of the wreck. Captain Wiggin and his wife reached San Francisco, Nov. 13th, on the *City of Tokio*.

Capt. John B. Joyce was in the *Lookout* until the end of 1856, after which Captain Hamilton had her one round voyage. Captain Sherwood succeeded, and was in charge for six voyages. Capt. R. McD. Nugent took command in the fall of 1863, continuing in her until she was sold in 1871.

LOTUS

CLIPPER ship, launched Oct. 26, 1852, by J. Taylor, at Chelsea, Mass.; 660 tons, British measurement. Owned by Dabney & Cunningham of Boston. Capt. John Leckie was in command during her whole career as an American ship.

Although one of the smallest of the clipper fleet, the *Lotus* proved to be a fast sailer, and her record in the trans-Pacific trade, in which she was employed for several years, is particularly good. She was built for trade with China and her maiden voyage was from Boston to Hong Kong, return being to New York. Taking her first departure, Nov. 30, 1852, she ran out to China in 115 days. Left Whampoa, Apr. 13, 1853, and Macao, two days later; passed Anjer, Apr. 30th; was off the Cape of Good Hope, 10 days; arrived at New York, Aug. 3rd, in 110 days from Macao and 42 days after clearing the Cape,—a very fine run. She was then diverted to the California trade and made four consecutive passages, arriving at San Francisco on the first, Jan. 14, 1854, in 121 days from New York. Entered port in company with the much larger, extreme clipper *Jacob Bell*, which ship was 122 days from Philadelphia. The *Lotus* was 15 days off Cape Horn in heavy weather, having planksheer split, cabin filled, etc. From San Francisco she was 53 days to Singapore and thence 25 days to Calcutta. Left the Sand Heads, May 24th, and arrived at Boston, Aug. 26th, in 94 days out. Sailed from Boston, Oct. 25th; was 30 days to the line; 63 days to 50° South; thence eight days to 50°, Pacific; thence 27 days to the equator; and arrived at San Francisco, Feb. 26, 1855, in 123 days' passage. Sailed, Mar. 14th, for Batavia; loaded at Foo Chow, from which port she took her departure Aug. 14th, and reached New York, Dec. 1st, in 109 days' passage; 74 days from Anjer, 46 from the Cape and 24 from the line. Sailed from New York, Feb. 14, 1856, and was 29 days to the line, 73 days to 50° South and 20 days off the Horn; had light winds in the South Pacific, being 25 days to the equator, and very light winds and calms from 14° North to port, being 38 days from the line to the Golden Gate. Arrived at San Francisco, July 5, 1856, 146 days out, entering port in company with the extreme clipper *White Swallow* which had made the run in 134 days. The latter had experienced much more favorable weather in the Atlantic and both ships made the run up from Cape Horn in about the same time. From San Francisco, the *Lotus* went to Hong Kong, in 50 days, and thence to Singapore; left the latter port, Dec. 28th, and arrived at

New York, Mar. 25, 1857, in 87 days' passage. Returned to San Francisco, arriving Oct. 19th, in 134 days from New York. Was 29 days to the line; in the South Atlantic was taken aback while running before the wind under close reefed topsails during a violent gale and was pooped by three heavy seas. The skylights were stove, cabin filled and 18 inches of water left in the hold, but no leak developed. From San Francisco she went to Hong Kong, in 42 days; thence to Manila; thence to Shanghai and back and arrived at San Francisco, July 5, 1858, in 58 days from Manila. Then crossed to Hong Kong in 56 days; loaded at Foo Chow and sailed Dec. 28th; was 107 days thence to New York.

Sailed from New York, June 30, 1859; was 36 days to the line; 69 days to the Straits of Le Maire and off the Horn for 26 days; had the forward house started, boat and bulwarks stove, and spare spars washed overboard; was not up to 50° South, Pacific, until the 90th day out; then had 22 days to the equator and arrived at San Francisco, Nov. 19th, in 138 days' passage. Other arrivals that day were: *War Hawk*, 144 days; *Shooting Star*, 142 days; *Cherubim*, 193 days; and *Wild Rover*, 178 days. The *Lotus* then became a regular packet between San Francisco and Hong Kong and made between December 1859 and April 1863, seven round voyages, always stopping at Honolulu, outward bound. Two westward runs were made in 44 days each and one in 45 days. On one occasion she was at Honolulu in 11 days from the Golden Gate. Returning eastward, her fastest passage was 41 days. Her whole time on the rounds, including detentions at Honolulu and in China, is, in regular order, 5 months, 17 days; 4 months, 3 days; 4 months, 25 days; 5 months, 12 days; 5 months, 3 days; 4 months, 22 days; 4 months, 16 days; a most excellent record.

The *Lotus* took her last departure from San Francisco, May 7, 1863. She crossed the equator, 20 days out; was up with Cape Horn, 50 days out, off which had very heavy weather; crossed the equator, 82 days out, and arrived at New York, Aug. 23rd, in 107 days' passage. Shortly after arrival she was sold on private terms and went under the French flag, without change of name, her hailing port becoming Marseilles and her owner R. de Fraisanet of that city. She was subsequently engaged in trade between New York and ports in the Mediterranean and her name appears in registers up to 1871.

End of Volume One.